FROM ADAM
TO ARMAGEDDON

The Bible world.

FROM ADAM
TO ARMAGEDDON

A SURVEY OF THE BIBLE

Second Edition

J. Benton White

San Jose State University

Wadsworth Publishing Company
Belmont, California
A Division of Wadsworth, Inc.

To my wife, Mary Lou,
whose affirming love and support have made whatever
I have accomplished or will accomplish possible.

Religion Editor: Sheryl Fullerton
Editorial Assistant: Andrea Varni
Production Editor: Vicki Friedberg
Managing and Cover Designer: Donna Davis
Print Buyer: Randy Hurst
Permissions Editor: Jeanne Bosschart
Text Designer: Irene Imfeld
Copy Editor: Jane Townsend
Maps: Martha Bredemeyer
Photos: J. Benton White

Map of the Bible world, p. ii, adapted from map, p. 228, in *Ways to the Center*, 3d ed., by Denise L. Carmody and John T. Carmody (Wadsworth, 1989).

All biblical quotations are from *The Jerusalem Bible*. Copyright © 1966, 1967, 1968, by Darton, Longman & Todd, Ltd., and Doubleday & Company, Inc. Reprinted by permission of the publishers.

Printed in the United States of America   49

1 2 3 4 5 6 7 8 9 10—95 94 93 92 91

Library of Congress Cataloging-in-Publication Data
White, J. Benton, 1931–
    From Adam to Armageddon : a survey of the Bible / J. Benton White.
    —2nd ed.
        p.   cm.
    Includes bibliographical references.
    ISBN 0-534-13884-5
    1. Bible—Introductions.   I. Title.
BS475.2.W52   1991
220.6′1—dc20   90-30573
                                                       CIP

CONTENTS

Maps ix
Preface x

PRELUDE 1

Approaches to the Bible 1
The Bible as History, Religious Document,
    and Scripture 2

Course Goals 3
Historic Outline and Biblical Order 3

Chapter 1: PREPARING FOR THE STUDY 6

The Bible's Meaning 6
Preconditions for the Bible's Origin 7
Scholarly Study of the Bible 8
Historical Development 9

The Order of the Books 12
The Arena out of Which the Bible Arose 14
Study Questions 17
Suggested Readings 18

Chapter 2: "IN THE BEGINNING . . ." 19

The Book of Genesis 19
Moses and the Pentateuch 25
Questions Raised by the Exodus Story 30

The Eyes of Faith 32
Study Questions 33
Suggested Readings 34

Chapter 3: SHAPING THE FUTURE: BECOMING A NATION 35

The Nature of the History 36
Joshua and the Conquest of Canaan 37
The Era of the Judges 38
Samuel: The Transitional Figure 39
Saul: The First King 40
David: A Dilemma 40
Solomon: In All His Glory 42

The Division of the Land 43
The Story of Israel 43
Judah: The Apple of Yahweh's Eye 47
An Overview of the Deuteronomic History 49
Study Questions 51
Suggested Readings 51

Chapter 4: THE PROPHETS 53

A Prophet Defined 53
The Tradition of the Prophets 54
Stages of Prophetic Development 57

Conclusions About the Prophetic Tradition 69
Study Questions 70
Suggested Readings 70

Chapter 5: FROM NATIONAL TO WORLD RELIGION 72

The Shaping of Surviving Judaism 72
The Exilic Prophets 75
The Chronicler 83

Study Questions 85
Suggested Readings 86

Chapter 6: THE LATE HEBREW BIBLE PERIOD 87

A Rationale for Our Study 87
Psalms 88
The Wisdom Tradition 90

The Literature of Wisdom 92
Study Questions 103
Suggested Readings 104

INTERLUDE: THE APOCRYPHA 106

Definition and History 106
Study Questions 111
Suggested Reading 111

Chapter 7: CHRISTIANITY: A SECT WITHIN JUDAISM 112

Postexilic Judaism 112
Diversity Within Judaism 116
The Birth of Christianity 117

Study Questions 122
Suggested Readings 123

Chapter 8: THE LETTERS OF PAUL 124

The Importance of Paul 125
Four Letters of Paul 129
Five Other Letters of Paul 138

Paul's Contribution 140
Study Questions 140
Suggested Readings 141

Chapter 9: THE SYNOPTIC GOSPELS: STORIES ABOUT JESUS 143

The Gospels Defined 143
The Occasion for the Gospels 144
The Interrelationship of the Gospels 145
Mark 148
Matthew 152

Luke 157
The Gospel Within the Gospels 163
Acts 164
Study Questions 166
Suggested Readings 167

Chapter 10: OTHER LETTERS AND A SERMON 169

The Nature of the Material 169
The Paulinists 170
Ephesians 172
1 and 2 Timothy, Titus: The Pastoral Epistles 173
The Catholic Epistles 176
James 176

1 Peter 178
2 Peter 178
Jude 179
A Sermon: Hebrews 180
Study Questions 181
Suggested Readings 182

Chapter 11: IN THE NAME OF JOHN 183

Common Elements 183
Traditions About John 183
The Gospel of John 184
The Letters of John 190

Revelation 192
Study Questions 196
Suggested Readings 197

POSTLUDE 199

The Forming of the Jewish and Christian
   Canons 199
The Standards of Canonicity 200
Pseudepigrapha and New Testament
   Apocrypha 202

The Transmission of the Bible Through the
   Centuries 203
Conclusion 204
Study Questions 204
Suggested Readings 205

Glossary 206

Index 223

MAPS

The Bible World ii

The Ancient Near East at the Time of the Patriarchs 15

The Route of the Exodus 31

Israel Under David and Solomon 42

The Divided Kingdoms of Israel and Judah 46

The Assyrian Empire in the Seventh Century B.C.E. 47

The Persian Empire in the Sixth Century B.C.E. 77

Palestine at the Time of Jesus 115

The Territory of Paul's Missionary Activity 128

PREFACE

In more than twenty years of teaching undergraduate courses on the Bible, one of my most difficult tasks has been finding a satisfactory textbook, particularly a single book on the entire Bible. I never totally succeeded, which led me to write this book. It includes those elements I found lacking in the other works, as well as elements that have always been helpful.

APPROACH

Perhaps the major difference between this text and others is the constant sense of connection. I not only explore the various individual segments of the Bible, but also show the continuing *relationship* of the works from the beginning to end. Recognizing that the Bible is first and foremost a religious document, an expression of the continuing development of the Judeo-Christian tradition, I attempt to show the interrelationships of the various works produced at separate moments in history. To do that, each work is placed in the proper historical context, showing how its moment reflects the maturing tradition, both depending on the past and shaping the future. In this way, we see that Christianity is indeed a child of Judaism and that Christian scripture is best understood with that common tradition in mind.

Thus, the sense of religious connection demonstrated in the examination of the Hebrew Bible extends to the last book of the New Testament. Although Christianity has become a religion distinct from Judaism, they share common roots, and thus their scriptures are related. The title of the book, *From Adam to Armageddon*, is the ultimate reflection of that viewpoint.

Based on the assumption that the Bible is best understood and studied as a product of the religious communities that produced it and as a reflection of their religious world views, the text concentrates on the Hebrew scriptures as Judaism has identified them and the scriptures concerning Christianity as that community has identified them. The apocryphal books are noted and discussed briefly, but the emphasis is on the works acknowledged as scripture by the communities that produced them.

I feel that the Bible can best be studied by using the historic-literary critical tools available to us. At the same time, I acknowledge the difference in established fact and intelligent assumption. I have tried to make the readers feel they have the right to draw their own conclusions based on the process I report to them. I have attempted to make them sensitive to the clues the Bible itself provides regarding sources, the various authors' religious world views, and so on.

I rely on the Bible to tell its own story, to make its own connections, and to reveal its own viewpoint. I have tried not to say more or less than the Bible seems to say about itself.

ORGANIZATION

The book's eleven chapters should fit well into a single semester. Each chapter could represent one week's assignment, except for Chapter 9, "The Synoptic Gospels," which could consume two weeks. This leaves some days for exams and other assignments or lectures that individual instructors may prefer. Some might want to transpose Chapters 8 and 9, using material on the synoptic Gospels before tackling the works of Paul.

The book contains a number of study aids. Each chapter contains study questions that help students identify important points and gain a deeper understanding of the material. The suggested readings section at the end of each chapter lists articles from readily available sources that provide in-depth treatments of the subjects covered in the chapter. The maps placed throughout the book provide a continuing reminder of the geography and shifting borders of the lands and empires important to the history of the Bible. Every important political change that occurs in Bible history is illustrated in those maps. The tables provide students with handy information at a glance. Finally, the photos scattered throughout the book allow students to see many of the historically important places discussed in the book.

NEW TO THE SECOND EDITION

Perhaps the most important change in the second edition is the substitution of the term *Hebrew Bible* for *Old Testament* whenever that term is the most accurate description of the material. When I refer to the Christian Bible as a whole, the traditional term that Christians apply to the Hebrew Bible (Old Testament) is maintained, because that is the term Christians use for that portion of their Bible.

It seems important for all of us to be aware of how value-laden our terminology is. The terms *Old* and *New Testament* clearly reflect the bias of the dominant Christian community that created them and are not an accurate description of the materials we are studying. There was no Christianity or New Testament—and thus no Old Testament—before the common era; the terms *Hebrew Bible* and *New Testament* are simple acknowledgment of what was historically true. My decision to use these terms reflects no intention to denigrate the Bible for Christians; it is an attempt to retain the literary/historical perspective evident throughout the text.

The second edition contains additional study questions, and I have attempted to make the questions from the first edition more precise; this will help students focus more clearly on the important aspects of each chapter. The bibliography at the end of each chapter has been expanded to include more recent scholarship to which students can refer. Some textual detail has been added throughout, as well as new illustrations and examples, all of which will help students better understand what lies behind the conclusions.

What remains important is that the text is brief enough so as not to overwhelm the student, while still containing the essential information needed in an introduction to the study of the Bible. Teachers will of course have their own agendas that they'll want to include to make the course meet specific teaching goals.

ACKNOWLEDGMENTS

Obviously no book of this nature could be produced without a great deal of help, support, and encouragement. First and foremost, I received a generous portion of all three from my wife and two sons, Tom and Matt. Even before that I was nurtured by my mother, who believed in my possibilities. San Jose State University granted me sabbatical leave so that I could devote myself to writing the first edition. Dr. Robert Woodward of San Jose State University was kind enough to read my first draft of that edition and make many helpful suggestions. My wife, Mary Lou, served as my typist throughout the process, an act of unmitigated devotion.

The help I received from those who read the original manuscript has been invaluable in shaping my work into a finished product of which I am very proud. The following people made many helpful suggestions regarding content and order that remain incorporated into this second edition: Alvin Denman, Antioch University; Warren McWilliams, Oklahoma Baptist College; and Robert Shofner, California State University, Northridge. They have my deep gratitude for sharing their critical insights with me.

I have benefitted from the helpful comments of a number of teachers who have used the first edition over the past few years. I appreciate the insights gained from Ronald Ballard, Texas Wesleyan University; Betty Griffin, Spartanburg Methodist College; and Thomas Indinopulos, Miami University of Ohio; whose specific suggestions were used in preparing this second edition.

I am particularly grateful to Sheryl Fullerton, Wadsworth's religion editor, for her help, patience, and professional skill in guiding a neophyte author to a successful conclusion in publishing his first book (the first edition). My production editor, Vicki Friedberg, was extremely helpful in guiding me through the difficult task of fine tuning the manuscript in both editions. I would also like to acknowledge the contributions of my copy editor, Jane Townsend, and the staff at Wadsworth.

One who teaches in the midst of the kind of faculty who surround me cannot help but be enriched by that continued contact. The religious studies faculty at San Jose State University have provided the academic and human environment in which this second edition was produced. I am fortunate to have colleagues who include Dr. Richard Keady, Dr. Kenneth Kramer, Dr. Christian Jochim, Dr. Mira Zussman, Dr. Richard Payne, Dr. Susan Mahan, Dr. Timothy Wadkins, Ms. Karen Voss, Dr. Norbert Firnhaber, and Dr. Sanford Rosen, all of whom provided the mental stimulation and encouragement that made this endeavor possible. I am grateful to all of them.

Finally, to the students who have tolerated me over the years as I have struggled to be a better teacher and whose helpful responses, probing questions, and deep interest provided the inspiration for this book, I express my deep thanks. This book is *for* them and in a real sense *from* them.

PRELUDE

Many people know some things about the **Bible,*** even some of what it contains, yet remain overwhelmed by the idea of dealing with the Bible as a whole. This book shares the experiences of myself and my students as we learned how to "tackle" the Bible and to finish that task with a sense of accomplishment. Many students, at the end of my course in Bible history and literature, have expressed deep personal satisfaction at having finally achieved a sense of the entire Bible.

APPROACHES TO THE BIBLE

My approach is simple and is designed to help introduce you to the most important literature of the Western world. This text emphasizes a constant sense of connection of the entire Bible. It not only deals with various segments of the Bible, it keeps in mind the continuing relationship of the works from beginning to end. Recognizing that the Bible is first and foremost a religious document, an expression of the continuing development of the **Judeo-Christian** tradition, it shows the interrelationship of the various works produced at separate moments in history. The works are placed in the context of the history out of which they were pro-

duced, showing how their moment reflects that growing tradition, both depending on the past and shaping the future. That process continues throughout the entire Bible, showing that **Christianity** is indeed a child of **Judaism** and that its scripture is best understood with that common tradition in mind. I do not depend on any one method, but use the most helpful insights I can find to lead you step by step through the entire Bible.

Each of you who approaches the Bible does so with personal motives, as well as with presuppositions based on prior religious training or attitudes. Try to set those presuppositions aside and enter the adventure of study with an open mind. Listen to what the material has to say, and don't be put off if you find words that seem to contradict your presuppositions. Many persons, both religious and nonreligious, miss much of the depth of the Bible simply because they try to make it either more or less than it is. My observations offer the means by which you can use your own critical faculties and are based on the work of scholars and the tradition that has existed around the material since it has been used as **scripture.**

Although not primarily a critical commentary, this book will cause you to appreciate the value of other approaches to the Bible and to realize that you have the capacity to make your own judgments with the same kind of reason. But scholars should be your guides, not your gods; I hope this book can make you more comfortable in drawing your own conclusions.

---

*Terms printed in boldface type are defined in the glossary at the end of the book

1

It is amazing what you can find in the Bible itself if you only know what to look for.

THE BIBLE AS HISTORY, RELIGIOUS DOCUMENT, AND SCRIPTURE

Norman Perrin has spoken of the **New Testament** as "a book and a collection of books."* That concept is equally applicable to the Bible as a whole.

The Bible is fascinating for many reasons. An anthropologist can find in its early pages stories resembling those found in traditions quite dissimilar from the Judeo-Christian tradition of which the Bible is a reflection. The Babylonians, for example, had both creation myths and a flood story that have striking parallels to the stories found in Genesis 1–11. Historians can gather valuable insights regarding times before there was formal history. Within the Bible is the story of the development of the Judeo-Christian tradition. The Bible introduces people who lived thousands of years ago and shows us how much we are like our ancestors and how much they have had to do with our own forming as a part of the human family. It shares their struggles, their victories and defeats; but most of all it is about their religious insights.

The Bible is primarily a religious book. The authors of the Bible were first and foremost religious authors. We must recognize that they speak to us from the perspective of **faith,** if we are to understand what the Bible does and does not say. Though there is much we can learn from it beyond religion, it was never intended for other purposes. The person who wrote the accounts that included the story of the Kings of Israel and Judah tells us quite clearly that if

*Norman Perrin, *The New Testament: An Introduction* (New York: Harcourt Brace Jovanovich, 1974), p. 3.

you want secular history you can go to the **Book of the Annals of the Kings of Israel,** or the **Book of the Annals of the Kings of Judah,** or the **Book of the Acts of Solomon.** Unfortunately those books are no longer available and all we know of their content is found embedded in the works of the Bible about the Kings (1, 2 Kings and perhaps 1, 2 Chronicles).

Many people have come to regard the Bible as a great deal more than a book of religious insights. It is their scriptures, the foundation for religious authority. Although this does not mean that everyone views scripture in the same way, those who accept the Bible as sacred writing do accept it as the defining authority for their religion.

It is through scripture that one begins to understand both Judaism and Christianity. It is the measuring rod both religions use to understand themselves, although it is not the only source to which one must refer to comprehend either religion. Found within both traditions are various ways of approaching the Bible as scripture and as authority. Those differences are the subject for another time, but they should be acknowledged here. These controversies about the Bible generally center on the issues of just how the Bible is to be interpreted and used as scripture or authority.

Within both Judaism and Christianity there are those who accept their scripture as the word of God. They tend to view their religion as **"revealed"** in the absolute sense of that term, and they approach scripture as the word of God in the most literal sense. Yet there are also those who accept scripture as authority while not being bound to it in the literal sense. They tend to view scripture as containing the word of God, and regard it as inspired in a broader sense. One can have either view of scripture and profit from the insights provided here.

One's viewpoint on scripture does not change what the Bible is and why it was produced. Though we recall history, recognize various literary styles, and make other observations about such things as authorship and literary process as we read the Bible, we must never forget that the Bible exists and has survived because it served the needs of the religious communities out of which it was produced and it continues to serve those needs.

COURSE GOALS

The intention of this book is to introduce you to the entire Bible: the Hebrew Bible (or to Christians the Old Testament) and the New Testament. The scope of that goal imposes certain limitations but also has some certain advantages. One of the most important advantages is that it makes those who are Christian take the **Hebrew Bible** more seriously and helps them better to understand Christianity as a child of Judaism. Those who come out of Jewish tradition seem to get a clearer picture of Christianity in its affinity to Judaism. Those whose roots are in neither tradition find a way of understanding both traditions and their impacts on our Western culture.

My goals for the reader are quite simple. When you have read this book, along with the suggested Bible readings, you will:

1. Know what the Bible contains

2. Know the differences between various kinds of biblical work, including differences in purposes

3. Have a sense of both the unity and diversity of the Bible

4. Have sampled each of the various works of the Bible, to acquire a sense of what they are

5. Have developed a sense of the history of the Judeo-Christian tradition (from universal to particular to universal)

6. Have a sense of the religious world view of the various works in the Bible

7. Have some understanding of the major theories of literary development of the Bible and know something of the questions and answers about such things as authorship, time, and purpose of the original works

8. Have some sense of how you can continue your study of various aspects of the Bible and where you can find resources for that study

I will provide the information I feel is most important to accomplish these goals. I will also point out sources of further information. As a study method, you might read the introductory portions of each chapter, the assigned Bible readings, and then the remainder of the text. You will get little out of this book if you do not read the Bible as well. Though I do not suggest that you read the entire Bible, I do recommend that you read a significant amount of its various works.

This book covers the works found in the Hebrew Bible (**Old Testament** to Christians) and the Christian writings (New Testament). It does not deal with the so-called **apocryphal works** in any depth, though it does not discount their importance. The selections are based on the assumption that Judaism should determine the limits of its scripture and Christianity should determine the scripture from the Christian era.

HISTORIC OUTLINE AND BIBLICAL ORDER

To keep you aware of the historical contexts in which the various works were produced, we sometimes deviate from the biblical order. This approach is valid because in both the Hebrew Bible and New Testament, books do not always appear in the historic order in which it is now believed they were written. The abbreviations B.C.E. (before the common era) and C.E. (common era) indicate a convention of dating. The common era begins with the year in

Table 1. Outline of Bible History

Event or Period	Approximate Dates	Historic Bible Reference
Abraham and the Patriarchs	1750–1700 B.C.E.	Genesis 11–50
Moses and the Exodus	1290–1250 B.C.E.	Exodus–Deuteronomy
Joshua and the conquest of Canaan	1210 B.C.E.	Joshua
The Judges (tribal confederacy)	1210–1020 B.C.E.	Judges
The monarchy	1020–587 B.C.E.	1, 2 Kings
The Prophets	1250–450 B.C.E.	
Division of Israel and Judah	922 B.C.E.	
The Babylonian exile	587–539 B.C.E.	2 Kings
The Postexilic period	539 B.C.E.–135 C.E.	Ezra–Nehemiah
The period of Hellenism	323–63 B.C.E.	
The Maccabean period	165–63 B.C.E.	
The Roman period	63 B.C.E.–135 C.E.	
The birth of Jesus	4 B.C.E.	Gospels
The founding of Christianity	30 C.E.	Acts
Paul's ministry	33–65 C.E.	Acts, letters of Paul
Development of Christian literature	50–120 C.E.	
Completion of the Bible	After 100 C.E.	

which early Roman historians believed Jesus was born (though the year 1 is now questioned as the date of the Nativity), and the term refers to a time common to the entire Judeo-Christian tradition. When the calendar we now use was introduced by Pope Gregory XIII in 1582, the birth of Jesus was considered significant enough to serve as the center point of all history.

An outline of that history, in its broadest sense, is provided here to help you get your bearings. That outline will be completed in the material provided throughout the text (see Table 1).

The Bible passed through a literary/historical process that brought it to its final form. Many scholars believe that we can detect in the Bible itself oral and written traditions that predate the final product, the materials used by the author/editors of the books that now constitute the Bible. I will talk about both authors and editors (those who brought earlier materials together but placed their own particular stamp on them) when I discuss the final product. Unlike some scholars, I do not believe we can speak with certainty about the form (written or oral) of the earlier material, but I will point out the possibilities and allow you to draw your own conclusions.

Our journey begins at the beginning, the Book of Genesis. Chapters 1–11 set forth the universal roots of the Judeo-Christian heritage.

Chapters 12–50 show the movement toward the concept of the particular, that is, a special people, the **Jews.** Judaism is further defined in the **Moses** story. In the definition provided in the Moses story, we see how Judaism tried to live out its vision in the midst of the world and the struggles (even debates) that occurred. In the period from Moses to the end of the monarchy, Judaism can probably best be described as a **national religion.** Only during the **Babylonian exile** did it really begin to be a **world religion.** Finally, Christianity was born out of Judaism. What began as a small sect within Judaism eventually became another world religion.

Neither Judaism nor Christianity was produced out of the Bible. Rather, their scriptures were produced after these religions were formed. Each religion produced scriptures, and Judaism and Christianity, respectively, determined what the scriptures of each contained. Judaism probably began to use scripture as scripture a short time before the period of the Babylonian exile. (There is a good clue about that use in the Bible itself, 2 Kings 21.) There is also biblical evidence that the traditions contained within those scriptures were used long before the days of **Manasseh** as authority or guides for Judaism, and that is probably why they survived to become scripture. Christianity began with the Hebrew Bible as its scripture, probably began to use the letters of **Paul** with the Hebrew Bible by the end of the first century, and had its own volume to accompany the Hebrew Bible by the end of the second century. It, too, had used the tradition contained in its final product as a guide or authority much earlier. Paul speaks in his letters of passing on what he had "received" (1 Cor. 15:3).

We will begin our study by reviewing just what the Bible is, its origins, ways it can be studied, and how it moved from religious literature to the status of scripture. As soon as we finish that task we will begin the study of the Bible itself.

The English translation of the Bible I have chosen, *The Jerusalem Bible: Reader's Edition*, has many advantages for a study of this sort. It distinguishes between poetry and prose. It contains many helpful footnotes and is well outlined. It has relied on the most recent biblical scholarship in its translation, while maintaining the power and beauty of the language of the original texts as well as a translation can. Its translators numbered scholars from both Judaism and Christianity. Other translations of the Bible can be used with this text, without doing harm to your study. So, now it is time to begin. I hope you will enjoy the adventure as much as I have enjoyed preparing it for you.

ONE

PREPARING FOR THE STUDY

THE BIBLE'S MEANING

The name "Bible" comes from the Greek word *biblos*, which means book. Actually the Bible is composed of sixty-six separate books. (Some religious traditions within the Judeo-Christian tradition have as few as thirty-nine books in their Bible, while others have as many as eighty.) Most of these books stand independent of one another, although there are demonstrable relationships between certain works.

The Bible consists of two sections that are commonly titled by Christians the Old Testament and the New Testament. Those titles indicate that Christianity has become a religion separate from Judaism and includes in its scripture books beyond those included in the Jewish **canon.** The titles Old and New Testament actually reflect a Christian bias, and because of that I will try to use more neutral terms when it seems appropriate and helpful. The descriptive terms that will be most commonly used will be Hebrew Bible (in reference to the so-called Old Testament) and New Testament in speaking of the scriptures produced by Christianity. (Whatever term seems most descriptive of our subject is the term I will use.) The word

testament comes from the Latin word *testamentum*, a translation of the Greek word *diatheke*, the normal word for **covenant** in the Christian writings. The designations "Old" and "New" reflect the Christian belief that with Jesus a new covenant was established, replacing that established through Moses.

The Hebrew Bible is honored as scripture by the entire Judeo-Christian community. Portions of Christianity include additional works that were a part of earlier Jewish scripture found in the Greek translation of Hebrew scripture (with the exception of 2 Esdras), the **Septuagint.** These works, which will be identified and discussed later, were not included in the official canon of Judaism as it was established at the **Council of Jamnia** in approximately 90 C.E. The New Testament includes those works Christianity has determined to meet the standards of canonicity, some twenty-seven books in all.

The Bible is a collection of works composed over a period of perhaps a thousand years. Many of these individual works have a literary history, having achieved the form in which we know them only at the end of a long editorial process. The literary history of the Hebrew

Bible encompasses many centuries. The works of the New Testament were composed within a span of one century. In both cases, the works existed as literature before they achieved scriptural status. Though most of them served the religious needs of the community in which they were preserved, they did not originally carry the authority of scripture. Canonical status came as a result of decisions within the religious communities that so designated them some time after the works themselves existed. Because it is considered sacred, scripture serves as an authority for any tradition that accepts it as such. In the Judeo-Christian tradition, scripture has usually been considered to have its source in God, revealed to the human family through those whom God chose for that purpose.

Even so, these works were written with religious purposes in mind: It is obvious that each of them was produced to preserve, interpret, or teach a religious tradition. It can be argued that none of the individual works found in the Bible was written for the purpose of being scripture, yet each serves that purpose well. In that sense the works served a scriptural role for some time before they achieved their official status.

The original religious purposes of these works have certainly influenced their style and content. Their intention is to recall history not for the sake of history, but for the sake of faith. Using history, they speak of that which causes history. It is through the eyes of faith that the stories are told—from faith to faith.

PRECONDITIONS FOR THE BIBLE'S ORIGIN

How did the Bible get to us? Unfortunately, we have little direct information about this lengthy process. Most of what is assumed is based on theory. From what is available scholars have speculated about the means.

The Hebrew Bible includes traditions that clearly date themselves across many centuries. Some of those traditions predate the literary period of the Hebrew culture, though it is not certain when these people became a literate society. If the Hebrews were anything like other **nomadic** cultures, they had a rich **oral tradition** long before they developed a **literary tradition.** It has been suggested that few Hebrews were literate until they ceased being nomadic and became a landed culture, after the period of Moses. If Moses was anything like the person portrayed in the **Pentateuch,** it is possible that he could and did write, perhaps preserving such things as the Covenant (the definition of **Yahweh's** relationship with Israel) and the **Law** (the rules that defined the behavior of those in Covenant) in written form. Certainly after the period of the **monarchy** the Jews became literate and began producing literature.

Armed with a rich oral tradition and a religious mentality according to which tradition ought to be preserved without perversion, the ancient Hebrews are believed by some scholars to have found the occasion of their establishment of a monarchy the appropriate time for the religious tradition to begin its literary period. Concern that the tradition might be polluted with ideas from the foreign cultures with which they must now intermingle led to the decision to preserve that tradition by putting it into writing. We know that from the beginning of the monarchy there were written records of kings, so it is not unreasonable to assume that the religious community carried on such activity with its tradition.

It is likely that from the beginning of the monarchy Israel maintained both an oral and a written religious tradition. Contained in that tradition were all those elements now embedded in the works of the Hebrew Bible that relate to those times. No one would be so bold as to suggest what remained in the oral tradition or what was written, or in what form the written tradition existed. Whereas the early traditions had originally been preserved in the **tribal** setting, and taught and passed on from generation to generation by whoever carried the responsibility for that function within the culture, after the time of Moses that function probably passed to those with special religious responsibilities. Such duties could have belonged to some of the **Levites,** although we have no direct clues about that.

Historical circumstances always seemed to play a part in the literary development of the works of the Bible. Regardless of the form in which these works might have existed originally, specific historical events led to their final shaping. As indicated earlier, the establishment of the monarchy may have prompted the translation of materials in the oral tradition into literary form. Perhaps the division of Israel and Judah was another such occasion, when each separate nation needed to preserve its understanding of its common religious tradition, and perhaps even to justify its own religious approach. The period of the Babylonian exile might have been another; however, this time history was reported in such a way as to show that it was not Yahweh's weakness but the people's stubborn disobedience that led to their fall.

Many scholars believe they observe in the Hebrew Bible some of the literary process that brought many of the works to their final form. Using the tools of **literary criticism,** they note that within the Pentateuch there are differences in style, that the name for God differs in different accounts, that there seems to be a blending of traditions in some stories, and that sometimes the same stories seem to be placed in different contexts. (Examples can be noted in Chapter 2.) In the historical books from Joshua to 2 Kings they also note such differences, as well as references to sources from which some of the information seems to have been derived. Similar differences are also noted

within the work of some of the prophets. Critical examination of the Gospels of Mark, Matthew, and Luke has produced theories that the authors of those books incorporated preexisting materials into their writings.

Critical scholarship has furthered the concept that the Bible has a literary history that should be understood as well as possible, to understand fully all that the final product can tell us. It is believed that by determining how and, if possible, when the process occurred, one can better understand the development of the Judeo-Christian tradition, as well as the message that the various authors intended to convey.

SCHOLARLY STUDY OF THE BIBLE

Critical study of the Bible has usually been carried on by those who have had an abiding interest in the Judeo-Christian tradition, not by persons who have sought to undermine its importance to the human family. The intention of such study has been to return as much as possible to the tradition in its original context. Though the results of these inquiries have often challenged traditional beliefs or assumptions, their intention has been not to destroy faith, but to enhance it. The controversies that have surrounded such study are well documented and remain unresolved. In whatever way one approaches the study of the Bible, critical decisions about its content and meaning are inevitable. The critical approach intends to enhance that process, whatever the motive of the one who uses it.

Literary criticism is not the only scholarly tool employed in the study of the Bible, and the insights derived from a number of critical approaches are shared in this study. An identification and definition of these tools may prove helpful. As a field of study, *literary criticism* includes many different endeavors, such as analyses of the text for the purpose of trying to determine its original source and efforts to understand the Bible simply as literature.

Historical criticism is an attempt to place the literature in its original setting. It is applied in conjunction with literary criticism to achieve a fuller understanding of the original intention or meaning of the work.

Textual criticism is the method used to try to determine, as nearly as possible, the original wording of the work being studied, as well as to report what has happened to the text through its transmission over the centuries.

Redaction criticism represents the attempt to separate the actual literary contribution of the redactor (editor) from the work he or she is editing. It shows when the editor has become the author and helps one determine the particular point of view or purpose of that author/editor.

Form criticism tries to recreate the biblical material in its original forms, literary or pre-literary, or to recapture the oral tradition. For example, it would try to determine as nearly as possible the form in which a parable of Jesus existed (either oral or literary) before it was placed in the context of a particular Gospel.

Hermeneutics is the discipline of explaining the meaning of a particular text, using the preceding critical tools. It is often used as the term for interpretation of the text. The term **exegesis** is also used for this process.

It should not be surprising to discover that those who employ such tools in their attempt to understand the Bible do not always come to the same conclusions. Thus, alternative conclusions are included when their implications seem important. It should always be kept in mind that theories are theories, based on careful and critical observation, yet having no claim to absolute truth. Ultimately, each of you must draw personal conclusions, weighing the evidence and using personal critical faculties. For the scholar, conclusions become not what is most comfortable, but what is most reasonable in light of all the evidence available. That is a helpful rule for any serious student of any subject.

HISTORICAL DEVELOPMENT

Steps to a Final Form

Using the resources of the scholars and critics, some things can be deduced about the process that brought the Bible to its final form. An outline of that process gives the reader a necessary overview with which to begin the study of the Bible:

I. The Hebrew Bible
   A. There was an oral tradition preserved within the Hebrew community for many centuries. Contained within that tradition are the stories found in Genesis 1–11, the history of the **patriarchs,** the story of the **Exodus,** as well as many later events (1700 B.C.E.).
   B. Around the time of Moses, a literary tradition began to develop, though it might have been very limited, and there is no evidence of its existence. It could have included many of the laws in the Pentateuch (1290 B.C.E.).
   C. The oral tradition continued to grow, now perhaps accompanied by a primitive literary tradition. These traditions, preserved by special persons in the religious community, incorporated current history with the existing tradition based on the belief that Yahweh, or God, was revealed in the midst of that history (1250 B.C.E.).
   D. With the establishment of the monarchy, much of the tradition assumed literary form. The oral tradition continued as well (1020 B.C.E.).

E. With the division of Israel into two kingdoms, **Judah** and **Israel,** there was also a division of the religious communities. Each community maintained its own traditions, both oral and written, and these traditions reflect the respective religious biases of North and South (922 B.C.E.).

F. Within the northern kingdom (i.e., Israel), the **prophet** played a central role. The tradition that surrounded the prophets maintained its own oral tradition about its heroes, those considered to be **"true" prophets.** By 750 B.C.E. the prophets began to record their prophecies in poetic form and these, too, were preserved by the ongoing prophetic community (after 922 B.C.E.).

G. The **priesthood** was the most prominent religious group in the kingdom of Judah, and it was that group which shaped and preserved its religious tradition (922 B.C.E.).

H. With the fall of Israel to the **Assyrians** in 721 B.C.E. some of those who maintained the religious tradition of Israel escaped to Judah. The Assyrians made Judah a vassal state after 703 B.C.E., and the religious leadership was forced into hiding. It was at this point the preservers of both traditions merged their religious insights (700 B.C.E.).

I. The religious traditions of Israel and Judah, now combined, reemerged and were introduced to the people during the reign of King **Josiah.** Portions of the Hebrew Bible began to assume the authority of scripture (621 B.C.E.).

J. The period of Babylonian exile provided a further opportunity for the blending of the traditions of North and South. The prophetic and priestly traditions were brought into harmony, both preserving their unique contributions to religious life. With the establishment of the **synagogue,** the preserved tradition became central to the worship life of the people (587 B.C.E.).

K. As Jews returned to **Jerusalem** in more significant numbers, they brought with them the works that informed the religious life in exile. The literary tradition began to replace the living prophet as Judaism sought religious understanding (450 B.C.E.).

L. With the **Hellenization** of the Middle East, Judaism continued to look to its past to understand and live out its covenant relationship with Yahweh. The past was used to argue the religious questions that the changing world imposed on those seeking to remain faithful Jews (after 323 B.C.E.).

M. Religious authority became rooted in tradition, that tradition now firmly entrenched in the literary works that compose the Hebrew Bible (165 B.C.E.).

N. Judaism set the limits of its canon. The Council of Jamnia determined which books would assume the role of scripture (90 C.E.).

II. The Christian Writings (New Testament)

A. Christianity had a scripture, the Hebrew Bible.

B. Stories about **Jesus,** as well as sayings of Jesus, some oral, some written, were preserved among those who believed Jesus was **Messiah** (33 C.E.).

C. More tradition about Jesus developed, particularly one that told of his passion and resurrection.

D. Paul wrote letters to churches. Jesus' sayings were applied with the authority of scripture (49 C.E.).

E. With the death of eyewitnesses, the

stories about and sayings of Jesus were placed into a formal literary volume (70 C.E.).

F. Further letters and other accounts about Jesus were produced (80 C.E.).

G. Persecution by the Romans prompted a Christian apocalyptic work (95 C.E.).

H. Paul's letters were used with the authority of scripture (100 C.E.).

I. Some of the other works now in the New Testament were being used, with the Hebrew Bible, as scripture (150 C.E.).

J. Christianity used some of its writings as scripture, although not all segments used the same books (200 C.E.).

K. The canon of the New Testament was fairly well settled within Christianity (393 C.E.).

The observations you have read rely on particular theories developed over the past two centuries of biblical scholarship. Particularly important is the four-source theory of the Pentateuch known as the Graf-Wellhausen hypothesis. Noting differences in names used for God, literary repetitions, or conflict in detail, particularly in the stories as they now stand, these authors suggested that the current accounts have been blended from what were previously separate sources. They identified those sources as "J," "E," "P," and "D." They suggest that each source had an individual existence before being blended into the final product. "J" is so identified because it uses the name Yahweh throughout. "E," on the other hand, uses Elohim as the name of God before the time of Moses. "D" is believed to be all or a portion of the Book of Deuteronomy and is identified as the document found in the **Temple** during Josiah's reform in 621 B.C.E. "P" is so designated because of the large amount of priestly legislation it contains, and it is assumed that

with its inclusion sometime after the Babylonian exile, the Pentateuch took its final form. The process suggested to you assumes the validity of such concepts while not specifically identifying the sources. Rather, the emphasis has been on the historical process that used sources to produce the Bible as it now is.*

Movement Toward Scripture

As the outline reveals, the Hebrew Bible has a much longer literary history than do the Christian writings. Both were used as scripture before they were officially designated as such. They were not documents that shaped the religious traditions they represent, but were rather the products of those traditions, produced to preserve the traditions themselves for future generations. Though Christianity continued to use the Jewish works as scriptures, its understanding of the Hebrew Bible differed from that of Judaism. Christianity interprets the Hebrew Bible in the light of the belief that Jesus was the promised Messiah, while for Judaism the Messiah is still to come.

It is difficult to remove both sections of Judeo-Christian scripture from the history of what people have come to believe about them. Immediately upon reading the New Testament one is countered with an interpretation of the Hebrew Bible. Most Christians know more about how early Christianity used and understood the Jewish scripture than they do about the Hebrew Bible itself. The critical methods defined earlier can be helpful in placing the works of the Bible into the proper context. They remind us that Judaism maintained a separate religious identity after Christianity

---

*An extremely helpful and readable book on the whole issue of Bible authorship is found in Richard Elliott Friedman, *Who Wrote the Bible?* (Englewood Cliffs, N.J.: Prentice-Hall, 1987).

was established. They also remind us that Christianity was, and is, a child of Judaism and that it cannot be understood unless one recognizes its roots in Judaism. Christianity had a Bible, the Hebrew Bible, before the New Testament was developed, and used that Bible to justify its own existence when it produced its companion works, the New Testament.

The movement of these works of literature to the status of scripture was an important process in both religious traditions. For Judaism that process probably began very early, but did not receive conscious affirmation until sometime after the Babylonian exile in 587 B.C.E. The Septuagint (the first Greek translation of the Hebrew scriptures during the Hellenistic era) is the first example we have of a collected body of the Jewish religious literature being used as scripture by those in Diaspora Judaism; that collection might well be more accurately described as the first Jewish canon.

In the case of Christianity the necessity for such an authority arose early, and by the middle of the second century the process was well under way, as the community sought to protect itself from error, or false teachers. In both cases, the final decision of what in their larger collections of religious literature ought to carry the authority of scripture was not made in an instant. Though there was a point in history when the decision was made, it was arrived at only after many years and the passage of generations of use and honor. The final designation of scripture was a recognition of the testimony of generations of faithful Jews and Christians of what had been found to be authentic in their lives. Though each established certain criteria by which works were included or excluded, the books that are in the scriptures of the Judeo-Christian tradition are there because they presented the elements most significant to the purity of that tradition as people understood and sought to be faithful to it in their own times.

THE ORDER OF THE BOOKS

The Jews had divided their literary tradition into three distinct categories and in the order they considered most important. The first five books, often called the Pentateuch, consisted of the books of the Law, followed by the **Prophets,** and concluding with the **Writings** (see Table 1.1, column 1).

Protestant Christianity, on the other hand, would probably classify some books differently (see Table 1.1, column 2). The Jerusalem Bible, which includes apocryphal works, has its own order reflecting their presence. Otherwise, it is ordered in the same manner as the **Protestant Bible** Old Testament (see Table 1.1, column 3).

When Christianity established the New Testament, it began with the life of Jesus, followed by the story of the early church. Next came the **Epistles** of Paul, the **general Epistles,** and finally, the **apocalypse.**

None of these orders will be followed in the absolute sense in this exploration of the Bible, though all the works will be explored in the context in which they can best be understood. The reasons for the ordering will become clear as each work emerges in its particular context.

The books of the Bible contain a variety of literary styles, and sometimes several styles exist in a single book. The early books of the Hebrew Bible are written in the form of narrative histories, but they contain what can be properly classified as **myths** or **legends,** poetry, biography, law codes, and **liturgy.** The prophetic books are chiefly poetry, some interspersed with narrative. The **psalms** are poems or hymns, while a portion of Daniel is **apocalyptic literature.** The Christian writings include a form unique to them, the **Gospel,** as well as letters, sermons, an occasional hymn, apocalyptic literature, and narrative history. Those who study the Bible primarily as literature would identify certain more technical literary designations, but they are beyond the

Table 1.1   The Order of the Books of the Hebrew Bible

Hebrew Bible	Protestant Bible	Jerusalem Bible (with *Apocrypha*)

The Law
  Genesis
  Exodus
  Leviticus
  Numbers
  Deuteronomy
	History
	  Genesis
	  Exodus
	  Leviticus
	  Numbers
	  Deuteronomy
	  Joshua
		The Pentateuch
		  Genesis
		  Exodus
		  Leviticus
		  Numbers
		  Deuteronomy

The Prophets
  The Former Prophets
    Joshua
    Judges
    Samuel
    Kings
  The Latter Prophets
    Isaiah
    Jeremiah
    Ezekial
    (The Twelve)
    Hosea
    Joel
    Amos
    Obadiah
    Jonah
    Micah
    Nahum
    Habakkuk
    Zephaniah
    Haggai
    Zechariah
    Malachi
	Judges
	  Ruth
	  1 Samuel
	  2 Samuel
	  1 Kings
	  2 Kings
	  1 Chronicles
	  Ezra
	  Nehemiah
	  Esther
		The Historical Books
		  Joshua
		  Judges
		  Ruth
		  1 Samuel
		  2 Samuel
		  1 Kings
		  2 Kings
		  1 Chronicles
		  2 Chronicles
		  Ezra and Nehemiah
		  Tobit
		  Judith
		  Esther
		  The First Book of Maccabees
		  The Second Book of Maccabees

The Writings
  Psalms
  Proverbs
  Job
  Song of Songs (Solomon)
  Ruth
  Lamentations
  Ecclesiastes
  Esther
  Daniel
  Ezra
  Nehemiah
  Chronicles
	Poetic Books
	  Job
	  Psalms
	  Proverbs
	  Ecclesiastes
	  Song of Solomon
	
	Major Prophets
	  Isaiah
	  Jeremiah; Lamentations
	  Ezekiel
	  Daniel
	
	Minor Prophets
	  Hosea
	  Joel
	  Amos
	  Obadiah
	  Jonah
	  Micah
	  Nahum
	  Habakkuk
	  Zephaniah
	  Haggai
	  Zechariah
	  Malachi
		The Wisdom Books
		  Job
		  Psalms
		  Proverbs
		  Ecclesiastes
		  The Song of Songs
		  The Book of Wisdom
		  Ecclesiasticus
		
		The Prophets
		  Isaiah
		  Jeremiah
		  Lamentations
		  Baruch
		  Ezekiel
		  Daniel (*with additions*)
		  Hosea
		  Joel
		  Amos
		  Obadiah
		  Jonah
		  Micah
		  Nahum
		  Habakkuk
		  Zephaniah
		  Haggai
		  Zechariah
		  Malachi

scope of this introduction. Here literary form is acknowledged when it is helpful in understanding the work being studied.

There is a sense of historic progression in the books that deal primarily with history. The first book of the Hebrew Bible begins with the story of creation and continues uninterrupted through the reestablishment of Judaism in the Holy Land after the Babylonian exile. The historic detail in the Christian writings begins with the Gospel accounts of the birth of Jesus and ends with Paul's imprisonment in Rome, near the end of the first generation of Christianity.

THE ARENA OUT OF WHICH THE BIBLE AROSE

A final consideration is important before we turn to the Bible itself, namely, the lands and the people of those lands out of which the Judeo-Christian tradition arose (see map, p. 15). Nothing happens in a vacuum, and the Jews and Christians were surely affected by their environment.

The land of Israel, known as **Canaan** before the invasion of Joshua and as **Palestine** after the Babylonian captivity, is the Holy Land for both Jews and Christians. It also holds a special place in the religion of Islam. One might wonder how this small and rather barren strip of land on the shores of the Mediterranean Sea has come to play such an important role in three major world religions. The answer to that question lies perhaps in location as much as any other factor: The Holy Land always served as a land bridge between the major civilizations of the ancient Near East. It was the access road for competing cultures, and control of this small area was of strategic military and commercial value. No wonder that throughout history, the larger and more powerful nations of the region viewed the control of land claimed

by the descendants of Abraham as important to their own well-being.

The Hebrew people were apparently native to the Sumerian civilization, which dates back to at least 3200 B.C.E. Centered in the valley of the Tigris and Euphrates rivers, and later renamed Mesopotamia by the Greeks, it was from Ur of the Chaldeans, a site in lower Mesopotamia, that we are told in Genesis 11:31 that Abraham's father moved his family. Sumerian origins of the Hebrews would account for the close similarities found in the Genesis accounts of creation and the flood and the Sumerian accounts found in the Gilgamesh epics, for both could be explained as being found in earlier Sumerian myths.

The Bible itself reports the ties of later Hebrews to Sumeria, pointing out that they were essentially nomads, not landed people, until their occupation of Canaan after the death of Moses. The initial settling of the sons of Jacob in Egypt coincides in time to the period when the Egyptians were dominated by a foreign group known as the Hyksos (approximately 1750 B.C.E.), and the enslavement of the Jews by a later Egyptian dynasty seems appropriate to the reemergence of Egyptian self-control (approximately 1570 B.C.E.).

If the followers of **Joshua** occupied Canaan in the thirteenth century B.C.E., they did so at a time when Egypt was preoccupied both internally and externally with more pressing affairs than dealing with a relatively small group of monotheistic rebels. The fates of Israel and Egypt, however, remained closely bound. There is every indication, in the Hebrew Bible and elsewhere, that Egypt was successful in dominating Israel and Judah when Egypt itself was dominant, that the Jews and Egyptians saw their fates intertwined in times of distress and entered alliances in such periods, and that simply because of their proximity, the two nations could never be totally free of each other.

During most of the historic development of

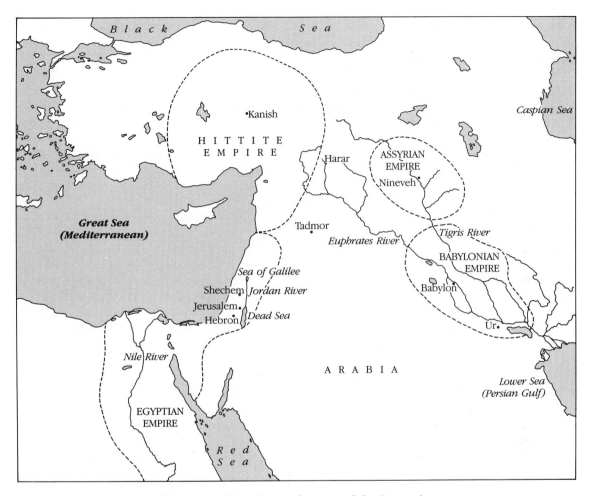

The ancient Near East at the time of the Patriarchs.

the Hebrew Bible, whatever power prevailed in the ancient Near East had a dominant influence on the history of the Jews. From the time of Moses it was the Egyptians. As Egypt declined in power the Assyrians became dominant, defeating the divided nation of Israel in 721 B.C.E., ending its history and making Judah but a vassal state during the first half of the seventh century B.C.E. With the decline of Assyria came the rise of the Babylonian Empire

(587 B.C.E.), followed by the Persians (539 B.C.E.), the Greeks (323 B.C.E.), and finally the Romans (67 B.C.E.). One can get a fairly good sense of the political history of the region by reading the Hebrew Bible carefully and with that question in mind.

The history of the period in which the Hebrew Bible was being formed can also be reconstructed with the aid of archeology, which has recovered artifacts of an astonishing variety from that area and that time period. It is through such discoveries that we know of the Gilgamesh epics, Hammurabi's Law (laws dating from the time of Abraham prepared by the famous Babylonian king, for which many striking parallels can be found in the Laws of Moses), the history of the dynasties of Egypt, and many other things contemporary to Hebrew Bible history. These continuing discoveries affirm that the writers of the Hebrew Bible did take history seriously, but it also affirms that they wrote that history with their own point of view and purposes clearly in mind. The writers clearly were not writing history for the pure sake of history, but to tell how Yahweh used history for his purposes.

During the Persian period of domination the Holy Land was known to outsiders as Palestine, and that has been the name used generally by non-Jews and non-Christians through the remainder of biblical history. By whatever name, it remains the Holy Land of the Judeo-Christian tradition and plays a very special role in both religious traditions. A portion of the land has been reoccupied by modern Jews and is known to us today as the state of Israel.

Rome, the occupying force in the Holy Land at the beginning of the Christian era, was the successor to the far-flung empire of **Alexander the Great.** All roads did indeed lead to and from Rome, and the unity of that empire was certainly a factor in the rapid spread of Christianity in its first few centuries of existence.

The Holy Land itself needs to be understood within the context of its internal history under the Judeo-Christian tradition. It became the homeland of Judaism at the time of Joshua's invasion of Canaan (1210 B.C.E.), and remained so until their expulsion from the land by the Romans in 135 C.E. Christianity, as a child of Judaism, inherited a special relationship to that land. In the early moments of history the twelve **tribes of Israel** occupied various portions of the land as their own, having no central government. The monarchy, a central gov-

ernment, was not established until the time of **Saul** (1020 B.C.E.) and the nation remained unified only through the reign of **Solomon.** On the death of Solomon (922 B.C.E.), Israel divided into two nations, Israel and Judah. Israel, the larger and more strategically located, fell to the Assyrians in 721 B.C.E. Judah, the smaller and more isolated portion of the land with Jerusalem as its capital, fell to Babylon in 587 B.C.E. Judaism survived within the tradition of Judah, thus its name, whose history continued after Persia defeated Babylon in 539 B.C.E. and allowed the Jews to return to the land from which they had been expelled. For all intents and purposes the Jews were not fully in control of their political destinies again in the biblical period, but at least some of them remained rooted in the land they believed destined for them by their God. Several maps throughout the text reflect the various borders and divisions during this turbulent history.

From the time of David, Jerusalem has been the Holy City of the Holy Land. It was in Jerusalem that stood the Temple of Yahweh, according to Jewish law the only appropriate place for sacrifices to Yahweh to be offered. Where once stood the Temple now stands the important mosque, the Dome of the Rock, and the Temple cannot be rebuilt while the Islamic shrine stands. That alone accounts for some of the modern tension among Jews and Moslems.

The geography of Israel is as diverse as its history. The coastal plain is interrupted by rising mountains whose backsides lead to a much more arid environment. The northern portion of the country is much more fruitful than the south, having a more ample supply of water. Where one lived had much to do with what one did, be it farmer, shepherd, or tradesperson. The **Philistines,** the perpetual enemies of Israel, occupied the coastal plain, but never seemed interested in the more arid portions of the country. The portion of the land that became Judah was located in the more hilly and less desirable portion of the area, away from

Dome of the Rock, located on the Temple Mount
in Jerusalem.

major trade routes and with less productive land, accounting perhaps for Judah's more tranquil political existence during much of its history.

All these factors are important to our total understanding of the Bible, which we are now better prepared to examine. Our study of the Bible begins where the Bible begins, and continues through the stages of the developing Judeo-Christian tradition. Guided by a sense of history, the journey begins with traditions common to much of humanity and ends with Christianity having emerged as a religion distinct from Judaism.

STUDY QUESTIONS

1. How would you explain the Bible to someone who is approaching that document for the first time?

2. How can the scholarly tools described in this chapter help one to better understand the Bible?

3. Identify the moments in the history of the Judeo-Christian tradition that you think are most important in helping one to understand the religious world views expressed in both the Hebrew Bible and New Testament.

4. How does the Hebrew Bible differ from the Christian Bible?

5. How can having a sense of history of the Jews and some knowledge of the geography and history of the land they occupied aid you in your study of the Bible?

6. Why would someone use such terms as *Hebrew Bible* or *Christian writings* to refer to writings more commonly known as the Old and New Testaments?

7. Explain the differences in the Jewish and Christian canons; include in your discussion an explanation of who determined the content of each.

8. What is meant by the idea that the authors of the Bible might have had sources from which they worked? Illustrate your response with an example that might suggest the use of sources within the Bible.

9. Explain why many call modern Israel the Holy Land.

SUGGESTED READINGS

Friedman, Richard Elliott. *Who Wrote the Bible?* (Prentice-Hall, Englewood Cliffs, N.J., 1987).

Goodspeed, Edgar J. *How Came the Bible?* (Abingdon Press, Nashville, 1979).

Juel, Donald, James S. Ackerman, and Thayer S. Warshaw. *An Introduction to New Testament Literature* (Abingdon Press, Nashville, 1978).

Mendenhall, George M. *The Tenth Generation: The Origins of the Biblical Tradition* (Johns Hopkins University Press, Baltimore, 1973).

Napier, B. Davie. *From Faith to Faith* (Harper & Row, New York, 1955).

Neusner, Jacob. *From Testament to Torah* (Prentice-Hall, Englewood Cliffs, N.J., 1988).

Trawick, Buckner B. *The Bible as Literature: The New Testament* (Barnes and Noble Outline Series, New York, 1968).

———. *The Bible as Literature: The Old Testament and the Apocrypha* (Barnes and Noble Outline Series, New York, 1970).

TWO

"IN THE BEGINNING . . ."

THE BOOK OF GENESIS

The Purpose of the Beginning

Judaism has maintained a sense of chosenness throughout history, dating its beginning to the time of **Abraham** and understanding its destiny in relation to the people's loyalty to the Covenant and Law delivered by Moses in the midst of the Exodus. Judaism also recognizes that its special role in history has implications for the whole human family. Yahweh says to Israel in calling it into covenant, "I will count you a kingdom of priests, a consecrated nation" (Exod. 19:6a). This is the moment in which Israel's future is shaped, and it is from the events included in that moment that Israel understands its destiny. Throughout the remainder of the Hebrew Bible, the authors look back to the moment in which Yahweh called Israel into covenant and delivered the Law, to understand the past and present and to project the future. Traditionally, both national and personal success and failure have been understood in relation to the loyalty of Israel, or the individual, to that moment in history. So central to the understanding of Judaism are those events that many begin their study of the Hebrew Bible with the material describing those events, the story of Moses and the Exodus.

When the story is recalled by Jews, however, they begin at the very beginning. Chapters 1–11 of Genesis tell a universal story, the history of all humanity. Chapters 12–50 tell the particular story of the Jews, separating the one people from the many. Before there can be a covenant there must be a community with which that agreement can be made. Genesis represents the collective memory of Israel as to how that community was formed. In the midst of human history, Yahweh chooses Israel for a special role, which was to be defined later. In the story is a blending of myth, legend, and history, and it is not always easy to separate one from the other. Whatever the form, however, the purpose is to give meaning to human existence. The story addresses the questions of why life is as it is, what brought people to the present, and what should direct their future.

The Pentateuch, or the so-called Books of Moses, are classified together and known as the Books of the Law or the **Torah.** In whatever ways they achieved their final form, it is obvious that those responsible for these five books understood them as being intimately interconnected. As the law is connected with the Covenant, so is the history that precedes both. It is because of this connection that it is not unreasonable to approach the Pentateuch as a whole, not in fragmented parts. The history of humanity has a common beginning, resulting in the world view of the Judeo-Christian tradition that presents its own understanding of how the creature is to stand in relation to the creator.

This study begins with Genesis, assuming an intentional link with the remaining books of the Pentateuch. The suggested readings allow the reader to have the sense of connection, without being burdened with the minute detail that might be explored later. The sense of connection should be kept in mind as the expanded dramatic history is explored. If the events of the Moses story are central, it must be remembered that Moses did not emerge in isolation. There was already a sense of community, a common heritage to which Moses could appeal. The materials found in Genesis are as close to that tradition as we are likely to come. For that reason alone it is appropriate to begin at the beginning, the stories of Genesis.

In the first section (Gen. 1–11) some of the stories have prototypes found in the remnants of other ancient cultures. Babylonia had both a creation and a flood story similar to those found in Genesis. Some scholars suggest that the Hebrews borrowed those stories for their own, while others take them as evidence of a tradition once held in common. Certainly the ancient Hebrews would not have quarreled over the source, for this was quite obviously the story of every person. It reflected recognition of the Israelites' common roots with the human family, of which they would be reminded again and again. In the New Testament (Acts 15), for example, early Christianity retains the common Jewish belief that the law given to Noah about eating meat with blood (Gen. 9:4) applies to all people, not simply the Jews.

Section II (Gen. 12–50) is special, for it directs itself to the establishment of a separate Jewish identity. Most scholars believe that the people in this story, unlike the characters in the first section, were real and that the places can be put into historical contexts. In broad strokes it tells the story of the Jews from their tribal, nomadic days to the point when they find themselves gathered in Egypt. Though few would rely on the details of this story to answer all their historic questions, most would recognize that the story is rooted in history as we know it. Like all biblical history, it is told for the sake of something more than history and that purpose must not be overlooked. History provides the arena to speak of the God of history.

The entire Book of Genesis should be read with imagination. If the stories are told to answer the "why" questions of life, they must be read with that in mind. Reaching back to a time before history, to a time accessible only through such traditions as are found here, the reader can find contact with much that still forms us today. Humanity has much in common with its ancient ancestors, the so-called primitive people from whom this tradition came. In fact, the reader will soon discover what an amazing influence those "primitive" people continue to exercise over our "modern" Western world, particularly because this tradition has continued to be preserved.

There is no question that if Genesis 1–11 were constructed by a twentieth-century writer, the stories would be significantly different. Who would believe a story of a lonely God perched in the midst of space, creating something out of nothing? For the past two centuries, people have been trying to reconcile the Bible stories with what is now thought to be a more accurate, "scientific" understanding of the origins of life. While some have clung to a literal understanding of these scriptures and have themselves attempted to use science to uphold their beliefs, others have dismissed the Genesis account as myth or legend, finding the stories useful in only limited ways. However, both sides tend to miss much of the point of the stories. If one reads with imagination, being open to the story as story, one can come very close to the power and purpose of these traditions as they have functioned throughout the Judeo-Christian tradition.

Imagine, if you will, sitting around a tribal campfire being told the stories of Adam and Eve and Cain and Abel as they are found here. To believe them literally, as most contemporary hearers likely did, does not rob them of their real purpose, which was to answer the questions of "why?" Those who were informed by these traditions, who shared them with succeeding generations, did so because they understood story as story, recognizing that value lay in the message, not the detail. There is good evidence that, throughout the Bible, "message" was preserved over detail, for message was the intention. Literalism for our ancestors did not get in the way of the story as story. It should not get in our way if we, too, allow story to function as story.

What do the stories convey when read with imagination? Some can find the answer while allowing the story to remain literal, whereas others are not able to do this. Remember, the Bible is not a neutral book, but an affirmation of a religious **tradition.** If one accepts those affirmations they become a part of that tradition, an act of faith. However, one can understand them without accepting them, and one's imagination will help in either case. In his conflict with the **Pharisees,** Jesus criticized them for their narrow, literal understanding of the Law. He seems to have said that one must live by the spirit of the Law, the intention of the Law, to be truly obedient to it. One must look behind the laws to find the Law. As this investigation of the Bible begins, you must try to look behind the stories to find the story.

Prehistory

✦ **READ**   *Genesis 1–11*

Genesis begins at the beginning with the story of creation (or two creation stories, according to some). After the introduction of the human

in creation, in the very image of God according to Chapter 1, came the **"Fall."** Whether the cause of the "Fall" was the human desire to be like God or simply disobedience, it had dire consequences not only for Adam and Eve, but for their heirs as well. Students of primitive religions will note that elements in these stories have much in common with religious myths of other cultures, and such observations can be helpful in finding the purpose of the stories. The traditions of most primitive cultures have creation stories that attempt to define not only the origins of those cultures, but the relation of the creatures of those cultures to the cultures' creator(s).

In the Creation story found in Genesis there are a number of observable parallels with the early Babylonian text entitled "Enuma Elish." Primeval chaos shrouded in darkness before the creation of light, the creation of the firmament, dry land, the luminaries, and humans are present in both accounts. A period of rest for the gods (God in the Hebrew version) concludes both accounts.

The story with the clearest parallel is one commonly referred to as the flood or deluge account (Genesis 6–9). The gods (God) decide to send a flood. Though the reasons for this action differ in the varying accounts, humankind has done something to disturb the gods (God). A person to be saved is identified, a boat is built, some humans and other animals are preserved in the midst of the deluge. All of the actions occur at the initiation of some divinity.*

The eleven chapters of Genesis can be divided into a simple outline, which will be

---

*Students may find it helpful to explore this topic in more depth; books on this single subject are plentiful. A helpful discussion on the similarities of the Hebrew and earlier Sumerian and Akkadian texts can be found in John Rogerson and Philip Davies, *The Old Testament World* (Englewood Cliffs, N.J.: Prentice-Hall, 1989), pp. 196–216.

helpful in keeping the continuing study in mind.

I. The Two Creation Stories (1:1–2:4; 2:5–25)

II. The Fall (3:1–24)

III. Cain and Abel (4:1–24)

IV. Seth (4:25–26)

V. Adam's Descendants (5:1–32)

VI. The Nephilim (6:1–4)

VII. The Flood (6:5–9:17)

VIII. Noah's Descendants (9:18–32)

IX. The Tower of Babel (11:1–9)

X. Genealogy to Abraham (11:10–32)

To provide a sense of connection, the outline above begins with the beginning, then turns to the problem of human alienation, keeping in mind the linkage of the generations of the human family. After sin has been defined, the consequences of sin are affirmed. The Flood story continues that theme, which is climaxed in the story of the Tower of Babel, which quite clearly incorporates all of humanity, not simply the Hebrew people. Just as clear is the importance attached to the naming of the various generations. As you will discover, it is out of the whole that the particular is to come; but just as clearly, the particular are affirming their common roots with all the human family. Each individual story has its own role, but all also have an obvious connection with what is to follow.

As you read Chapters 1–11, list the questions you believe the stories are designed to answer. Then, using the stories themselves, answer those questions. At the conclusion of such an exercise, you will have developed the general world religious view out of which the Judeo-Christian tradition emerged. List now the various affirmations of those observations.

Your list will probably include at least some of the following:

1. God is the source of all creation.

2. Humanity was created in the image of God.

3. Creation was good.

4. Humanity was given dominion over the earth.

5. Evil came because humanity forgot that it was the created, not the creator.

6. As a consequence of its disobedience, humanity lives in battle with the creation in which it once enjoyed a harmonious relationship.

7. Further consequences of the continuing disobedience bring further suffering.

8. At one time all humanity acknowledged dependence on Yahweh.

9. Humanity continued in disobedience, making Yahweh sorry he had created it.

10. Yahweh sought to cleanse creation of its wickedness, and his anger brought great devastation.

11. Yahweh again sought obedience from his creatures as he delivered the First Covenant.

12. Later history was determined by the faithful and faithless relationships of those who had a vision of Yahweh.

13. Humanity continued to try to assume the role of God; thus the enmity among themselves, as well as alienation from their Creator.

Your list could be much longer; it might well be different. That does not make it wrong. Like the preceding outline, however, the list above includes elements common to the religious mentality of the world three thousand years ago. It contains at least some of the common roots to which later Judaism would give more specific definition. It includes the affirmation that the Judeo-Christian tradition had more universal roots and would have more universal responsibilities. For, as will be discovered, if the later community that preserves this tradition is to define itself in more narrow terms, it retains common roots with all and is still to play a universal role among the human family.

It is not too early to observe how the stories that make up the ongoing story have individual functions, as you have seen above. Each of the episodes that you read and easily remember, such as the serpent in the Garden of Eden or the flood, has embedded within it its own moral or religious lesson(s). Each answers a question as to *why*, while at the same time connecting with the other episodes to make a related account that has a broader function. Students will find it helpful to explore the function of individual stories even as they ponder the overall message these stories in combination impart.

It is from individual stories that many of you have learned about your own religious tradition, and it is in those traditions that many of you have learned how those stories can be understood within their own context. It is also at this level that one finds many of the religious traditions developing their own understanding of the meaning of the particular text. While this is an important function of the Bible for the religions that use it as scripture, it is not the primary function of this text—although it will be important at times in developing an overview of the Bible. That certainly should not deter you from examining this aspect further. After all, the original function of the story was to pass on a religious value system.

The Patriarchs

◆ **READ**   *Genesis 12–50*

Genealogies appear often as you read through the Bible. They have essentially two functions: to acknowledge the common link of all humanity, and to identify those who are a part of the community that Yahweh set aside for his special purposes, namely, the Jews, or the children of Abraham. Abraham and his immediate descendants are known to us as the patriarchs.

If Chapters 1–11 acknowledge common human beginnings, representing the universal story of humanity, Chapters 12–50 introduce us to the sense of the chosen, the story of the Jews and their special place in the human family. The story begins with Abram (Abraham) and continues through to **Jacob** (Israel) and his twelve sons (tribes). By the end there is a sense of chosenness, a dream of a land, and a gathering in Egypt in preparation for the defining moment of their history.

Unlike the earlier portions, this part of the story might well be dated, assuming that the events and people portrayed correspond to concrete historical incident. This is not to suggest that nothing that precedes Abraham has a historic reference point or that everything that follows is literal history. Yet with the introduction of Abraham, history becomes more like history as we know it. Although the purpose of these chapters of Genesis is obviously to relate the story of Yahweh, not Abraham, **Isaac,** or Jacob, it is more likely that the patriarchs' stories are told with a stronger sense of the context of history in mind. It is for this reason that many scholars are willing to suggest a date in history for Abraham and his successors.

The story of Abraham and his offspring is the story of nomadic tribal people among whom a dream was implanted. That dream bound succeeding generations with a sense of destiny, still somewhat unformed when this story ends and the next begins.

It is possible to read these stories with the same imagination appropriate to the stories that preceded them. What is their purpose, what questions do they address, or what values do they affirm? Why did Yahweh choose Abraham? Better still, why would a God of compassion and love make a father take his favorite son to the top of a mountain and have him believe that he was going to have to put him to death? Again a list to record and answer such questions will be helpful to the reader. The single story about Abraham's sacrifice of Isaac is itself the subject of a number of scholarly and religious books.

There is a clear sense of connection between the succeeding generations these stories encompass. Moreover, the people in these stories are not the perfect images of religious heroes. In the story about Jacob acquiring his birthright, for example, there is a reality that should be noted, for it will help in understanding the true purpose of all the stories.

An outline of this portion of Genesis reveals its movement:

I. Abraham (12:1–25:11). Yahweh chooses Abraham to be "Father of Jews." The promise that the people will possess the land of Canaan is introduced, as well as the covenant of circumcision. Dimension of covenant relationship is introduced, though not defined. Included in the account are stories explaining the enmity between later Jews and **Ishmaelites,** the Moabites, and the **Amorites.** The story of Lot, Sodom, and Gomorrah is also found in this sequence. At Abraham's death his son Isaac receives his inheritance.

II. Isaac (21:1–22:15, 24:1–67, 35:22–29). The most prominent story about Isaac involves him only passively, as Abraham prepares to sacrifice his son as proof of Abraham's faithful obedience to Yahweh. Otherwise, Isaac's story has no great moments, and he appears only as a transitional figure in the Book of Genesis.

III. Jacob (Israel) (25:19–35:29)
A. Here is the story of one of the less exemplary characters in the Hebrew Bible, yet it is Jacob who fathers the twelve tribes of Israel. This sly, conniving son of Isaac shows all the attributes of a nomadic survivor, but hardly what one would imagine for the soul of a religious hero one would create. Not only does he obtain his inheritance by deceit, but he also tricks Laban, his father-in-law, out of some of his wealth. Together with his wife, he steals Laban's household goods.
B. The narrator is not unaware of the darker side of Jacob, and there are some efforts to justify him in the story itself. For example, it is implied (25:29–34) that Esau did not value his birthright. Jacob even wrestles with a supernatural being (later referred to as God), after which his name is changed to Israel. He fathers twelve sons, who are to be progenitors of the twelve tribes of Israel.

Joseph

◆ **READ** *Genesis 37–50*

Joseph is the focus of the concluding chapters of the story of the patriarchs. Favorite of Jacob's twelve sons, **Joseph** enjoys special favor with his father. He is sold into slavery by his jealous brothers, who report to his father his death. Transported to Egypt as a slave, he eventually rises to great prominence in Pharaoh's court. Wise and chaste, he foregoes vengeance against his wicked brothers, instead bringing his entire family to live in Egypt, thus allowing them to survive a severe famine in Canaan. As Joseph's story ends, the Jews are in Egypt; in future years they become slaves, to be delivered by the next hero, Moses.

As you recall the broad outline above, you will note how much detail it omitted. You will want to include more detail in your own outline, perhaps entitling the individual stories (such as the story of Jacob's dream, or Joseph's resistance to seduction). At the same time you will want to keep in mind the connection among individual stories, focusing on how they combine to build a particular religious world view, one that is particularly well articulated in the Moses story.

MOSES AND THE PENTATEUCH

The Shaping of a Religion

◆ **READ**   *Exodus 1–24, 32–34; Numbers 10–14, 20–25; Deuteronomy 32–33*

In discerning how Judaism understands its emergence from the whole, we have shared in the story of how Jews acquired a sense of specialness within a religious understanding of themselves. Yet, the Book of Genesis does not provide a great deal of definition in regard to the content of that religion. The remainder of the Pentateuch, through Moses, supplies that definition.

The opening of Exodus introduces us to Moses. You will want to remember, however, that the story is not about Moses. It is about Yahweh and his dealing with Israel. These next four books of the Bible, Exodus through Deuteronomy, reflect the shaping and defining of the relationship of Yahweh with his chosen. It becomes, as you will discover, the standard by which Israel will always understand itself. That discovery is embedded in stories throughout the Hebrew Bible, and you will be shown its presence throughout our study. Whether we examine the work of a prophet such as **Amos** or a literary masterpiece such as the Book of **Job,** the standard by which Israel is measured is found in the story of the Covenant and the Law, which we now explore.

The suggested readings begin with the historic details of the Exodus and conclude with the death of Moses. You have also been given a sample of the law—enough to impart a sense of the all-encompassing nature of the law in the Hebrew religion. An outline of the material suggests the various aspects of the material you are reading.

  I. Preparation for the Exodus
    A. The Hebrews become slaves (Exod. 1:1–22)
    B. The introduction of Moses (2:1–22)
    C. The call of Moses (2:23–4:17)
    D. Moses' return to Egypt (4:18–31)
    E. The first encounter with Pharaoh (5:1–5)
    F. The ten plagues (7:8–10:29, 12:29–34)
    G. The institution of the Passover (12:1–28, 43–51)

 II. The Exodus
    A. The departure from Egypt (Exod. 13:17–14:14)
    B. Crossing the Sea of Reeds (14:15–31)
    C. The desert experience (15:22–18:27)

III. The Covenant and the Law
    A. The arrival at Sinai (Exod. 19:1–2)
    B. The Covenant promised (19:3–8)
    C. The Ten Commandments (20:1–7)
    D. The Book of the Covenant (20:22–23:19)
    E. The Covenant affirmed (24:1–18)

 IV. The First Failure
    A. The golden calf (Exod. 32:1–35)
    B. The relation of the Covenant to the Law (34:10–28)

  V. The Departure from Sinai
    A. Leaving Sinai (Num. 10:1–36)
    B. Spying out Canaan (13:1–33)
    C. Rebellion, and the consequence (14:1–38)
    D. The unsanctioned invasion of Canaan (14:39–45)

 VI. Moses' Farewell (Deut. 32:1–47, 33:1–29)

The prominent Hebrew Bible scholar Bernhard Anderson says that in the events surrounding the Exodus we have the outline of Mosaic theology that informs the remainder of the history of Israel. Included in that theology are the following points:

1. Yahweh is the Lord of history and makes himself known through the events of history.

2. Yahweh has chosen Israel for a special role.

3. For Israel there is but one God, Yahweh.*

One should probably add that in the chosen relationship Yahweh provided for Israel, the rules for the covenant relationship are found in the Law. This Law, by the way, is more than a set of rules to be followed. It is really the guide to a way of life. That will be discussed later in this text but needs to be acknowledged here. Law is teacher, guide, the measure by which Israel is judged in relationship to the holy obligations it assumes in the Covenant.

As Anderson and others properly observe, Exodus, Covenant, and Law are intricately bound to one another and must be understood in that binding relationship. If the story of Abraham begins the story of Judaism, the events of the Moses story surely define what it is to be. If all these stories are grounded in real history, they surely are told by those who believe that history has meaning beyond the events themselves. We are reading **experienced history,** history written by those who are more concerned with meaning than event, who provide meaning as event is recalled. We can probably rehearse the history of Israel quite well in the Hebrew Bible, however, knowing that we do not have the report of unbiased observers. If we remember that the history is both selective and interpreted, we can garner a fairly good

sense of what must have happened from Egypt to Canaan and understand as well how the events were understood by the participants.

Of course all history is interpreted, and no history is free of bias. No historian can report an event without finally, in one way or another, interpreting. Therefore, a knowledge of our biblical writers' understanding of history is all the more important. If they truly believed that Yahweh was the Lord of history and made himself known through the events of that history, they took history very seriously. Remembering this point of view will be helpful in your study of the Bible, for it applies equally throughout the Bible, even in books that probably make no claim to be historic.

If you have read these selections from the Pentateuch with an awareness that the stories issue from the experience of the community that has repeated them for us and reflect the community's particular understanding of their meaning, you have dealt with its original intention. Yahweh, the Lord of history, chose Israel to play a special role in the midst of history, to be a kingdom of priests, a holy nation. To enable them to perform this role, he delivered his people from their oppressors and gave them a covenant bound by their responsibilities defined in law. We need to look at the various parts as well as the sum, and that is what we will do next.

The Story of Moses

When people who are to have special roles in the Bible are introduced, the stories often give the reader clues: Isaac is a gift to Abraham and Sarah when Sarah is beyond the child-bearing years; Joseph is born to Rachel, Jacob's true love who had been barren; and Moses is saved from death by being hidden in the bulrushes, to be raised finally in the court of Pharaoh. Later **Samuel** is the answer to the prayer of a barren woman, young David slays a giant, **John the Baptist** is born to aged parents, and Jesus is

*See Bernhard W. Anderson, *Understanding the Old Testament,* 3rd ed. (Englewood Cliffs, N.J.: Prentice-Hall, 1975), pp. 95–97.

Michelangelo's portrayal of Moses.

portrayed as being born of a virgin. As in every case, the early events in Moses' life are indeed a portent of things to come.

Moses was indeed a historic person, the chief architect in the shaping of Judaism. Many scholars suggest that at least in the form we now have, much of the particular law that the Bible attributes to Moses postdates the life of the patriarch. It is generally agreed, however, that Moses himself passed on to the people the concepts of Covenant and Law. For the defining ingredient within the Jewish religion, his story is really quite brief. This story, honed through years of telling, includes only the elements essential to its point. Like most biblical narrative, every detail has purpose, so that brevity becomes its greatest asset.

Exodus begins by placing Israel in Egypt. Having grown rich and powerful, the Israelites now pose a threat to their hosts. A king, "who knew nothing of Joseph," enslaves them. As they continue to multiply, the king orders the killing of all the male children born to these slaves. Moses, born to a family of Levites, is hidden for three months and then put into a papyrus basket in the reeds of the River Nile. Found by the daughter of Pharaoh, he is kept as her own by the young woman, who hires his natural mother to nurse him.

Moses grows up as a prince in the court of the Egyptian king. Aware of his roots, he kills an Egyptian who is abusing a Hebrew slave. To avoid death at the hand of the Pharaoh, he flees to **Midian,** where he marries the daughter of a Midianite priest and becomes a shepherd.

In the meantime, the Israelites cry to Yahweh for deliverance. In response, Yahweh reveals himself to Moses in a "burning bush," ordering him to return to Egypt and rescue the people. In this encounter Yahweh reveals his name to Moses (Exod. 3:13–15), with the understanding that the name implies a God who is involved in history. Some suggest that the name itself can be interpreted "He who causes to be," an indication of an understanding of a God whose very name indicates his continued involvement in history.

Armed only with his staff, which Yahweh has empowered, Moses reluctantly returns to Egypt to intercede with Pharaoh on behalf of his people. In a strange interlude that occurs on the journey, Yahweh tries to kill Moses. He is saved by his wife, Zipporah, who circumcises their son and touches the genitals of Moses. The story reflects the importance for Jewish identity of the covenant of circumcision, which was not fully a part of Jewish tradition at the time.

On his arrival in Egypt, Moses meets his brother **Aaron,** and they together inform the sons of Israel of Moses' mission. Almost immediately Moses and Aaron begin a series of encounters with Pharaoh in which the king is told that Yahweh demands the release of his people. Declining to acknowledge Yahweh, Pharaoh refuses, instead increasing the burden of the slaves. The Israelites moan at the burden, and Moses responds in his own frustration to Yahweh.

Parts of Chapters 6 and 7 seem to recount another version of Moses' commission, interspersed with a genealogy. Highlighted is the fact that only here does Israel learn God's name, Yahweh; thus Israel is able to learn his nature.

Following is an account of the ten plagues, or signs, in which Yahweh shows that his power is superior to that of the gods of Egypt. Pharaoh remains unconvinced because Yahweh has "hardened his heart," obviously to allow a display of God's awesome power. Each plague is more devastating. Though the first two plagues are matched by the magicians of Pharaoh's court, none of the rest can be duplicated, showing how much more powerful is Yahweh than the gods of Egypt. The final plague, the death of the firstborn, is the basis for the Jewish festival of the **Passover.** It is also the factor that led Pharaoh to tell the Jews to leave Egypt.

The story reports that six hundred thousand men—not counting their families—left Egypt, along with their flocks and herds. Moses establishes the Passover, indicating that it is to be celebrated only by Jews, either by birth or conversion via circumcision. The consecration of the firstborn is also established at this point in the story.

The people are led into the wilderness, so that they will not have to fight the Philistines and lose heart, preceded by a pillar of cloud by day and a pillar of fire by night. Reaching the banks of the Red Sea (called the Sea of Reeds in the Jerusalem Bible), the Israelites are pursued by Pharaoh and his army, which Yahweh intends to use to display once again his mighty power. Already terrified, unconvinced of Yahweh's capacity to save them, the Israelites cry out in despair. As the Egyptians approach from the rear, Yahweh parts the waters to allow the Hebrews to escape. When the Egyptians pursue, they are swallowed by the sea as Yahweh releases the water upon them. Chapter 15 contains a hymn, or liturgical poem, that celebrates the event in later Judaism. Verse 21, known as the Song of **Miriam,** is believed to be a couplet dating back to the event it extols, perhaps the oldest bit of poetry in the Bible.

The Israelites now find themselves in the desert, complaining bitterly of their uncomfortable circumstances. Water and food, in the form of **manna,** are provided by Yahweh. Quails are even provided as meat for the hungry people. Moving through the wilderness, the Israelites are attacked by the Amalekites. Yahweh provides them with victory, just as he had provided them with material sustenance.

Jethro, the Midianite priest and father-in-law of Moses, arrives in camp to comfort and advise Moses. On his suggestions, the people are organized to share some of the burdens Moses has thus far carried alone.

Three months after the departure from Egypt, the people arrive at the wilderness at Sinai. Though it is a relatively short time, the period at Sinai consumes an inordinate portion of the literature: From Exodus 19 to Numbers 10 are materials devoted to the events that purportedly took place at this stop in their journey.

It is in Exodus 19:3–8 that the Covenant is delivered, followed in Chapter 20 with the beginning of the Law expressed in the **Ten Commandments.** Exodus 20:22–23:19 is known as the Book of the Covenant. It contains **absolute law** and **conditional law, ritual, moral,** and **religious laws.** Its location so close to the Covenant is an indication that for Judaism every aspect of human behavior is under Yahweh's authority, that law governs one's relations with neighbors as well as with God.

The Covenant is ratified before the people, and Moses departs to the mountain to receive the Law from the very hand of Yahweh. An interlude includes laws in reference to worship and establishes Aaron and his sons in the role of the priesthood. While Moses is away, the people become afraid they have lost him. They, with Aaron, erect a golden calf (probably to represent Yahweh), thus violating one of the laws they have already received. Yahweh expresses his anger, but Moses intervenes in behalf of the people. Yahweh's judgment is withheld. When Moses enters the camp and observes the people paying homage to the idols they have created, he breaks the tablets of stone on which the laws were recorded. Moses orders that some be killed for their sin, proving that those who transgress the Law shall not go unpunished.

Moses goes back to the mountain to have Yahweh replace the Law, once again encountering Yahweh and again receiving the Law. Upon his return, Moses' face shines brightly, an indication that he has indeed been in Yahweh's presence.

The materials from Exodus 35 to Numbers 10 (incorporating the whole book of Leviticus) have to do with laws, prescribing in detail the religious obligations that are to be followed in obedience to the covenant relationship. These materials contain prescriptions for everything from the erection of the tent of the meeting, the responsibility of the Levites, to rules for conjugal relationships.

The Israelites leave Sinai in Numbers 10:33. The people continue to whimper and moan, complaining every step of the way. At the borders of Canaan, a reconnaissance team composed of one person from each of the twelve tribes is formed. Only Joshua and Caleb bring back a positive report, while the others tell stories of a veritable land of giants, saying that the Canaanites are too powerful to overcome. The people become fearful at the reports, evoking the wrath of Yahweh because of their lack of trust in him. Moses tries to intervene on their behalf once again. Though not disowning the people entirely, Yahweh decrees that this

generation (except for the faithful Joshua and Caleb) shall not enter the **promised land.** Though some have second thoughts and attempt to invade Canaan, their efforts fail, for they have neither Moses nor the **Ark of Covenant** with them.

The history of the next forty years is contained in the remainder of Numbers. The account of these wilderness years explains why Moses and Aaron will not enter Canaan (they failed to give Yahweh proper credit), reports the deaths of Miriam and Aaron and the early conquest of lands across the Jordan, tells the story of **Balaam** and his ass, describes the Jewish feasts that were to become a part of their national life, and assigns portions of Canaan to the various tribes. Chapter 33 reviews the stages of the Exodus.

Numbers ends with the Israelites camped across the Jordan from Canaan, ready to claim the inheritance long awaited. Deuteronomy, the last book of the Pentateuch, is purported to be the farewell sermon of Moses. In many respects it is really a summary of the three preceding books. It not only rehearses the history, it repeats much of the Law as well. Set into three discourses (1:1–4:40, 4:41–28:69, 29:1–33:29), it is a fitting preparation for Israel as she awaits to live out her destiny. It reminds the people what brought them to this moment in history and what they must do to achieve a successful future. Chapter 34 describes the death of Moses after he has been allowed to view the promised land, which he has been forbidden to enter.

The importance of this story to the understanding of the remainder of the Bible cannot be emphasized too strongly; it is no exaggeration to say that the rest of the Bible is understood through the world view expressed in the Pentateuch. As many have stated, "Once one has come to grasp the central importance and meaning of the story surrounding the Exodus, all the rest of the Bible can be regarded as commentary." It will not hurt to review some important points.

That Yahweh is a God of history is implicit from the story of creation. The very nature of the ongoing story reemphasizes Yahweh's revealing presence in history. In case the point was missed, however, the language of the Covenant reminds you, "You yourselves have seen what I did with the Egyptians, how I carried you on eagles' wings and brought you unto myself. From this know that . . ." (19:5–6).

The second important point is that Yahweh has chosen Israel. That, of course, is first articulated in the story of Abraham but is dramatized in the story of the deliverance of the Jews from the hand of Egypt. Until the time of the Covenant expressed in Exodus 19, one might say that Israel had a sense of being chosen but no definition of what it meant to be chosen. In the Moses story that definition is given in the language of the Covenant: "I will count you a kingdom of priests, a consecrated nation" (19:6).

Directly related to the Covenant relationship is, of course, the Law. If you obey my voice and hold fast to my Covenant, Yahweh is saying, then . . .

If you read the rest of the Bible and keep in mind the history out of which it was created, you will discover that it articulates this concept of a world view to future generations (see the first verses of Joshua as a restatement of the values imbedded in the Moses story), teaches this view and its implications to those within the tradition (Proverbs provides a helpful example), or reports and interprets history based upon this world view (the Deuteronomic view of history that will be discussed in the next chapter). When scholars say that "all else is commentary," they simply mean that the rest of the Bible (and that includes the Christian writings) is indeed a series of explanations and interpretations that seek to define, for example, what it means to be a kingdom of priests.

An answer to that question is probably what turned Judaism into the world religion it is today, but that story will come later. The remainder of this text assumes that the reader understands the world view imbedded in the ongoing story found in the Pentateuch. This point will become clearer as our exploration of the Bible continues.

QUESTIONS RAISED BY THE EXODUS STORY

Although tradition attributes the authorship of the Pentateuch to Moses, even the casual reader is led to question the idea that the material is the work of a single writer. For example, the story of Moses is told in the third person. The death of Moses is reported, something he could hardly have done himself. As observed earlier, the Book of Exodus gives two accounts of Moses' call by Yahweh (Chs. 3 and 6). Chapter 15 contains a longer and shorter version of the Song of Miriam. The list is extensive, and the reader can make his or her own. The question is not so much whether Moses was the final author of the Pentateuch (literary evidence alone belies that) but what connection he had with the materials represented there. If he was not the final author, was Moses at least the spiritual father of the Pentateuch? The answer to that question is probably yes.

The material in Genesis clearly is more ancient than Moses. If he was the author of a portion of the Pentateuch, he was more an editor than an author in Genesis. In the case of the next four books, many scholars suggest that this codification represents the Law at a much later period of development in Hebrew history, a law fully developed over the years as a landed culture. At the same time, however, the concepts of Covenant and Law surely were introduced by Moses and, in that sense, we can truly speak of "the Law of Moses."

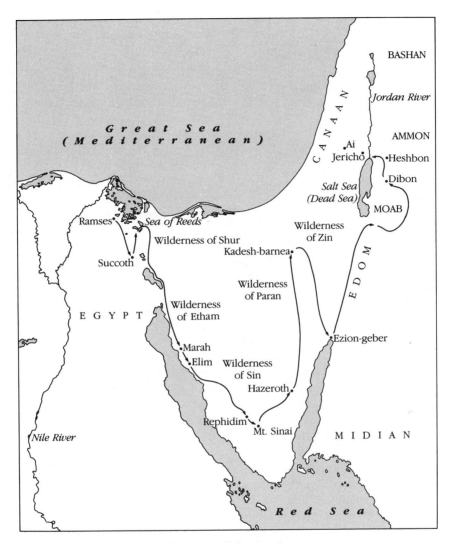

The route of the Exodus.

The date and route of the Exodus, as well as the number of participants, are all open to question, though few doubt that an Exodus took place (see map above). If one were to rely solely on the materials of the Pentateuch, the event would have to have occurred earlier than the date now assumed by most scholars, namely, nearly 1250 B.C.E. The confusion over the route comes from the inability to link our imprecise knowledge of ancient geography with the biblical records. The almost two million people reported in Exodus (600,000 men, plus women and children) seems an exaggeration to many scholars, simply because of the logistics involved in such a massive move. Questions have also been raised about the ten plagues. Some suggest that the occurrences reported (except for the slaying of the firstborn) are all natural phenomena, repeatable and observable at other moments in history. It also has been suggested that the manna described in Exodus resembles a honeylike substance commonly found in the desert.

THE EYES OF FAITH

Even if all the alternatives suggested above are true, as opposed to the literal version of the Exodus, the integrity of the story is not challenged; we have simply been given a better understanding of the viewpoint of the story-teller. That viewpoint is of central interest for the student of the Bible, and it remains intact whether the story is dealt with literally or critically. The viewpoint affirms the belief that Yahweh is indeed the Lord of history and uses history for his purposes. What might be explained in one way by one who lacks the sensitivity is viewed entirely differently by one who knows this is the work of Yahweh. The very name by which God identifies himself at the burning bush, the name Yahweh, is important. Not only is the name revealed, the meaning of that name is also provided. This is a God active in history, one who is the cause behind what is, and to know his name is to know his nature. The story itself tells us that those who were a part of the Exodus did not appreciate the true meaning of that experience, and it remained for Moses to try to help them understand. The people are reported as constantly complaining, or being afraid. In the midst of the experience they did not always sense the presence of Yahweh in their midst. This remains true throughout the Hebrew Bible. There must always be someone standing among them pointing to the true meaning of the event,

and we read history that has been interpreted through the **"eyes of faith."**

"Why," some have asked, "is there no mention of the Exodus in Egyptian records?" Perhaps the occasion was not significant to the Egyptians. On the other hand, it was in the midst of this event and the understanding of it that Judaism was shaped. History, viewed through the eyes of faith, takes on an entirely new meaning for those who share this perception. What might seem natural to others becomes supernatural to those who truly believe that the hand of Yahweh causes history to happen as it does. This is history written not for the simple sake of history, but for the sake of faith.

Using the Pentateuch, one could reconstruct the history of the Exodus and come to conclusions entirely different from those of our author. The detainment of the Israelites in the wilderness, for example, could be explained by pointing out that the generations that left Egypt were not numerous enough or strong enough in military power to overcome the fortified cities of Canaan. The author/editor of the Pentateuch, as we know, cites the failure of the people to trust Yahweh. Strangely enough, each conclusion could be true in its own context. One is a statement of history, one a statement of faith; they are not contradictory. In the Bible the eyes of faith look beyond history; they look to what they understand to be the cause of history to report history, for they believe God is the God of history, using it for his purposes. That viewpoint remains consistent throughout the Bible, and it must be understood if the Bible is to be understood. The Bible reports God's activity through the eyes of those who have been spiritually sensitized to perceive that activity in the midst of what others perceive as an ordinary world. Here Moses provides the spiritual insights. Later others will report history, not as neutral observers, but as people of faith.

Viewed through the faithful eyes of our storyteller, the key to understanding the meaning of all the events reported is found in Exodus 19:3–8:

> Moses then went up to God, and Yahweh called to him from the mountain, saying, "Say this to the house of Jacob, declare this to the sons of Israel. 'You yourselves have seen what I did with the Egyptians, how I carried you on eagles' wings and brought you to myself. From this you know that now, if you obey my voice and hold fast to my covenant, you of all the nations shall be my very own, for all the earth is mine. I will count you a kingdom of priests, a consecrated nation!' Those are the words you are to speak to the sons of Israel." So Moses went and summoned the elders of the people, putting before them all that Yahweh had bidden him. Then all the people answered as one, "All that Yahweh has said, we will do." And Moses took the people's reply back to Yahweh.

Thus, the Israelites are now a people of the Covenant. The Covenant is based on Yahweh's deliverance from the Egyptians and will be bounded by the Law, the means by which the people will express their faithfulness to Yahweh as their king.

Very soon in the story the people break the bounds of the covenant relationship, and the consequences are immediate. Chapter 32 begins the story of the golden calf, the first of many instances of an unfaithful Israel. Unfaithfulness has its own consequences, and Israel will continue to understand its low moments in history in that sense. In delivering the Jews from the Egyptians, Yahweh has shown who he is, calling the sons of Israel into covenant. To be Yahweh's people, they must live in faithful obedience to him, for it is only in such obedience that they can serve his purposes. Observance of the Law is the means by which such obedience is to be reflected.

Much of the remainder of the Pentateuch delivers the Law, which was all encompassing. It was not, however, just a set of rules that removed responsible decision making from the individual. As becomes clear, the Law was a way of life reflecting the kingship of Yahweh for this holy community, which was to be his witness to the world. Obedience to the Law represented the people's faithfulness to the task they gladly assumed in response to Yahweh's call. Though they would often lose their way, the Law was to remain the standard by which they understood all that occurred.

STUDY QUESTIONS

1. How does Genesis 1–11 differ from the remainder of Genesis in scope and purpose?

2. Who are the patriarchs, and why are their stories important to our study of the Hebrew Bible?

3. What elements of the stories about Abraham and Sarah do you consider most important in regard to the continuing study of Judaism, and why?

4. Explain the importance of the story of Jacob to the continuing story of Judaism.

5. How would you defend Jacob as a religious hero, and what problems would you encounter?

6. Identify Moses and explain his major contributions in the definition of what it means to be a Jew.

7. What is meant by the Covenant and the Law, and how are these concepts important to our understanding of the Bible?

8. What is meant by "the composite nature" of the Pentateuch?

9. How would you summarize the religious world view presented in the Pentateuch as a whole?

10. Explain what is meant by the statement that the story of the events surrounding Moses and his life provides the focal point for all the rest of the Bible, and "all else is commentary."

11. Identify the connection between Covenant and Law as it is expressed in Exodus 19.

12. How would you explain the purpose of the story of the golden calf in the context of the ongoing story of Moses and the Exodus?

SUGGESTED READINGS

Albright, W. F. *From Stone Age to Christianity*, 2nd ed. (Johns Hopkins University Press, Baltimore, 1946).

Buber, Martin. *Moses: The Revelation and the Covenant* (Harper & Row, New York, 1958).

Dentan, R. C. "Numbers, Book of," *The Interpreter's Dictionary of the Bible*, Vol. 3 (Abingdon Press, Nashville, 1962).

Eissefeldt, O. "Genesis," *The Interpreter's Dictionary of the Bible*, Vol. 2 (Abingdon Press, Nashville, 1962).

Freeman, D. N. "Pentateuch," *The Interpreter's Dictionary of the Bible*, Vol. 3 (Abingdon Press, Nashville, 1962).

Hunt, Ignatius. *The World of the Patriarchs* (Prentice-Hall, Englewood Cliffs, N.J., 1967).

Kikawada, Isaac M., and Arthur Quinn. *Before Abraham Was: The Unity of Genesis 1–11* (Abingdon Press, Nashville, 1985).

Nicholson, Ernest W. *God and His People: Covenant and Theology in the Old Testament* (Oxford University Press, New York, 1986).

Pagels, Elaine. *Adam, Eve, and the Serpent* (Random House, New York, 1988).

Pritchard, J. B. *Ancient Near Eastern Texts* (Princeton University Press, Princeton, N.J., 1955).

Sarna, Nahum M. *Exploring Exodus: The Heritage of Biblical Israel* (Shocken Books, New York, 1986).

Thompson, Thomas L. *The Origin Tradition of Ancient Israel: The Literary Formation of Genesis and Exodus 1–23* (JSOT Press, Sheffield, 1987).

von Rad, Gerhard. *Genesis* (Westminster Press, Philadelphia, 1961).

Wright, G. E. "Exodus, Book of," *The Interpreter's Dictionary of the Bible*, Vol. 2 (Abingdon Press, Nashville, 1962).

THREE

SHAPING THE FUTURE: BECOMING A NATION

◆ **READ** *Joshua 1–10, 23–24; Judges 1–21; 1 Samuel; 2 Samuel 1–20; 1 and 2 Kings*

The books from Joshua to 2 Kings (except for Ruth, which will be dealt with in another context) cover the period from the invasion of Canaan by the Israelites (1250 B.C.E.) to the end of the monarchies (587 B.C.E.), the period some call the golden era of Jewish history.

The Jerusalem Bible has chronologies and maps to which you can refer from time to time to keep historic moments in perspective. Although you will find that not all such materials are in absolute agreement, these guides do afford a general sense of historical context.

The suggested readings for this chapter include the major events of this history but may exclude some things you consider important. It would be well to read this entire section of the Bible. Again, an outline of what is contained in these books should be helpful as you review these materials (see also Table 3.1):

I. Joshua
  A. Preparation for conquest (1:1–5:12)
  B. Conquest of Jericho (5:13–7:26)
  C. Conquest of Ai and other events (8:1–9:29)
  D. North and South subdued (10:1–12:24)
  E. Land apportioned and tribes described (13:1–21:45)
  F. End of Joshua's rule (22:1–24:31)

II. Judges
  A. Summary of settlement of Canaan (1:1–2:5)
  B. Age of the Judges (2:6–3:6)
  C. The individual judges (3:7–16:31)
    1. Othniel (3:7–11)
    2. Ehud (3:12–30)
    3. Shamgar (3:31)
    4. Deborah (4:1–5:31)
    5. Gideon (6:1–8:35)
    6. Abimelech's abortive kingship (9:1–57)
    7. Tola (10:1–2)
    8. Jair (10:3–5)
    9. Jephthah (10:6–12:7)
    10. Ibzan (12:8–10)
    11. Elon (12:11–12)
    12. Abdon (12:13–15)

13. Samson (13:1–16:31)
D. Danite and Benjamin stories
(17:1–21:25)

III. 1 Samuel
A. The story of Samuel (1:1–7:17)
B. Samuel and Saul (8:1–15:35)
C. Saul and David (16:1–31:13)
1. David flees (22:1–26:25)
2. David among the Philistines
(27:1–31:13)

IV. 2 Samuel
A. David becomes king of Judah
(2:1–4:12)
B. David king of all Israel (5:1–8:18)
C. History of David and his family
(9:1–20:26)
D. Other events (21:1–24:25)

V. 1 Kings
A. Solomon becomes king (1:1–2:46)
B. Solomon's reign (3:1–11:43)
1. The wisdom (3:1–4:1)
2. The builder (5:1–9:25)*
3. The trader (9:26–10:29)
4. The king's decline (11:1–43)
C. The divided kingdom (12:1–22:54)
1. The two kingdoms until Elijah
(14:1–16:34)
2. The Elijah cycle (17:1–2 Kings
1:18)

VI. 2 Kings (the divided kingdom continued)
A. Stories about prophets (1:1–13:25)

1. Elisha cycle (2:1–8:29)
2. Anointing of Jehu (9:1–37)
B. Till the fall of the North
(14:1–17:41)
C. Till the fall of the South
(18:1–25:30)

THE NATURE OF THE HISTORY

As the stories remind you throughout, this is not a simple history of the **Hebrews** as they invade Canaan or establish themselves as a nation. The Jews evidently did produce such histories, and the writer or writers of these books we now study have made use of them. Note the suggestion to go to the Book of the Annals of the Kings of Israel or Judah to get more detail about the secular history. The story the biblical writers chronicle focuses on the religious dimension of the history of the period, a Mosaic or prophetic view of history. As will be suggested in the next chapter, the version of these books we now read was probably the work of a member of a prophetic school, who used three major sources for his work. Beyond the Books of Annals was probably a tradition of the prophets that well could have included both oral and written materials.

It is well worth repeating that the world view behind all the Bible is the concept that Yahweh is the Lord of history and makes himself known in the midst of that history. The history we read here is intended to help us understand Yahweh. He is the central subject matter. Though you read about people and events, these are only vehicles to speak about something beyond them.

The story begins with Joshua as he leads the exiles into the promised land. It is followed by the tradition of the **Judges,** which leads to the stories about the establishment of the monarchy and its history. If Moses is the spokesman for Yahweh during the Exodus, Joshua assumes

---

*On occasion, the texts from which the Jerusalem Bible was translated have verses that differ in order from the standard St. Jerome Latin version of the Bible. When this occurs the previous numbering appears in italics along with the new numbering dictated by the texts being used. This accounts for the double numbering of verses you find in portions of the Jerusalem Bible and explains why verse numberings may vary slightly if you use another translation of the Bible.

Table 3.1 Major Moments in Jewish History

Approximate Date	Important Event
1750 B.C.E.	Abraham called to his role
1250	Exodus led by Moses
1210	Invasion of Canaan led by Joshua
1210–1020	Period of tribal confederacy
1020	Saul becomes first king of Israel
1000	David becomes king
961	Solomon becomes king
922	Israel and Judah divide
721	Israel falls to Assyria
621	Josiah's reform
587	Judah falls to Babylon
539	Jewish exiles return to Jerusalem
520–515	Temple rebuilt
458 or later	Period of Ezra and Nehemiah
332	Alexander the Great conquers Palestine
167	Maccabean War
63	Palestine becomes a Roman protectorate
70 C.E.	Temple destroyed
90	Canon of Jewish scripture established
135	Jews expelled from Palestine

only supplies some historic detail, but explains the why of the history. You will note that the story does not give all events or persons equal attention, and it is appropriate to ask why that is so. Note, as well, that there are no unblemished characters in the stories. Even **David,** the king against whom all others are measured, is presented with all his faults, and the facts selected for telling about his life would probably not lead many of us to the conclusions the author draws about him. On the other hand, Saul does not seem as villainous as the contemporary judgments made about him would indicate. These biases, in themselves, help the reader to be sensitive to the point of view with which they are to be presented. Of course, the summaries about the Kings, as well as the reasons given for the fall of Israel, are also clear indications of the viewpoint that dominates these books.

This viewpoint—which affirms that individuals of the community would be blessed by Yahweh if they remained faithful and were punished when unfaithful—is introduced in the concluding chapters of Joshua, expressed again in the stories of the Judges, and repeated on numerous occasions through the remainder of the stories. The standard of faithfulness, of course, consisted of the Law and the Covenant. It is a confirmation of the observation made in Chapter 2 that the events surrounding the Exodus became the constant focal point of Israel's self-understanding.

JOSHUA AND THE CONQUEST OF CANAAN

Beginning with the affirmation of the death of Moses, the story of Joshua is a continuation of the Pentateuch, and it is apparent that it was composed by someone richly steeped in tradition. Yahweh's opening address to Joshua reminds us of the preceding events:

that role during the invasion, as do the prophets in the later history. The role of the Judges in this respect is less clear, as we shall see.

Bible scholars refer to this section of the Hebrew Bible as the **Deuteronomic history,** suggesting that it had a sense of connection and is dominated by a particular point of view, probably provided by its final editor or author. It not

Only be strong and stand firm and be careful to keep all the Law which my servant Moses laid on you. Never swerve from this to right or left, and then you will be happy in all you do. Have the book of Law always on your lips; meditate on it day and night, so that you may carefully keep everything that is written in it. Then you will prosper in your dealings, then you will have success. Have I not told you: Be strong and stand firm? Be fearless then, be confident, for go where you will, Yahweh your God is with you. (Joshua 1:7–9)

Not only does this view dominate the material you study now, it is the standard for everything to follow. That point is made early in Joshua. As soon as **Jericho** has been captured, the Jews move on to take **Ai.** Though intelligence reports indicate that victory should be easy, Joshua's troops are at first repulsed. Joshua's lament to Yahweh asks why and he is told, "Israel has sinned; they have violated the Covenant I ordained for them" (7:11). Only after the sin is removed are they able to continue their conquest of the land.

One gets the impression from Joshua that Canaan is well in the hands of the Hebrews, subdued at least to the point where the individual tribes can possess the lands assigned to them without the aid of the other tribes. At the end of the initial conquests and the distribution of the land, followed by a period of peace, Joshua assembled the twelve tribes at **Shechem.** Chapters 23 and 24 seem to report two different events, though they could fit together: Chapter 23 is Joshua's farewell sermon; Chapter 24 reports the events of the **convocation at Shechem.** In the first Joshua reminds the people of the standards by which they must live and the consequences of failure in this regard, while in the second he leads all the people in a ceremony of covenant renewal, again reminding them of the consequences of failure. In the second is something very close to a liturgy used in Israel from a time as early as Joshua. The priest might well have repeated

the words of Joshua, while the people made the appropriate responses.

The convocation at Shechem provided the ingredients for whatever political unity existed in Israel during the period of the Judges. It is conjectured that the tribes assembled on a regular basis at Shechem, rehearsed their history, and renewed their Covenant vows. Some suggest further that it was on such occasions that converts were initiated into Judaism; the words of the ritual certainly lend themselves to such an assumption.

THE ERA OF THE JUDGES

The era of the Judges was a period of transition, during which the highly independent, tribal people found that they needed a greater sense of unity if they were to survive as a nation. After the story found in Joshua, the reader assumes that the tribes are well established in the new land. The Judges' account indicates that the tribes of Israel had a great deal more to do before the land was securely in their hands. Again, the story is told from the religious perspective, through the eyes of faith. If the land was not easily conquered, the fault lay not in Yahweh, but in the unfaithfulness of the people. In the story of each judge we are informed that it was the lack of faithfulness on the part of the people that caused Yahweh to deliver them into the hands of their enemies. It was only after the people repented and turned again to Yahweh that he provided them with victory.

None of the Judges seemed to have presided over all of Israel, and neither were they jurists in the usual sense of that term, **Deborah** perhaps being the exception. The role, as described in the Bible, seems to be that of tribal warlord rather than settler of legal or religious disputes. They are not associated with religious leadership, although the last judge, Samuel, may well have played a variety of roles. Judges did not inherit their positions; rather, they are described as being raised up by Yahweh to deliver his people at a particular moment in history. By the time of Samuel, however, there seems to have been a change in the nature of succession, for it is said that his sons were not worthy of succeeding him.

During the period of the Judges no judge presumed continuing or central power. The story of **Gideon** has a ring of verisimilitude when it suggests that the people tried to make this popular and successful judge their king. Gideon's son **Abimelech** apparently found a following among some of the tribes, for he became king of a portion of Israel for a short time. Though this writer does not acknowledge Abimelech's kingship as legitimate, the episode recognizes the problem that existed during this period of relative disorganization. The term "tribal confederacy" describes the form of government in Israel during the period of the Judges. There was no central government, and only a loose sense of tribal unity seemed to have arisen during periods of threat from outsiders. In these insecure times, the various judges provided whatever leadership existed across tribal lines. Israel was apparently never totally secure politically or nationally during this time. Plagued by others who had claim to the same lands and lacking the strength of total unity of resources, those who had lived with the promise of a land they believed destined to them by their God found their expectations unfulfilled.

You will note that though twelve judges are listed, little is said about many of them. Some scholars have therefore devised categories of major and minor judges, based on the space allotted to their respective stories. Obviously Deborah and Gideon were considered to be the most important of the lot by the Deuteronomic historian if that standard is applied. **Samson,** who hardly qualifies as a judge by our standards, also receives a great deal of attention. His large presence might represent the continued popularity of this folk hero embedded in the tradition of Israel, for the story certainly presents an enigma to most scholars who try to explain the important place of Samson in the Book of Judges.

The other oddity found in Judges is that the last four chapters are obviously a postscript to the main body of the story, used to explain how the **Danites** settled into their territory and how the **Benjaminites** became outcasts among the tribes of Israel. The sin of Benjamin can be likened to the story of Sodom and Gomorrah, while the compromise that allowed the Benjaminites to obtain wives from the tribes of Israel is representative of the customs of other tribal peoples who have excluded from their midst those found to be morally repugnant. The stories have the ring of tribal history about them, and there is no reason not to treat them as essentially authentic.

SAMUEL: THE TRANSITIONAL FIGURE

Samuel's importance is indicated in the way his story is introduced. The story of this man, who plays many roles, from priest, to warrior/judge, to prophet, to almost king, begins when he is born in answer to the prayer of the previously barren Hannah. The young Samuel is dedicated to the service of Yahweh as an expression of Hannah's gratitude.

Samuel, who is of the tribe of **Ephraim,** not a Levite, serves the priest **Eli** and assumes a priestly role in the history told about him. Thus the role of priest was not assigned exclusively to the Levites at this time in history.

The story implies that the high priest has a political as well as a religious role, and Eli is the nearest thing to a king Israel has at the time. Eli's sons were assumed to be the natural successors to their father's religious and political leadership. Indeed, they appear to have usurped some of this power in Eli's later years. Abuse of that power, however, caused the dissatisfaction among the people and could well have been a cause for the change from the priestly leadership of the nation to an eventual monarchy. Samuel became the transitional figure in that change.

Samuel is called by Yahweh to be the successor of Eli. The text refers to his call as that of a prophet, but the description of his role is much broader and includes the priestly function. A series of dramatic events results in the death of Eli's sons and the capture of the ark by the Philistines. On hearing the news, Eli falls over and dies, having ruled Israel, we are told, for forty years.

Twenty years later, Samuel emerges as leader/judge. He leads the people to victory over the Philistines in his warlord role, while offering priestly sacrifice. This part of the story of Samuel very obviously is drawn from two sources, one much more favorable to the establishment of the monarchy than the other. After we are told that Samuel was judge over Israel for as long as he lived, the next episode relates the events that lead to the establishment of the monarchy.

Like Eli, Samuel has sons who assume some of his functions as judge in his later years. They, like the sons of Eli, do not live up to the high standards of their father. In the first story (Chapter 8) the people ask Samuel to appoint a king. Samuel seeks the guidance of Yahweh, who says that the requests represent not a rejection of Samuel, but a rejection of Yahweh "from ruling over them." Samuel points out the disadvantages of monarchy, but the people insist. In the ensuing events Yahweh is portrayed as identifying Saul to Samuel and being responsible for providing them with a king, while at other times it appears that Yahweh allows a king while accepting such a move as a rejection of his kingship over Israel.

SAUL: THE FIRST KING

There are two clear and continuing traditions about the monarchy, one more favorable to the idea than the other. In the more favorable account Saul is gifted with the spirit of ecstasy, appearing like one of the prophets (1 Sam. 10: 9–12). In the other tradition Saul is rejected from his kingship because he assumed the role of priest and sacrificed in the absence of Samuel. A careful reading of this portion of Israel's collective memory will provide numerous examples for the reader, the sum of which will be commented on later.

Saul becomes a rather tragic figure in this history. Elevated to the monarchy, he suffers the consequences of assuming the new role among some who would preserve individual freedom over collective security, and others who believe that politics must remain secondary in a nation built on a religious precept. He was obviously a rather popular leader and must be judged a success as a monarch despite the poor grade assigned him by the Deuteronomic historian.

The account of Saul found in 1 Samuel describes both his successes and failures. His success as a political leader is unquestioned, while his loss of favor with Yahweh is a religious judgment. The story of his loss of favor with Yahweh (1 Sam. 13:8–15; 15:1–23) is accompanied by the introduction of David. The remainder of 1 Samuel is the adventure of David as the groundwork is laid for his assumption of the throne.

DAVID: A DILEMMA

The story of David is perhaps the most intriguing history about one person found in the Hebrew Bible. This son of **Jesse,** who might not even qualify as a Jew by the strict standards set by **Ezra** and **Nehemiah** at a later stage in Hebrew history, is truly a folk hero. Told through the eyes of faith, the story nevertheless includes many aspects that another storyteller (the author of 1 and 2 Chronicles) chose to exclude. David, who becomes the standard against whom all future monarchs are to be measured, is presented here with all his warts and pimples. One cannot accuse the biographer of overglamorizing his hero.

As Yahweh realizes his mistake in choosing Saul, he identifies David to Samuel as the one to be anointed as the next king. Saul loses favor early in the story, but it is not until his death that David can assume power. Even then, it is some time before he is accepted as king over all the tribes of Israel. It would be hard to create a figure such as David, had he not existed. Handsome, strong, bright, politically astute, an accomplished warrior, charismatic, and with the soul of a poet, David, with the aid of Samuel, sets out to become the king Yahweh has anointed him to be. The story of this man, with all the inner struggles dictated by his complexity, is brilliantly told. Again, the blending of traditions is apparent in such instances as David's introduction to the court of Saul, as well as his escape from Saul's jealousy.

David is anointed by Samuel after Yahweh has withdrawn his favor from Saul. Saul remains king and enjoys the support of most of the people for some time. In the meantime, David, the anointed, spends his life on the run, even living for a time among the hated Philistines and apparently serving them, although we are told that David remained loyal to his own people. Upon the death of Saul, David is proclaimed king over the **tribe of Judah,** and Ishbaal, a son of Saul's, is made king over the remaining tribes of Israel. Israel and Judah battle, with David as successful politically as he is militarily. David finally becomes king of all Israel seven years after his assumption of power in Judah and rules over the united tribes for thirty-three years.

It would be a mistake to ignore what the story tells us of David's reign. Although the author indicates that Yahweh gives the house of David his special blessing through the **court prophet Nathan** (2 Sam. 7), indicating that it is to exist forever, David did not have a tranquil monarchy. Much of the remainder of 2 Samuel recalls events in David's monarchy. Many scholars suggest that it uses a court history of David's reign as one of its sources. There is probably also a prophetic memory of those days that provides some of the information included. The story tells us of military successes, of internal strife, and of eventual tranquility in the king's later years. Although David is presented as a religiously sincere lover of Yahweh, his devoutness does not prevent him from coveting the wife of another man and plotting the man's death so that **Bathsheba** can become his bride (after he has made her pregnant). Politically astute, David also reclaims the daughter of Saul as his wife, after he had earlier abandoned her, to secure a stronger claim to the kingship of all Israel. He is obliged to flee his own household and his son **Absalom** in the midst of his monarchy. It is, indeed, a story of contradictions, interpreting history as it is told. What is remarkable is that so many concrete events are retained in such a way that one can perceive history as it was actually experienced. Such is the advantage of having a storyteller who truly believes that it is in the concrete events of history that Yahweh is revealed.

The story of David begins to draw to a close at the end of 2 Samuel. The later chapters include poetry attributed to David as well as some isolated and seemingly unrelated events associated with his reign. Although there is little question that David was a poet of some consequence, there is doubt that the psalm found in Chapter 22 is his work. It seems to reflect a time after the construction of the Temple and a theological standard more akin to the Deuteronomic historian than to David. The other poem (2 Sam. 23:1–7), however, could be from the pen of David.

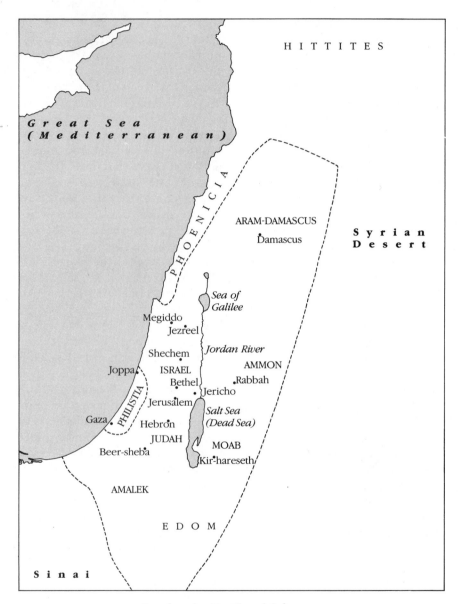

Israel under David and Solomon.

SOLOMON: IN ALL HIS GLORY

The First Book of Kings begins with the last days of David and the intrigues of ensuring that Solomon would succeed him to the throne (see map above). Nathan the prophet and Bathsheba the queen approach David and remind him of his promise that Solomon was to be his heir. Solomon is given David's blessing and anointed king, even while his half-brother

Adonijah is making plans to ascend the throne. The first two chapters detail the events that ensure Solomon will be secure on the throne. Chapter 3 begins the story of the events that make Solomon and his reign significant in the history of Israel.

Solomon is portrayed as a pious leader, granted wisdom as an answer to prayer, blessed by Yahweh for his humble request. He is portrayed as a gifted administrator and wise king, builder of the Temple in Jerusalem as well as a permanent royal palace. This prayer at the occasion of the Temple dedication (Chapter 8) is a theological reflection of the times.

Like his predecessors, Solomon was not perfect, nor was his reign without difficulty. Although Israel enjoyed a time of peace and prosperity during his reign, life as a nation among nations was not without costs. Forced conscription of laborers for Solomon's enormous building programs created internal discontent. His many foreign marriages, probably for the purpose of building political alliances, brought religious problems. The sin of Solomon—allowing his foreign wives to bring their own religions, even erecting places of worship and participating in such worship himself—was a portent of things to come. In the eyes of our storyteller these were the actions of an unfaithful man, and they would have significant consequences. However, a new ingredient had been added to the formula in Yahweh's blessing of the house of David, and it would alter Yahweh's dealing with the transgression of the Law.

THE DIVISION OF THE LAND

Solomon's sin must be punished. Though the consequences are to be experienced by future generations, they serve as a constant reminder that Yahweh will not be rebuked. The tribes gather after the death of Solomon to affirm their allegiance to his heir, **Rehoboam.** The story has already prepared us for what is to follow. **Jeroboam,** representative of the discontent caused by the more repressive aspects of Solomon's reign, speaks for the people before Rehoboam at Shechem, the site of the original tribal convocation. Unwilling to accede to the people's demand for more freedom, Rehoboam pledges an even heavier handed monarchy, resulting in the division of Israel into two separate nations, Israel and Judah. Judah, the smaller kingdom, was to consist of the tribes of Judah and Benjamin, keeping its capital in Jerusalem, the City of David and the site of the Temple. A son of David would be their king. The northern kingdom, Israel, would be composed of the remaining ten tribes and have no continuous monarchy. It would experience a much less tranquil history (see Table 3.2).

The remainder of 1 and 2 Kings chronicles selected events from the two monarchies, giving more attention to Israel than to Judah until Israel falls to the Assyrians in 721 B.C.E. After the fall of Israel the story continues until the defeat of Judah by the Babylonians in 587 B.C.E.

THE STORY OF ISRAEL

The majority of the attention of the history of the divided kingdoms is directed to Israel. Only when the northern kingdom falls does the southern kingdom of Judah receive its appropriate notice. Among the numerous suggestions for this uneven emphasis are:

1. Judah had a fairly tranquil history, with little noteworthy about it.

2. Israel was the apostate state, and its history serves as an example of Yahweh's judgment.

3. Israel's history is concerned more with its prophets than its kings, and their interpretive presence makes that story more significant.

Table 3.2   Kings of Israel and Judah*

Saul 1020–1000 B.C.E.
David 1000–961 B.C.E.
Solomon 961–922 B.C.E.
Division of Monarchy 922 B.C.E.

Israel: Ten Tribes Northern Kingdom, c. 922–721 B.C.E. (fell to Assyria)	**Judah:** Two Tribes Southern Kingdom, c. 922–587 B.C.E. (fell to Babylon)
Jeroboam c. 922–901	Rehoboam c. 922–915
Nadab c. 901–900	Abijah (Abijam) c. 915–913
Baasha c. 900–877	Asa c. 913–873
Elah c. 877–876	Jehoshaphat c. 873–849
Zimri c. 876 (7 days)	Jehoram c. 849–842
	Ahaziah c. 842
OMRI DYNASTY	Athaliah† c. 842–837
Omri c. 876–869	Joash c. 837–800
Ahab c. 869–850	Amaziah c. 800–783
Ahaziah c. 850–849	Uzziah (Azariah) c. 783–742
Jehoram c. 849–842	Jotham (regency) c. 750–742; (king) c. 742–735
	Jehoahaz (Ahaz) c. 735–715
JEHU DYNASTY	Hezekiah c. 715–687
Jehu c. 842–815	Manasseh c. 687/6–642
Joahaz c. 815–801	Amon c. 642–640
J(eh)oash c. 801–786	Josiah c. 640–609
Jeroboam II c. 786–764	Jehoahaz II (Shallum) c. 609 (3 mos.)
Zechariah (6 mos.) c. 746–745	Jehoiakim (Eliakim) c. 609–598
Shallum (1 mo.) c. 745	Jehoiachin (Jeconiah) c. 598–597 (3 mos.)
Menahem c. 745–738	Zedekiah (Mattaniah) c. 597–587
Pekahiah c. 738–737	Judah falls 587 B.C.E.
Pekah c. 737–732	
Hoshea c. 732–724	
Israel falls 721 B.C.E.	

*Scholars do not agree on the exact dates of the reigns of the kings of Israel and Judah. These dates here represent one attempt to fit the kings into the context of history as we can best now reconstruct it. The variance of these dates from those provided in the Jerusalem Bible reflects the lack of agreement among scholars about the exact dating of these events. Such differences can be observed in almost every chronology one might find of the kings. These dates presented here are consistent with the information provided in this book.

†Mother of Ahaziah; her reign represents a break in the line of David.

4. Israel was the larger and had a more volatile history, its very size and location making events there more important.

5. The entire national history is about Yahweh's dealing with his people as understood by the prophetic heart; thus, where the prophet was, so was the history remembered.

There are probably other theories equally adequate, but the prophetic aspect of this work is certainly central to any answer. Although the next chapter will make that aspect more clear, one can get a sense of the role of the prophet in the preservation of this material without any aid beyond the material itself, for a prophetic view of history dominates the story, and stories about the prophets are more significant than the story of any king. The prophets are certainly held in a more favorable light than are the kings.

1 and 2 Kings chronicle the entire history of the divided kingdoms (see map, p. 46). The reign of each king is summarized and the religious faithfulness of the monarch assessed. Very few made passing grades in the category in which they were judged. The reader becomes quickly aware that although all kings are included, this is not a history of the monarchy. That information, we are told, is found in the Book of the Annals of the Kings of Judah or the Book of the Annals of the Kings of Israel. Unfortunately, these source books for our author/editor are not available to us.

The story of Israel begins with the reign of Jeroboam (1 Kings 11:26). He is encouraged in his revolt by the prophet **Ahijah,** who prepared him for his task before the death of Solomon. Jeroboam gets an "F" from the Deuteronomic historian, his major sins being the offering of sacrifices beyond the Temple, making visible images of Yahweh, and establishing a priesthood outside the house of Levi. These are obviously the judgments of those who believed that the Temple at Jerusalem was the only appropriate location for sacrifice, the Levitical priesthood the only one allowed by Yahweh, and any visible representation of Yahweh an abomination. Whether right or wrong, the judgments represent an orthodox point of view at a later moment in history and should not be automatically interpreted as the abandonment by Israel of the exclusive worship of Yahweh. There are moments when such condemnation seems appropriate, but the reign of Jeroboam does not appear to be one. Embedded in this story is the recital of the struggle of a divided nation over what are appropriate religious practices, and out of that struggle will develop the concept of **orthodoxy.** The ground rules have been established at the time 1 Kings was written, but they were not agreed on in their own time. How would one honor Yahweh without the Temple or an established priesthood? Jeroboam could have been a pious and well-intentioned king who simply failed the test of a later orthodoxy.

Almost immediately we find interspersed in the story about kings stories about prophets, and indeed, it is the prophet in Israel who plays the more significant role as he speaks in behalf of Yahweh. One detects that the prophet is very much involved in the ongoing political life of Israel, a reminder that the true king of this "holy nation" is Yahweh. The people do not stand in awe of the human king, nor do they believe that Yahweh has endowed the throne with a special blessing, as do their counterparts in Judah. As a result, monarchies are overthrown regularly, internal strife is typical, and constant tension is felt between the body politic and the religious community.

Illustrative of that tension is the large amount of attention devoted to two prophetic heroes of the time, **Elijah** and **Elisha,** who exert considerable political power. It is Elisha who is ultimately responsible for the fall of the **House of Omri** and the establishment of the **House of Jehu.** The entire period is dominated by stories about the prophets. When Jehu becomes king

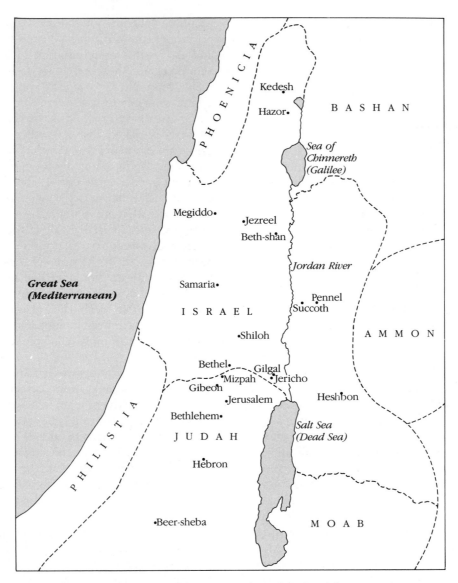

The divided kingdoms of Israel and Judah.

he institutes a religious reform by destroying the followers of **Baal,** although even he did not pass the test of complete religious orthodoxy.

Israel obviously enjoyed some military success. Stability did exist at times, although internal and external strife seemed to have been endemic. Israel's national problems could have been created by its size and location as much as by religious turmoil or unfaithfulness. We are reading a religious judgment made on history after the fact.

Israel was located on an important trade

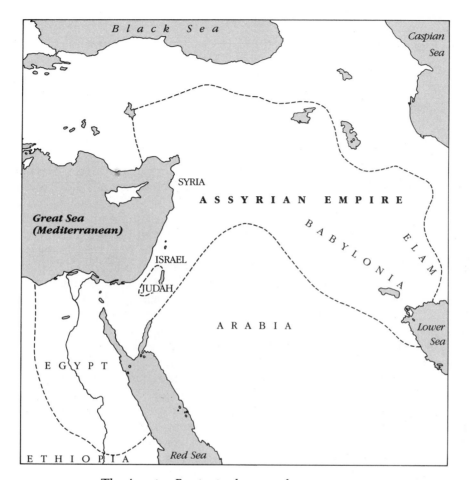

The Assyrian Empire in the seventh century B.C.E.

route in the Mideast and had a population large enough to pose a military threat to those who would dominate the area; its national history was ended by the Assyrian conquest in 721 B.C.E. (see map above). The story is found in 2 Kings 17:1–41. Again, remember that you are not reading an unbiased account. Our author tells us specifically that Israel was destroyed because it had transgressed the Law. In what seem like two accounts of that judgment, the specifics are outlined. Before the accounts end, however, one more detail is added. The presence of the dreaded **Samaritans** is explained,

making certain that the reader understands that they are really not Jews, although they call on the name of Yahweh.

JUDAH: THE APPLE OF YAHWEH'S EYE

Concurrent with the story of Israel is an account of Judah. Though there had been warring between Israel and Judah, as well as between Judah and others, one senses that Judah's national life had been fairly tranquil. A son of

David had been upon the throne except for the brief queenship of **Athaliah** when the House of David was threatened with extinction. Though its monarchs do not get much better grades than those of Israel, they are treated a bit more kindly. The House of David comes nearer the orthodoxy of our judge than do the various houses of Israel. The role of the prophet does not become prominent in the telling of Judah's history until after the fall of Israel, suggesting perhaps that the prophets escaped to Judah in the wake of the conquering Assyrians.

If Judah had enjoyed a degree of tranquility before the fall of Israel, such was not to be the case for the remainder of its national existence. Judah survived the siege of the Assyrians, probably because it did not pose as great a threat as did larger, and more centrally located Israel. Survival was purchased at a high cost, however, for Judah was subjugated to the Assyrians for at least sixty years.

Soon after the fall of Israel, **Hezekiah** became king of Judah. He is one of the few kings to get an uncompromising grade of "A" from our narrator. The leader of a significant religious reform, he also resisted Assyrian domination. It was during his reign that Jerusalem was put under siege by the Assyrians and was seemingly doomed. Hezekiah faithfully followed the advice of the prophet/priest **Isaiah,** the only prophet who seemed fully to support the royal theology of the House of David, based on Yahweh's promise that Jerusalem and the House of David would survive, as they did. This fulfilled promise was to give Judah a false sense of confidence when later it faced the Babylonians.

Judah's survival was not without costs. If there are degrees of failure, Manasseh, Hezekiah's heir to the throne, received the lowest "F" of any king of Judah. Under him, Judah was to maintain its national identity, but probably not much else. We have no record of the prophetic voice. Manasseh's Judah was a mere vassal of Assyria, and the sins of Manasseh are interpreted as an expression of that situation. The religion of Judah was the target of the Assyrian dominance. The Temple was desecrated by the introduction of foreign religion, and there was active persecution of those who resisted such intrusions into their culture. It was not a happy history as long as the Assyrians were powerful.

The story changes as the Assyrians lose their place of dominance and Judah is able to reassert its sense of national independence during the reign of Josiah, another king who receives a favorable grade from our interpreter. Only eight years old when he ascends the throne, Josiah rules for thirty-one years. It is during his reign, in 621 B.C.E., the one-hundred-year anniversary of the fall of Israel, that Josiah orders the cleansing and revamping of the Temple, to rid it of the devastating influence of Assyrian domination. During the cleansing a scroll of the Book of Law is discovered in the Temple and is eventually delivered and read to the king. When it cannot be determined whether the writing is truly representative of the religious tradition of Judah, it is taken to the prophetess **Huldah,** who confirms its authenticity. This discovery of the Book of the Law becomes the occasion for a religious reform, for the Law is reintroduced as a part of Judah's religious tradition. The story seems to indicate just how much had been lost during the period of Assyrian domination, at least to the mass of Judah's population. With the reinsertion of the Law as central comes a verification of the Temple of Jerusalem as the only appropriate place for sacrifice, as well as a reinstitution of the Passover, a most appropriate ceremony for keeping the religious tradition alive. This appears to be a moment when a certain orthodoxy was beginning to be shaped among the Jews.

The remainder of Judah's history is quite sad. Josiah is killed in battle as Judah is caught in a struggle among the more powerful nations seeking political dominance of the area. Until its national history ends in 587 B.C.E., Judah is to be but a pawn in that power struggle. Much of our knowledge of contemporary political and religious life is derived from the writings of prophets during those years. We will examine those works in the next chapter.

2 Kings concludes with the report of a series of national disasters. Josiah was succeeded by Jehoahaz II. Three months later Pharaoh Neco of Egypt captured Jehoahaz and replaced him on the throne with Josiah's son Eliakim, renaming him **Jehoiakim.** Jehoiakim's eleven-year reign saw him become a vassal to **Nebuchadnezzar.** He was succeeded by his son **Jehoiachin,** whose reign in Judah lasted but three months, for Jehoiachin was taken in exile into Babylon, along with much of the national leadership. The well-meaning **Zedekiah** was to rule over Judah for its last ten years of existence. At the end of his reign, his sons were slaughtered, his eyes were put out, and he was taken to Babylon in chains.

Left in Judah are but a few common folk, tillers of the land. For all practical purposes, Judah has no identity of its own. But of course we know that this does not end the story. Apparent defeat is to become a very different kind of victory. With the defeat of the nation comes the triumph of the religion. Before we go on to that story, however, we need to make a few observations about this portion of the Hebrew Bible and to return more closely to an examination of the tradition of the prophets.

AN OVERVIEW OF THE DEUTERONOMIC HISTORY

In numerous places in the books that compose the Deuteronomic history the reader has the impression that a single event is being told from different points of view. A few of those have been identified, and you have probably noted others. Some of the more obvious cases are found in the stories about Samuel, Saul, and David, where one account seems more favorable to the idea of a monarchy for Israel than does the other. As another example, the judgments made about the kings of Israel and Judah tend to be kinder to the kings of Judah, the line of David.

All this has led scholars to conjecture how this tradition reached its final form, which they believe was achieved during the period of the Babylonian exile, soon after the last event it reports, namely, the release of Jehoiachin from imprisonment. The story itself identifies two of the sources it has used, the book of the Annals of the Kings of Judah and the Book of the Annals of the Kings of Israel. In addition to the detailed accounts of the reigns of David and Solomon, two other sources are assumed, the court histories of those two kings. The large amount of material about the prophets found in the various books could indicate a separate tradition about the prophets available to the final author/editor. It is also important that Israel and Judah became separate nations early in their national histories, each having a distinct religious tradition. In Judah the Temple at Jerusalem, the Levitical priesthood, and the throne of David all were important parts of the religious tradition. The tradition of Moses, nurtured in the circle of the prophets, seemed to be the predominant religious force in Israel. All these elements are, of course, found in our stories, for they represent the tradition at the end of the historical period it reports, and these elements have now been blended into a single tradition. It is not likely that such was always so.

During the periods of Joshua and of the Judges, Israel was bound not by national unity but by religious devotion. Gathering, perhaps yearly, at a place such as Shechem, they renewed their religious vows, revived their collective commitment to uphold one another as an expression of their devotion to the dream provided them by Yahweh, and even initiated others into the community by allowing them to accept the covenant condition established by Yahweh, making the history on which that covenant was based their own history. "Choose today whom you wish to serve" (Josh. 24:15).

The arrangement of this loose tribal confederation did not offer the kind of political security people sought, and another system seemed more desirable. Thus a monarchy was proposed and, indeed, instituted. These fiercely independent people who for centuries had enjoyed the freedom that tribal life offers now chafed under the demands imposed by nationhood. It was not long until a large portion of them rebelled, returning to the more independent life, at least in the northern kingdom of Israel. Distrust of the monarchy had both cultural and religious roots. Israel was never to give great respect to any sitting king, often toppling a current monarch at the instigation of a prophetic leader. Judah did maintain a respect for the monarchy, because the idea that Yahweh was to bless their land through the House of David was firmly entrenched.

As the two nations existed side by side, they never lost their sense of kinship. Both called on the name of Yahweh, the one they viewed as the God of history. Israel, lacking the Temple, developed its own **cultic life.** Judah maintained its devotion to the Temple, established early in its history; thus its cultic life was more central to its religious life. The priestly figure assumed the central role in the worship life of Judah, while the prophetic figure was more prominent in Israel. Each nation preserved the religious tradition inherited from their common ancestors, yet circumstances probably dictated the emphasis placed by each on various aspects of that tradition.

With the fall of the northern kingdom to the Assyrians, it is likely that at least some of Israel's prophets sought sanctuary in Judah,

taking with them their cherished religious tradition and their understanding of it. Although this immigration would not have been received with great enthusiasm by the established religious leadership of Judah, circumstances would change. Those who had used the Mosaic standard to understand their own demise would find a more receptive audience under the reign of Manasseh, possibly as the result of the probable martyrdom of the highly respected prophet/priest Isaiah. Religious persecution certainly occurred, for the House of David became a puppet of the hated Assyrians, and the Temple a center of pagan worship. The religious leadership, driven out of the public eye in fear of their lives, saw an appropriate time for the remerging of the traditions that had gone their separate ways for too long. Armed with their collective insights and having viewed history out of their collective judgments, they were prepared to lead God's chosen people along the right path when the opportunity presented itself. That opportunity came very soon.

With the decline of Assyrian power, Judah was able to reestablish its independence. Led by the boy king Josiah, who was raised under the tutelage of the religious community, Judah was returned to the true worship of Yahweh. On the occasion of the cleansing of the Temple of the foreign elements introduced by the Assyrians, a scroll was found, as recounted previously. When its genuineness was accepted, the scroll became one of the foundations for a renewed religious consciousness in Judah. Combined with the reestablishment of Temple worship and the reintroduction of important cultic feasts, Judaism was to emerge with more vigor than its various parts had possessed in its past. Its tradition, now at least in part in literary form, served as a constant measure of its religious health. Fortified with that vision, Judaism was able to enter one of its most traumatic moments and survive. It could view events with the understanding that present travail was not a sign of the weakness of Yahweh, but a sign of his strength. Yahweh was not to be mocked, but neither were his purposes to be defeated. To understand the past would give a clue to and a hope for the future. Thus, our author/editor, using the collective wisdom derived from the long struggle of the people of Yahweh living out their national experiences, sat down to recall that history as only the faithful could do. The results are the Books of Joshua through 2 Kings, our Deuteronomic history, told with the bias of one who has a prophetic understanding of history. It is appropriate now to look specifically at his predecessors the prophets, who established and passed on that tradition in the centuries before.

STUDY QUESTIONS

1. Describe the period of the Judges and identify the major problems encountered by Israel during that period.

2. Discuss the role of Samuel as the transitional figure between the end of the tribal confederacy and the beginning of the monarchy in Israel.

3. Evaluate Saul as the first king of Israel in light of what is reported about him in 1 Samuel.

4. What makes David so prominent in Jewish history? How is his hero status made difficult to accept by the accounts about him in 1 and 2 Samuel?

5. Explain the strengths and weaknesses of Solomon's reign and indicate how they help us better understand Jewish history.

6. Explain the division of Israel and Judah. What do you consider to be the major effects of that division?

7. Summarize the most important points in the history of the northern kingdom of Israel as reported in 1 and 2 Kings.

8. Discuss briefly the history of Judah and try to explain why it survived longer than its sister, Israel.

9. Tell what happened to Israel and to Judah and identify the religious judgments made by the Deuteronomic historian on the fate of each.

10. Explain what is meant by the term *Deuteronomic history,* indicating what the history includes and what point of view it seems to represent.

SUGGESTED READINGS

Freeman, D. N. "Deuteronomic History, The," *The Interpreter's Dictionary of the Bible,* supplementary volume (Abingdon Press, Nashville, 1976).

Good, E. M. "Joshua, Book of," *The Interpreter's Dictionary of the Bible,* Vol. 2 (Abingdon Press, Nashville, 1962).

Halpern, Baruch. *The First Historians: The Hebrew Bible and History* (Harper & Row, San Francisco, 1988).

Kraft, C. F. "Judges, Book of," *The Interpreter's Dictionary of the Bible*, Vol. 2 (Abingdon Press, Nashville, 1962).

Szikszai, S. "Kings, I and II," *The Interpreter's Dictionary of the Bible*, Vol. 3 (Abingdon Press, Nashville, 1962).

———. "Samuel," *The Interpreter's Dictionary of the Bible*, Vol. 4 (Abingdon Press, Nashville, 1962).

———. "Samuel, I and II," *The Interpreter's Dictionary of the Bible*, Vol. 4 (Abingdon Press, Nashville, 1962).

Welch, A. C. *Kings and Prophets of Israel* (Butterworths, London, 1952).

West, James King. *Introduction to the Old Testament*, 2nd ed. (Macmillan, New York, 1981), pp. 199–262.

FOUR

THE PROPHETS

Before we deal with events of the Babylonian exile, we need to pause to consider the **tradition of the prophets.** The role of the prophet goes back at least to the time of Moses, although many scholars suggest that neither the term nor the concept became part of the Hebrew tradition until contact with the Canaanite culture had occurred, after the time of the Judges.

The Hebrew Bible itself suggests many things about the importance of the prophets in the development of Judaism. Their role throughout the period of the monarchy is suggested by the stories about them in 1 and 2 Kings. It is even possible that a member of the prophet school was responsible for the Deuteronomic history. Thus we need to define "a prophet," to be aware of the continuing prophetic tradition, and to have some sense of its influence on the shape of Judaism.

The suggested readings out of the written prophets are intended to give you a sense not only of their works, but also of their influence on one another. You will want eventually to read all the works of the prophets, but for now an overview within the prophetic tradition will be helpful.

A PROPHET DEFINED

Stated most simply, a prophet within the context of Judaism is one who speaks on behalf of God. For example, it becomes clear very early that the story of Moses is really not about Moses. Moses is simply a vehicle to reveal the will of Yahweh. Moses is not the deliverer, nor is he speaking for himself. He acts in behalf of Yahweh, always under his guidance.

We are told in 1 Samuel (9:11) that "a man who is now called a 'prophet' was formerly called a 'seer.'" This statement indicates that the function existed before the term. Though the literary evidence is somewhat sketchy, it is possible to get a sense of the development of the prophet's role in the history of Judaism.

As suggested, Moses was the prototype for the prophets. He spoke on behalf of Yahweh. According to the tradition, Moses told people of a future beyond their existence in Egyptian bondage, but his main function was not to predict the future. He spoke, first and foremost, to his own time, and by linking the concepts of the Law and the Covenant, he laid the foundation for what has come to be known as prophetic theology.

There is some suggestion that, after Moses, leaders of Israel did not automatically assume the prophetic role that Moses had established. Joshua, his successor, is described primarily as a military leader, although his farewell address at Shechem (Joshua 23–24) indicates that he served a religious function as well. The Judges, the charismatic tribal leaders, are portrayed as being appointed by Yahweh to deliver the people out of political turmoil, and it is implied that they might well have provided religious leadership as well, but not like Moses. By the time of Samuel, there are indications that the roles of political leader and prophet had become competitive. Samuel had a political and a religious role in the life of the twelve tribes, similar to Moses, and the formal separation of those two roles seemed to take place at his time in Israel's history. Of the two explanations of why Yahweh rejected Saul as king (1 Sam. 13:8–15, 15:1–23), one has to do with Saul making a sacrifice, the other with Saul's disobedience. Saul had legitimate reason for both the actions that led to his rejection. Though there are numerous theological explanations, including the commentaries in the stories themselves, it is not unreasonable to suggest that we are reading a prophetic view of history. The division of the secular and the sacred, however, was to present a continuing problem for Israel throughout the history of the monarch, and Saul's fall from Yahweh's favor was a portent of events as Israel sought to become a nation like other nations. The religious judgment shared through the Hebrew Bible tells us that the division of function really never worked, and our attention to the prophetic tradition is our best clue to this understanding.

After Samuel there is a clear distinction between king and prophet, though Samuel seemed to embody many roles in his own career. The stories about prophets appear after the establishment of the monarchy, and prophets are often those most directly in conflict with the monarchy, especially in the northern kingdom of Israel. As you read 1 and 2 Kings you might have thought that "Prophets and Kings" would be a better title. The stories about the prophets (prophets who are named as well as those who remain identified only by their roles as prophets) are as prominent as those about kings. Near the end of Kings we have stories about two of the written prophets, Isaiah and **Jeremiah,** who figure prominently in the prophetic tradition as a whole.

If you have continued to read these stories with imagination and have been willing to ask questions (Where did these stories come from? How were they preserved? Who was responsible for getting them to us in this form?), it is not hard to form reasonable suppositions. Add to those the questions about the preservation of the written prophets, and some of the following possibilities occur.

THE TRADITION OF THE PROPHETS

The tradition of the prophets is as old as Israel's history as a nation, if not older. The religious vision of Israel as a holy nation, a people in covenant with their God and bound in that covenant by the Law, brought by Moses, remains the standard by which Israel understands itself. No king, no matter how holy or favored by Yahweh (David and Solomon are good examples), can live out the Covenant in his own life, nor can he keep Israel in the bounds of the covenant relationship. The prophet, on the other hand, is Yahweh's measuring stick and spokesperson, reminding Israel, individually and collectively, of how far it has strayed.

The prophetic tradition became especially

strong in the northern kingdom of Israel, which lacked the theological premise that Yahweh favors the established monarchy. Because Israel was without the strong priesthood of Judah and the Temple in Jerusalem, the prophet was its chief religious leader. It was not an easy task, for what was viewed as good for Israel and what was right to please Yahweh did not always coincide. Remembering that we are dealing with the judgment of who was a true prophet, we find clues that even then some said what people wanted to hear, while others spoke out of a sense of religious conviction.

By the eighth century B.C.E., some of the prophets began to write down their prophecies, perhaps to gain a wider audience for their pronouncements. Amos (approximately 750 B.C.E.) was the first of the new tradition, which with the fall of Israel (721 B.C.E.) sought refuge in Judah. Thus we have the emergence of the written prophets, all of whom use the standard of Moses, the father of the prophetic tradition, as their theological guideline. Though one of their number, Isaiah, comes from the southern tradition of Judah, with its belief that Yahweh had favored the House of David, the tradition remained essentially Mosaic in its outlook. During the reign of Manasseh it had to go underground to survive, and it was during this time that there was some accommodation between the strong Mosaic tradition of the north and the more Temple-centered religion of the south. With the return to relative political autonomy of Judah after the period of Assyrian domination, the Jews had to be reintroduced to their own religious tradition. It was at the time of Josiah that this took place. Judah, so bound by its Davidic and Temple theology and affected by the alien influences of Assyria, did not accept the scroll found in the Temple in 621 B.C.E. (the centennial of the fall of Israel) as a part of its religious tradition until its authenticity was confirmed by the prophetess Huldah

(2 Kings 20:11–20). Prophetic theology, at this point, became the basis for the religious reform that swept Judah, although final victory would only come during the period of the exile.

These suppositions can be extended even further. Let us imagine a **"Prophetic School of Theology,"** which would date at least back to Samuel. In such a group the tradition of Moses could be kept alive. Along with that, the memory of the tradition itself could flourish, its heroes could be remembered, and its history could be maintained. Here the works (both oral and written) of their number could be treasured and even built on, with new religious insights appropriate to the time emerging. Their timeless visions spoke to every generation, and thus must be kept alive.

It is not hard to imagine other possibilities. Amos, the first prophet of the literary tradition, has been described properly as a "prophet of doom." A contemporary of Amos, **Hosea,** shares this sense of doom, but he also includes hope, a characteristic of **remnant theology.** I Isaiah, a southern prophet, is deeply influenced by his own upbringing and still trusts in Yahweh's promise to David through the prophet Nathan; thus he introduces a messianic dimension to his religious visions. One cannot read the eighth-century prophets without sensing their awareness of their predecessors in the faith, yet each has another aspect to add to the building aspects of prophetic theology. **Habbakuk** speaks to the individual, while Jeremiah adds to that the concept of a future covenant written on the heart. Obvious as well is the growing sense of the idea of Israel as a religion, rather than a nation, found in the later chapters of Isaiah, and although there is a bit of a return to some nationalistic tendencies in the later prophets, what has been done by their predecessors can never be fully undone.

In a very real sense the prophets were the interpreters of the already established religious

Table 4.1 The Prophets of the Literary Tradition

Date (B.C.E.)	Prophet	Audience	Basic Message
750	Amos	Israel	Doom
750	Hosea	Israel	Doom, and survival of a remnant
742–700	I Isaiah	Judah	Messiah, one of David's line, will be agent as Yahweh prevails
722–701	Micah	Judah	Justice, kindness, and humility
628–622	Zephaniah	Judah	Attacks complacency
626–561	Jeremiah	Judah	New covenant, written on the heart
612	Nahum	Judah	Against Assyria
605	Habakkuk	Judah	The just shall live by faith
593–573	Ezekiel	Judah and those in exile	New beginnings—restoration
After 587	Obadiah	Judah's exiles	Against Edom
540	II Isaiah	Exilic community	Strong messianic dimension
520–515	Haggai	Postexilic community	Attacks religious apathy
520–515	Zechariah	Postexilic community	Attacks complacency
After 500	Joel	Postexilic community	Day of Yahweh's judgment
After 500	Malachi	Postexilic community	Plea for sincere worship

tradition of their times. They did not create new theology as much as they spoke out of the dominant Mosaic theology of which they were the guardians. Although historic circumstances changed, the concept of people living out the covenant relationship within the boundary of the Law remained. Not only were people and nation to be judged by their obedience to that covenant/law demand, but future history also would be formed by the judgments of the God who placed those demands upon the people. The prophets did not articulate new rules as much as they spoke of Yahweh's judgment under the old rules, which the people seemed to find difficulty living within. Even with the introduction of the messianic dimension within the prophetic theology, one finds not so much new demands as much as a new *under-standing* as to how Yahweh's will will be finally accomplished. As you read the prophet oracles against the people or the nations, you will find that there is not a judgment made that cannot not be related to an existing law. The prophet does not issue new demands; rather, he shows the people how they are measuring up to established demands. This shows us again how, after Moses, "all else is commentary."

The "Prophetic School of Theology" preserved the work of the prophets listed in Table 4.1, but it was also probably responsible for the Pentateuch and the Deuteronomic history in the form in which we now have it (Genesis through 2 Kings, with the exception of Ruth). Not only have they formed much of the literary tradition of the Old Testament as it now exists, but they have also laid the foundation for the remainder of that tradition, illustrating again how the Mosaic theology dominates. As the prophets tell the story of how Yahweh continues to reveal himself in the midst of the history of Israel and Judah, as is done in 1 and 2 Kings, they make certain that the reader does not miss the presence of Yahweh's judgment within the pages. The evaluation of the reign of all the kings (a powerful example is found in 2 Kings 21:10–16) is but one example of the prophet judgment based upon the standard of Law and Covenant being made in the midst of the telling of history.

STAGES OF PROPHETIC DEVELOPMENT

Most of the theories about the growth of the prophetic tradition in Judaism suggest that this tradition passed through a series of stages. It is believed by some that the Israelites, a nomadic people, copied from the traditions of the Canaanites' landed culture, which they were seeking to dominate. At the same time, they were bound by the religious vision provided by Moses. Let us examine those prophetic stages.

The Early Tradition

Moses. Moses was the founder of the prophetic tradition and provided its theology, regardless of whether he was known as a prophet in his own time. He stood in the midst of Israel and pronounced the will of Yahweh. He spoke on behalf of Yahweh as he interpreted the events of history, linking it to the Covenant and the Law. The Covenant was to become the theological standard by which all future prophets would be judged, as well as that by which they would judge Israel.

Joshua and the Judges. Joshua assumed at least some of the prophetic role of Moses, but his function as described in the Deuteronomic history was more to keep alive the teachings of Moses than to deliver a new tradition. The Judges' role is less clear, although the judgment placed on the tribes in the Book of Judges is based on the Mosaic standard.

Samuel. The Hebrew Bible applies the term *prophet* to Samuel, who indeed described more in a prophetic role than anyone since Moses, particularly when he establishes the monarchy and replaces Saul with David. After Samuel we are told about prophets such as Nathan, Elijah, Elisha, Isaiah, and Jeremiah acting in the pages of the Deuteronomic history as Yahweh's spokespersons as they have some influence on ongoing Jewish history.

Saul and the Ecstatic Prophets. In 1 Samuel (10:9–12), Saul is reported to be overcome by ecstasy, beginning to prophesy with the established prophets. This story has led some scholars to suggest that early Hebrew prophets copied their form from the **ecstatic prophets** of Baal then present in Canaan. It is believed that in the state of ecstasy, the prophets received the message they were to proclaim. The manifestation of such ecstasy would be considered a sign that they were truly possessed by a divine spirit. Some suggest that such ecstatic fits were accompanied at times with self-abuse, such as flagellation, or that such practices led to the ecstatic trance. The evidence is skimpy, but some form of charismatic behavior is indicated in what we do know.

There is a slight hint that David might have been overcome by a spirit of ecstasy as he danced before the Ark (2 Sam. 6:5). It is equally clear that Samuel, and the prophetic school that preserved his tradition, did not believe that the roles of prophet and political leader should be combined. Rather, they asserted that political leaders should be guided by the realization that Israel was judged by the concept of the Covenant and the Law, the understanding of which was guided by the religious and not the political leaders.

The Court and Cultic Prophets

The prophets assume a more distinct role in the remainder of the Hebrew Bible. Nathan, the prophet in the court of David, speaks on behalf of Yahweh. Examples include his blessing of the House of David and the judgment of David on the occasion of the Bathsheba affair. It has been suggested that the role of court prophet was a formal role, one that was always occupied in subsequent Hebrew history. The evidence is not totally clear, but it is not an unreasonable assumption. Since the Hebrew nation was based on a theocratic concept, it would be unusual *not* to have the religion represented in the court of the king. However, if it was represented, our authors did not have high regard for the representatives, for they receive little or no attention after Nathan.

Cultic prophets are defined as those having formal religious responsibilities during the period of the monarchy. It has been suggested that such a group worked at the Temple, offering intercessory prayer on behalf of the people. It is my contention that the cultic prophet was found in both Judah and Israel and is best understood as the continuing tradition of the prophets whose heirs preserved that tradition for us. The Deuteronomic history clearly implies that these prophets had a formal role in the religious life of Israel at least from the time of the monarchy. They well could have had formal training in the tradition of Moses, then assuming the responsibility of keeping the Mosaic tradition alive from generation to generation. In time, the measure of their prophetic authenticity came to be firmly based on theological authority rather than a state of ecstatic behavior. Our authors judge true and false prophets by the standard of Mosaic theology, and they preserve for us stories about those who maintained that standard over time. The passing on of the mantle of prophet from one generation to the next is illustrated in the story of Elijah and Elisha.

Thus it is likely that the prophetic tradition was based in Israel after the division of the kingdoms. That would explain why most of the stories about the prophets in 1 and 2 Kings deal with the kings of Israel. The tradition, however, was not exclusive to Israel, for there was obvious religious and cultural intercourse during the period of the divided monarchies. If it was centered in the North, it obviously did not disappear upon the fall of Israel. As suggested in Chapter 3, some of the prophetic school could have escaped the Assyrians by fleeing to Judah, taking with them the tradition with which they had been entrusted, including the works of Amos and Hosea. The significance of their influence in shaping the future of Judaism is illustrated by their strong presence in the materials we now study.

The Literary Tradition: Before the Exile

Beyond the tradition about the prophets in the books we have read, a number of books in the Hebrew Bible are purported to be the writings of the individual prophets whose names they bear. Most of these books date themselves, or can be dated by the events to which they direct themselves. Why the prophets began to write their messages becomes a matter of speculation, but the fact that most of them are in the form of Hebrew poetry offers a helpful clue. Cast in poetic form, a message could be remembered and passed on to an audience larger than its initial hearers, while maintaining its original dramatic impact.

It is not suggested that the tradition about the prophets had not been expressed in written form before its insertion in the Hebrew Bible. From the eighth century B.C.E. until the exile, however, the work of the prophets is quite different and deserves individual consideration. We will review the work of these prophets in the order in which they appeared in history and then make some observations about their relationship to one another. You may wish to consider the prophets according to three stages: those who wrote before the Babylonian exile (**preexilic**), those whose careers were in the period of exile (**exilic**), and those who lived after the return of the Jews to their own land (**postexilic**). You will find that there is a commonality among those groups, at least in the sense of the common history to which they were addressing themselves. Viewed in that context, it is easy to discern how the history in which they were declaring their message had a profound influence on the content of that message. Whether they were looking forward to Yahweh's judgment, or were looking back on the accomplishment of that judgment, it remained clear that Yahweh had a strong hand in history, that one was to learn from that history, and that Yahweh was still in command.

◆ READ *Amos 1–3, 7:1–9*

Amos. The work of Amos is dated at approximately 750 B.C.E., almost thirty years before Israel's fall to Assyria. Amos says that he is not a professional prophet, but a shepherd and dresser of sycamore trees who was called by Yahweh (7:14–16).

Amos stands strongly in the Mosaic tradition. He has been called the "prophet of doom" and his work merits such a title. Whether he believed that there was hope beyond the retribution that Yahweh would visit on Israel for transgressing the Law is a matter of a debate among scholars. Some suggest that the most hopeful part of Amos (9:9–15), in which there is remnant theology, is a later addition, not a part of the original work. However a few instances in the earlier part of the book in which Amos calls for repentance (see 4:5) lead others to believe that Amos was not a prophet of complete doom. The most remembered portion of Amos are his famous lines:

This is what the Lord Yahweh showed me:
a man standing by a wall,
plumb line in hand.

"What do you see Amos?" Yahweh asked me.
"A plumb line," I said.
Then the Lord said to me,
"Look, I am going to measure my people
Israel by plumb line;
No longer will I overlook their offenses.
The high places of Isaac are going to be ruined,
the sanctuaries of Israel destroyed,
and, sword in hand, I will attack the House of Jeroboam." (7:7–9)

The plumb line is obviously the Mosaic law, the violation of which Amos has chronicled throughout his work. The overwhelming sense of doom is recorded when Amos states that Yahweh says of Israel ("the pride of Jacob"), "Never will I forget a single thing you have done" (8:7). Amos's message obviously finds Israel wanting when measured by the Mosaic standard.

There are at least two other noteworthy elements in the theology of this prophet. The first is its universality. Yahweh is the God of all creation, and all must pay for their sins, not just Israel. Early in the poem are judgments against the enemies of Israel, who are no less subject to Yahweh than is Israel, to whom the majority of the message is addressed. Then there is the social dimension of Amos's message. The sins for which Israel must pay are social: rich taking advantage of poor, failure to care for the oppressed:

For the three crimes, the four crimes of Israel
I have made my decree and will not relent:
because they have sold the virtuous man for
silver and the poor for a pair of sandals, because they trample on the heads of ordinary
people and push the poor out of their path,
because father and son have both resorted to
the same girl, profaning my Holy name.
(2:6–7)

These are obvious violations of Mosaic law, but perhaps not considered with the same regard as more religiously oriented laws delivered by Moses. (Verse 7 might refer to Baal prostitutes, or it might be an allusion to the sins of the idle rich.)

Amos's message was delivered at the time of tranquility and prosperity in Israel. Few could believe that its destruction was near, only thirty years away. In the midst of plenty, Amos proclaimed Yahweh's judgment on a contented people. There is no hint that Amos's words had much impact on their contemporary audience, yet they became a measure by which people could understand the later devastation they were to endure. Yahweh would not be mocked; his justice would be satisfied. Amos and his successors were to provide means by which the events of succeeding generations could be understood and survived without a complete loss of faith.

✦ **READ** *Hosea 1–3, 14*

Hosea. Hosea was a contemporary of Amos, their prophetic careers being almost simultaneous. Hosea's career should also be dated as beginning circa 750 B.C.E., yet continuing for a somewhat longer period than that of Amos. Hosea directed his prophecy to Israel, as did Amos. He was more likely of the ongoing prophetic tradition of Israel, a professional prophet.

His work, like that of Amos, is poetic in structure, with a few prosaic moments interspersed to provide a context for his message. One of the more unusual characters in the Bible, Hosea marries the prostitute **Gomer** on orders from Yahweh and with her has children. Again under instructions from Yahweh, he names his first son **Jezreel,** after the site of Jehu's slaughter of the House of Omri, indicating that Israel was to pay for this sin. The second child, a daughter, was named Lo-Ruhamah (translated "unloved") to symbolize Yahweh's withdrawal of his love from Israel. The third child, a son, was named Lo-Ammi ("no-people-of-mine"), indicating that Israel was no longer to be Yahweh's people.

After a prose introduction, Hosea expresses the judgment on Israel. In the end, however, those whom Yahweh has rejected he will love again, for judgment is not without reason, and those who accept judgment and return to more faithful ways will experience the loving protection of Yahweh once again. If there is doubt whether Amos truly saw hope in the future, there is no question in regard to Hosea. His marriage to Gomer becomes the illustrative point. She abandons him for her old life. Yahweh sends him to seek her out, and once again to give her love. There is a time of chastisement to allow for cleansing, after which Gomer is restored fully to the household (3:1–5).

Nor is there doubt that the sins of Israel must be punished, or that those who accept the chastisement offered in that punishment will be restored. Hosea's list of the sins of Israel is longer than that of Amos, and perhaps more typically religious in nature, though the consequences are the same. As Hosea used his marriage and the naming of his children as a vehicle to pronounce Yahweh's judgment, he used names to pronounce survival of a faithful remnant.

> In the place where you were told, "You are no people of mine," they will be called, "the sons of the living God." The sons of Judah and Israel will be one again and choose themselves one single leader, and they will spread far beyond their country; so great will be the day of Jezreel. To your brother say, "People-of-Mine," to your sister, "Beloved." (2:1–3)*

The overall message of the book is summarized well in its closing chapter:

> Israel, come back to Yahweh your God; your iniquity was the cause of your downfall. Pro-

---

*See the Jerusalem Bible, p. 1260. These verses are found at end of Chapter 1 in other translations of the Bible.

vide yourself with words and come back to Yahweh. Say to him, "Take all iniquity away so that we may have happiness again and offer you our words of praise. Assyria cannot save us, we will not ride horses any more, or say, 'Our God!' to what our own hands have made, for you are the one in whom orphans find compassion."

I will heal their disloyalty, I will love them with all my heart, for my anger has turned from them. I will fall like dew on Israel. He shall bloom like the lily, and thrust out roots like the poplar. His shoots will spread far. He will have the beauty of the olive and the fragrance of Lebanon. They will come back to live in my shade; they will grow corn that flourishes, they will cultivate vines as renowned as the wine of Helbon. What has Ephraim to do with idols any more when it is I who hear his prayer and care for him? I am like a cypress ever green, all your fruitfulness comes from me. (14:2–9)

There is no clue that Hosea had any more immediate impact on Israel than did Amos. Yet his message, along with that of his contemporary, provided the means whereby some of those who experienced the devastation that he prophesied could survive it without losing faith in Yahweh.

Perhaps you are beginning to understand the world view of the prophet, which was so important to the survival of Judaism in the dark days to come. More of that view is revealed as we sample the works of the prophets who addressed Judah after the fall of Israel.

It is mainly an accident of history that the remainder of the prophets we discuss address themselves to Judah. Since the tradition of the written prophets did not begin until shortly before the fall of Israel in 721 B.C.E., the theology of the remaining prophets, with the possible exception of I Isaiah, is compatible with the northern prophetic tradition already described. Yahweh, after all, had chosen all of Israel and entered into a covenant with all its tribes, and Judah was not exempt from his judgment.

✦ **READ** *Isaiah 1–9, 36–39*

I Isaiah. The first of the prophets of Judah is Isaiah, whose prophetic career expanded over forty years, 742–700 B.C.E. It appears that Isaiah was a priest before he was a prophet, receiving his prophetic call while tending to his priestly duties in the year that King Uzziah died (see 6:1–13). The book that bears Isaiah's name is for a number of reasons perhaps the most difficult of all the prophetic books to comprehend:

1. The material is not neatly ordered, and it is sometimes difficult to set particular prophetic oracles in any historic context.

2. It is generally believed that the Book of Isaiah is a composite of prophetic works composed over a period as long as two hundred years. Many accept Chapters 1–39 (i.e., I Isaiah) as belonging to the time of the prophet, but they date Chapters 40–55 (**II Isaiah**) in the Babylonian exile and place Chapters 56–66 (**III Isaiah**) even later. These theories are based on changes of literary style and poetic meter, as well as on the widely separated historic circumstances the work addresses.

3. Some have suggested that prophets are best understood in the context of their own times, that they did not intend to be "long-range forecasters." Although that is an oversimplification, it is probably true that they would think of their messages as predictions not of precise events, but rather of general consequences ("If you disobey you will face Yahweh's judgment, if you return he will restore . . ." and so on). There is certainly a timeless dimension to their messages, and it is that dimension that most continues to speak to the religious communities that use them as scripture. For instance, although the prophet could have believed that Yahweh would use Babylon to punish Israel, or even that Yahweh would later raise up a nation to restore the repentant, the deliverer's surname (Cyrus in the case of Isaiah) would not necessarily have to be known. Chapters 40–55 (or 40–66 for some) have several elements, including very specific references to a later period of history, that have led many to suggest that portion of the work should be assigned to a later prophetic writer.

The Book of Isaiah raises the whole question of how all the prophets are to be read and understood. Students of the Bible know that the Christian writers viewed the prophets as foretellers and used their works to portray Jesus as the Messiah foretold by the prophets. Students of the history of religion know that at the time of the birth of Jesus a strong sense of messianic expectation had developed within Judaism, out of an understanding that the prophets, and the later apocalyptic writer of the Book of Daniel, were indeed foretellers. The works of the prophets themselves lead to such an understanding, for they forecast both doom and redemption. The question then is, What was in the mind of the prophet?

In most cases we can find in the immediate historic context out of which the prophet spoke actual events to which to relate their pronouncements. At the same time, as noted earlier, there is a timeless dimension to their work. If the prophet was pronouncing the general judgment of Yahweh, almost any disaster could be related to that judgment were one to assume that Yahweh continues to use history to reveal his will. Surely the prophet spoke from the context of history, viewed the arena of history as the platform of Yahweh's revelation of himself, and believed that Yahweh would use that arena to make his judgments known. That in itself explains how the prophets came to be viewed as foretellers long before the end of the literary period of the Bible. It necessitates having to decide how specifically one is to understand the prophets. The Jews agree

that Isaiah spoke of a messiah who would have an important role in the accomplishment of Yahweh's will in history, and much of Judaism still looks for that messiah. One has only to turn to Christian scripture to know that the early Christian writers believed Isaiah spoke specifically of Jesus of Nazareth as that messiah, predicting even how he would be born and how he would die. Two religious communities that shared that prophetic work understood it differently. That is the case not only between religions, but within particular religions as well. All of Christianity does not approach the prophets in the same way. The mention of **Cyrus of Persia** by name (44:28–45:1) in Isaiah does lead some to attribute that part of the work to a later author, someone contemporary to Cyrus, not Isaiah. Obviously how this issue is resolved by the individual reader will have an effect on how one reads and understands all of the written prophets.

For those who would divide Isaiah, attributing Chapters 40–66 to persons who wrote in his name while trying to be faithful to his prophetic vision, the value of the entire work is not diminished. They assume that those who added to the original text were responsible for the preservation of the original and that they spoke in the spirit of the vision provided by the prophet to new moments in the historical life of Judah. One could think of it as the **"Isaiah School of Theology,"** perhaps a branch of the "Prophetic School of Theology" suggested earlier.

However one chooses to understand the prophets, it must be kept in mind that their value to the Judeo-Christian tradition has always lain more in the world view they present than in any events they might or might not predict. It is that world view on which we will concentrate, for it remains intact in either approach. At the same time, we will deal with Isaiah as a document produced by more than one hand, turning our attention first to Chapters 1–39, that is, I Isaiah.

You will note that most of I Isaiah consists of prophetic **oracles,** set in poetic form. Some chapters, such as 6–9, set their own historic context, while others are quite general and the setting of a context is more difficult. The style turns to prose in Chapters 36–39, with the inclusion of some poetic oracles fitting for the occasion. These chapters deal with the siege of Jerusalem (703–701 B.C.E.) and Isaiah's role in the events surrounding it. Chapters 6–9, known as the Book of Immanuel, were written earlier in Isaiah's ministry, and that section contains the clue to how Isaiah's work was preserved and even added to:

I bind up this testimony,
I seal this revelation,
in the hearts of my disciples.
I wait for Yahweh
who hides his face from the House of Jacob;
in him I hope.
I and the children whom Yahweh has given me
are signs and portends in Israel
from Yahweh Sabaoth
who dwells on Mount Zion. (8:16–18)

Although Isaiah was clearly part of the ongoing prophetic tradition, his priestly background brought a blending of the northern and southern traditions in a way not visible in any other prophetic work. Added to the measure of Mosaic theology is the continuation of the belief that Yahweh was to continue to use the House of David in a very special way. It is this extrapolation that makes Isaiah unique and is responsible for his greatest individual contribution to prophetic theology, the adding of the messianic dimension.

The early Christian writers quote extensively from Isaiah, using him as their proof text in establishing Jesus as the fulfillment of messianic prophecy. The stories of the virgin birth obviously have Isaiah in mind. Much of the material found in Isaiah 6–9 is used by Christianity, as is much found in II Isaiah (Chs. 40–55). Whether Isaiah addressed his prophecy to **Ahaz** and his own time is really

now beside the point, for it was in this and later portions of Isaiah that Judaism, and later Christianity, began to look for a messianic figure who would be the deliverer of Yahweh's people. Obviously Judaism continues to wait for the Messiah, while Christianity believes that Jesus was that messianic figure.

After receiving his call to be a prophet, Isaiah has a long career. Chapter 7 is set in the context of a siege of Jerusalem during the time of Ahaz. This is not the later Assyrian siege—the enemy here is Israel and Aram (Damascus). Sent to Ahaz by Yahweh, Isaiah counsels the king to resist, foretelling the fall of Israel. "Ask for a sign," Isaiah says, but Ahaz refuses. Isaiah speaks of the sign nevertheless, pronouncing the famous Immanuel prophecy (7:13–25), which has become so prominent in messianic theology. Chapter 8 includes prophetic pronouncements in regard to Assyria's defeat of Israel. Chapter 9 seems to reiterate the Immanuel prophecy of Chapter 7 (see 9:1–7), again speaking of a child of the House of David who will lead Judah to a time of peace, justice, and integrity.

Reading through the prophetic oracles reveals their collected nature as well as the difficulty of dating them at any particular time in Isaiah's long ministry. Some scholars suggest that some of this material does not belong to Isaiah at all, but to a later period of Judah's history. The mostly prosaic portion found in Chapters 36–39, however, not only is dated, but describes the siege of Jerusalem during the reign of Hezekiah. Here Isaiah speaks to the king on behalf of Yahweh, asking him to rely on Yahweh for his protection. It seems that these chapters include a blending of two accounts of the same event, lending some credence to the idea that the work of Isaiah took its final form from the hand of a later editor. Isaiah assures Hezekiah that Jerusalem will not fall for Yahweh's sake and "for the sake of my servant David." Jerusalem is spared; Isaiah is vindicated.

Chapter 39 predicts the eventual fall of

Judah to Babylon and is a fitting introduction of the beautiful poetic assurances addressed to a despairing people in II Isaiah (40–55), which we examine in Chapter 6. For now, we acknowledge that with Isaiah comes a new dimension in prophetic theology, the concept of a Messiah.

◆ READ   *Micah 1–4, 6:1–8*

Micah.   A contemporary of Isaiah whose prophetic career extends from 722 to 701 B.C.E. is the prophet **Micah.** Very much in the tradition of Amos and Hosea, he speaks of Yahweh's judgment first against Israel for its violation of the Law, particularly in regard to the exploitation of the poor by the rich, yet with a strong sense of a future role for the surviving remnant.

Chapter 6 of Micah is the best known of this small, powerful book of the eighth-century prophet. It is here that Israel (apparently, all the twelve tribes) is put on trial:

> What is good has been explained you, man;
> This is what Yahweh asks of you:
> Only this, to act justly,
> To love tenderly
> and to walk humbly with your God. (v. 8)

Micah adds nothing new to prophetic theology, but he expresses most eloquently the judgments of that theology on the people, while encouraging them to return to the standards that would allow them to live out Yahweh's purposes in history.

◆ READ   *The Book of Zephaniah*

Zephaniah.   There is a period of prophetic silence after Micah and Isaiah, probably as the result of the harsh reign of Manasseh. We have no written prophets for the next seventy years, and then a series appears in rapid succession. That is not to suggest that the prophets were inactive, but rather that they were conducting their activity out of the public eye in order to survive. With the return to some sense of auton-

omy in Judah, the prophets came once again onto the public scene, beginning with **Zephaniah** in 628 B.C.E.

The Judah to which Zephaniah addressed himself was badly in need of religious reform. The apostasy created by the Assyrian domination was still quite strong, and Zephaniah attacked the religious complacency of his time, calling for a religious revival:

> Seek Yahweh
> All you, the humble of earth,
> who obey his commands.
> Seek integrity,
> seek humility:
> you may perhaps find shelter
> on the day of the anger of Yahweh. (2:3)

True to his prophetic predecessors, Zephaniah speaks of the judgment of Yahweh, while affirming that the future is to be found in loyalty to the race to which Yahweh has called his people.

◆ READ   *Jeremiah 1–4, 31–38*

Jeremiah.   One of the four major prophets (the others are Isaiah, Ezekiel, and Daniel*), Jeremiah was the second prophet to emerge during the reign of Josiah. His prophetic career began in 626 B.C.E. and continued until after the fall of Judah to Babylon in 587 B.C.E. The prophetic oracles found in the book that bears his name encompass that period. As with Isaiah, it is difficult always to place the writings in order, or to give them specific dates in the ministry of Jeremiah. There are moments of prose, many of which serve to interpret or to describe historical moments, indicating that the final work comes from the hand of someone other than Jeremiah.

---

*Daniel, though listed among the prophets, is best described as an apocalyptic work. The reason Daniel is classified as a prophet is because of the predictive nature of the visions in the later portion of Daniel. We will deal with Daniel in another section.

Jeremiah had a secretary named **Baruch** (36:32), to whom is attributed much of the prose, as well as the final form of the work.

Jeremiah stands strongly in the tradition of the earlier prophets. It is obvious that that theology now incorporates not only the Mosaic, but the messianic dimension prominent in Isaiah. The entire House of Israel (Israel and Judah) shall be restored under a virtuous branch of David, loyal to the covenant relationship into which they had been called (33:15–16).

It is in the time of Jeremiah that a subtle shift in the thinking of the prophets seems to occur. Israel and Judah can be regarded in the book of Jeremiah more as a religion than as nations, or at least as much a religion as a nation. The most significant of all Jeremiah's prophetic utterances is perhaps found in his words about the new covenant, a vision that moves Judaism beyond the bounds of a national religion to the stage of a world religion:

> See, the days are coming—it is Yahweh who speaks—when I will make a new covenant with the House of Israel (and the House of Judah), but not a covenant like the one I made with their ancestors on the day I took them by the hand to bring them out of the land of Egypt. They broke that covenant of mine, so I had to show them who was master. It is Yahweh who speaks. No, this is the covenant I will make with the House of Israel when those days arrive—it is Yahweh who speaks. Deep within them I will plant my Law, writing it on their hearts. Then I will be their God and they shall be my people. There will be no further need for neighbor to try to teach neighbor, or brother to say to brother, "Learn to know Yahweh!" No, they will all know me, the least no less than the greatest—it is Yahweh who speaks—since I will forgive their iniquity and never call their sin to mind. (31:31–34)

Jeremiah has added a new dimension to prophetic theology, that of the new covenant written on the heart.

The stories about Jeremiah are as informative as his prophetic utterances. One senses the developing conflict between those now considered to be "true prophets," whose stance and message were confirmed by history, and the so-called **popular prophets,** who said what people wanted to hear. It is obvious from the laments found in Jeremiah itself, as well as in the book called Lamentations, which is attributed to the prophet as well, that Jeremiah did not enjoy his prophetic role. It was not a happy task to pronounce the judgment of Yahweh on a nation that Jeremiah so obviously loved. His loyalty to the prophetic message led to his imprisonment, almost to his death, charged with treason. The story recounted in Chapters 37 and 38 illustrates the point well, and it gives the accusation made against Jeremiah: "You are deserting to the Chaldaeans" (37:13).

The parallel between Chapter 39 of Jeremiah and 2 Kings (25:8–21) suggests that both authors relied on a common source, illustrating once again how biblical materials used existing traditions to mold the final product.

The latter chapters of Jeremiah (46–51) are a series of prophetic oracles "against the nations," and though they probably are the work of the prophet, they are difficult to date. They are further illustrations of the stylistic differences found in this book, the poetic oracles and the prosaic history. Chapter 52, which is prosaic, reports the history of the last days of Jerusalem and selected events in the exile, indicating that the book did not take its final form until after 561 B.C.E., when Evil-Merodach pardoned Judah's King Jehoiachin.

✦ READ *The Book of Nahum*

Nahum. The prophecy of **Nahum,** one of the three contemporaries of Jeremiah, should probably be dated 612 B.C.E. This small book is reflective of the strong presence and activity of the prophetic school in the last days of Judah.

Nahum prophesied against the dying Assyrian empire. The opening poem is a psalm that extols the wrath of Yahweh against his enemies and foretells the fall of **Nineveh,** obviously as a result of Yahweh's displeasure.

◆ **READ** *Habakkuk 1:1–2:4, 3:1–19*

Habakkuk. Although the prophetic work of Habakkuk, another contemporary of Jeremiah, does not date itself, many scholars place it at about 605 B.C.E. The brevity of this prophetic book belies its power and impact.

Habakkuk, standing strongly in the Mosaic tradition, struggles with the seeming contradictions provided by life. He observes the prosperity of the wicked, while the righteous suffer. Like Jeremiah, he sees the Babylonians (Chaldaeans) as an instrument of the wrath of Yahweh on Judah, yet he still has trouble discerning how justice is being worked out in the context of history.

Habakkuk brings his petitions before Yahweh, seeking answers to the dilemmas that history poses. In the answers come the most famous of Habakkuk's contributions to prophetic theology. Habakkuk has asked about individual righteousness, pointing out the seeming injustice of having to suffer for the sins of one's neighbor. Yahweh responds:

> "See how he flags, he whose soul is not at rights,
> But the upright man will live by faithfulness." (2:4)

Those who are familiar with the works of Paul in the New Testament will immediately recognize that it is Habakkuk whom Paul is quoting when he builds his case for a theology of justification by grace through faith. Long before Paul, however, Habakkuk contributed to prophetic theology the case for individual righteousness, with each person judged for his or her own behavior. This is certainly an important element in the evolution of Judaism into the sphere of world religions, and it has close connections with Jeremiah's new covenant theology. Combined, these two elements are significant in the shaping of the future understanding of the Judeo-Christian tradition.

The Literary Tradition Continues: During the Exile and Afterward

◆ **READ** *Ezekiel 1–7, 33, 37*

Ezekiel. The final contemporary of Jeremiah, **Ezekiel** did not receive his call to be a prophet until he was captive and exiled in Babylon. We have little difficulty finding the historical context of Ezekiel's prophetic oracles, for they are dated for us. The book progresses naturally from beginning to end. Ezekiel's prophecies span a time from before the fall of Jerusalem to a period after the exile in Babylon. This chronology should be noted as one reads the message Ezekiel delivers, for there is a dramatic change in that message after the fall of Judah.

The imagery used by Ezekiel is markedly different from that of any other prophetic figure, and that should be understood as well. Ezekiel was a mystic. If he had lived among us we might well have thought him eccentric, perhaps even insane. We probably would not have wanted him for a next-door neighbor, nor would we have allowed our children to play in his yard. Yet it is that very quality of intense personal participation in unearthly experiences that raises his work to the level of the highly dramatic and gives his poetry such enduring power. Those qualities should be appreciated.

Called to be a prophet in approximately 593 B.C.E., this priest/prophet speaks from his new home by the river Chebar in Babylon. His first prophetic vision, the means by which he is always to receive the word of Yahweh, is so symbolic that it has led some to speculate that it is in Ezekiel that we have the first written report of an encounter with a flying saucer. It is probably more helpful to seek the more significant message symbolized within the vision, that of being called to his prophetic role, "a sentry to the House of Israel" (2:17). Awestruck with the magnitude of the responsibility, Ezekiel accepts the prophetic mantle. Like his predecessors, he finds the role difficult but does not turn aside. Struck dumb, he does not speak until Yahweh wants him to speak. Following the instructions of Yahweh, he lies in the midst of the city for 190 days on his left side, then for one year and one day on his right side, symbolically bearing the sins of Israel and Judah. This and other rather bizarre acts are, for Ezekiel, a means of dramatically illustrating the message of Yahweh. Like Jeremiah, he is convinced that Jerusalem and Judah must be chastised for their sins, thus Babylon will prevail. All of history, however, is under the control of Yahweh and, whether in victory or defeat, it should be understood that his will is displayed in all events. As he destroys, he does so with purpose, "and so you will learn that I am Yahweh."

Just as Yahweh is to be discerned in tragedy, so will he be revered in future restoration. Engrained with a theology of a new covenant (11:14–21) much akin to that of Jeremiah, Ezekiel declares that after Yahweh has chastised, so will he restore, again so that "then you will learn that I am Yahweh."

To read Ezekiel you might want to begin with his first vision (1:4–3:21) and follow it with his vision of the dry bones (37:1–14). These two very distinct episodes illustrate how it is Ezekiel expresses the message he seeks to convey. If the dry bones are symbolic of the whole House of Israel, so too is the fiery figure described in Chapter 1, or the eating of the scroll in Chapter 2. The writer often provides the clue to his symbolism and is always clear in expressing the final message. For Ezekiel, Yahweh controls history and can be known through its events. Yahweh has called Ezekiel to speak in the midst of that history, to show how it is to be understood. The fall of Judah

does not signal the weakness of Yahweh, but shows instead that he is God and will not be betrayed. Just as he has the power to destroy, so also has he the power to restore, and indeed he will do so. Yahweh has exhibited his power in the judgment cast upon Judah and he will be known as well in its restoration, for Yahweh is the Lord of all history, using it as he will.

Ezekiel is the last of the prophets whose work is preserved in his name until after the period of the Babylonian exile. Those who wrote in the name of Isaiah during this period, and perhaps even later, are considered in our next chapter. Before we proceed to the last of these prophets, however, let us note that Judaism was never again to be bound exclusively to a land after the Babylonian exile, and it is easy to see how the prophets had prepared the people for that reality over the centuries preceding their exile. Had Judaism remained more like the national religion it seemed to be before the first destruction of Jerusalem, we would now study it as a religion of the past, a phenomenon of another age. That, of course, is not the case. Rather than viewing the fates, first of Israel and then of Judah, as proof that Yahweh was inferior to the gods of the Assyrians or the Babylonians, the prophets had provided new lenses through which history could be viewed. Rather than a sign of weakness, it was a sign of the great power of Yahweh, using what and whom he pleased to accomplish his purposes. If Yahweh was boundless, he was also omnipresent, and he could be found wherever his people were, a point that will be pursued in our next chapter, but one residing in the theology of his servants the prophets.

◆ **READ** *The Book of Obadiah*

Obadiah. Some time after 587 B.C.E. **Obadiah** pronounces destruction upon Edom, a habitual enemy of the Jews. Much of this short book is paralleled in Chapter 49 of Jeremiah. The **Edomites** appropriated some of Judah after the destruction of Jerusalem, and the prophet says that when the day of Yahweh arrives, Israel will have its vengeance on the hated invaders.

II *Isaiah*. This portion of Isaiah is believed to have been written during the period of the exile and will be read and discussed in Chapter 5.

◆ READ *The Book of Haggai*

Haggai. **Haggai** was one of the two prophets who were a part of the community that participated in the initial return to Jerusalem after the Babylonian exile. This work probably should be dated around 520 B.C.E. Although the people have been back for some time, the Temple continues to lie in ruins. The prophet urges the people to get on with the restoration of the Temple, promising prosperity as a result.

The work reflects the rather drab existence of the early returnees. Its optimistic outlook seems to predict the nearness of the messianic age, even indicating that **Zerubbabel** would serve a messianic role (1:20:23).

◆ READ *Zechariah 1–4*

Zechariah. A contemporary of Haggai, **Zechariah** should be dated at the same time, though the internal dates of the book would extend it for a slightly longer period. The book offers some difficulty even for the casual reader. Chapters 1–8 deal with the same subject as Haggai and apparently belong to the same period. Chapters 9–14 are difficult to set into a historical context, leading some scholars to suggest that these chapters represent an addition to the work, perhaps two hundred or more years later. While there is much evidence to support the concept of a later addition, there is also much within the material itself to allow it to be considered the work of the prophet himself.

As in many of the works of the Hebrew Bible that can be dated after the fall of Jerusalem, the idea of Judaism as a world religion seems to underlie the view of the writer. There is a certain sense of universalism in regard to

Yahweh's power and call, leaving the idea that although those born to Judaism have a special place in Yahweh's heart, he will not reject any who call on his name. That sense of universalism spans all of Zechariah.

There is much in the book to create confusion. There are moments when the author seems to identify Zerubbabel (4:6–10) as a messianic figure, while at other times that role, and the total role of spiritual and political leadership, seems to be vested in Joshua, the high priest (3:7). In addition, Zechariah says that the walls of Jerusalem are not to be rebuilt (though this later was done), for Yahweh would be its protecting wall (2:8). The later chapters are apocalyptic, predating the time most scholars believe that apocalyptic thought resided in Judaism.

Haggai and at least a portion of Zechariah were written to attack the religious apathy of the time, encouraging the restoration of the Temple and Judah's role as a holy nation. If Judah would assume her responsibilities, she would enjoy the blessings of Yahweh.

◆ READ *The Book of Joel*

Joel. The Book of Joel does not date itself, and placing it has always been a subject of debate among scholars. There is enough in the book to lead us to call it a postexilic work, though its placement in time—probably between 500 and 350 B.C.E.—is no more than a guess.

The occasion that prompted the prophetic work was the devastation of the land by a plague of locusts. The plague is viewed as a judgment of Yahweh, and the people are called to repent, fast, and pray. The calamity seems to be viewed as a sign of the nearness of the "day of Yahweh." In the midst of the calamity Yahweh responds, the plague is removed, and the land becomes productive again. This leads the prophet to declare in behalf of Yahweh:

"After this
I will pour out my spirit on all mankind.

Your sons and daughters shall prophesy,
your old men shall dream dreams,
and your young men see visions.
Even of the slaves, men and women,
will I pour out my spirit in those days."
(3:1–2)

Very much in the spirit of the earlier prophets, yet with a strong sense of Yahweh's universal concern, Joel declares that Yahweh will soon come to punish his enemies while vindicating the righteous. He will dwell in Zion, his home. Obviously aware of the work of Isaiah, Joel turns to the words of the earlier prophet (Isaiah 2:4), when he charges those who have plundered Judah:

Hammer your plowshares into swords,
your sickles into spears,
let the weakling say, "I am a fighting man."
(4:10)

✦ **READ** *The Book of Malachi*

Malachi. The book that appears last in the Hebrew Bible, and perhaps the last of the written prophets, **Malachi** takes its name from the Hebrew word "my messenger" and probably was not the name of the writer. This is another book that is not easily dated, although it seems to belong in the postexilic period, many scholars suggesting between 500 and 450 B.C.E..

The message seems to be addressed to a period highlighted by an undistinguished priesthood and poor worship habits. It expresses Yahweh's dismay at the shoddy religious practices it describes. The writer is distressed not only by such practices, but by the people's general lack of faith. The evil prosper, while the righteous flounder; yet that will not always be the case. There will be a day when sin is punished and righteousness rewarded. The author of Malachi looks to the day of judgment, to be heralded by Elijah the prophet, whose ministry will give the people one last chance to turn again to the ways of Yahweh.

✦ **READ** *Isaiah 56–66*

III *Isaiah.* Many scholars believe that this portion of Isaiah should be attributed to an author even later than the exile, perhaps as late as the fifth century B.C.E. Within these chapters is a strong universal view of Judaism, including Yahweh's concern for whoever would acknowledge him, not just those who were a part of the original tribes of Israel.

Jonah and Daniel. Included with the works of the prophets in at least some of the Judeo-Christian community, the books of **Jonah** and Daniel are dealt with in a context more appropriate to their understanding (see Chapter 6).

CONCLUSIONS ABOUT THE PROPHETIC TRADITION

It has been suggested that the prophetic movement was responsible for its own preservation, as well as much of the tradition we know now as Judaism. Its spiritual father was Moses, and the Mosaic view dominated the theology of the prophets. Included in the tradition kept alive by those who assumed the prophetic responsibility over the centuries was the memory of their spiritual ancestors, as well as the literary products of some of them. We probably do not possess all the tradition or literature, but only that which was judged to be the work of true prophets, those whose prophetic vision was vindicated by history. The true prophets provided a means by which Judaism could survive and even prosper out of national disaster. Their view of history assured a religious future beyond individual moments of disaster, acknowledging that Yahweh controls all history to accomplish his purposes. If Yahweh was the God of all history, he was also God of all people. The prophets' view helped move Judaism past a narrow nationalism into the arena of the world religions, again helping assure its survival. The shape of the future was to be carved in one of the most severe crises Judaism was ever to face, the period of exile in Babylon. It is to that moment, and beyond, that we now turn our attention.

STUDY QUESTIONS

1. Define a prophet within the tradition of Judaism and indicate how an individual came to be judged a true prophet.

2. Identify the various stages of propheticism within the history of Israel and identify one person who exemplifies each of those stages of development.

3. It has been suggested that the prophets we have discussed wrote with their predecessors in mind. Illustrate how these prophets built on the theology of one another as they spoke to their contemporary situations.

4. Discuss the major contributions of the eighth-century prophet Isaiah.

5. Identify and evaluate the contributions of the prophet Jeremiah to the ongoing prophetic tradition.

6. Distinguish the works and contributions of the exilic and postexilic prophets from those whose careers preceded the fall of Jerusalem.

7. Based on your own reading of the prophets, either defend or refute the concept of a "Prophetic School of Theology" as discussed in the text.

8 Explain how the tradition about the prophets as well as the written works were preserved and passed on to succeeding generations.

9. Discuss how the written prophets of Judaism might or might not best be considered as predictors of specific future historic events and indicate upon what you base your assertions.

10. Discuss what is meant by the term *the individual dimension* (in regard to prophetic theology) and indicate when and by what individuals that dimension was introduced.

11. Discuss the impact of the individual written prophets on their own times and contrast that to the long-term impact on their own religious traditions.

12. What would you suggest as the major contributions of the prophets to their ongoing religious traditions?

SUGGESTED READINGS

Anderson, Bernhard W., and Walter Harrelson, Eds. *Israel's Prophetic Heritage* (Harper & Row, New York, 1962).

Buber, Martin. *The Prophetic Faith* (Macmillan, New York, 1949).

Heschel, Abraham J. *The Prophets* (Harper Torchbooks, New York, 1962).

Howie, C. G. "Ezekiel," *The Interpreter's Dictionary of the Bible*, Vol. 2 (Abingdon Press, Nashville, 1962).

Leslie, E. A. "Habakkuk," *The Interpreter's Dictionary of the Bible*, Vol. 2 (Abingdon Press, Nashville, 1962).

———. "Micah, The Prophet," *The Interpreter's Dictionary of the Bible*, Vol. 3 (Abingdon Press, Nashville, 1962).

———. "Nahum, Book of," *The Interpreter's Dictionary of the Bible*, Vol. 3 (Abingdon Press, Nashville, 1962).

———. "Zephaniah, Book of," *The Interpreter's Dictionary of the Bible*, Vol. 4 (Abingdon Press, Nashville, 1962).

May, James Luther, and Paul J. Achtemeier, Eds. *Interpreting the Prophets* (Fortress Press, Philadelphia, 1987).

Muilenburg, J. "Jeremiah, The Prophet," *The Interpreter's Dictionary of the Bible*, Vol. 2 (Abingdon Press, Nashville, 1962).

———. "Obadiah, Book of," *The Interpreter's Dictionary of the Bible*, Vol. 3 (Abingdon Press, Nashville, 1962).

Neil, W. "Haggai," *The Interpreter's Dictionary of the Bible*, Vol. 2 (Abingdon Press, Nashville, 1962).

———. "Joel, Book of," *The Interpreter's Dictionary of the Bible*, Vol. 2 (Abingdon Press, Nashville, 1962).

———. "Malachi," *The Interpreter's Dictionary of the Bible*, Vol. 3 (Abingdon Press, Nashville, 1962).

———. "Zechariah, Book of," *The Interpreter's Dictionary of the Bible*, Vol. 4 (Abingdon Press, Nashville, 1962).

North, C. R. "Isaiah," *The Interpreter's Dictionary of the Bible*, Vol. 2 (Abingdon Press, Nashville, 1962).

Petersen, David L., Ed. *Prophecy in Israel: Search for an Identity* (Fortress Press, Philadelphia, 1987).

Smart, J. D. "Amos," *The Interpreter's Dictionary of the Bible*, Vol. 1 (Abingdon Press, Nashville, 1962).

———. "Hosea," *The Interpreter's Dictionary of the Bible*, Vol. 2 (Abingdon Press, Nashville, 1962).

FIVE

FROM NATIONAL TO WORLD RELIGION

The materials discussed in this section either were produced during or after the Babylonian exile, or contain information that refers to that period of Israel's history. The exile, when Judaism was essentially without a country, was followed by a slow drift back into the land of the forefathers. At the same time, Judaism now existed as a religion beyond the borders of Israel or Judah. Jews had undergone a profound change in how they understood themselves in relation to the role of Covenant and the Law in their lives. To understand the significance of this change, we must examine the events that occurred during and after the exile.

Although we have material that traces Judaism from its inception with Abraham until its defeat by the Babylonians, there is no comparable biblical material for the period of the exile or beyond. The books of Ezra and Nehemiah do resume the history at the end of the exile and continue it through the era of Ezra and Nehemiah, though even the books of the prophets leave a large gap in the story. Because of this, the assumptions made about the events of the exile and consequent history are based on intelligent conjecture, aided by material found in the books of the Hebrew Bible be-

lieved to have been written during and after the period of the exile.

THE SHAPING OF SURVIVING JUDAISM

The Problem

That Judaism survived at all is something of a miracle. According to tradition, the Jews' relationship with Yahweh had, from the time of Abraham, included the concept of possessing their own land. As late as the decade before Judah's defeat by the Babylonians, it is apparent that popular religion still clung to the belief that Yahweh would never allow his people or his Holy City, Jerusalem, to be destroyed. That strong popular belief is evidently what caused such trouble for Jeremiah the prophet with the religious and political establishments. As pointed out in Chapter 4, had it not been for the theology of the prophets that provided a way of dealing with the great national disaster, we would probably be studying Judaism as a "dead" or "ancient" religion, rather than as a vital, living religion.

Consider what the popular religion thought at the time of the defeat by the Babylonians:

1. That Yahweh had promised them their land

2. That the throne of David would exist forever

3. That Yahweh was present among the people, residing in the Temple of Jerusalem

4. That Yahweh, as the Lord of history, was all powerful and had always intervened in behalf of his chosen ones

In addition, at least up to this time, the religion of Israel was much more a "national" than a "world" religion.* This limited view of Judaism is illustrated in many ways throughout that portion of the Hebrew Bible you have already read. Indeed, the common Jews were probably not yet purely monotheistic (note how they constantly are criticized for worshiping other gods). Thus, it is easy enough to imagine them simply assuming that the gods of the Babylonians were superior to Yahweh, with some switching allegiance to those gods. Undoubtedly some Jews abandoned their religion for that of their captors, but during this period of extreme crisis Judaism not only survived, it blossomed. It was, as has been suggested, the moment when Judaism became a true world religion. One could now be a Jew anywhere, neither limited by national boundaries nor tied to the Temple in Jerusalem.

---

*Some have suggested that only so-called missionary religions (i.e., Christianity, Buddhism, Islam) should be called world religions, while nonmissionary religions should be designated as nationalistic or ethnocentric traditions. The term *world religion* is used here in the broad sense. It includes any religious group that is open to anyone who would adopt its affirmations, whose practice is not limited to one geographic location or ethnic group, and that understands that its message has universal implications. This describes Judaism after the Babylonian exile.

The Solution

To understand this change in the Jews' religious concepts, you need to review our previous discussion. Remembering some of the points made about the prophets will be especially helpful. Let us summarize the most important points:

1. The theology of the prophets had always assumed that Yahweh rewarded obedience and punished disobedience.

2. Prophetic theology had provided a means of reconciling the fall of Israel with the continued perception of Yahweh as God, omnipotent.

3. Prophetic theology had begun to separate the individual from the community in regard to one's final destiny.

4. The remnant theology of the prophets encouraged continued loyalty while offering a way of understanding temporary devastation.

5. The prophets Habbakuk and Jeremiah had allowed the Covenant to be interpreted on an individual basis.

6. Thus it followed that a Jew could survive apart from the Temple or the Holy Land.

Few would suggest that Judaism developed new concepts during this period. It is more likely that the Jews began to understand the established tradition in new ways. Moses remained the source of the content of the tradition, but his successors provided fresh and significant ways of appropriating that tradition into the lives of its adherents.

The exile was indeed a catastrophic moment in Jewish history. Their leaders had been deported in 597 B.C.E., most of the rest in 587 B.C.E. Their home was now Babylon, and they now had no control of their political destiny. They evidently lived in relative freedom, being allowed to participate in the new society at least in a limited way. Some probably blended totally into Babylonian society, losing their Jewish identity forever. From then on, to be a Jew would depend more on religious commitment than on place of residence. Thus it was important to define again what it meant to be a Jew, and to relearn how to express one's faith. These considerations lead to the conjecture of what indeed happened among the Jews in Babylon.

First, we know that despite the loss of the Temple, Jews continued to worship. As has been pointed out earlier, Israel maintained its form of Judaism without a central temple for two hundred years, while Judah's worship was much more Temple centered. If, as has been suggested, the tradition of the prophets was blended with the priestly tradition after the fall of Israel in 721 B.C.E., we can perhaps understand how the Jews found a way to approach Yahweh without the Temple, as had the people of Israel since 922 B.C.E.; for it was during the exile that the tradition of the synagogue seems to have been established. As far as we can tell, from this time forward Jews did not attempt to offer sacrifices away from the Temple, for such sacrifices had been especially criticized in 1 and 2 Kings. Worship without sacrifice would be an appropriate compromise between prophetic and priestly religions and would preserve the integrity of both. In any event, such an adjustment was necessary if Judaism was to break out of the national boundaries that had confined it, especially in Judah.

We know that the past traditions came closer to their present forms during this period. The Deuteronomic history (Joshua through 2 Kings) was probably put in its final form. Reading those books, you must have been aware of the constant explanations of why things happened as they did. These explanations are a reflection of how Judaism was appropriating its history, gathering meaning, and extending its ability both to survive and to prosper. Obviously, such understanding developed under the guidance of those who shared the Mosaic or prophetic view of history.

The continued honoring of the prophetic tradition and the addition of the tradition about the prophets with the other historic traditions that had taken literary form assured the preservation of this prophetic tradition. The energetic continuation of this tradition can, in fact, be seen in the later work of Ezekiel (the portion after the exile) and the portion of Isaiah (40–55) that seems reflective of the exile period. Indeed, most of the prophets are introduced in a historic context that identifies the prophet and the time during which he prophesied. This context might well have been provided by those who treasured and preserved their works.

Obviously, the priesthood survived. It was probably at this point that the roles of priest and prophet were more fully combined, the priest assuming a broader role than he had enjoyed during the more tranquil days of Judah. Ezra, whom we will meet later, is an example of the new priesthood.

The changes that took place brought problems, however, that become apparent as we examine the remainder of the Hebrew Bible. The major problems, of course, are those associated with moving from a national to a world religion. Much of the continued dispute about defining what it means to be a Jew centers in this expanded view of Judaism.

The Jews did return to their land, yet things were never to be quite the same again. No king from the line of David would preside, nor would the Jews ever be totally independent of foreign domination again during the biblical period. As far as we know, no one who went into Babylonian captivity was to return. Those who "returned" were in fact a new generation of Jews.

Having read all of this, the student needs to

be aware that there are other views of this history. Some would argue that Judaism never was as universal as has been implied here, that it was always more tied to the Holy Land than the preceding discussion would lead one to believe. Whether Judaism ought to be described in world religion terms or as an ethno-religious nation is an issue that has existed both within and outside Judaism since the period of the second Temple.

The argument extends to the question of who properly qualifies as a Jew. One side supports the more narrow definition articulated in Ezra-Nehemiah; the other, the broader acceptance of converts reflected in the story of Ruth. Is a Jew anyone who calls on the name of Yahweh, or is being a Jew something that brings special responsibilities to the person born into that community? Is the existence of Israel necessary for the continued existence of the religion, and how important was/is the Temple to ongoing Jewish life?

The position offered here suggests that Judaism had an independent existence after the Babylonian exile from the nation Israel. Clearly Israel did not exist as a Jewish homeland for centuries after 135 C.E. Even when it did, not all of the people who claimed the title "Jew" were a part of the nation. There were more Jews in Diaspora Judaism than there were in Palestine after the period of the exile. Even today the majority of the world Jewish population does not live in Israel.

None of this suggests that the land of Israel has not remained an important part of the religion, nor that the Temple has not maintained a central place. The Holy Land has been just that, and the idea that the future is not somehow associated with the reoccupation of the land and the rebuilding of the Temple has never occurred to religious or nonreligious Jews.

What is suggested, however, is that before the Babylonian exile being a Jew always involved a direct association with one's place of residence. After the exile that definition had much less to do with where one lived and a great deal more to do with an understanding of one's religious responsibilities. The nation Israel remained important, but in different ways. The messianic future proclaimed by Judaism has always included the restoration of the throne of David as well as a reestablishment of the nation Israel and the rebuilding of the Temple. Those associated with the land and the Temple after the exile always held a special place of honor and authority in postexilic Judaism. None of these facts should be ignored in any understanding of the subject. Nevertheless, Judaism has survived beyond the land and without the Temple, and the people and events that helped form Judaism before the exile helped make that survival possible.

The books of Ezra and Nehemiah provide information about Judaism's return to its own land. However, portions of Ezekiel present the prophetic view during the early exile, and II Isaiah (Chs. 40–55) gives us the prophetic view shortly before the initial return. An examination of all these works provides some helpful clues, and they shall be our guide.

THE EXILIC PROPHETS

Ezekiel After the Fall

◆ **READ** *Ezekiel 33–37*

As Ezekiel began his prophetic ministry, his message affirmed, with Jeremiah, the inevitable fall of Judah to the Babylonians, "so they will learn I am Yahweh." Chapter 33 of Ezekiel addresses the period during and after the siege of Jerusalem, and we learn that Jerusalem has fallen "so men will learn that I am Yahweh, when I reduce the land to desert and desolation on account of all their filthy practices" (33:29).

Immediately the message changes, however, as Ezekiel seeks to offer comfort and hope to a despairing people. Condemning the established leadership for their spiritual failure, he indicates that Yahweh himself will assume the shepherd role and that the line of David will be restored:

> I, Yahweh, will be their God, and my servant David shall be their ruler. (34:24)

After a condemnation of the Edomites for occupying the land of Judah and mocking Yahweh's apparent lack of sufficient strength to protect his people, Ezekiel again prophesies the restoration of Israel. In what is one of the more moving and dramatic portions of the Hebrew Bible, he recites his vision of the dry bones, which tells how the whole House of Israel is to be restored:

> Then [Yahweh] said, "Son of man, these bones are the whole House of Israel. They keep saying, 'Our bones are dried up, our hope has gone: we are as good as dead.' So prophesy, say to them, 'The Lord Yahweh says this: I am now going to open your graves; I mean to raise you from your graves, my people, and lead you back to the soil of Israel. And you will know that I am Yahweh, when I open your graves and raise you from your graves, my people. And I shall put my spirit in you, and you will live, and I shall resettle you on your own soil; and you will know that I, Yahweh, have said and done this—it is the Lord Yahweh who speaks.'" (37:11–14)

Ezekiel later prophesies the restoration of the Temple and the reestablishment of the faithful portion of the levitical priesthood. Finally, Jerusalem is to be renamed "Yahweh-is-there."

A review of Ezekiel helps us understand how Judaism survived catastrophe. The defeat was not a sign of Yahweh's weakness, but of his strength. He will punish sin. The events provide a means of cleansing, after which the dream would be restored. Yahweh, the Lord of history, reveals himself in his anger and in his continuing love. One having the spiritual sensitivity of the prophet, the spiritual sentry

mentioned in Chapter 33, would be the vehicle to inform.

II Isaiah

✦ **READ** *Isaiah 40–55*

Armed with the view of history provided by the earlier prophets and reinforced by Ezekiel, the religion of the Jews survived and flourished. Gathering together to remember the past and to prepare for the future, they fully expected that the hand of Yahweh would soon return them to their land. With the death of Nebuchadnezzar and the accompanying political disarray in Babylon, the time seemed propitious, especially in view of the rise of Persia as a world power and its early successes in campaigns to wrest control of the Mideast from the Babylonians (see map, p. 77). In the midst of that situation we are given a window through which to view the religious mind of exilic Judaism in the poetry of one who is known to us as II Isaiah, the author of Chapters 40–55 of the Book of Isaiah. Nourished by the religious tradition of his ancestors and excited by the current events of history, this highly spiritual member of the prophetic school saw in those events the hand of Yahweh.

In 550 B.C.E. Cyrus of Persia had begun the military campaign that was to culminate in the defeat of Babylon in 539 B.C.E. Cyrus was not only a very successful warrior, he also was an astute politician and statesman. As a result, the empire he established lasted for more than two hundred years. It is known that Cyrus allowed people in the territories he conquered to return to their ancestral lands, taking with them their religious traditions and treasures. The account in the Book of Ezra of Cyrus allowing the Jews to return to Judah is consistent with this policy. Although Cyrus himself worshiped Marduk and believed his military campaigns to be guided and sustained by that

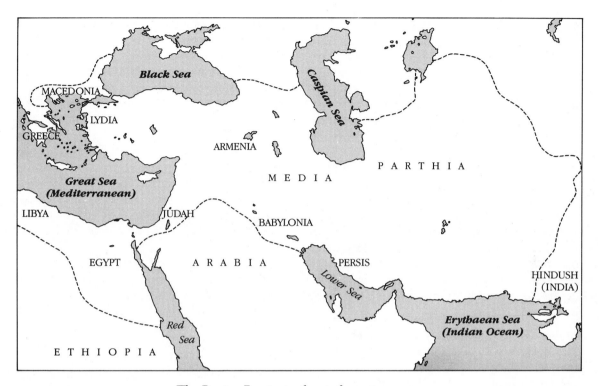

The Persian Empire in the sixth century B.C.E.

deity, his policy of religious toleration probably led him to encourage the reestablishment of prior religious traditions as a means of making conquered peoples more comfortable in their vassalage to the Persian Empire. The policy was successful and was continued well beyond the years of Cyrus.

It is believed that II Isaiah belongs to the period of the triumph of the Persians over the Babylonians. Remember that most of I Isaiah (i.e., Chs. 1–38) directs itself to the events of the eighth century B.C.E. Chapter 39 reports the receipt of a gift by Hezekiah from Merodach-Baladan, king of Babylon, on the occasion of the king of Judah's recovery from illness. Isaiah appears in Hezekiah's court, inquiring where the gift bearers had come from. He then pre-

dicts the Babylonian exile. Chapters 40–55 change in mood, circumstance, even poetic style. They seem to speak to present circumstances and to future events. The captivity is a realized fact, and the initial mood is one of despair:

> "Console my people, console them,"
> says your God.
> "Speak to the heart of Jerusalem
> and call to her
> that her time of service is ended,
> that her sin is atoned for,
> that she has received from Yahweh
> double punishment for all her crimes."
> (40:1–2)

Deliverance seems to be at hand. A king from the east is already on the move, subduing the nations, although it is really Yahweh who is directing history. Though Israel (from this time forward all the people of the Covenant are called Israel, not just Judah) deserved the punishment it has received, the time of redemption is at hand. Cyrus is mentioned twice by name (44:28, 45:1), supporting the position that this section of Isaiah dates from the exilic period.

Included in these poetic oracles are indications of two significant developments within Judaism during the period of the exile. The first is the appearance of a sense of messianic expectation stronger than anywhere earlier in the Hebrew Bible. The second is an insistence on absolute **monotheism,** accompanied by a universalizing of the religion of Moses. Both deserve our special attention before we move further.

Messianism. Few doubt that I Isaiah introduced the messianic dimension into prophetic theology. It is also obvious that that vision was shared by many of the eighth-century prophet's successors, including Ezekiel. Nowhere, however, is **messianism** so prominent in the Hebrew Bible as it is in what have come to be known as the **servant passages** of II Isaiah. "The servant" is sometimes referred to in individual terms, while in other passages Israel is identified as the servant. In both cases servanthood is identified as the role to be assumed upon delivery from oppression, and the concept could well incorporate not only the new role Israel must play in history but also an anticipation of a Messiah to lead Israel in that role.

Before the specifics are examined, we must recognize that at no time in Judeo-Christian history has there been absolute agreement on the identity of the servant. When the early Christians proclaimed Jesus as Messiah they made constant use of this portion of Isaiah to show what they believed to be the ways Jesus' life fulfilled these prophecies. The strong sense

of messianic expectation that existed in Judaism at the beginning of the Christian era is an affirmation that the Jews themselves looked for an individual Messiah, probably under the influence of the Book of Isaiah. The fracture that occurred in the first century, which eventuated in the emergence of Christianity as a religion separate from Judaism, began a tendency within Judaism to see itself in a messianic role and has led some modern Jews to abandon entirely the idea of the individual Messiah. Throughout, however, there was a strong sense of expectation after the exile of a Messiah who would lead Israel in its proper role as a restored nation.

There is an overlooked aspect of the servant image in Isaiah. As you read this portion of Isaiah you might want to give attention to the role the Messiah is to play in the future life of Judaism rather than to the question of who the Messiah is envisioned to be. Whether an individual or the community, the Messiah's role is to be that of servant. In the first of the servant songs, we read of Yahweh's servant:

. . . that he may bring true justice to the nations. (42:1)

And again:

I, Yahweh, have called you to serve the cause of right, . . .
I have appointed you as a covenant of the people and
light of the nations,
to open the eyes of the blind,
to free captives from prison,
and those who live in darkness from the dungeon. (42:6–7)

This theme is continued in the second song:

. . . "You are my servant (Israel)
in whom I shall be glorified"; (49:3)

. . . he who formed me in the womb to be his servant,
to bring Jacob back to him,
to gather Israel to him:

"It is not enough for you to be my servant,
to restore the tribes of Jacob and bring back
the survivors of Israel;
I will make you the light of the nations
so that my salvation may reach to the ends of
the earth." (49:5a–6)

The third song begins:

The Lord Yahweh has given me
a disciple's tongue. (50:4)

Read the fourth song in its entirety (Isa. 52:
13–53:12), and then consider these verses:

With you I will make an everlasting covenant
out of the favors promised to David.
See, I have made of you a witness to the
peoples, a leader and master of nations.
See, you will summon a nation you never
knew,
those unknown will come hurrying to you,
for the sake of Yahweh your God,
of the Holy One of Israel who will glorify
you. (55:3b–5)

Isolating what it is the servant will do, as
set forth above, there begins to emerge not
only the concept of a servant but the implication that the servant will fulfill a religious role.
The purpose of servanthood is to make Yahweh known and honored by all people. That
role is directly related to the other significant
considerations, namely, monotheism and
universalism.

Monotheism/Universalism. Now that you
have read so much of the Hebrew Bible, I want
to ask you a question: When did absolute
monotheism become a part of Judaism? I am
not asking whether Moses was a monotheist,
or the authors of the books that you have read,
but when the people we call Jews reached that
point. They certainly had not done so during
the era of the Judges. They do not appear to
have been monotheistic during the period of
the monarchies. While they might have ac-

knowledged Yahweh as their only God in their
better moments, they did worship the gods of
surrounding cultures long after Moses, at least
up to the time of Josiah's reforms (621 B.C.E.).
While they might have considered Yahweh superior to other gods, there is little clue that the
common people thought he was the only God
until very late in this ongoing history. The beliefs of the religious leaders are not easily discerned, but there are clues that even many of
them did not arrive at a sense of absolute
monotheism until late in the monarchy. There
is no question that Judaism did espouse an absolute monotheism after the exile, with its accompanying sense of the universal demands of
such a concept. If there is but one God, he
must be acknowledged by all, hence must be
made known to all. Let's examine the case:

1. Moses says that Israel must worship only
Yahweh. He does not say that there are no
other gods. Though Moses' view of Yahweh is
consistent with absolute monotheism, those
who accepted his vision might not have
understood the message in that sense.

2. The Hebrews worshiped the gods of the
lands they occupied, while still acknowledging Yahweh.

3. Elijah's contest with the Baal priests (1
Kings 18:16–40) proved that Yahweh was
superior, more powerful. Did it prove to
the people of the time that he was the only
God?

4. The prophets continued to berate the
people of Judah and Israel for their worship of
gods other than Yahweh.

5. There is no indication that the Jews tried
to export their religion, to share their vision
of Yahweh with other nations at any time
through the period of the monarchy, although
they appear to have allowed some outsiders to
become Jews.

You could add to the list. These are but examples. In the story you have read until now, Judaism can be better described as a national rather than a world religion. Yet this will no longer be the case. As the prophets who immediately preceded the exile would affirm, Yahweh used whom he would to accomplish his purposes. The Babylonians were considered the rod of Yahweh's anger directed at his stubborn and disobedient people, who had failed in the obligations imposed by the Covenant and had transgressed the Law. "You," Yahweh had said, are to be a "kingdom of priests, a consecrated nation," and it is not until Isaiah 40–55 that there emerges a fresh understanding of the priestly role first identified in the Book of Exodus.

We need not infer that a new dimension was added at this point in history, but II Isaiah does suggest a new dimension in the understanding of the existing religious tradition. Being a "kingdom of priests" now more clearly meant that Israel was to be the light of Yahweh for the world. Yahweh was not the best or most powerful national god, he was the only God. His concern for Israel was continuing, but as the creator of all things, Yahweh was concerned for all. Israel was to be the vehicle to make that concern known, "a light to the nations." The priestly role was to take on an evangelical dimension: The servant of Yahweh was to bring knowledge of God to all people.

As Israel faced the possibility of release from captivity, it prepared to assume its covenant role to the fullest. The release itself would serve as a sign as Yahweh delivers his people:

> Then the glory of Yahweh shall be revealed
> and all mankind shall see it. (Isa. 40:5)

Absolute monotheism is emphasized:

> Thus says Israel's king
> and his redeemer, Yahweh Sabaoth:
> I am the first and the last;
> there is no other God besides me.

> Who is like me? Let him stand up and speak,
> let him show himself and argue it out before me.
> Who from the very beginning foretold the future?
> Let them tell us what is yet to come.
> Have no fear, do not be afraid;
> Have I not told you and revealed it long ago?
> You are my witness, is there any other God besides me?
> There is no Rock; I know of none. (44:6–8)

Yahweh, the only God, calls all to judgment:

> Pay attention to me, you peoples,
> listen to me, you nations.
> For from me comes the Law
> and my justice shall be the light of the peoples. . . . (51:4)

Armed with this new vision, the people are prepared to resume their covenant role in history. It is a role that does not require a location within national boundaries, nor does it require political autonomy. It is essentially a religious role, which can be assumed by one who remains in Babylon as well as by one who returns to Judah. Thus we see that the servant's role can be ascribed to an individual or to Israel as a holy nation. Perhaps both are assumed by the prophet as he speaks of the future of Judaism.

The Return

✦ **READ** *The Books of Ezra and Nehemiah*

Cyrus did, indeed, defeat the Babylonians in 539 B.C.E. The Jews were allowed to return to their land and to their Holy City. It does not seem that they rushed back in droves. After all, most of those who had gone into exile had died in Babylon, and the new generation had known only life in Babylon. The historic reality is that not all the Jews were to return, some choosing to remain in the lands of their birth but still acknowledging the religious heritage of their ancestors. It is apparent that the Jews no longer felt that to be a Jew required living in a particu-

Model of the restored Temple at Jerusalem after
the Babylonian exile.

lar place, for Judaism was now truly a world religion. What is known of that early return is
found in the books of Ezra and Nehemiah, as
well as the prophetic books believed to have
been produced at that time. Let us look to
them for help in this continuing story.

Chapter 1 of Ezra describes the return. The
account is consistent with what is known of
that history, except that Cyrus is said to have
invoked the name of Yahweh.* Led by **Sheshbazzar,** one of the line of David, the Jews set
out for Jerusalem, bearing the Temple treasures. Almost fifty thousand returned, according to Ezra, although many scholars suggest
this figure represents instead the total who
made their way back over the century or so until Ezra himself arrived. The genealogical lists
here and elsewhere reflect the abiding interest
of the author in identifying the true Jews. They
can be skipped, but remember that they are important to the author's overall purposes.

One needs to be aware that the first portion
of Ezra deals with the period immediately after
the return. Later portions deal with history at
the time of Ezra and Nehemiah, a period dated
as many as one hundred years later. With fewer
than six chapters describing more than a hundred years of history, it is obvious that the report is highly selective, including only events
considered essential to the total story. Thus
we are told that upon their return the Jews
gathered in Jerusalem to restore the Temple.

---

*There is no evidence outside the Book of Ezra and the
apocryphal Bel and the Dragon that Cyrus was a wor-
shiper of Yahweh. Rather, as indicated previously, he is
believed to have honored the Babylonian god Marduk
(Bel).

The first task, that of rebuilding the altar, was accomplished, but the people who currently occupied the land resented the returning Jews. The rebuilding of the Temple and the eventual rebuilding of the city walls (but not for another one hundred or so years) meant to the people who had made Jerusalem their home that the Jews were attempting to regain political control.

Although the altar was completed and celebrations of sacrifice reinstituted almost immediately, the Temple was not completed until 515 B.C.E. The project appears to have been all but abandoned for a period, for both Haggai and Zechariah chided the people to get on with that task. The delay was occasioned by the hostility between the returning exiles and the current residents, enhanced perhaps by the haughty attitude of the Jews toward the Samaritans, who thought of themselves as Jews but were not perceived as such by the returnees. Accusing the returnees of attempting to reestablish their own government at the expense of allegiance owed to the Persians, the Samaritans appealed directly to **Xerxes**, ruler of the Persian Empire. The building project did not begin again until the second year of the reign of **Darius**, 520 B.C.E., and was not completed until 515 B.C.E., just in time for the Passover celebration of that year.

The story now skips to the period of Ezra and Nehemiah, leaving no clue to what happened in the intervening years. We do, however, have the writings of the two prophets **Joel** and Malachi, two of the prophetic books that do not date themselves but are believed to have been written after 500 B.C.E. Both reflect a Judaism not at its highest point. Joel was written at a time of plague and Malachi at a low period in the priestly tradition. Both look to a day of Yahweh, a day when Judah will reflect its past glory, but neither writer views his own moment as very glorious. Those two books give the clearest picture available of the conditions in the years between 515 B.C.E. and the admin-

istration of Nehemiah as governor of Jerusalem.

A number of scholars suggest that the stories of Ezra and Nehemiah should be reversed, that Nehemiah preceded Ezra, who did not arrive until Nehemiah's second term as governor. That arrangement is reasonable, and it is the one followed here to describe the events for which these two persons are remembered and honored within Judaism. There is no consensus regarding exactly where Ezra and Nehemiah should be placed chronologically. Depending on which Persian **Artaxerxes** is assumed by the individual scholar, the beginning of the story is dated as early as 458 B.C.E. or as late as 397 B.C.E.

Even if Nehemiah preceded Ezra, the contributions of the two were made in concert. Nehemiah was a political figure, supported by the authority of the Persian Empire, whereas Ezra was a priest. Nehemiah's major accomplishment was the supervision of the rebuilding of the tattered walls of Jerusalem. He, with Ezra, had an even greater accomplishment, however: namely, the rebuilding of the tattered image of Judaism. Some call Ezra the "father of modern Judaism." Probably that title should be shared, for Ezra and Nehemiah together were responsible for the revitalization and redefinition of Judaism as truly a world religion, providing it with a new sense of purpose and with the means of maintaining its identity amid most difficult circumstances.

Nehemiah, after completing the restitution of the walls of the Holy City, recognized the need of a religious authority to help dispel the apathetic religious atmosphere that continued to exist. Ezra brought with him the Law. Ezra and Nehemiah set about to rid Judaism of the foreign influences that had plagued it since its earliest existence, and that meant the casting out of foreign wives. Only those who were of pure stock could consider themselves Jews. Intermarriages were dissolved now and forbidden in the future. Sabbath observance was reinforced, and the Temple reinserted as central to the worship life of the people. Nehemiah and Ezra established the standard by which the Jews would measure their authenticity:

1. By being of pure Jewish blood
2. By loyalty to and support of the Temple
3. By devotion to the Law

Some have suggested that this was really a step from redefining Judaism as a world religion, while others view the events recounted in this story as ensuring the survival of Judaism. There is some truth in both views, as you will discover. Suffice it to say here that although Ezra and Nehemiah had a major impact on the shape of Judaism beyond their own time, they were not without critics among their contemporaries. These criticisms will be examined in the next chapter. First, however, you need to know a bit about the theory of how the books of Ezra and Nehemiah reached their literary form and why it is an important consideration.

THE CHRONICLER

◆ **REVIEW**   *1 and 2 Chronicles*

Those who were already familiar with the Hebrew Bible, or have now read 1 and 2 Kings and 1 and 2 Chronicles, probably have wondered about the similarity of the Kings and Chronicles accounts. That similarity, along with the similarity of literary style and the thematic consistency of 1 and 2 Chronicles, Ezra, and Nehemiah, has led most scholars to conclude that these books are the work of one author/ editor, who is known as the **Chronicler,** a person with a strong priestly interest in the formation of Judaism as a "kingdom of priests."

This author/editor includes the genealogy of Judaism from the time of Adam, making certain that a true Jew can be identified by the standard of Ezra and Nehemiah, the standard of birth. He establishes, as well, the linkage of those designated for specific religious roles in the society. He shares the view of the Deuteronomic historian that the exile was a result of faithlessness; obviously he relied on this material as he recorded his own account of history from the time of the monarchy, but his own point of view is nevertheless easily detectable. He mentions Saul but gives him little attention, beginning his story with David. The picture the Chronicler paints of David is much more positive than the earlier view we have received. In Chronicles David builds the palace but only designs the Temple, which is said to be the work of Solomon. The relationship with Bathsheba is not reported, nor are many other events found in our earlier account. What is highlighted is Yahweh's blessing of the throne of David and David's pious devotion to Yahweh. 1 Chronicles deals with genealogy, the prominence of David, and the role of various groups in setting precedent for what was to follow.

2 Chronicles begins with the reign of Solomon and continues to the Edict of Cyrus, which freed the Jews from their Babylonian exile. The dominance of the priestly interest in this history is illustrated in an abundance of ways, even to the casual reader. When Israel and Judah are divided, for example, all priests and Levites abandon their own dwelling places to reside in Jerusalem, the place of the Temple. This story includes a condemnation of Jeroboam for allowing sacrifice at places other than the Temple. The account of the prophet **Abijah's** condemnation of the division (Ch. 13), not found in Kings, reveals further the point of view of the author. The kings of Judah are treated somewhat more kindly in this account, though they are not without sin. The priest's role in fostering Yahweh worship is honored, as is illustrated in the portion of the Jehoshaphat story found in Chapter 19. Chapter 23 recounts the priestly resistance to the illegitimate queen Athaliah, providing more detail than the account found in Kings. The story of

the prophet **Obed,** not found in Kings, shows that Yahweh favors Judah over her sister Israel. The reinstitution of the Passover takes place much earlier in Chronicles than it does in Kings, and although Manasseh is judged as wicked, he is portrayed as repentant, even beginning some religious reform to atone for his sins.

For one who uses the Bible to seek history, 1 and 2 Chronicles create more problems than they solve. They illustrate, however, that none of our biblical authors wrote merely for the sake of history. The Chronicler, for example, did not create a new David. He reported the details important to his point of view, ignoring circumstances that did not serve his purposes. Perhaps he was more a story writer than a story teller at points. Some scholars suggest that his knowledge of or interest in history was not as strong as that of the writers out of the prophetic tradition, simply because his passions did not make history as important as it was for a prophet.

What sources did the Chronicler use? It has been suggested that one source was 1 and 2 Kings. Another, obviously, was the priestly tradition itself. The first-person accounts of Nehemiah suggest to many that the governor of Jerusalem left a diary that was available to his near-contemporaries. The same is suggested in regard to the material about Ezra, although there is much less agreement among scholars on that matter. It is believed, however, that after the period of Ezra and Nehemiah this account reached its final form, shaped by someone who would affirm the view of Judaism as a religion with its heart in Jerusalem and the Temple, its true leaders the priests, its people born, not made, and its devotion to the Law as an expression of Covenant obedience.

The unity of the material becomes clear when one reads 1 and 2 Chronicles, Ezra, and Nehemiah as a unit. The priestly point of view literally jumps off the pages, much as does the prophetic viewpoint of the Deuteronomic history. As a whole, the work of the Chronicler defines Judaism much more in religious terms, doing away with many of the nationalistic tendencies that can be found in other places. The Jews maintain a special role in history, as the protectors and carriers of the tradition to which they have been entrusted in their covenant relationship with Yahweh. To ensure the purity of that tradition, the Jews must be pure themselves, thus needing to rid themselves of any foreign influence that would distort their message. Because they had gone astray by allowing false religions in their midst, by incorporating elements of surrounding cultures, and by marrying those outside the faith, they must now purify themselves, casting out any possibility of such distortion in the future by affirming that only the pure seed of Abraham will remain in their midst. To be true to the covenant of priesthood from which their specialness derived, the Jews must set aside all distractions and forbid them in the future. The casting out of foreign wives in Ezra and Nehemiah was for this purpose, and the avoidance of such dangerous intermingling would help ensure the purity sought. The seed of Abraham had a special place in human history; to be born a Jew meant that one was born to a special responsibility, which could not be ignored.

From this time forward, a sense of separateness in Jewish history was to be both a blessing and a curse, according to one's point of view. Our own historical perspective makes us acknowledge that without the sense of exclusiveness that developed in the era of Ezra and Nehemiah, Judaism might not have survived in the form in which it now exists. At the same time, the expansion of Judaism as a world religion was hampered when many insisted that the only true Jew was one born within the faith.

The result of the formal literary introduction of this point of view within Judaism was the establishment of boundaries of a religious debate that continues to this day within that community. Whether this began the debate or simply reflected an already existing argument, from the time of the second Temple forward the question of who truly qualifies as a Jew became a passionate argument among those within Judaism. The narrow answer, the one attributed to Ezra/Nehemiah, would respond that it is someone with pure Jewish blood. Those who would counter this definition point out that David would not qualify as a Jew under such a narrow definition, because his great grandmother was a Moabite. (See our discussion of the Book of Ruth in Chapter 6.)

Although the works of the Chronicler provide a view of Judaism that some would consider narrowly exclusive (and certainly those works have been used as the source of authority by those within Judaism who would argue for a narrow definition), there is perhaps another way those works can be understood. Rather than to cut Judaism off from the world or cause it to become aloof, the real intent of those works might be understood as to define those of Jewish blood (the children of Abraham by birth) as being chosen for a special role in history. Thus, although all humanity is to honor and worship Yahweh, only the children of Abraham have the responsibility to make Yahweh known so that he can be honored and worshiped. This is what it means, some would declare, to be a Kingdom of Priests, a Holy Nation. To be a Jew, a child of Abraham, means that one is born into a priestly responsibility and is to be the light of Yahweh to the nations.

To successfully carry out that awesome responsibility, Jews must remain free of contamination from the seductive world; thus, they cannot be married to those whose culture might contain bogus religious visions. After all, one has only to review the history to know that much of the reason for their downfall, even from the prophetic point of view, was that they gave in to the temptations of the surrounding cultures (see 2 Kings 17). Jews must live the life befitting their responsibilities, honoring the Law as their teacher and living the pure life of service Yahweh has set aside for them.

Understood in the way just described, the view put forth by the Chronicler does not have to be understood as narrowly exclusive. Clearly, however, some within Judaism did become aloof, encouraging other Jews to disassociate themselves from the evil world. This was not the final word for all Jews, however.

Subsequent history and literature show us that while **Palestinian Judaism** seemed to accept the more narrow definition of Judaism these books provide, other segments of the Jewish community, particularly those who did not have the Holy Land as their home, resisted such a limited interpretation. Much of the remainder of the literature of the Old Testament provides clues to the continuing debate the narrow view provoked. It also suggests clues to other developments that give shape to modern Judaism as a world religion.

STUDY QUESTIONS

1. Identify the problems created for Judaism by the Babylonian exile and indicate how the people dealt with those problems.

2. Discuss the change in the prophetic message of Ezekiel after the final Babylonian exile.

3. Identify the material of II Isaiah, explain why it is so designated, and tell what it contains.

4. Explain why it is suggested that absolute monotheism was not a part of all Judaism until the period of the Babylonian exile and that II Isaiah did much to solidify that concept for the Jews.

5. Discuss the "servant" so prominent in Isaiah 40–55, including the identity and role of that servant.

6. Identify the problems of constructing Jewish history after the exile.

7. Identify Ezra and Nehemiah and indicate their major contributions to ongoing Judaism.

8. Who is the Chronicler? What point of view does the material attributed to him represent, and which books of the Old Testament are attributed to him?

9. Explain how one can understand the defining of a Jew within Ezra/Nehemiah as the defining of future Jewish religious responsibility.

10. Identify those things within II Isaiah that would lead one to describe its message as having "universal dimensions," and explain what that means.

11. Indicate what is found in the message of the written prophets that leads some to suggest that those prophets provided Judaism with an understanding of its history that would not destroy its faith when it lost its land and Temple.

12. Summarize what you believe to be the best way to explain how the events of the exile transformed Judaism from a national to a world religion.

SUGGESTED READINGS

Bickerman, Elias. *From Ezra to the Last of the Maccabees: Foundations of Post-Biblical Judaism* (Schocken Books, New York, 1962).

Blenkinsopp, Joseph. *Ezra-Nehemiah: A Commentary* (Westminster Press, The Old Testament Library, Philadelphia, 1988).

Koch, Klaus. *The Prophets, Vol. II, The Babylonian and Persian Periods* (Fortress Press, Philadelphia, 1984).

McKenzie, John L. *Second Isaiah*, Anchor Bible (Doubleday, Garden City, N.Y., 1968).

North, Christopher. "Isaiah," *The Interpreter's Dictionary of the Bible*, Vol. 2 (Abingdon Press, Nashville, 1962).

Pfeiffer, R. H. "Chronicles, I and II," *The Interpreter's Dictionary of the Bible*, Vol. 1 (Abingdon Press, Nashville, 1962).

———. "Ezra and Nehemiah, Books of," *The Interpreter's Dictionary of the Bible*, Vol. 2 (Abingdon Press, Nashville, 1962).

Schuller, Eileen. *Post-Exilic Prophets* (Glazier, Wilmington, 1988).

Smart, James D. *History and Theology in Second Isaiah* (Westminster Press, Philadelphia, 1965).

Talmon, S. "Ezra and Nehemiah, Books and Men," *The Interpreter's Dictionary of the Bible*, supplementary volume (Abingdon Press, Nashville, 1976).

SIX

THE LATE HEBREW BIBLE PERIOD

A RATIONALE FOR OUR STUDY

The series of readings in this chapter concludes our investigation of the Hebrew Bible. These materials seem to have been among the last books written (not including the apocryphal works, which are noted separately) that are included in the Jewish canon. Though some of these materials probably have a direct relation to tradition much more ancient than the period during which they took their literary form, they likely find their place in the scriptural tradition fairly late in the Hebrew Bible period.

It will be helpful to recall the suggested chronology of the literary development of the Hebrew Bible until this time:

1. Oral tradition (before Moses)

2. Beginning of a written tradition (Moses to the monarchy), including some form of the Law and the Covenant

3. Expanded literary tradition, preserving the oral tradition in literary form, with the beginning of the shaping of the Pentateuch

4. The court history of David, followed by the Annals of the kings of both Judah and Israel

5. The prophetic tradition preserved in oral and literary form, including stories about the prophets as well as the books attributed to the individual prophets

6. The Book of Deuteronomy, perhaps the scroll found in the Temple during Josiah's reign

7. The Deuteronomic history, reaching its final form during the exile

8. The other literary events of the exile, as well as the works of the later prophets

9. The work of the Chronicler

10. The remaining books of the Hebrew Bible

We will examine the books in the last category in the following order, mainly as a matter of convenience (there is no scholarly consensus on when each work was produced or became a part of Jewish scriptural tradition):

Psalms

The Wisdom Books (Proverbs, Ecclesiastes, and Job)

Jonah

Ruth

Esther

Daniel

Song of Songs

Lamentations

These works lack accompanying historical books against which we can measure them. In fact, they provide us with the sense of history of the times out of which they were produced. That alone makes their dating important.

The placing of these works at the end of our study of the Hebrew Bible does not indicate that they are less important than the works previously examined, nor that their roots are not as deep in the tradition of emerging Judaism. (Some are among the more important books of Jewish scripture, while others play a less important role.) Together they provide the final touches of our picture, and none can be ignored if we are to gain a total understanding of the Judaism out of which Christianity emerged, which provides the foundation of the more modern forms of itself.

These works differ from the Apocrypha because they are more closely tied to the earlier tradition, often consciously placing themselves in the midst of it. We can often make that connection ourselves. Though the Book of Psalms, for example, did not reach its final form until the period of the second Temple (probably after the days of Ezra and Nehemiah), many of the individual psalms are easily placed at a much earlier date. The story of **Ruth** might not have achieved the form in which we have it until after 400 B.C.E., yet the historical roots of the story clearly predate David. A people rooted in history and tradition continued to draw on both history and tradition as they sought to find their way in a changing world, relying on whatever had defined them. There was always another story from which one could find meaning, an-

other tradition that could guide and sustain. Let us now examine them.

PSALMS

✦ **READ** *Psalms 1, 2, 6, 8, 22, 32, and 150*

The Book of Psalms is best understood as a hymnbook. It contains the liturgy of Israel's worship life in a collection that spans a number of centuries. Though most of the psalms have traditionally been credited to David, it is probably more accurate to say simply that they emerged out of the worship life of Judaism. Although David is remembered as a poet and it is possible that he wrote some of the psalms, no one can say with assurance who penned any particular psalm. The designation of authorship tells us more about what was traditionally believed about the material's origins than it does about those origins themselves.

It is known, however, that the psalms provided the formal liturgy in Temple worship. Composed over the centuries, they offered a means for the people to acknowledge their faith in Yahweh in their formal devotions. It is obvious that some psalms were composed for particular occasions, such as special holy festivals, while others reflect historic moments of crisis in the life of the people. No one assumes that we have all the psalms of Israel; rather, the Book of Psalms more likely represents a particular collection at a specific moment in history. Some have called the Book of Psalms the hymnbook of the second Temple, and that seems a good description of what it represents and of the time in which it was put into the form we now know and use.

Remember that in the Judeo-Christian tradition, liturgy is the formal guide to community worship, the collective affirmation of religious devotion. It represents the moments when people turn to the object of that devotion for the purpose of religious encounter. It is in the worship life of a community that we find just what people believe and how they respond to that belief. It is in their praise and prayer that we come to understand how they comprehend deity and how they respond to that comprehension. It is in the content of worship that we find truly what people believe.

Up until this point in the study of the Hebrew Bible we have learned what Moses, the prophets, and the priests taught. Now we have the opportunity to be in touch with the individual who was the recipient of these lessons. The psalms offer us an insight into the life of individual Jews as they invite us into their worship life. They show us how Yahweh was understood and how that understanding led people to respond. They answer the question "So what?" and offer us a sense of the meaning of all that the people have affirmed.

How did the individual child of Abraham understand Yahweh? The answer is in the psalms. Make a list of the various ways Yahweh is described in the psalms and you have that answer. Yahweh is not unidimensional, nor is he aloof from his people. He takes care of the virtuous, provides protection, inspires fear, works wonders for those he loves, expresses displeasure with wickedness, and will not tolerate social injustice. He is the final judge, the source of all wisdom, a shield in time of trouble. The list can go on and on. The Book of Psalms might well be called the theology book of the Hebrew Bible, for it includes every aspect of the theology of the Judeo-Christian tradition, every facet of the understanding of the nature of God found in that combined tradition.

Those of you familiar with Christianity know that there are some within that tradition who assert that through Jesus and the New Testament, Christianity brought new dimensions to the personality of God not before revealed. You can find suggestions that the God of the Old Testament is more a God of judgment, while the God of the New Testament is more a God of love and compassion. For one familiar with the psalms it is difficult to accept the idea that Christianity introduced new aspects to existing Jewish theology. The worshiping Jew perceived of Yahweh as father, understood that there was mercy as well as justice in his nature, and felt his compassion. In fact, it might be helpful to take a few moments to go through the various psalms and simply identify the various words used to describe God as he is being addressed in worship; the list will quickly become quite long. The psalms reveal how much alike the combined traditions truly are. One must look elsewhere to explain their separation, not in what they believed about the nature of their God.

The context and structure of the psalms themselves provide our best clues to how or when these hymns were used in Israel's worship life. Scholars have developed classifications for the various types, such as psalms of praise, laments, and psalms of thanksgiving, and have used those classifications to describe the function of psalms in Jewish liturgy. Such classifications can be helpful for certain purposes but are beyond the scope of this study. Obvious in the psalms are certain indications of how such determinations were made and how the psalms were originally used in the context of worship. Psalm 6 serves as an example. Verses 1–7 are a lament. Evidently after this lament the worship leader pronounced assurance, for verses 8–10 reflect a new mood. The lament has been heard, Yahweh has responded, and the reason for sadness removed. There is now a mood of thanksgiving.

In the one hundred fifty psalms one can find something appropriate for every mood or occasion in worship. Some are meant for community gathering; many are obviously appropriate for individual worship. Even community worship becomes very much an individual affair as each person seeks privately to relate to the object of worship. The psalms have well served both purposes—community and individual worship—in the Judeo-Christian tradition since they were first produced. Not only were they the hymnbook of the Temple, they formed the early hymnody of Christianity as well. An examination of the liturgy of the combined traditions shows their dominant influence in the worship life of the Judeo-Christian tradition over the centuries and how much those traditions have a common world view.

The psalms reveal the religious dimension of the Judeo-Christian tradition more fully than any other portion of the Bible, for they carry us into the most private place in the life of the community, the place of the individual at worship. There we find the struggles, the anguish and despair. There, also, we find the hope, the faith, the comfort of those who affirm Yahweh as the Lord of history. They take us beyond ideas to the intimate response of those who accept those ideas as true. They bare the soul of the religion they proclaim. While revealing the human condition, they reach beyond that condition to show us how the faithful at least were able to overcome its obstacles. The power of the psalms is not in their beauty, but rather in their content. The worship life of any religion provides us with the best clue to what empowers it and preserves it in the lives of those who accept it. The psalms give us that clue in the Bible.

THE WISDOM TRADITION

Wisdom Defined

Wisdom is defined as knowledge and good judgment based on experience. We use words such as learning, erudition, prudence, and discretion as synonyms. In Acts 7:22, Moses is characterized as powerful because of his knowledge of the wisdom of the Egyptians. Wisdom is also a form of literature common to the ancient Near East. As it is dealt with here, however, wisdom is really something more and, in some respects, something different. To understand the wisdom literature of the Judeo-Christian tradition, it is necessary to understand the **wisdom tradition** in its historical context.

Wisdom in Israel

Like so many of Israel's traditions, the wisdom tradition is best understood by exploring its likeness to similar usages found in surrounding cultures and its own uniqueness among those traditions. Although most of the information that is needed is provided by the Hebrew Bible itself, that information does not jump from the pages to inform us, nor is it always distinguishable from other portions of the tradition.

Solomon is revered in the Hebrew Bible as the father of the wisdom tradition. His prayer to Yahweh in which he asks for wisdom, "to discern between good and evil," and the famous story of how he proves his wisdom (1 Kings 3:4–28) provide our best clue to the distinctive nature of Hebrew wisdom and its important role in religious history.

Solomon was not the first of Israel's wise men, nor was he the last. Joseph has the distinction of playing that role initially, while **Daniel** is the last of such Hebrew Bible characters. Moses and Aaron, many of the prophets, and some kings also can properly be identified with the tradition, for in Israel the most distinguishing characteristic of wisdom is the ability to discern the will of Yahweh. We need to trace the tradition through its various stages and to explore how it achieved its uniqueness.

Being a wise man was a profession in the ancient Middle East, and undoubtedly some in Israel, at least during the period of the monarchy, served that profession. Joseph well could have been a professional wise man in the court of Pharaoh, as Daniel was in the court of Nebuchadnezzar. Both men were brought to the attention of the monarchs they served by their ability to interpret dreams. When Moses went before Pharaoh, the king was surrounded by his own sages, sorcerers, and magicians who attempted to give counsel and to counter the magic of Moses and Aaron. Daniel, **Shadrach, Meshach,** and **Abednego** are described as being selected out of the youth of Israel to be ". . . trained in every kind of wisdom, well informed, quick at learning, suitable for service in the palace of the king" (Daniel 1:4). They were also to know the language and literature of the Chaldaeans. All these elements contribute to our understanding of the context of professional dispensers of wisdom and to those who served as wise men in the courts of the kings.

Professional wise men gave counsel to kings. The source of their knowledge was believed to be the God of gods, whom they honored, and they had means to demonstrate the source of their knowledge. The contest between Moses and Pharaoh serves as an example. To demand the release of the Jews, Moses went before Pharaoh armed with the signs and wonders Yahweh had provided in the power of his staff. The attendants at Pharaoh's court were able to reproduce some of the signs of Moses, though never to the same degree. Soon, however, they were unable to duplicate Moses' efforts, and they reported to Pharaoh, "This is the finger of God" (Exod. 8:19), acknowledging that Yahweh was more powerful than the gods of the Egyptians. Earlier Moses had said to Pharaoh that his signs (plagues) were intended to show Pharaoh "that Yahweh our God has no equal" (Exod. 8:10). In other stories when Joseph and Daniel proved to be correct in their interpretations, their standing at court was enhanced, the gift of wisdom for which they credited their God having brought respect and honor. Nebuchadnezzar even acknowledges Yahweh as "the God of gods" (Dan. 2:47), thus recognizing the source of Daniel's wisdom.

In all this, whether through magic, the cast-ing of lots (another way of discerning Yahweh's will), or the interpreting of dreams, the purpose was to determine the will or intention of the "God of gods," the will of Yahweh. And of course this is the same role that the prophet played in the life of Israel. In a culture that views Yahweh as the God of history, known through the events of history, prophet and wise man play complementary, if not identical, roles. Add to that the understanding of Israel's special covenant relationship with Yahweh, a Covenant bound by the Law, and the uniqueness of Israel's wisdom tradition begins to emerge.

The source of wisdom in Israel is Yahweh. Wisdom itself is the ability to discern Yahweh's will or way. Deeply embedded in Israel's religious tradition is the belief that Yahweh rewards obedience and punishes disobedience. Thus it can be said that wisdom in Israel is the ability to discern the will of Yahweh and to determine the responsibility of those who must follow that will: Do this and there will be reward; failure to so act will result in punishment, as is demonstrated in history itself, at least history as told by those within Israel's own religious tradition. The wisdom tradition, then, is just another way of expressing Mosaic or prophetic theology; it is totally consistent with the religious mentality of its people. It may be described most easily as the popular means by which the values of that tradition were preserved and passed from generation to generation, giving special honor to those whose discerning abilities were especially acute.

The wisdom literature of Israel is a reflection of that tradition and of the serious philosophical arguments raised by such a view over the years. It expresses what is known as a traditional view of **wisdom.** Throughout the Hebrew Bible, it presumes a way of understanding the will and way of Yahweh within the Covenant and Law and assuming a world view that explains good and evil, reward and punishment, based on one's adherence to the covenant relationship expressed by the Law. It assumes that good will be rewarded and evil punished, as it always has been, a fact obvious to the sensitive observer of Israel's own history. The purpose of wisdom literature is to teach the ways of Yahweh so that the pitfalls of life can be avoided or, as in the case of **Ecclesiastes** and Job, to question these assumptions; for although all the wisdom literature begins with the same assumptions, they are not always accepted as valid.

THE LITERATURE OF WISDOM

✦ **READ** *Proverbs 1–5; Ecclesiastes 1–3, 12; Job 1–7, 38–42*

The literature of wisdom is of two sorts. The first, of which the Book of Proverbs is our example, is an expression of **traditional wisdom.** The second, to which Ecclesiastes and Job belong, challenges that traditional view.

Proverbs

Traditional wisdom is the expression of the practical, living application of Mosaic or prophetic theology. "Live," it says, "by the precepts of Covenant and Law and you will be rewarded. Otherwise you will be punished." Reward will be in the form of material blessings, good health, and long life. Punishment will consist of trouble and sorrow. It assumes that one's life is a reflection of such behavior. Since wisdom literature includes instruction on what the Covenant and the Law demand in personal behavior, it is in its own way indirectly teaching both. Cast often as advice of parent to child, it serves as a means of teaching the practical application of the world view that informs it, at the same time citing the consequences of the behaviors described.

Like the psalms, wisdom literature invites us to a personal encounter with the community who accepted the Mosaic view of history, showing us how they understood that such a view directed their lives. Although Proverbs 1:1 attributes these sayings to Solomon, and some scholars try to date the work in monarchical times, it is probably best understood as the traditional wisdom of Jewish culture, collected over the centuries. Indeed, beginning in 22:17, the collection is attributed to "the sages," probably a reference to those who have professionally played the role of wise men over the centuries in Israel. Chapters 30 and 31 are credited to the wisdom traditions beyond Israel, and if nothing else, such attributions lead to the assumption of the collected nature of the work. Scholarly agreement on this matter is lacking, however.

One often reads of the influence of the Judeo-Christian tradition on the Western world. Looking at that world, it is often difficult to find specific examples. They abound, obscure yet visible, embedded in the value system of our societies. Many of us have lost an immediate sense of their origins, yet one does not have to dig deeply to discover their beginnings. Traditional wisdom is much like that. To appreciate it fully, one must remain sensitive to its religious roots even when those roots do not declare themselves. With that in mind, let us examine Proverbs.

The purpose of the **Proverbs** is declared at the beginning:

for learning what wisdom and discipline are,
for understanding words of deep meaning,
for acquiring an enlightened attitude of mind
—virtue, justice and fair dealing;
for teaching sound judgment to the ignorant,
and knowledge and sense to the young;
for perceiving the meaning of proverbs and obscure sayings,
the sayings of sages and their riddles.
Let the wise listen and he will learn yet more,
and the man of discernment will acquire the art of guidance. (1:2–6)

The source of wisdom is also acknowledged:

For Yahweh himself is giver of wisdom,
from his mouth issue knowledge and
discernment. (2:6)

The role of the family in passing on the values of the religious society is revealed in the language of the teachings. Father and mother are the teachers, the young the pupils. Some have suggested that traditional wisdom is the reflection of the family values of the upper class of society, yet this seems to be too harsh and limiting a judgment. The earlier suggestion that it represents the practical aspect of the theology of Moses and the prophets is perhaps more fair. For enlightenment, try to relate Proverbs to the particular laws they reflect. Having done that, compare the consequences they affirm to the view of history you have encountered to this point in the reading of the Hebrew Bible. You will find a remarkable consistency:

[Yahweh] keeps his help for honest men,
he is the shield of those whose ways are
honorable;
he stands guard over paths of justice,
he keeps watch on the way of his devoted
ones.
Then you will understand what virtue is,
justice, and fair dealing,
all paths that lead to happiness. (2:7–9)

The message is quite simple. Honor Yahweh, follow his ways, and reward will be yours. Forsake his ways and trouble will follow. Avoid the things that would entice you from the Covenant and the Law. The seven sins that Yahweh abhors (6:16–19)—the haughty look, lying tongue, the shedding of innocent blood, weaving wicked plots, hurrying to do evil, lying, and the sowing of dissension—are all in disregard of the Law. Much of the advice about avoiding evil women seems to be directed against association with those who do not share the values of the Jewish culture, the aliens whom Ezra and Nehemiah cast out, those who would seduce one from the righful worship of Yahweh.

It is too simplistic to suggest that traditional wisdom offers a comfortable orthodoxy based on a balanced view of rewards and punishment. There is constant warning against the prideful arrogance of so simple a view and the reminder that material reward is not the object of a good life (see 8:12–21). Yet it is important to recognize that an uncritical reading of the sage advice could lead and has led to the idea that prosperity and good health are signs of Yahweh's pleasure, whereas poverty and despair indicate divine displeasure. Surely some readers took the simplistic view, thus missing the deeper meaning found in these powerful teaching tools of Hebrew society. The Hebrew Bible, however, contains two other wisdom books that attempt to correct the distortions that had crept in. These works are designated **nontraditional wisdom,** a phrase describing their role in trying to correct the popular distortions that had arisen in their own day.

Ecclesiastes

The first of these nontraditional wisdom books is Ecclesiastes. Described by some as the work of a cynic and reflecting a religious agnosticism, it can be understood in ways that might prove more helpful—for example, as a book that challenges some of the basic assumptions of traditional wisdom.

Ecclesiastes is ascribed (1:1) to Qoheleth (the Preacher), son of David, king in Jerusalem. While some have assumed this was a claim for authorship by Solomon, most regard it as a literary device to associate Ecclesiastes with the father of Hebrew wisdom. It is likely the work of a Hebrew sage who wrote it to challenge the traditional wisdom view espoused by Proverbs and perhaps distorted by the popular religion of its own day, thus making it a very late book in the chronology of Hebrew Bible literature. Scholars do not agree on a date for this work. Some have suggested that the book had no religious theme at its inception and that the few passing references to God at its conclusion are the work of a later pious editor who had missed the essential message or was trying to make the work acceptable in the religious community. It is just as likely that the work we have stands much like the original, if its intention was to challenge the popularized religious assumptions of traditional wisdom.

The work itself is the best argument for the idea that someone in the religious community of Israel wanted to correct the distortion of important theological principles that was perceived to be developing. Those who would date it in the third century B.C.E. suggest that it has a great affinity with the Greek philosophy of that time and affirm such an influence. It does not seem to occur to them that the influence could have been in the other direction, or that Ecclesiastes can be as easily explained as a sensitive response to a religious problem by one who was a part of the Jewish tradition and cared for it deeply.

Traditional Hebrew wisdom, as has been observed, is based on the idea that obedience within the covenant relationship would assure Yahweh's pleasure and blessing; disobedience, his displeasure and curse. Yet perhaps the heart of the matter lies not in the assessment of any given consequence as "good" or "evil" but in the assumption that the will of God—what *is* good, or evil?—can be known. There are numerous, if subtle, examples of the struggle Judaism had with its understanding of the demands of the Law, the instrument understood as the guide to Yahweh's will for his people.

Although one does not have to interpret traditional wisdom simplistically, it does lend itself to the notion that one can do good and be rewarded, or fail and suffer the consequences.

Of course this point of view can lead to a complacent stance in which all life is viewed as revealing the signs of good and evil, providing simple answers to complex problems. However, the truly wise know that what seems clear is often hidden. Doubt is not a sign of unfaithfulness as much as it is a symbol of our human condition.

The author of Ecclesiastes speaks in favor of the human condition, avoiding the easy clichés as he attempts to deal with the reality with which we all must cope. He says that things are not always as they seem, that the easy answer is not always the best. True wisdom is elusive, if not unavailable, and it is better to acknowledge that than to fall into the trap of easy answers that will betray one in time of trouble. It is better to realize that our knowledge is limited, that life is complex, than to rely on assumptions that prove false in crises. Though cynical in tone, Ecclesiastes is perhaps not as cynical as it first appears. Perhaps the Preacher is more realistic than cynical.

"There is nothing new under the sun," we are told. "What was will be again," though we may forget. Having tasted all aspects of life, from folly to virtue, we learn that all produce vanity. The same fate comes to all: Life ends, and there is little in the quality of life that makes that consequence change. The ways of God are difficult to fathom by observing life around us—the rain falls on the just as on the unjust; the good despair while the evil prosper.

The author implies that it is better to accept life as it is than to try to explain the unexplainable. God's ways are not as easily discerned as some would have us believe, and neither good nor evil is simply explained. The concluding words are consistent with this summary:

. . . fear God, and keep his commandments, since this is the whole duty of man. For God will call all hidden deeds, good or bad, to judgment. (12:13–14)

In sum, Ecclesiastes says that the testimony of life itself challenges the simple assumptions one might make from traditional wisdom. One might be wiser to accept life without trying to analyze its meaning, to live the best one can, and to leave judgment to God, whose ways are not always clear. The Preacher does not counsel neglecting the Law. Rather, he warns that the rewards one might expect are not guaranteed, nor should they be the goal, for such expectations may lead to disappointment. Ecclesiastes does not challenge the value on which traditional wisdom is based, the values of Covenant and Law, but only the mistaken assumptions to which those values can lead.

Job

The other challenge to traditional wisdom is the Book of Job. Unlike its companion, Ecclesiastes, Job makes direct use of the arguments of traditional wisdom themselves. The unknown author of this work takes the prosaic story of the pious Job, an Edomite, and adds to it a poetic section in which the point of view of the author is revealed.

There is no scholarly agreement on the source or time of Job. It has been suggested that the prose portion may well be rooted in a period as early as the patriarchs and that the work was resurrected later to provide a setting for the author's questioning of the simple assumptions accompanying traditional wisdom. This suggestion has much to commend it in the work itself. The ancient folk tale makes an excellent setting for the arguments provided in the poetic section.

The Book of Job has been hailed as a literary masterpiece of the ages; this powerful work is an expression of the finest of the literary tradition of the Hebrew Bible. Dealing, as it does, with the problem of human suffering, Job has become the prototype of much of the literature on that subject through the centuries. Because of the high drama revealing the travail of Job, many have sought to use this book as the Bible's answer to the question of suffering, although a careful reading will show that it is not fully satisfactory in that regard. The phrase "the patience of Job" reflects another poor reading of the book, for Job was anything but a patient man. An examination of its contents best provides us with a sense of its true purpose.

Job is divided into five parts:

1. Prologue, in prose (Chs. 1–2)

2. Dialogue with Job's friends, in poetry (Chs. 3–31)

3. The **Elihu** speeches, in poetry (Chs. 32–37)

4. The speeches of Yahweh, in poetry (Chs. 38–42:6)

5. The epilogue, in prose (Ch. 42:7–17)

If the prosaic portions of the work were indeed adopted by the poetic author to provide a setting for his message, perhaps the prosaic ending (42:7–17) is an even later addition, put there by a scholar who had missed the point of the book and felt the need to uphold the traditional wisdom point of view. That possibility will be discussed at the end of this survey. The poetic section contains three distinct parts, each with its own role.

The prologue introduces us to the righteous Job, who is rich in the things of the world, yet pious beyond question, "a sound and honest man who feared God and shunned evil" (1:1) Not only did Job do all the things required of a religious Jew in the patriarchal period, he did more, making certain that neither he nor his family did anything to offend Yahweh.

The setting now shifts to heaven, the scene of the heavenly council. Satan returns from a visit to earth and Yahweh asks him if he has observed God's righteous servant, Job. Satan indicates that he has indeed seen Job and raises a major issue: "Job is not God-fearing for nothing," Satan challenges, pointing out that Job has been well blessed for his righteousness. "Take away his blessings," Satan suggests, "and Job will curse you." Although insisting on the protection of Job's person, Yahweh allows a series of tragedies to be visited on Job and his family, oxen and servants, sheep and camels. Even his children are killed. The pious Job responds to the news:

> "Naked I came from my mother's womb,
> naked I shall return.
> Yahweh gave, Yahweh has taken back.
> Blessed be the name of Yahweh!" (1:21)

We are reminded that in all this "Job committed no sin nor offered any insult to God" (1:22).

Once again, Satan returns from earth to the heavenly council. Yahweh again extols the virtues of Job, and Satan suggests that if Job is burdened with physical affliction he will reject God. Yahweh allows Satan to test this hypothesis, only demanding that his life be spared. Job is then struck with malignant ulcers from the soles of the feet to the top of the head. His wife counsels, "Do you now still mean to persist in your blamelessness? Curse God, and die" (2:9). Job refuses, uttering no sinful word. Three friends arrive to console Job, but seeing his great distress they only sit in silence for seven days.

It will help in your understanding to know that Satan in the book of Job is not to be understood as the Devil. Rather, he is portrayed as a member of the Heavenly Council whose major responsibility is to keep an eye on the earth for Yahweh and report to him its activities. While Satan can be considered an adversary of humans (he accuses humans before God in the heavenly Council), he is not portrayed here as an adversary of Yahweh. That relationship comes later and is clearly present in the New Testament. The change has taken place by the time of Jesus, but exactly when and where it

happens is still a matter of scholarly speculation. Most suggest that Satan assumed that role in Jewish mythology sometime in the postexilic period, illustrating our need to have a way of explaining evil as a competing force against that of the good God. That issue is a matter that a student of the Bible will want to understand as the subject continues to emerge.*

Chapters 3–31 report in poetry the dialogues of Job with **Eliphaz, Bildad,** and **Zophar.** The dialogues begin with Job cursing the day of his birth, for his suffering is unbearable and cannot be explained. This begins the speeches of his friends, who express the assumptions of traditional wisdom that there is not suffering without guilt. They constantly suggest that Job will be restored if he will appeal to God and willingly confess his guilt. Job, in his responses, insists on his innocence, as firmly established in the prosaic introduction. Job, like his comforters, argues from the point of view of traditional wisdom. Yet whereas their arguments suggest guilt in Job, his arguments protest his innocence, leading him to question God's justice. Neither argument presumes another way of understanding Job's predicament, for both accept the assumptions that good is rewarded and evil punished. Thus, the friends assume Job's guilt, and Job concludes God's injustice as he continues to affirm his own righteousness.

Chapter 32 introduces the speeches of Elihu. The friends of Job had given up too easily, and the angry young Elihu takes over the defense of the justice of God. Again he argues from the point of view of traditional wisdom, insisting that Job must have some secret sin. Chapter 36 is especially powerful as Elihu chronicles the contentions of the wisdom tradition his speeches represent. Job remains silent.

---

*A short but helpful article on Satan is James E. Efrid, "Satan," *Harper's Bible Dictionary* (New York: Harper & Row, 1985), pp. 908–909.

Yahweh himself begins to speak in Chapter 38. It is in his words we find the clues to our author's message. Up until this point the entire study has been based on the assumptions of traditional wisdom. Job, his friends, and Elihu all assume that they understand the will and ways of Yahweh. Now Yahweh will set them straight! As Yahweh speaks out of the tempest (whirlwind), we get to the heart of the matter. The message is simple: Job and his friends have made the same mistake of thinking that they can understand the ways of God.

The message of Yahweh chides any who feel that they can discern his ways. Job acknowledges his frivolity, and Yahweh speaks again, condemning the arrogance of any who believe that they understand God's ways. Job answers:

> I know that you are all-powerful:
> what you conceive, you can perform.
> I am the man who obscured your designs
> with my empty-headed words.
> I have been holding forth on matters I cannot
>   understand,
> on marvels beyond me and my knowledge.
> (Listen, I have more to say,
> now it is my turn to ask questions and yours
>   to inform me.)
> I knew you then only by hearsay;
> but now, having seen you with my own eyes,
> I retract all I have said,
> and in dust and ashes I repent. (42:2–6)

If Job had sinned, his error lay in presuming to discern the ways of Yahweh. The foolishness of the entire debate is revealed. Much like the message of Ecclesiastes, the Book of Job seems to say that the ways of Yahweh are not easily discerned, that there are no simple answers to life's complex problems, that things are not always as they seem to be. Job's repentance is such an acknowledgment.

In both Job and Ecclesiastes the question is not whether one needs to be righteous. Righteousness is assumed. One just need not expect that righteous behavior is necessarily going to produce reward. One should not judge God or others based on the assumption that the "whys" of life are clear.

In the epilogue (42:7–17), Job's righteousness, which has never been in doubt, appears to receive material vindication. Some understand this as a reaffirmation of the values of traditional wisdom, but others see it as a part of the original prose that the author borrowed. However it is understood, its presence need not detract from the essential point of view of the book that is revealed through the voice of the tempest, and against which the other portions of the book must be judged.

Other Examples of Late Hebrew Bible Literature

Let us now examine the remaining books listed earlier that deserve some attention before we leave the Hebrew Bible.

✦ **READ** *The Book of Jonah*

Jonah. The Book of Jonah is included in the collection of the minor prophets, yet it is quite different from the other prophetic works. It is really a story about a prophet (or Jewish missionary) rather than a recording of prophetic teaching. The historical Jonah can be placed at the time of Jeroboam II, and portions of his story can be related to events in the life of the ruler. Many scholars cite the contents of the book as the basis for their belief that Jonah was written in or after the fourth century B.C.E. by an unknown author for the purpose of arguing against the narrow definition of Judaism credited to Ezra and Nehemiah.

Jonah is one of the most familiar stories of the Hebrew Bible. Yahweh speaks to Jonah, instructing him to go to Nineveh, a non-Israelite city, and condemn the citizens for their wickedness. Jonah runs away instead of obeying for, as we learn later, he fears Yahweh's mercy on the people of Nineveh. He boards a ship bound for Tarshish (Spain), but the ship encounters a terrible storm. The passengers cast lots to determine the one responsible for the storm. The lot falls on Jonah, who is cast into the sea and swallowed by a great fish. After three days in the belly of the fish, Jonah is coughed up onto the shore. Again called by Yahweh to go to Nineveh, this time Jonah goes. He tells the people of Yahweh's displeasure, they repent, and Yahweh withholds his judgment. Jonah becomes enraged, telling Yahweh he knew that would happen all along, because he knew of Yahweh's tender compassion. Pouting, he finds shelter under a plant, which Yahweh withers, bringing Jonah more discomfort. Jonah's continued complaint gives Yahweh the opportunity to make the point of the story:

> God said to Jonah, "Are you right to be angry about the castor-oil plant?" [Jonah] replied, "I have every right to be angry, to the point of death." Yahweh replied, "You are only upset about a castor-oil plant which costs you no labor, which you did not make grow, which sprouted in a night and has perished in a night. And am I not to feel sorry for Nineveh, the great city, in which there are more than a hundred and twenty thousand people who cannot tell their right hand from their left, to say nothing of all the animals?" (4:9–11)

Here the story abruptly ends. The point has been made. Yahweh has universal concern for mankind rather than a narrow view that would exclude all but the Jews.

◆ READ *The Book of Ruth*

Ruth. Many would link the book of Ruth to the same period as Jonah, citing the same purposes. At a time when many Jews were accepting the more narrow and exclusive view of their religion, another unknown author reaches back in Judaism's history to recall a story that was probably already known by most, a story set in the period of the Judges. The two main characters are **Naomi,** a Jew, and Ruth, her

Moabite daughter-in-law. Naomi, her husband, and their two sons have left Judah to live in Moab. The two sons marry Moabite women, but the men die, leaving three widows. Naomi plans to return to Judah, urging her daughters-in-law to return to their families. One daughter-in-law, **Orpah,** does leave, but Ruth responds with the famous words:

> "Do not press me to leave you or to turn back from your company, for
> wherever you go, I will go,
> wherever you live, I will live.
> Your people shall be my people,
> and your God, my God.
> Wherever you die, I will die
> and there I will be buried.
> May Yahweh do this thing to me
> and more also,
> if even death should come between us!"
> (1:16–17)

They do return. Eventually Ruth marries a Jew, **Boaz,** a kinsman of Naomi on her husband's side, and a son, Obed, is born to the couple.

This is a beautiful story of a loving relationship between a woman and her daughter-in-law. It is, however, not religious in the traditional understanding of that term. Aside from Ruth becoming a convert to Judaism, there is no deep or hidden revelation as to matters concerning Yahweh or the human relationship to divine. There is no direct reference to how Yahweh might be involved in the matters related in the story. What, then, is it doing in the Hebrew Bible? The clue may well be in 4:17: "and they named him Obed. This was the father of David's father, Jesse." Some take this as an indication that David himself, the ideal king in whose line the hope of Israel lay, would not by the more narrow definition qualify as a Jew. The Book of Ruth, it is believed, is included in the canon as an argument against the absurdity of a concept of Judaism that would exclude even David from its ranks.

Ancient Jewish tombs located outside the walls of
Jerusalem.

✦ **READ** *The Book of Esther*

Esther. If the Book of Ruth seems to lack a re-
sounding religious message, the Book of **Esther**
has none at all. It contains no reference to God
or religious practice. It is really a story about
Jewish survival, hence it had difficulty finding
a place in both the Jewish and the Christian
canons. It has been suggested that its canonical
status was granted mainly because the story is
the basis of the popular Jewish festival of **Purim.** The religious elements of Esther in the Jerusalem Bible are later additions and will be
noted in the next section.

Esther was a Jewish woman of such great
beauty that she became a queen of Persia, wife
of Xerxes. With the counsel of her cousin **Mordecai,** she was able to intervene in behalf of her
people when the evil **Haman** had tricked
Xerxes into ordering the extermination of the
Jews. Thus Esther was successful in saving her
people. In addition Xerxes gave the Jews the
right to arm themselves and use deadly force in
their own defense (8:10–12).

The Book of Esther tells the story in detail,
thus explaining the foundation of the holiday
that celebrates these events. In the context of
our current discussion, however, we can understand Esther as a book that argues on the other
side of the debate reflected in Ruth and Jonah,
affirming a more narrow definition of Judaism
by recognizing the hostile environment that
would destroy the Jews except for their own
watchfulness. Certainly, the book has served

as a symbol of hope for those who believe it is important for Judaism to survive, remembering a time when its very existence was imperiled.

There is no absolute scholarly consensus as to when Esther was written. Most would agree that it belongs to the very late Hebrew Bible period, perhaps the second century B.C.E. Its story, which fits well with a period in which Judaism was threatened with annihilation, would certainly be encouraging to those who faced the severe persecution of **Antiochus IV,** the same period that stimulated the **Maccabean Revolt** and in which it is believed the Book of Daniel was also produced.

✦ **READ** *Daniel 1–2, 7–12*

Daniel. The Book of Daniel is one of the more controversial books of the Hebrew Bible, not only because of its last chapters but also because of the seeming errors in its history and the ambiguity of its role in Hebrew literature. The book is divided into two parts. The first is the story of Daniel and his friends (Chs. 1–6), the second the visions of Daniel (Chs. 7–12). If you are using the Jerusalem Bible you will find additional materials incorporated in the book; these are discussed in our next section.

The Book of Daniel has been described as the only truly apocalyptic work in the Hebrew Bible. The term "apocalyptic" describes a particular dualistic world view that is eschatological, as well. The dualism is cosmic, regarding the world as caught up in a struggle between the forces of good and evil. **Eschatology** views history as expressed in two distinct ages, time and beyond-time. Common to the apocalyptic view of the Judeo-Christian tradition, good is represented by God, while evil is under the guidance of Satan. The outcome of the struggle is never in doubt, because God is obviously superior to Satan. The outcome of the struggle will bring a climactic end to history as we know it, with a new beginning in which evil will be destroyed and only good will remain. In this view "time" is strongly influenced by evil, and even the righteous will suffer. However, in "beyond-time" evil will not exist, and righteousness will be rewarded. Hope is in "beyond-time," not in the present age. Apocalyptic literature is the literature that incorporates that world view. Daniel represents its most complete expression in the Hebrew Bible, Revelation in the New Testament.

Scholars suggest that an apocalyptic view of history in Judaism came as a result of the influence of the Persians, for such thought was very prominent in their religious world view. The view was certainly compatible with existing Jewish thought, and perhaps it can as easily be explained as a natural outgrowth of prophetic theology. It simply implies that one has to live by the consequences of one's choices. If one lives within the bounds of the covenant relationship, bound by the Law, then when temptation comes and one succumbs by the rejection of Yahweh, one has to pay the penalty. Times of trouble can be viewed as times of trial, the domination of foreign powers seen as tests of one's loyalty to the Law and Covenant. Yahweh will reward faithfulness and punish unfaithfulness, the same view expressed by the prophetic author/editor of the Deuteronomic history. The later view most fully explains why Daniel is grouped among the prophets in the Christian Bible.

The questions of the dating and authorship of the book form the basis of the controversy that surrounds it. If it is assumed to have been written by Daniel during the Babylonian exile, it must be viewed one way. If produced in the second century B.C.E., as some believe, it must be understood entirely differently. Though those questions have not been answered in the same way by all biblical scholars, the majority now views Daniel as a product of the second century B.C.E., written by a member of the Palestinian Jewish community. If that interpretation is correct, it leads to other conclusions about the book, some of which will be reviewed here.

Judaism was being threatened with extinction during the period of Antiochus IV (175–164 B.C.E.), an aggressive hellenizer who sought, among other things, to undermine Jewish exclusivism. The policies of Antiochus resulted in religious persecution of the Jews, with some attempts to eliminate Judaism entirely. There are stories about the desecration of the Temple by the forces of this hated ruler, as well as an attempt at eradicating Judaism by the destruction of its sacred literature when it could be found.

Because of these policies, the Maccabean Revolt took place, after which Judaism came to enjoy again the sense of independence in its own land. It is to such a setting that those who would give Daniel its late date believe the book addressed itself. When Judaism was faced with extinction, one who believed that Yahweh would not abandon his faithful people would recall another moment in history when things were equally dark. Looking back to the time of the Babylonian exile and recalling the story of the heroic Daniel, a story many believe to have had an independent existence before the canonical work, the author incorporates the history of the past with his apocalyptic vision of the present.

Those who hold this view cite varied pieces of evidence. First the book seems to be a composite of accounts, referring to Daniel in the third person in places, in the first person at later points. The inaccuracy of the history, especially that dealing with the kings in Chapters 1–6, suggests that the author was not one completely familiar with the history of the time of Nebuchadnezzar. Evidence of the use of more than one language in early manuscripts further supports the theory of a composite origin. The very nature of apocalyptic literature is another affirmation, for it uses history for apocalyptic purposes. Recognizing the book to be highly symbolic, especially after Chapter 6, many are convinced that placing it at a late period provides the clues to the symbolism and thus explains the book. If these assumptions are correct, they lead to the following synopsis:

1. During the period of severe Jewish persecution under Antiochus IV, one who was committed to the salvation of Judaism produced the Book of Daniel.

2. This author appealed to the memory of Judaism, imploring the people to recall other moments of crisis they had survived, particularly the time of the Babylonian exile.

3. The author used the example of the faithfulness of the pious Daniel and his friends to demonstrate a case of divine intervention on behalf of Israel. God in the past had not allowed the destruction of those who had maintained their faithful devotion to him.

4. The visions of Daniel predicted future travail, when again the faithful were to be threatened because of their faithfulness to a God not acknowledged by would-be conquerors. Though it might seem that evil was about to triumph, goodness would ultimately prevail and faithfulness be rewarded. If such a message were read in the second century, it would surely seem the time for those things that Daniel had envisioned.

5. The message was a call to faithfulness. Using an apocalyptic view of history, the writer rehearsed history (time) as the arena of the conflict between Yahweh and Satan, promising that in the world to come (time-beyond) Yahweh will rule and their faithfulness will be rewarded. Good triumphs over evil. Those who waver will suffer in the

defeat of the evil they have joined in their unfaithfulness.

Those who view Daniel in this way suggest that all apocalyptic literature made broad use of symbolism. This symbolism, they explain, was to confound those who were outside the faithful community, for they would not share this view of history or understand the meaning of the symbols. Of course, not all within the Judeo-Christian community have interpreted apocalyptic literature in the same way, nor are they likely to in the future. Some believe that in Daniel (and later in Revelation) lie the literal clues to what is to happen in human history. One needs only to find the proper key to the symbols. Differences in interpretation have led to apocalyptic groups arising in both traditions. Almost every generation has produced some who have been convinced that they were/are living in the last days and that the signs of their time have been revealed in apocalyptic books of the Bible.

The real value of the apocalyptic view has never been in being able to state when history as we know it will end. Apocalyptic literature has survived and has been honored as scripture in the Judeo-Christian tradition because it remains consistent with the theology of that tradition. It contains a theology of hope. As Jeremiah and Ezekiel had earlier spoken of individual survival in righteous behavior, so the apocalyptic writer emphasizes such a message. A people who are being tested in their faith are reminded of the rewards of faithfulness. Convinced of the eventual triumph of Yahweh, it encourages those who are his people not to yield in time of trouble, assuring them that they will share in the final triumph. In whatever way the book is understood, the essential message remains the same—that Yahweh rewards faithfulness and punishes unfaithfulness—and that message is shared by later apocalyptic works.

◆ **READ** *Song of Songs 1:1–3:5*

Song of Songs. One book that usually receives little attention in the study of the Hebrew Bible is the **Song of Songs.** Purported to be written by Solomon, it is more likely a collection of poetic units by no single author, celebrating nuptial and prenuptial love. Some have attempted to allegorize the songs as expressions of divine love, yet they more likely are lyric poems collected for use at Hebrew weddings, which for that reason became associated with the scriptural tradition.

It would be difficult to date the poems, though one (3:6–11) may have been composed for use at one of Solomon's many weddings. The final collection we have was most likely assembled during the period of the Second Temple, like the Book of Psalms. There has always been dispute over whether these works ought to be considered religious, even when they were considered for inclusion in the Jewish canon.

The poems seem to honor monogamy, and they celebrate rather unashamedly the physical aspects of the marital relationship. While some young people are titillated by its verses, the material is by no means either crude or lewd. It would be an appropriate part of the liturgy of marriage for a culture of Israel as we know it, a culture not yet trapped by our more modest social mores.

◆ **READ** *Lamentations 1:1–22*

Lamentations. Jeremiah has been given the name "the weeping prophet," and the Book of Lamentations has been traditionally attributed to him, thus accounting for its location in the Christian Bible. The Hebrew Bible places it among the writings.

The entire collection, which is in the form of laments, could have been associated with the liturgy of the Second Temple. It seems clear that these laments were composed at the time of or soon after the destruction of Jerusalem by the Babylonians in 587 B.C.E. There is a very real question as to whether the work ought to be attributed to Jeremiah, but there is no question about its value as a guide to repentant behavior. The verses were most likely composed to be used in the annual lament held to remember the fall of Jerusalem to the Babylonians. Their purpose is to assuage the grief felt over that tragic moment in the history of Judaism. They, in the spirit of traditional Judaism, acknowledge that the despair is a result of the sin of Israel. To lament is to acknowledge the guilt and to hope for Yahweh's future mercy to the repentant. As Yahweh must punish guilt,

surely he will also restore the remorseful. The sense of utter disgrace felt by the defeated peoples is reflected in the laments, as is the need to repent from the behavior that brought on such devastation.

With Lamentations we conclude our study of the Hebrew Bible. Before we move on to our reading of the New Testament, however, it is appropriate to acknowledge the existence of other works, some of which were used as scripture by some Jews before they established their own canon. Many of the works discussed briefly in the Interlude that follows have been included in the scriptures of some portion of Christianity and are known to us as the Hebrew Bible's **Apocrypha.**

STUDY QUESTIONS

1. Explain why the Hebrew Bible books discussed in this chapter are included here in our study of Jewish scripture.

2. What was the function of the psalms in the worship life of Israel, and how is that reflected in their content?

3. Define wisdom in the context of the Hebrew tradition.

4. Identify the wisdom books of the Hebrew Bible and indicate what is unique about each.

5. What is the major purpose of the Book of Jonah, and how is that purpose expressed within the work?

6. What factor does Ruth's Moabite origins play in the message of the book?

7. If the Book of Esther has no religious dimension, why is it in the Hebrew Bible?

8. Discuss Daniel as an apocalyptic work and show how that understanding determines one's interpretation of the message of the book.

9. Why do you suppose it is more difficult to place within a context of history the books of the Hebrew Bible that we studied in this chapter, and thus more difficult to come to a common agreement as to how they should be understood?

10. How would you explain the function and message of the book of Lamentations in the Hebrew Bible?

11. How does the content of the individual psalms help in one's understanding of how the Jews of the second Temple understood the nature of Yahweh?

12. Explain why the author of this text suggests that the study of the psalms reveals that the Judeo-Christian tradition shares a common understanding of the nature of God—that one does not include elements excluded by the other.

SUGGESTED READINGS

Aufrecht, Walter E., Ed. *Studies in the Book of Job* (Wilfred Laurier Univ. Press, Waterloo, Canada, 1985).

Blank, S. H. "Ecclesiastes," *The Interpreter's Dictionary of the Bible,* Vol. 2 (Abingdon Press, Nashville, 1962).

———. "Proverbs, Book of," *The Interpreter's Dictionary of the Bible,* Vol. 3 (Abingdon Press, Nashville, 1962).

———. "Wisdom," *The Interpreter's Dictionary of the Bible,* Vol. 4 (Abingdon Press, Nashville, 1962).

Brueggemann, Walter. *The Message of the Psalms: A Commentary* (Augsburg Press, Minneapolis, 1984).

Collins, John J. *Daniel: An Introduction to Apocalyptic Literature* (W. B. Eerdmans, Grand Rapids, 1984).

Fox, Michael V. *The Song of Songs and the Ancient Egyptian Love Songs* (University of Wisconsin Press, Madison, 1985).

Frost, S. B. "Daniel," *The Interpreter's Dictionary of the Bible,* Vol. 1 (Abingdon Press, Nashville, 1962).

Gordis, Robert. *The Book of God and Man: A Study of Job* (University of Chicago Press, Chicago, 1965).

———. *The Song of Songs and Lamentations* (KTAV Publishing House, New York, 1974).

Gottwald, N. K. "Lamentations, Book of," *The Interpreter's Dictionary of the Bible,* Vol. 3 (Abingdon Press, Nashville, 1962).

———. "Song of Songs," *The Interpreter's Dictionary of the Bible,* Vol. 4 (Abingdon Press, Nashville, 1962).

Hanson, Paul D. *Old Testament Apocalyptic* (Abingdon Press, Nashville, 1987).

Harvey, D. "Ruth, Book of," *The Interpreter's Dictionary of the Bible,* Vol. 3 (Abingdon Press, Nashville, 1962).

Hayes, John H. *Understanding the Psalms* (Judson Press, Valley Forge, 1976).

Hempel, J. "Psalms, Book of," *The Interpreter's Dictionary of the Bible,* Vol. 3 (Abingdon Press, Nashville, 1962).

Miller, Patrick D. *Interpreting the Psalms* (Fortress Press, Philadelphia, 1986).

Neil, W. "Jonah, Book of," *The Interpreter's Dictionary of the Bible*, Vol. 2 (Abingdon Press, Nashville, 1962).

O'Connor, Kathleen M. *The Wisdom Literature* (Glazier, Wilmington, 1988).

Pope, M. H. "Job, Book of," *The Interpreter's Dictionary of the Bible*, Vol. 2 (Abingdon Press, Nashville, 1962).

Russell, D. S. *The Method and Message of Jewish Apocalyptic* (Westminster Press, Philadelphia, 1964).

Saunders, E. W. "Esther, The Book of," *The Interpreter's Dictionary of the Bible*, Vol. 2 (Abingdon Press, Nashville, 1962).

von Rad, Gerhard. *Wisdom in Israel* (Abingdon Press, Nashville, 1962).

INTERLUDE:
THE APOCRYPHA

DEFINITION AND HISTORY

Readers who have used a Bible without the Apocrypha probably were surprised or confused to find in the Hebrew Bible portion of the Jerusalem Bible books or additions to books (such as in Daniel) that do not appear in all Bibles. Those who are exploring the Bible for the first time need to be aware that all editions of the Bible do not include the same material in the same order. The reason lies in the sources of the materials from which the Bible was translated into the various English editions. It is appropriate now to recognize these differences and the reasons for them, and to note briefly the works that are not fully explored in our study.

First, the Jerusalem Bible contains the following books or portions of books not found in all Bibles:

Tobit

Judith

Esther (portions in italics)

1 and 2 Maccabees

The Book of Wisdom, or the Wisdom of Solomon

Ecclesiasticus

Baruch

Chapter 6 of Baruch (Letter of Jeremiah)
Daniel
    3:24–90 (Prayer of Azariah; Song of Three Children)
    Chapter 12 (also known as Susanna)
    Chapter 13 (also known as Bel and the Dragon)

Not included in the Jerusalem Bible but found in some others are:

1 and 2 Esdras

Prayer of Manasseh

3 and 4 Maccabees

What are these works? These are books and portions of books found in Greek translations of the Hebrew Bible (Septuagint), but not in the later Hebrew canon. They were accepted by those who used the Septuagint, though some of the later books were not in all copies of that work. The Jews did not include these works in their scripture when the Hebrew Bible was canonized at the Council of Jamnia in 90 C.E. The Christian church continued to use them as such, although there has always been some dispute about their place as scripture, even in Christianity. Only **Tobit, Judith,** the Wisdom of Solomon, and **Ecclesiasticus** were included in the canon of the **Eastern Church,** that decision being made at the Council of Jerusalem in 1672. **1** and **2 Esdras** and the **Prayer of Manas-**

seh were not included in the Roman Catholic canonical list adopted at the Council of Trent in 1548. Works that appear in the Septuagint and are not included above are Psalm 151 and **3** and **4 Maccabees,** though you might find them included in some modern translations of the Bible.

Where these works belong in the arrangement of the books of the Bible is also a matter of dispute. When Martin Luther translated the Bible into German, he worked from a Greek New Testament and a Hebrew Bible. With regard to the Old Testament, he simply moved the material found in the Latin **Vulgate** but not in the Hebrew Bible to the end of his Old Testament translation. This practice was followed by many of Luther's Protestant successors. The Vulgate, on the other hand, relied on an earlier translation of the Septuagint for its translation of the Jewish scriptures and left the works ordered as they were in that work. This different ordering also reflects the tension that erupted among Christians at the time of the Reformation, and the Protestants' either complete removal or relegation to a lesser place of these apocryphal works had both political and spiritual implications. Psalm 151 and 3 and 4 Maccabees were omitted because the early Latin translation used by **St. Jerome** to produce the Vulgate did not include these works.

The Apocrypha in Brief

What do the apocryphal works contain? The most helpful approach is to place the works into their respective historical contexts and provide some information about their contents. We use the ordering of the Jerusalem Bible, which is as good as any for these purposes.

Tobit

Though the story of Tobit is set in the eighth century, most believe it was produced in its present form after the rise of Alexander the Great (323 B.C.E.) and the ensuing period of Hellenization. Tobit was a Jew living in the northern kingdom of Israel who nevertheless remained loyal to the Temple of Jerusalem. He made a yearly pilgrimage to Jerusalem to observe the Passover and to carry his tithe (he took more than required). When Israel was captured by the Assyrians, he was exiled to Nineveh, where he rose to a place of wealth and prominence, becoming buyer for the king. Tobit lost his high standing at court, however, because of his insistent pious loyalty to his religion. He became blind and poor, a pathetic figure. Remembering that he still had money secured with a friend in Media, Tobit sent his son **Tobias** to recover these funds. The real adventure is found in the story of Tobias, his love and experience. Intended to encourage Jews not to abandon their devotion to their religion in a period when the prevailing society valued **syncretism** above exclusiveness, the story has much in common with other works found in the Hebrew Bible. This short book is fascinating, and you should find time to read it.

Judith

You should not use the Book of Judith to gather a sense of history, for it seems to have been composed by someone who knew tradition better than history. Probably produced by a **Diaspora Jew** during the Hellenistic period, it portrays Nebuchadnezzar as king of Assyria with his capital in Nineveh. Its heroine Judith, a most pious Jewish widow, is portrayed as never violating the Law, even when she lives among the enemy. This beautiful and well-to-do lady comes to the aid of her people when they are under threat of extinction by the armies of Nebuchadnezzar. She gets into the enemy camp by means of deception and, finally, into the tent of Holofernes, the commanding general. While he lies drunk upon his couch she beheads him with his own sword. Judith returns to her people, and by showing them the head of Holofernes, gives them courage to take the situation in hand and drive the enemy away.

The point of the story seems similar to that of Tobit, recalling examples of the past when faithfulness was rewarded and Judaism persevered in time of great distress. It is another call for faithfulness.

Additions to Esther

If you read Esther without the portions called the **Additions to Esther,** you might well ask what is religious about a book that does not mention Yahweh, a book that tells about Jews who do nothing particularly religious. The story is really about the survival of Judaism, and it explains the story behind the very popular Jewish holiday, Purim.

Now if you read the story with the additions, or the Rest of Esther, as it is also called, the question about the religious nature of the book is answered. The two major religious additions are Mordecai's prayer and the prayer of Esther.

1 and 2 Maccabees

Here we do have a valuable source of history. **1** and **2 Maccabees** are set in the period of the Maccabean Revolt (second century B.C.E.) and the establishment of the **Hasmonaean dynasty.** Not a continuous narrative, the two books tell the same story from two different points of view, that of the **Sadducees** (1 Maccabees) and the Pharisees (2 Maccabees).

2 Maccabees, which obviously used 1 Maccabees as a source, carries the story to the point at which religious freedom is reestablished for the Jews, having much less interest in politics than its predecessor. It well could have been produced after Palestine had become a Roman protectorate, and its lack of political interest reflects the contemporary reality. Both books, however, offer some historic insight into the communities that produced them as well as the events they report. The kind of Pharisee portrayed in 2 Maccabees represents the uncharitable Phariseeism of which Jesus was so critical in the New Testament.

The Book of Wisdom

Though attributed to King Solomon, the **Book of Wisdom** probably was produced by a Hellenistic Jew in the last century before the Christian era. It is divided into three sections. Chapters 1–5 deal with wisdom and human destiny; Chapters 6–9 with the origin, nature, and effects of wisdom, and Chapters 10–19 with wisdom and God in history. It remains in the spirit of Hebrew wisdom and is quoted on occasion in the New Testament. It is considered perhaps the finest of the literature of Diaspora Judaism.

Some suggest that this work was written when Jews were being actively persecuted by Hellenists. Unlike the seeming cynicism of Ecclesiastes, the Book of Wisdom presents a hopeful outlook for a life to come and gives meaning to the sufferings of martyrs.

Ecclesiasticus

Ecclesiasticus was produced in Jerusalem at the beginning of the second century B.C.E. by Jeshua, son of Sirach. This marvelous philosophy of the pious Judaism of the day is the longest of any works of the literature of wisdom. It includes advice on everything from how to behave at a banquet to how to be a successful speaker.

Probably the best-known lines in the Apocrypha are found in the Praise of Famous Men (Chs. 44–50). This is, again, one of the finest pieces of Jewish literature and one that would enrich your life by its very beauty.

Baruch

Now dated after the fall of Jerusalem in 70 C.E., the Book of Baruch bears the name of the secretary of the prophet Jeremiah and purports to have been written in 582 B.C.E., five years after the conquest of Jerusalem by the Babylonians. According to this book, the Temple in Jerusalem has survived and priests still offer sacrifices there. Baruch has recovered some of the Temple utensils and sent them back to Jerusalem. Those remaining in exile are reminded of the reason for their distress: They had ignored the laws of God, and they had ignored the prophets by trying to throw off the yoke of the Babylonians. There is hope in the future, however, for Yahweh will restore what has been taken away, and people will learn wisdom by returning to the Law. "Peace through integrity, and honor through devotedness" is the theme of the long wisdom poem found in this work.

Chapter 6 purports to be a letter written by Jeremiah to those in exile. Believed by some to have been a separate work that was later attached to Baruch, the letter reminds the people that the gods of the Babylonians are shams and have no true power. It simply warns people not to worship such false gods.

If this work is the product of the first century of the Christian era, its intention seems to be to discourage Jews from continuing in political subversion. If, instead, they remain as law-abiding citizens of the Roman Empire, God will ultimately relieve their distress.

Additions to Daniel

The "extra" sections not found in the Hebrew Bible are Ch. 3 : 24–90; Chapter 12, also known as **Susanna;** and Chapter 13, also known as **Bel and the Dragon.**

In the Jerusalem Bible Chapter 3 of Daniel has two additions not found in the Hebrew scripture. The first, known as the **Song of Aza-** riah* in the Furnace, is a prayer seeking deliverance. The second, known as the **Song of the Three Young Men,** is a unison prayer of Shadrach, Meshach, and Abednego, essentially a hymn of praise.

Susanna is a story of the beautiful wife of Joakim. Her great beauty roused the desires of two prominent elders in Babylon, who sought a way to seduce her, but she refused their advances. The elders falsely accused her of unfaithfulness, and she was sentenced to death. Daniel was able to prove Susanna's innocence as well as the treachery of the elders, who were executed.

Chapter 14 (Bel and the Dragon) is another story that points out that the gods of Babylon are false gods. Daniel has refused to worship the gods of Babylon and through his ingenuity proves them to be powerless. On one occasion he demonstrates to Cyrus that the idol Bel does not consume the food offered to him. Later, a concoction Daniel prepares for a dragon who was an object of worship causes the dragon (or large snake) to burst. At the end of the story Daniel is once more cast into the lion's den, and again he miraculously escapes.

Susanna probably addressed the need of some reform in the Jewish judicial system, pointing out that it was not without flaw. Bel and the dragon, on the other hand, is very compatible with the rest of Daniel insofar as it ridicules idolatry and commends faithfulness to God.

1 and 2 Esdras

"Esdras" is the Greek rendering of the name Ezra. 1 Esdras seems to be a compilation of portions of Chronicles, Ezra, and Nehemiah. The

---

*In Nebuchadnezzar's court the Israelites Daniel, Hannaniah, Mishael, and Azariah were renamed Belteshazzar, Shadrach, Meshach, and Abednego (Dan. 1 : 7).

significant addition to those accounts is what has come to be known as the story of the three guardsmen. These three Jews, who had become guards of King Artaxerxes, spent the night debating what was the strongest thing in the world. After discussing the merits of wine, monarch, and woman, they decided that truth was indeed strongest. The result of the debate was the rewarding of the third guardsman, who turns out to be Zerubbabel, by allowing him to return to Jerusalem to rebuild the Temple. Though 1 Esdras confuses the order of the Persian kings, it does reflect the memory of Diaspora Judaism of the times when faith overcame overwhelming obstacles and allowed them to restore themselves in their own land.

2 Esdras is probably a compilation of a number of works ranging from as early as 66 C.E. to as late as 270. Martin Luther had no use at all for the book and said that he had discarded it. It is a series of apocalyptic visions addressed to people under severe persecution.

The Prayer of Manasseh

A short psalm of fifteen verses has been ascribed to King Manasseh, based on the recounting of his repentance found in 2 Chronicles (33:11–17). Whether Manasseh should enjoy the reputation of repentant sinner is questionable. This short prayer serves to enhance such a view if that is its source. Most would date the material to a time of postexilic Judaism; the reason for its attribution to Manasseh is not clear.

3 and 4 Maccabees

3 Maccabees seems to be designed to encourage Jews in their religious steadfastness, while at the same time warning would-be persecutors that the Jews are under the protection of a God who is not to be mocked. Filled with exaggerations, this work nevertheless seems to have

a fairly good sense of the history of the times in which its story is set. The story itself reports three instances of conflict between **Ptolemy Philopator** and the Jews. The first involves Ptolemy's unsuccessful attempt to enter the Jerusalem Temple, the second his persecution of **Alexandrian Jews,** and the third his attempt to exterminate the Jews living in Egypt. The Jews prevailed in all instances, remaining faithful to their religion and prospering.

The source of 4 Maccabees, a philosophic discourse in support of rational religion, is unknown. However, at times the work has been attributed to the Jewish historian Josephus. 4 Maccabees argues that the Law is the truest expression of real philosophy. Reason is identified with religious wisdom, the source and essence of which is piety:

> Reason, then, is the intelligent choosing with correct judgment the life of wisdom; wisdom is knowledge of things human and divine and their cause. Such wisdom is education in the Law, through which we learn things divine reverently and things human advantageously. (1:16–17)

Rich in moral philosophy, this work advocates the Jewish way of life as the best reasonable expression of that philosophy. Judaism demands the virtues of prudence, justice, courage, and self-control. The people's loyalty to these virtues is demonstrated in their devotion, even to the point of martyrdom, something the religion itself encourages. This powerful book deserves your attention.

These apocryphal works have had an impact on the Judeo-Christian tradition regardless of whether they have been included in the canons of any particular religious expression of that tradition. They are a part of the total literary tradition and are important to your full understanding of the Judeo-Christian communities that produced them.

STUDY QUESTIONS

1. Define what is meant by the Apocrypha and indicate what it includes.

2. Explain why some suggest that the books of the Apocrypha had the status of scripture for at least a period of their literary history.

3. How can one distinguish the apocryphal portions of regular books of the Hebrew Bible as they are presented in the *Jerusalem Bible?*

4. Do the works reviewed in this interlude have the status of scripture in any of the religious traditions represented in the Judeo-Christian tradition? Explain.

5. How would you explain the additions to Esther that make up the apocryphal portions of that book?

SUGGESTED READING

Sparks, H. F. D. *The Apocryphal Old Testament* (Oxford University Press, Oxford, 1984).

SEVEN

CHRISTIANITY: A SECT WITHIN JUDAISM

Now that we have become familiar with the so-called Old Testament, as the Hebrew Bible is designated by those within the Christian community, it is time to examine the "New Testament," that portion of the Bible used as scripture exclusively by Christians.

While the Hebrew Bible serves as scripture for both portions of the Judeo-Christian tradition, those traditions do not always understand and interpret it in the same way. The designations "Old" and "New," as has been stated earlier, reflect the belief among Christians that another chapter in the story of Yahweh's relationship with humanity has taken place in the arena of history. Christians believe that the Messiah has come (and is coming again), whereas Jews continue to look for the Messiah or believe that the messianic role will be played by Judaism itself in its capacity as "holy nation." Christians believe that the life and ministry of Jesus gave humanity a new covenant, or a radically new way to understand the old.

It is important to review some of our discoveries from the study of the Hebrew Bible as we prepare to study the scripture that is exclusive to Christians. To put the New Testament in

clear perspective, we must know about the history of Judaism in the late Hebrew Bible period, as well as the history of primitive Christianity. In addition, we must acquire a sense of the **Jesus of history,** the central figure in a belief system that led to the emergence of Christianity as a religion separate and distinct from Judaism.

POSTEXILIC JUDAISM

What happened between the time of Ezra and Nehemiah (450 B.C.E.) and the beginning of the Christian era? Obviously Judaism survived and prospered in those intervening years, yet not without change and not without being affected by the surrounding cultures. Scholars do not agree on the nature or the degree of that change, yet all acknowledge the occurrence of change. For example, the religion became more personalized, and the apocalyptic view of history, with its accompanying connection to a growing sense of messianic expectation, became more widespread. Though the depth of Greek influence remains a point of debate, such influence was definitely present. The translation of the Hebrew scriptures into Greek (the Septuagint) for the use of Jews outside Palestine who had lost their linguistic abilities in Hebrew is but one example. Even so, changes in the internal circumstances of Judaism (some, of course, brought about by outside forces) are also observable and need to be considered. Some of the circumstances that are important in understanding these changes can be listed as follows:

1. The Jews who returned to their land after the Babylonian exile remained under the benevolent rule of the Persians until the time of Alexander the Great (323 B.C.E.).

2. Judaism was now a world religion, not merely a national religion, with perhaps more Jews in Diaspora Judaism (those who had not returned from the Babylonian dispersion but had maintained their Jewish religious identity) than in Palestinian Judaism (see below).*

3. The Palestinian Jews continued to define Judaism in the more narrow terms of Ezra and Nehemiah, while those outside Palestine tended to be more liberal and inclusive in their definition.

4. Palestinian Judaism was less affected by outside cultural influences, such as Hellenization, than was Diaspora Judaism. For example, the Septuagint emerged in the Diaspora community.

5. Hellenization influenced all of Judaism and, for a brief moment, threatened to extinguish it. While the impact is more observable in what we know of Diaspora Judaism, it had an impact in Palestine, as well. (Persian and Babylonian influence is also acknowledged by most scholars, although the exact

nature of those influences are not universally agreed on.)

6. Palestinian Judaism achieved a brief period of self-rule (167–63 B.C.E.), but not under the line of David. The chief priest was a major political and religious leader throughout the period after the return.

7. Palestine became a protectorate of the Roman Empire in 63 B.C.E. and remained in this status until the expulsion of Jews from Palestine in 135 C.D.

8. Judaism was a religion of the book, without living prophets, probably from the time of Ezra and Nehemiah. Jews looked to their literary tradition, which was now being used as scripture, to guide their religious life. As a result, there arose within Palestinian Judaism several groupings that represented ways of understanding and interpreting religious tradition. At the time of Jesus there were four major religious groupings. A very brief description of each would include:

a. Usually associated in the popular mind with the Dead Sea Scrolls, the **Essenes** most likely emerged from the **Hasidim** during the Maccabean period (middle of the second century B.C.E.) as a result of their belief that the Hasmonaean dynasty had corrupted the high priesthood. Initially led by one known as the Righteous One, their philosophy of cosmic dualism was much akin to apocalyptic thought. The Essenes lived on the shores of the Dead Sea, attempting to create in their monastic community an atmosphere into which the expected Messiah could come. Among the Essenes' practices were ritual cleansing and a common meal, two factors that have led some to speculate that they had an influence on early Christianity. Many suggest that John the Baptist came out of the Essene community.

b. The Sadducees (perhaps named after

*There is one suggestion that there were four million Diaspora Jews in comparison to five hundred thousand Palestinian Jews in the first century. See Joachim Jeremias, *Rediscovering the Parables* (New York: Charles Scribner's, 1966), p. 102.

Ancient ruins of the Qumran community overlooking the Dead Sea.

Zadok, David's high priest) consisted of the upper class of Judaism. This priestly party upheld the most conservative interpretation of religious tradition. Its members were responsible for the appointment of the high priest and controlled the Temple activities in Jerusalem. The Sadducees made up the major portion of the **Sanhedrin.** Much like some modern biblical literalists, the Sadducees rejected any oral tradition and beliefs associated with it. As a result, they did not hold a belief in life after death (they found no basis for it in scripture), accepting only the most literal understanding of the written tradition. The Sadducees were politically conservative, as well, holding that the survival of Temple religion was more important than political autonomy, and trying to accommodate to the reality of the Roman occupation rather than opposing it.

c. The Pharisees were the majority religious party of the day. The only group to survive the destruction of the Temple in 70 C.E., they became the source of modern Judaism. More liberal in their understanding of tradition, the Pharisees accepted much of the oral law and believed in life after death. They developed the **Mishnah** and the Talmud and are credited with setting the limits of the Jewish canon at their Council of Jamnia in 90 C.E.

d. Probably more political than religious, the **Zealots** seemed to play heavily on the strong contemporary sense of messianic expectation. They advocated the use of military means to free Palestine of its oppressors (perhaps harkening back to the successful Maccabean revolt against seemingly overwhelming odds). In seeking political autonomy, they incited the Jewish war with the Romans, which led to the destruction of Jerusalem and the Temple in 70 C.E. Zealotism might have reemerged for a short time (132–135 C.E.) under the leadership of Simon Bar-Kochba, creating events that resulted in the expulsion of Jews from Palestine by the Romans. Some have speculated that Judas Iscariot was a

Palestine at the time of Jesus.

Zealot and have attempted to explain his betrayal of Jesus in light of that assumption.*

---

*Students will want to understand the entire setting of first-century Judaism better as they explore the Bible in more depth. A helpful book will be Jacob Neusner, *From Testament to Torah* (New York: Prentice-Hall, 1988).

No one can date the transition precisely, but by the time of Jesus (i.e., during the Roman occupation), the land of the Jews was commonly known to those outside its borders as Palestine. The change happened gradually after the conquest of the territory by the forces of Alexander the Great and was most likely a reflection of the Greek attempt to rid the land of its narrow religious and cultural bias, which the Greeks viewed unfavorably. The name "Palestine" itself reflects the earlier presence of the Philistines as the dominant force in Canaan during the later portion of the second millennium. Although the Philistines' real presence was mostly in the coastal plains of Canaan, those outside Canaan had referred to Canaan as Palestine in recognition of their dominant position. Later, when Israel—that is, Israel and Judah—made the land their own, they gave it their own names. After the Babylonian exile the Jews themselves referred to it as Israel, while others seemed to return to the earlier designation, acknowledging the reality that Israel was no longer in control of its political destiny. The name Israel, or Judah, had both religious and political connotations that were obviously not acceptable to those who were in political control, thus leading them to use the earlier designation by which the land had been known (see map, p. 115).

DIVERSITY WITHIN JUDAISM

An important implication in the points listed above is the development of varying ways in which Jews came to understand their tradition. Naturally enough, Judaism, in moving on to the world scene as a religion among religions, affirming itself as the correct or superior way of understanding life both in this world and beyond, did not remain monolithic. The diversity was particularly great when one considers the Jews outside Palestine, who married foreigners, opening the doors for conversion into Judaism. There is evidence, too, that some became Jews simply because they viewed the religion as reasonable and attractive, becoming a part of the covenant by religious affirmation apart from marriage or birth. Some seemed to have entered partially into the Jewish community, perhaps in worship and ethical practice, while

not accepting circumcision or strict dietary restrictions. (These people were referred to as "**God fearers**" and seem to have been objects of strong Christian missionary activity a bit later.)

Those whose impressions of the groups listed above are based solely on a reading of the New Testament need to be reminded that the Christian view of those groups was not unbiased: Jesus himself was often in conflict with the established religious leadership of the day, and the Sadducees and Pharisees represented that establishment. Thus the view of these groups provided in the New Testament reflects the continuing tension between the infant Christianity and established Judaism, as well as the actual conflict experienced by Jesus.

What at least three of these groups had in common (the Sadducees might be the exception) was a strong sense of messianic expectation. The messianic concept, introduced by the prophet Isaiah in the eighth century B.C.E. and expanded by his successors in the prophetic tradition, had reached full bloom by the first century. Judaism had again lost control of its political destiny, this time at the hands of the Romans. It was increasingly difficult to feel optimistic about the course of history, having only the brief period following the Maccabean revolt to look back on as providing a favorable political atmosphere. Even then the Jews' internal political turmoil did not allow much room for a revival of religious vigor. Hope began to be placed in an apocalyptic view of history, a time when God himself would intervene in human affairs, ending history as it was known and beginning anew, a messianic age. Fortified by the imagery found in works such as Daniel, part of the agenda of each group was to prepare for the coming of the Messiah, by putting the world in the order that would allow that age to come.

Two other groups within the Palestinian Jewish community need to be identified to complete a sense of that diverse community.

They are the Samaritans and the **scribes.** The Samaritans were introduced much earlier, as the inhabitants of Israel after its fall to the Assyrians in the eighth century B.C.E. (2 Kings 17). According to the account in the Hebrew Bible, they were not really Jews, but rather persons imported by the Assyrians who adopted the worship of Yahweh while still clinging to their former religions. The truth is probably more complicated, and the Samaritans might not deserve as poor a press as they received from the Deuteronomic historian. They certainly did not fit the orthodox standards of Palestinian Judaism, either by birth or religious practice, and official Judaism had defined them as outside the community. However, the Samaritans considered themselves to be Jews; they did not accept a definition of Judaism that limited membership to the standard of birth, nor did they evidently limit the place of sacrifice to the Temple of Jerusalem. It is likely that such unorthodoxy, along with refusal to cast out their foreign wives at the time of Ezra and Nehemiah, brought about the exclusion of the Samaritans from mainstream Judaism. Their acceptance of only the Pentateuch as scripture also differentiated them from their coreligionists. Their presence was a constant irritation to other Palestinian Jews, and they were regarded with the disdain granted heretics by their other Jewish neighbors in Palestine.

The scribes, on the other hand, had a prominent role in Palestinian Judaism in the period that marked the emergence of Christianity. They were responsible for teaching and interpreting the Law. It is possible that they emerged out of the priestly class and, by the time of Jesus, had become closely associated with the Pharisees and their way of understanding the Law. They were evidently a part of the Sanhedrin and, as such, became the "attorneys for the tradition." They seemed to have been the official interpreters of the Law in Palestinian Judaism and also to have borne the responsibil-

ity of keeping the tradition alive. By recording and transmitting the Law, they were able to preserve their holy scriptures during the period of Hellenism.

THE BIRTH OF CHRISTIANITY

Out of the dynamics surrounding Palestinian Judaism, a new religion was born. We know that religion as Christianity, but it did not always have that identity. Christianity began as a part of Judaism, "a sect within Judaism" as some have described it, and did not achieve its separate identity until some years after the death of Jesus.

What made Christianity new was its belief that Jesus of Nazareth was indeed the promised, long-expected Messiah. In most other respects it probably looked like another Jewish party to outsiders. Its earliest followers continued in the Law, offered sacrifices at the Temple, and were Palestinian Jews. It might have been as long as twenty years before this group began to be known as other than Jews, and it was at least that many years more before it produced a scripture that stood along with the Hebrew Bible to supplement the tradition of its ancestors. It was this new community, one that had emerged from the old, that produced the books of the Bible we know as the New Testament.

The reality that Christianity is indeed a child of Judaism is important to any study of the New Testament. The world view of Judaism, the view that Yahweh is Lord of history and uses history to reveal himself, remained essential. The difference was now in what one believed history to be revealing. For Judaism the center of history remained in the events surrounding Moses, whereas for Christianity Jesus and the events surrounding him became the center.

It was this Christianity, and that of the generations to follow, that produced the New

Testament as further scripture to convince others of the belief in a new chapter in Yahweh's encounter with his creation. Believing that in Jesus God had completed his **revelation,** Christians felt compelled to share this vision, first with their fellow Jews and, later, with those outside Judaism as well. It was in this sharing that the New Testament was produced.

The scripture exclusive to Christianity was probably not written for the purpose of supplementing the Pentateuch. Most of the earliest Christians were convinced of the imminent return of Jesus and the nearness of the establishment of the **kingdom of God** on the earth. Through their writings, however, we find our best understanding both of early Christianity and the people and events who produced it.

All the earliest Christians were Jews, though certainly not all first-century Jews were Christians. Christianity grew first among Jews as early believers convinced other Jews, both Palestinian and Diaspora, that Jesus was the Messiah. As far as can be determined, the Samaritans were included in Christianity before it opened its doors to those totally outside Judaism, the **Gentiles.** The movement began as **apostles** and their followers shared their belief in Jesus' messiahship, using stories about him and telling what they believed those stories to mean. These earliest sharings were likely part of an oral tradition at first, while there were eyewitnesses still alive. Interspersed in the stories about Jesus were recollections of his teaching, for clues to his messiahship were found in all aspects of his life.

Most of the New Testament, in the form in which we now have it, was not produced until most of the principal eyewitnesses to the life of Jesus had died and the Christian community had begun to accept a view of itself as distinct from Judaism. The most ancient literary portions of the New Testament, the letters of Paul, do not seem to have been written with the idea of achieving canonical status, yet they were serving such a purpose by the end of the first century. Most of the books now in the New Testament were being used as scripture by at least some people by the middle of the second century. Written originally to preserve the new tradition, to defend it from distortion, and to share it with others, these works became scripture because they served those needs for those who called themselves Christians.

What was distinguishing about early Christianity was the belief that Jesus was the Messiah. What was distinguishing about the works of the New Testament was the affirmation of that belief and its implication for the life of the world. Paul summed up the early teachings of Christianity in his first letter to the church at Corinth:

> Well then, in the first place I taught you what I had been taught myself, namely that Christ died for our sins, in accordance with scriptures; that he appeared first to Cephas [Peter] and secondly to the Twelve. Next he appeared to more than five hundred of the brothers at the same time, most of whom are still alive, though some have died; then he appeared to James, and then to all the apostles; and last of all he appeared to me too; it was as though I was born when no one expected it. (1 Cor. 15:3–8)

This creed probably represents the earliest Christian teaching about Jesus. The Gospels, which we study later, reflect further teachings about him and can help in our attempt to understand Jesus. Before turning to our study of Jesus and the beliefs about him, however, we should be aware of the problem and promises the investigation has in store. Some preliminary observations about Jesus are, therefore, appropriate.

Jesus: History and Faith

To understand Christianity one has to understand what early Christians believed about Jesus, both the person of Jesus and his significance in the midst of human history. Some would insist that one has to understand Jesus himself but, as will be shown, that is not an easy matter. Scholars have long distinguished between the "Jesus of history" and the **"Christ of faith,"** and most have concluded that the "Christ of faith" is the more easily discerned, the "Jesus of history" the more elusive. Although the Gospels set the story of Jesus in the context of history, that story is told through the eyes of faith. The Gospel writers believed that Jesus was (and is) the promised Messiah and wanted others to share this belief. Convinced that God is the God of history, revealing himself through the events of history, those writers reported not only history but their understanding of its meaning as well. That will become more clear to the reader through an examination of the individual Gospels.

Although the Jesus of history may remain elusive, he is not absent from the stories about him. The problem is in separating what the community believed about Jesus (the "Christ of faith") from what he said and did, and when (the "Jesus of history"). However, our major source of information, the Gospels, deals only with some aspects of Jesus' life, and not always with the same aspects. **Mark** and **John** begin their stories at the time of Jesus' baptism. **Matthew** has a birth narrative and some infancy narratives, then takes up the story where Mark and John begin. **Luke** has his own account of Jesus' beginnings, different from that of Matthew, adds an account of an incident during the youth of Jesus, and then moves to the more common material. Even after arriving at the portion of the life that all the Gospels include, one finds the material to be quite sparse. All Jesus' teachings as recorded in the Bible could be read aloud in little more than two hours.

The Gospels do not seem to agree on the length of Jesus' ministry, ranging from less than a year in Mark to at least three years in the Gospel of John. Neither is there agreement among the Gospels on the order or locations of the events of that ministry. The writers seem to be more interested in conveying meaning than in providing a sense of order. Though the Gospels of Matthew and Luke do seem to follow the order of Mark, they often depart from that order to make a particular theological point. The earliest traditions indicate that Mark's author did not concern himself with order when he wrote his account.*

Do the discrepancies mentioned above indicate that the "Jesus of history" is irretrievable? Probably not. While we cannot know everything about the historic aspects of Jesus, some things can be affirmed with reasonable assurance. The Judeo-Christian tradition did take history seriously. It was (and is) in the arena of history that Yahweh made (and makes) himself known, and one must look to history to find what Yahweh is saying. Our difficult task is to separate history from the faith proclamations embedded in its telling.

Without showing you how each of these matters is resolved, it can be reported that most scholars agree on the following points about the "Jesus of history":

1. That he was born between 7 and 3 B.C.E., probably in **Bethlehem**

2. That he grew up as a Jew in **Nazareth**

3. That he began his formal ministry in conjunction with his baptism by John the Baptist

4. That he gathered disciples

5. That there was an apocalyptic dimension to his ministry, illustrated by the abundance of references to the kingdom of God in his **parables**

---

*From Eusebius, *Ecclesiastical History* (III. 39) as reported by C. E. B. Cranfield, "Gospel of Mark," *The Interpreter's Dictionary of the Bible*, Vol. 3 (Nashville: Abingdon Press, 1962), p. 267.

6. That he taught in parables

7. That his teaching placed him in conflict with established Judaism, especially with the Pharisees

8. That he died on a cross at the hands of the Romans, probably for the crime of sedition

9. That there was a messianic dimension to his ministry, though it is not clear that he made direct claims to being the Messiah

No serious scholar has ever doubted that there was a historic Jesus. Scholars disagree about what we can know about him, but they do not question his existence as a historical figure. They are more clear about the "Christ of faith." Christianity began as a sect within Judaism, proclaiming Jesus to be the long-awaited Messiah. Belief in his messiahship was based on the conviction that Jesus had overcome death on the cross, that he had risen from the dead. Jesus as Messiah, confirmed by his resurrection, was the foundation belief of early Christianity, and the understanding of the meaning of that belief was to produce the "Christ of faith." History was to become more than history; it was to be the vehicle to proclaim ultimate reality for those who believed Jesus to be the Messiah. To them, Yahweh had acted once again to reveal himself, this time in the life of one they believed to be God's chosen instrument. They found, as will be later observed, a close proximity in the life of Jesus and the vision of the "suffering servant" found in II Isaiah (Chs. 40–55). Armed with the scriptures of their tradition (the Hebrew Bible), they began to interpret those works in light of their belief in Jesus' messiahship. Very quickly, some have suggested, the "Jesus of history" was transformed into the "Christ of faith." Obviously, the separation is not complete, and the suggestion that the "Jesus of history" is the vehicle used to proclaim the "Christ of faith,"

while including a truth, is not completely true. The sensitive reader can observe both while reviewing the pages of the New Testament.

Christianity Produces Its Scripture

Although Christianity had its roots in Palestinian Judaism, its ranks were to include a majority outside Palestine by the end of the first century of the common era. Equally important, by the same time the majority of Christians were of Gentile, rather than Jewish, background. Not only did Christianity pass beyond national boundaries, it passed beyond religious boundaries as well. It should be noted that the followers of Jesus were not known as Christians during the life of their leader; the first use of this label is reported in Acts (11:26).

Christianity spread rapidly beyond the borders of Palestine after 50 C.E. Among the new Christians were Diaspora Jews, God-fearers, and Gentiles. Receiving the message from Christian missionaries who traveled to foreign lands to declare their belief in Jesus as Messiah, the new converts established spiritual communities, nourished by their missionary teachers. They also seem to have developed an indigenous religious leadership. It seems likely that at first the missionaries began to preach among the Diaspora Jews, with whom they and their message would have affinity, moving into the broader community only after they had achieved whatever success was possible among their fellow Jews.

The early success of the movement among those of Jewish background was not maintained. A Jew either did or did not accept the belief in Jesus as Messiah. Those who did became Christians. Those who did not become Christians became hostile to Christianity, regarding it as a **heresy.** Those who became Christians were excluded from the Jewish community and formed new communities, which served as centers of Christian missionary activity, now directed to those beyond the confines of Judaism. Beginning with the "God-fearers," Christians soon expanded their audience to those who had no previous relationship with Judaism, the people we know as Gentiles.

It is a common view that the people of the Roman Empire were irreligious, or pagan. That simply is not the case. Religion flourished in the **Greco-Roman world.** People were very open to religious ideas and ideals, though such ideas were not always compatible with the values of the Judeo-Christian tradition. Monotheism was not prevalent, nor was it deemed important. Long influenced by Hellenistic syncretism, people often accepted a variety of religious visions as part of their own world view, finding something of value in each. The approach to religion was pragmatic, using beliefs and practices that enhanced the quality of life. There was no lack of morality, although the standards of morality varied from place to place. It is not surprising that Gentiles found attractive elements in both Judaism and Christianity.

Whether formerly a Jew or a Gentile, the new Christian was becoming a part of a different religion. One of the tasks of the early missionary-teachers was to help potential converts understand the difference between the new and the old, as well as the implications of that difference in their lives. They used a common tradition for this purpose. That tradition, some oral and some written, was later to become a part of the literature of the New Testament. The earliest of the works of the present New Testament were expressions of missionary teaching, letters written by the missionary Paul to give advice and guidance to churches he had established. These works were valued by the recipient communities, saved, and shared among the people. It is assumed that later someone traveled among the churches with which Paul had corresponded and collected his letters, thus making them available for the broader church to use eventually as scripture.

Paul, however, was not the person around whom Christianity was formed. That person was Jesus. Paul and his fellow missionaries carried the message of Jesus as Messiah to the far reaches of the Roman Empire. While Paul had not been an eyewitness to the life of Jesus, many others had. Persons such as the twelve disciples also served a missionary role, recounting what Jesus said and did, trying to convince nonbelievers that in all aspects of Jesus' life were affirmations of his true messiahship.

Apparently the early believers thought that Jesus would return in their lifetime to usher in the **apocalyptic age.** It was only after some of the eyewitnesses began to die that the need to preserve the eyewitness tradition surrounding Jesus' life became apparent. Most scholars assume that the death or old age of eyewitnesses prompted the writing of the traditions about the life of Jesus, the Gospels. To serve the needs of a community now far beyond the borders of Palestine and including many who did not share the religious background of Judaism, a literary tradition was necessary both to preserve the memory and to protect it from distortion.

From very early times Christianity had a problem within, the problem of heresy. Just as faithful Jews regarded Christians as heretics, some Christians so regarded certain people who claimed their own faith. Heresy is simply defined as "wrong belief." Belief, or the proper way of interpreting the meaning of the historical events around which Christianity centered, became important to Christians. There are many examples of the problem in the New Testament itself, beginning with the letters of Paul. False teachers (people who would distort the meaning of the **Christ-event** in history) were a constant threat. In such an atmosphere the life and teachings of Jesus were recalled, not only to keep the memory alive, but to protect it from error as well. Event and meaning were woven together to provide the community with the means of understanding of how to appropriate the Christ event into their own lives.

Christianity continued to grow throughout the first century of the common era. Although we probably do not have a totally accurate picture of its scope or composition, it is safe to say that it was present in most portions of the Roman Empire and was composed of a majority from the Gentile ranks by the end of the first century. It was during the latter portion of the century that most of the New Testament was produced. It is possible that some portion of it was being used by Christians with the authority of scripture (along with the Hebrew Bible).

It was during the same period that some Christians began to suffer persecution because of their faith. For example, the New Testament reports some cases of Palestinian Jewish Christians who underwent abuse at the hands of Palestinian Jews, who regarded them as heretics (Acts 3:11–4:31). Roman history reports that **Nero** used the Christians of Rome as a scapegoat after he had burned Rome. However, persecution did not seem to be widespread until later in the first century, under the direction of the Roman emperor **Domitian.** The cause was the demand of emperor worship by Domitian. The Jews were excluded from compliance because of their status as adherents of an "**official religion**" in the Roman Empire. Christians, however, had no such protection because they were no longer regarded by the Romans as just another Jewish sect, but as a separate religion. They could not accede to the emperor's demand and maintain their faith. Their failure to respond brought about a view of them as politically disloyal and placed them ironically in the same category as their Jewish ancestors at earlier moments in this continuing history.

The circumstances of history had an impact on the early Christians and played a part in shaping the literature that was to become Christian scripture. In that literature, the New Testament, lie the best clues to the history that shaped it. Now we turn to the writings that were produced out of the community known as Christians, a community born from Judaism but distinctly different.

STUDY QUESTIONS

1. Identify the problems faced by Judaism after the Babylonian exile.

2. What were the major parties in Palestinian Judaism at the time of the common era? Describe the distinguishing marks of each.

3. Explain why one would call Christianity a "sect within Judaism."

4. What distinguishes the "Jesus of history" from the "Christ of faith"?

5. Explain how and why Christians produced a scriptural tradition.

6. Explain why the term *New Testament* is used by Christians to designate that portion of the scriptures exclusive to them.

7. Why was Pharisaic Judaism the most popular expression of that religion in the first century?

8. What would lead one to suggest that John the Baptist was associated with the Essene sect of first-century Judaism?

9. Identify the Samaritans and discuss why it is helpful to know something about them when studying the first-century Judaism out of which Christianity arose.

10. Why was there such a strong sense of messianic expectation in the first-century Judaism out of which Christianity emerged?

SUGGESTED READINGS

Briggs, R. C. *Interpreting the New Testament Today* (Abingdon Press, Nashville, 1973).

Bultman, R. *Primitive Christianity in Its Contemporary Setting* (Meridian, New York, 1956).

Callon, Terrance. *Forgetting the Root: The Emergence of Christianity from Judaism* (Paulist Press, New York, 1986).

Fredriksen, Paula. *From Jesus to Christ: The Origins of the New Testament Images of Jesus* (Yale University Press, New Haven, 1988).

Grant, F. C. "Jesus Christ," *The Interpreter's Dictionary of the Bible*, Vol. 2 (Abingdon Press, Nashville, 1962).

Kee, H. C. *Jesus in History: An Approach to the Study of the Gospels*, 2nd ed. (Harcourt Brace Jovanovich, New York, 1977).

Pelikan, Jaroslav. *Jesus Through the Centuries: His Place in History and Culture* (Yale University Press, New Haven, 1985).

Roetzel, Calvin J. *The World That Shaped the New Testament* (John Knox Press, Atlanta, 1985).

Russell, D. S. *Between the Testaments* (S.C.M. Press, London, 1960).

Segundo, Juan Luis. *The Historical Jesus of the Synoptics*, John Drury, Trans. (Orbis Books, Maryknoll, N.Y., 1985).

Thompson, William. *The Jesus Debate: Survey and Synthesis* (Paulist Press, New York, 1985).

EIGHT

THE LETTERS
OF PAUL

We begin our study of the New Testament with a group of letters written by someone who was not even an eyewitness to the life of Jesus. Paul was a second-generation apostle, a convert to Christianity some three years after the death of Jesus. You might well ask, "Why begin here?"

There are two principal ways to approach the New Testament. One is to begin with the Gospels, go next to Acts and the letters of Paul, and end with the other writings. The general reason for following the order of the books found in the Bible is that Jesus and the beliefs about him are central to the New Testament; thus one should begin with the Gospels, which relate to his life and teachings. The second approach, the one taken here, deals with the books in the order it is believed they were written. There is no absolute agreement among scholars, however, about the dates of composition of all the works of the New Testament or about the identities of their authors. (Those uncertainties will be reflected as the various works are explored.)

Beginning with the works of Paul has certain advantages: allowing one to observe how Christianity expressed itself in its early years, giving a view of how Christianity varied its message according to circumstance and background of the community being evangelized, and showing the struggle of Christianity in forming its own identity. Jesus is no less important to Paul than to the writers of the Gospels, but the fact that Paul makes little mention of Jesus' life or teachings can prepare you to view the Gospels a bit differently from readers who begin with the books of the **evangelists.** Paul's works remind us immediately that the meaning of the "Christ event" in history, the understanding of the "Christ of faith" that is the theme of all the New Testament, was the focus of early Christianity. As you will see, Paul approaches this theme in one way, the Gospels in another. All the authors, however, shared the faith that Jesus was the Messiah and proclaimed implications of that faith to believer and nonbeliever alike.

The books now included in the New Testament were written within a span of seventy to one hundred years after the death of Jesus. The genuine works of Paul are usually considered to be the first works produced, followed by the Gospels (at least the **synoptic Gospels**—Matthew, Mark, and Luke), the other letters, John's Gospel, and Revelation. Because there is no general consensus about authorship of the works or their date of composition, you will find disagreement in the lists that order the works of the New Testament.

There is not even total agreement about whether Paul wrote all the works that bear his name. Although thirteen works in the New Testament make internal claim to having been written by Paul and another was included in the New Testament canon because it has been attributed to Paul, we will not deal with all those works now. Where serious question of Paul's authorship exists, we have made another category, and the reasons for so classifying certain works are explained later.

In this section our attention is directed to:

Galatians

Romans

1 and 2 Corinthians

1 and 2 Thessalonians

Philemon

Colossians

Philippians

In the later section we will examine:

Ephesians

1 and 2 Timothy

Titus

Hebrews

Few suggest that Paul thought he was producing scripture for a burgeoning religion when he wrote letters to churches that he had helped establish or from which, as in the case of Romans, he was soliciting support. As you read the letters themselves you develop a sense of their original purposes, which were always immediate and direct. After Paul died, however, his letters were collected and given wider circulation, such that they began to assume the authority of scripture (2 Peter 3:15–17), perhaps as early as the end of the first century.

To determine why the works of someone who had not been an eyewitness to the life of Jesus became so prominent so early in the life of the Christian community, we must know something about this remarkably influential first-century Christian.

THE IMPORTANCE OF PAUL

Paul was born in the town of **Tarsus** in the province of **Cilicia** on the southeastern coast of Asia Minor. Although he testified that he never met Jesus, he did claim to have encountered the resurrected Christ in a very special experience (Acts 9:3–9), an encounter that led to his conversion and his later activity as a Christian missionary. His importance came, therefore, not out of an association with the "historical Jesus," but from the impact he had on early Christianity, particularly as it spread beyond Palestine.

Some assert that Paul was the most important first-century Christian, more important than the original twelve **disciples** of Jesus, who were eyewitnesses to and pupils of the "historic Jesus." It has been further suggested that Paul was really a second founder of Christianity, the person who shaped what Christianity was to become, as well as how it was to understand itself. The term "**Pauline Christianity**" is based on such assumptions and is cause for continuing debate among those who try to understand the emergence of Christianity out of Judaism.

Paul referred to himself as the apostle of the Gentiles; it is in that role that he stands distinguished in early Christianity. He certainly was the major influence in the expression or interpretation of Christianity in the Gentile world. It is probably more accurate to view Paul, therefore, as the major force in the way an already established Christianity would present itself to the world beyond Judaism, so that it would be understood and accepted.

Roman aqueduct at Caesarea, which supplied water to Paul during his
imprisonment in Palestine.

Details of Paul's Life

Certainly Paul's background had prepared him
for such a task. A Diaspora Jew, originally
named Saul, he went to Jerusalem at about the
age of fifteen to be trained in the rabbinic tradition under the famous Pharisee Gamaliel.
Thus he would have been in Jerusalem at the
time of Jesus' crucifixion. Paul's conversion
took place some two or three years after the
death of Jesus, while he was on a journey to
Damascus as an official of Judaism for the
purpose of persecuting the followers of Jesus,
whom the Jews considered to be heretics.

Paul gives some details of his life in his letter to the Galatians, written at a time when he
was defending his apostolic authority against
detractors of his message. In that letter (see
Gal. 1:11–2:14) he tells us:

1. He was a practicing Jew.

2. He had persecuted the followers of Jesus
because of his enthusiasm for his own tradition (Judaism).

3. He experienced God's revelation. (The full
story of the conversion of Saul of Tarsus is
given in Chapter 9 of Acts.)

4. He went to Arabia after his conversion, not
discussing his conversion with other Christians, and then back to Damascus.

5. Three years later he went to Jerusalem and
spent fifteen days with Cephas (Peter), seeing
no other apostles but **James** the brother of
Jesus.

6. He then went to Syria and Cilicia, still not
known by sight to the churches of Christ in
Judaea.

7. Fourteen years later (it is not clear if this is
from time of conversion or from his first
visit), spurred by a revelation, he went to Jerusalem a second time, privately laying before

the leading men the message he had been preaching among the pagans.

8. Titus, a convert who accompanied Paul, was not required to be circumcised.

9. Paul was harassed (spied upon) by **Judaizers.**

10. He presented his message to the uncircumcised, and reports that the Jerusalem church added nothing to that message.

11. It was recognized that Paul had been called to preach to the uncircumcised (Gentiles), just as Peter had been called to preach to the circumcised (Jews).

12. Paul's ministry was given approval and he agreed to remember the poor in Jerusalem.

13. Peter (Cephas) later came to visit Paul in Antioch, joining in meals with uncircumcised. However, when friends of James came from Jerusalem, Peter withdrew from table fellowship in fear of those "who insisted on circumcision." For this, Paul chided Peter.

The personal references in Paul's letters are helpful in revealing something of the man. The Book of Acts also directs a good deal of attention to Paul and his missionary activity, and, despite points on which those two sources do not totally agree (cf. Gal. 1:11–2:14 with Acts 15), one can in the broad sense get a view of Paul from Acts as well. Luke, the purported author of Acts, seems to have been a companion of Paul for at least a portion of one of his missionary journeys (see the **"We" section of Acts**) and could have derived much of the information he supplies from that acquaintance.

According to Acts (13:1 ff, 15:36 ff, 18:18 ff) Paul took three separate missionary journeys. By the end of the third journey he had helped bring Christianity to much of the Roman world, from Palestine to the borders of Rome (see map, p. 128). Luke's account ends with Paul a prisoner in Rome, having been arrested in Jerusalem at the conclusion of his third mission-

ary journey on charges of defiling the Temple. The fate of Paul is not revealed in the New Testament, although according to tradition both he and Peter died martyrs' deaths in Rome during the reign of Nero.

Paul and the Law

Paul played a major role both in carrying Christianity beyond the borders of Palestine and in helping to make Christianity a major world religion. In regard to the second accomplishment, Paul presented Christianity to the Gentile world in a way that made it attractive to them. That was particularly true in the way that Paul dealt with the ethical dimension of the religion.

You know the Law was and is central to Judaism. You also know there was a debate within Judaism itself as to how the Law was to be understood and applied. As you study the Gospels you will see how Jesus is portrayed as being in conflict with the established Judaism of his day in regard to the Law. He and his disciples are portrayed as being accused by the leaders of Palestinian Judaism of ignoring the Law by doing such things as healing on the Sabbath, or not practicing ritual cleansing before eating. Likewise, Paul was accused by some within the Palestinian Jewish Christian community of not having a strong enough regard for the Law. There were those in early Christianity who insisted that one had to become a Jew, or at least abide by the laws of Moses as did the Jews, in order to be a faithful Christian. They accused Paul of being lax in that regard—for instance, by not requiring Gentile converts to be circumcised. The tension created by such criticism is reflected in Paul's letters and is observable in the reports about him in the book of Acts.

Not only was Paul criticized in his own lifetime, but others have later suggested that Paul indeed abandoned the Law. They quote such passages as Romans 3:31–41, suggesting that

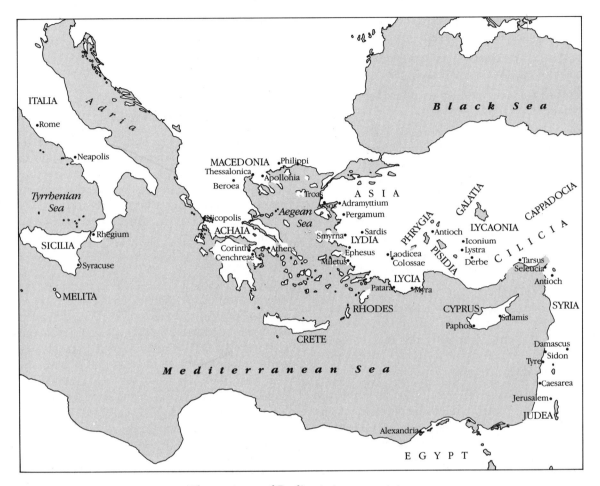

The territory of Paul's missionary activity.

Paul taught that one is now justified by faith, not by obedience to the Law. However, it is probably more precise to say that Paul did not suggest that the Law should be abandoned, but brought forth an understanding of its role that was different from that of some other early Christians. Careful examination will, in fact, show that Paul's approach to the Law was quite similar to that attributed to Jesus in the Gospel of Matthew, particularly the **Sermon on the Mount.**

It is a good thing to be circumcised if you keep the Law; but if you break the Law you might as well have stayed uncircumcised. If a man who is not circumcised obeys the commands of the Law, surely that makes up for not being circumcised? More than that, the man who keeps the Law, even though he has not been physically circumcised, is a living condemnation of the way you disobey the Law in spite of being circumcised and having it all written down. To be a Jew is not just to look like a Jew, and circumcision is more than a physical operation. The real Jew is one who is inwardly a Jew, and the real circumcision is in the heart—something not of the letter but of the spirit. A Jew like that may not be praised by man, but he will be praised by God. (Rom. 2:25–29)

Paul's decision not to require converts to Christianity to be circumcised was symbolic of his approach to the meaning of the Christ event in history and the function of the Law in light of that event. One could say that he applied the teachings of Jesus in regard to the Law in a practical way to those whom he persuaded to Christianity, and in that sense he stood very much in the Judeo-Christian tradition that saw the God of history as acting in history in ways having implications for all people, not just a chosen few. Paul's teachings should not be considered strange coming from one whose roots were in Diaspora rather than Palestinian Judaism.

FOUR LETTERS OF PAUL

The letters of Paul were simply letters. Each was written at a particular moment to address the practical needs of a particular Christian community. There is no indication that they were intended to be scripture. How then did they achieve that status? The most obvious answer is that they gave spiritual direction to the broader Christian community, as they had done for their original recipients. Because the human condition is shared, because the spiritual pilgrimage continues to have many of the same ingredients in every age, what applied to specific cases had a universal dimension. Paul, an acknowledged spiritual giant in primitive Christianity, could speak beyond his own time because he spoke out of a sense of timelessness to his own time. What was true for the Corinthians remained true to people of later times and places who consulted Paul's words to find meaning for their own lives.

The works of Paul to which special attention is devoted are but a sample of his writings. Since you will want to read all his writings at a later time, some information is supplied about all of them to aid in that examination. The works chosen for this study represent Paul's correspondence with three early Christian communities, two of which he had helped found.

The letter to the Galatians has been dated by some as Paul's earliest letter, but the majority of scholars place its writing at the same period as the letter to the Romans in 55 or 56 C.E. Albert Barnett suggests that Galatians was the first letter, written immediately after Paul's return from his first missionary journey and in which he most strongly defends his apostolic authority.* Whenever it was written, it does exemplify Paul's conflict with the Judaizers, which continued throughout his ministry. It is in the midst of that conflict that Paul's theology in regard to the "Law" is most practically expressed.

The Corinthian correspondence probably includes a fairly long series of letters Paul wrote to that church, which he had founded, and which struggled to live out its new faith in a world hostile to its commitment. Surely consisting of more than two letters (suggestions range from four to a dozen), this material gives us insight into Paul's methods of teaching and of his leadership.

The Epistle to the Romans was directed to a church that Paul had not founded. In introducing himself and his approach to Christianity to a church whose support he was seeking, Paul made the most complete statement of his theology that is available. Therefore Romans is extremely important to our understanding both of Paul and of Gentile Christianity as it

*Albert E. Barnett, *The New Testament: Its Making and Meaning* (Nashville: Abingdon Press, 1946), pp. 25–28.

existed outside Palestine. Students of the New Testament will want to compare the theological statements of Romans with the affirmations about Christianity found in the Gospels and in other works not attributable to Paul. The clue to whether Paul's theology was consistent with that of his Christian contemporaries lies most completely in this work.

Galatians

✦ **READ** *The Letter of Paul to the Church in Galatia*

The letter of Galatians was written with great passion. As with all Paul's letters, the best clues to its purpose are found in the letter itself. A careful reading, with the following questions in mind, elicits as much information as scholars can provide:

1. Who wrote it?

2. To whom was it written?

3. When was it written?

4. Why was it written?

5. In light of the above, what was Paul's message?

We approach Galatians by allowing the letter to provide the initial answers, and then revealing the questions scholars raise about some of those answers, to show some of the difficulties inherent in Bible scholarship.

1. *Who wrote it?* The letter purports to be written by Paul. Verse 1:1 provides that information. Verse 6:11 indicates that Paul had dictated the letter and was adding a postscript in his own handwriting, a characteristic practice (see also 1 Cor. 16:21 and Col. 4:18).

Those who use the tools of critical analysis to compare the works attributed to Paul agree that the letter to the Galatians should be counted among Paul's genuine works. The language, ideas, and circumstances all compare favorably with what can be known of Paul.

2. *To whom was it written?* The letter is addressed (1:1) to the churches of **Galatia.** The problem is in determining just where those churches were. There are two possibilities: the northern province that was associated with the name for at least two centuries before the common era, and the Roman province of Galatia, a much larger territory.* Paul, who was himself a Roman citizen, touched both territories on his first missionary journey and most likely used the name of the Roman province as he did on other occasions (see 1 Cor. 16:19; 2 Cor. 8:2 or 2 Cor. 9:2). The issue is not crucial to a full understanding of the letter.

3. *When was it written?* Those who believe the letter to be Paul's first base this opinion on their reading of 1:6. Here Paul indicates, they believe, that he is writing soon after his original visit during which he had established the churches. The statement that the writer is "astonished at the promptness with which you have turned away" is taken to indicate an early date. These critics also note that in the letter Paul reports having visited Jerusalem only twice. Others, however, assign a later date to Galatians on the basis of the close linguistic similarity of this letter to the letter to the Romans, indicating that Galatians represents a higher stage of development of theological thought than the earlier Paul. They also point out that the conclusions Paul reports from the controversial Jerusalem visit correspond to those of the visit designated in Acts as the third.

4. *Why was it written?* The first clue is found

---

*Raymond T. Stamm, "The Epistle to the Galatians," *The Interpreter's Bible*, Vol. 10 (New York: Abingdon-Cokesbury, 1953), p. 435.

in 1:6, and other clues abound. A list might help:

1:6–12

2:15–21

3:1–5

5:1–6

5:15

These verses show us that the recipients had been told by others that Paul's initial teaching had been incomplete. Paul has taught that righteous standing before God is found in accepting the gift of God represented in Christ's death, not in observing the Law. In believing this message, the Galatians had found freedom. Now someone had been telling them that to complete their salvation they had to be circumcised, to become observant Jews. This had created disharmony in the community, threatening to destroy it.

5. *In light of the above, what was Paul's message?* Paul repeated what he had originally taught, that one was justified in the sight of God by accepting the free gift of God's love demonstrated by the sacrifice of Christ on the cross. According to Paul, the purpose of the Law was to specify crimes until the promise made to Abraham, namely that justification would come by faith, was expressed in the midst of history. "The Law was to be our guardian until the Christ came and we could be justified by faith" (3:24). The distinction has now been removed among all people; now all are the posterity of Abraham, the heirs he was promised. The distinction of Judaism has been removed and God's promises apply universally.

After using arguments to prove his point in classic rabbinical fashion, Paul makes it quite clear that although the Law does not lead to salvation (being pleasing to God), the ethics it expresses continues to be important. As he does in most of his writings, Paul includes a section on behavior (ethics), pointing out that freedom from the Law does not imply license to abuse that freedom. To live in the spirit, Paul counsels, is to relinquish the self-indulgent life. New life is brought in Christ. "It does not matter if a person is circumcised or not; what matters is for him to become altogether a new creature. Peace and mercy to all who follow this rule, who form the Israel of God" (6:15–16). The same theme is developed more fully in Romans and will be given fuller attention at that point.

The letter to the Galatians contains the first clue to what Paul taught about Christianity. It is clear that Paul did not want to be viewed as a libertine, that his insistence that the Law was not a means of salvation did not diminish the importance of righteous human behavior. Ethics simply comes from a different motivation, a point on which we elaborate in the study of Romans.

Galatians also affords a good look at the divisions that were already developing within Christianity. Here Paul is plagued by those who teach that Law remains primary (Judaizers), while he insists that it no longer is binding where superseded by the exercise of faith. You will note other divisive elements within the Christian community in other letters attributed to Paul. The letters also illustrate the problems that a religion new to its adherents created among the faithful. Nowhere are these examples more abundant than in Paul's letters to the Corinthians.

1 and 2 Corinthians

◆ READ *The Letters of Paul to the Church in Corinth*

As indicated earlier, many scholars believe that Paul wrote more than two letters to the Corinthians. The letters themselves provide the clues that have led to such speculation. For example, 1 Corinthians 5:9 refers to an earlier letter and identifies its contents. In addition, Chapters 10–13 of 2 Corinthians violate the spirit of the earlier portion of that epistle. While some scholars believe they detect even more examples, it is generally agreed that the examples cited establish the presence of four letters in what are now combined into two. Separating those four and reading them in the order of that separation will be helpful in the study of these works. The suggested order of reading is as follows:

1. 2 Corinthians 6:14–7:1

2. 1 Corinthians

3. 2 Corinthians 10–13

4. 2 Corinthians 1–9 (except 6:14–7:1)

The reason for this order can be found in the works themselves, but a few observations will be helpful. Paul had founded the church at **Corinth** and had spent a good deal of time living there (Acts 18:1–17). His continued relationship with that church is suggested in further sections of Acts (18:28; 19:1; 20:3–6). The Corinth that Paul missionized was a relatively new city, founded in 46 B.C.E. on the former site of (Old) Corinth, which had been destroyed in 146 B.C.E. A center of commerce and government, the city had a reputation for licentiousness and, like ancient Rome, it had a variety of cultures. The church that Paul founded reflected this mixture and included both former Jews and "pagans." Paul had difficulty in helping these new converts to Christianity break away from their former lives, withstand the temptations of their environment, and live as he believed was fitting for Christians. Apparently after Paul left Corinth he kept a special eye on this new church. Concerned for its welfare, he sent emissaries through which he maintained communication. 1 and 2 Corinthi-

ans contain, it is believed, at least a portion of that correspondence.

In 1 Corinthians (5:9) Paul mentions a previous letter in which he had warned against association with people living immoral lives. A later passage (2 Cor. 6:14–7:1) fits the description of such a letter very well. Moreover, these verses seem out of place in their present location, for the surrounding material is of a much different tone. Verse 13 of Chapter 6 of 2 Corinthians can be joined to verse 2 of Chapter 7 without any sense of interruption, whereas the insertion of the six verses we now have (i.e., 6:14–7:1) breaks the spirit. This discrepancy has led to the assumption that the "missing" letter consisted of the exhortations now found in 2 Corinthians.

1 Corinthians is a letter that seems to elaborate on the first. Paul had sent **Timothy** to Corinth, in the meantime having received word from the church. Part 1 (Chs. 1–6) seems to respond to matters brought to Paul's attention by a messenger from **Chloe,** while Part 2 (Chs. 7–16) seems to answer a letter from the Corinthian church. It is obvious that Paul is seeking to help resolve some internal church problems that are troubling to him.

2 Corinthians 10–13 represents a third, and rather harsh, letter. The Corinthians continued to struggle, and Paul felt the need for more firmness. He takes the church to task for its continued resistance to his advice. Timothy had now visited the church. Neither his visit nor Paul's first two letters had accomplished the desired results. Paul himself had returned to the city, a painful visit, which he felt was unsuccessful. Now he hoped to accomplish by letter what he had failed to do in person.

2 Corinthians 1–9 (except 6:14–7:1) represents the last of the correspondence and differs in tone from the earlier work. Paul was traveling again to Corinth. During the journey he received word that the Corinthians had finally

come around, becoming what Paul wanted them to be. Delighted, Paul wrote a letter to precede him to the city, perhaps hoping to end some of the bad feelings he felt had been generated by his constant criticism of the church. This letter is most conciliatory, very different in tone from what are now the closing chapters of 2 Corinthians.

Having given a different order to our reading of these letters, let us now deal with some of the same questions we answered regarding Galatians.

1. *Who wrote the letters?* Both letters claim to be written by Paul (1 Cor. 1:1; 2 Cor. 1:1). If the multiple letter theory has merit, it must be assumed the salutations of the first and third letters have been lost. It has been suggested that Paul's letters were stored together, that their pages were intermingled and portions lost. Their current order is said to have been decided by the person responsible for their inclusion in Paul's collected letters.

Although it is generally agreed that these letters belong to Paul's genuine collection, some recent scholars suggest that certain fragments have been written by others. The arguments for multiple authorship are not convincing, nor is the view that there are more than four letters. The content is certainly consistent with what is known of Paul, as are the style and language.

2. *To whom were they written?* 1 Corinthians identifies its audience as the church at Corinth (1 Cor. 1:2). 2 Corinthians identifies the church at Corinth and those in the province of Achaia, of which Corinth was the capital (2 Cor. 1:1). Presumably Paul intended his letters to be shared by the surrounding churches. The circumstances they address are certainly consistent with all that is known about Corinth.

The church, which evidently consisted of some former Jews (1 Cor. 7:18), as well as former pagans (1 Cor. 12:2), was the object of continued missionary activity that had brought some internal conflict of its own (1 Cor. 1:10–16). There is also some suggestion that most of its membership came out of the lower classes of the city (1:26–31).

3. *When were they written?* Our earlier discussion has dealt with that question. The first letter obviously was written after Paul had left Corinth. The second letter responded to a conference and a letter. The third letter came after a return visit by Paul himself, and the fourth preceded his final visit to the city.

The Book of Acts suggests that Paul founded the church and remained there in 50–51 C.E. The letters must fall between his leaving and his last visit in 55, making it probable that they were written between 53 and 55.

4. *Why were they written?* Again, our earlier discussion about the order of the letters suggests why they were written. They covered the practical problems facing the Corinthian church as it attempted to live out its commitment to its adopted faith while surrounded by a seductive culture and torn by internal strife. Compelled to give direction to the church he had founded, Paul was also responding to specific questions that the church itself had asked Paul, who was its spiritual adviser.

5. *In light of the above, what was Paul's message?* Here, of course, one must speak in the plural, for there is a series of letters.

Letter One (2 Cor. 6:14–7:1). This short letter has a single message: Do not associate with people living immoral lives. Quoting from the Hebrew Bible to make his point, Paul counsels the Corinthians to maintain their purity.

Letter Two (1 Cor.). This letter contains multiple messages, for it responds to a series of situations and questions.

The first problem addressed is the division within the church, evidenced by some looking to Paul, some to **Apollos,** some to Cephas for spiritual guidance. Paul counsels that unity lies in Christ and factions should not be allowed to develop in the church (1 Cor. 1:10–4:21).

The second problem involves incest in the church (a man living with his father's wife), a practice contrary to the normal morality of the day and expressly forbidden by Jewish law. Paul advises getting rid of the bad before the whole is polluted (5:1–13).

The third problem consists of church members taking one another to civil court to settle their disputes. Paul says they should be ashamed of the fracture in their life together. Their concern, states Paul, should be God's kingdom, and not civil justice (6:1–11).

His final response to concerns expressed by the message from Chloe has to do with the religious significance of the body. He warns the readers to avoid prostitutes, indicating that fornication is a violation of one's own body, which is now God's property and should be used for his glory (6:12–20).

The remaining chapters are responses to a series of questions posed in a letter from the church. The questions, enumerated below, have topics as widely variant as sex and eating meat that has been offered to idols. Paul's answers are practical, based on the circumstances in which the people found themselves, and he makes quite clear at times that his responses are suggestions, not rules. It is obvious that Paul believes he is living in the last days. That consideration is important to remember, especially in regard to marriage.

The questions to which Paul seemed to be responding were:

1. *7:1–40: What about the propriety of marriage for Christians?* Paul's response is that it is better to remain single, but not at the cost of sinning. He makes clear what is his advice and what are the commands of Jesus, counsel-ing that Jesus forbade divorce and remarriage. All the other rules are the advice of Paul in light of the present circumstances. Though he prefers celibacy, he has only his advice and "no directions from the Lord," he says.

2. *8:1–10:33: Should one be free to eat food that has been offered to idols?* This is of course a problem that arose out of the circumstances of the day. The markets of Corinth sold the carcasses of animals that had been offered in pagan temples in rites of sacrifice. The Christians had asked Paul whether the consumption of such meat constituted worship of the diety to which it had been sacrificed. Paul said that as long as one was not participating directly in the ritual, eating such meat did not constitute idolatry; but if by eating sacrificial meat one were to have an appearance of idolatry or to "cause others to stumble" (by causing them to violate their consciences) it should not be done. One's example must always be positive and must never lead others into actions that would compromise them.

3. *11:2–14:40: The third question addresses decorum in public worship.* A number of elements are included in the question. The first portion (11:2–16) deals with the participation of women, and Paul's advice reflects the accepted standards of Hellenistic culture. The advice is certainly not intended for all time, nor is it antifeminine. It is given in the same spirit as the answer to the question regarding meat.

Verses 17–22 indicate that the communion service had become an occasion for contention and the expression of factionalism. Paul admonishes the Corinthians to return to the example of the tradition out of which the Lord's supper arose and the spirit in which it was first celebrated (23–34).

The final portion of the question deals with the gifts of the spirit. They, too, had become a bone of contention, with those expressing various gifts competing with one another. While all gifts are important, Paul observes, each must be exercised "with propriety and in order." Love is the standard by which each gift must be applied and measured.

In addition, Paul was asked to clarify his teaching on the resurrection, a topic more clearly understood by Jews and early Christians than by the predominantly Greek Corinthian community. Paul reminds the Corinthians (15:1–58) of the resurrection of Christ as the foundation of their belief. Indicating the difference between the corruptible physical body and the incorruptible spiritual body, he notes a difference between the now and what is to be.

The remainder of 1 Corinthians deals with personal matters between Paul and the church, including the collection for the church at Jerusalem and his impending visit. He ends by signing the letter with his own hand, suggesting that he had used a secretary in its composition.

Letter Three (2 Cor. 10–13). The third letter is the harsh letter discussed earlier. In defending his apostolic authority against a slanderous attack by detractors, Paul is driven to boast of his spiritual accomplishments. Chapter 12 reveals what we would describe today as an "out-of-the-body" experience, followed by a reference to the physical malady ("thorn in the flesh") that evidently plagued Paul throughout his ministry. This severe letter attempts to do what the apostle had failed to do in person, namely, set the Corinthians on the right track.

Letter Four (2 Cor. 1–9, except 6:14–7:1). The final letter is written in the spirit of reconciliation and joy, for Paul has received word from Titus that all is well in Corinth. Paul boasts of the new spirit and calls for a continuing sense of the harmony that has been created. His final plea is that the church express this spirit of harmony by generously sharing their resources with the poor in the Jerusalem church.

Although each of these letters is directed to a specific situation, it is not difficult to discover why they enjoyed continuing popularity in Corinth and among the surrounding communities. Practical advice on specific matters also could have universal application. The principles on which the advice was predicated had application far beyond questions of proper attire or behavior in worship, or what spiritual gift should be most highly honored. It was that universal dimension that made these works of continuing importance to the church at Corinth and led to their later status as scripture for all of Christianity.

Romans

◆ **READ** *The Letter of Paul to the Church in Rome*

The letter to the Romans reveals a number of interesting things about itself. The exercise of letting the work answer as many of our questions as possible will provide some insights.

1. *Who wrote it?* Again, the letter identifies its author as Paul (1:1). Its similarity to the letter to the Galatians, which is obvious to even the casual reader, has led to a scholarly consensus that it is Paul's work. If Paul wrote any of the letters attributed to him, he surely wrote this.

2. *To whom was it written?* The audience is identified as the church in Rome (1:7). Paul indicates that he knows the church by reputation and desires to bring his message to them in person. There is some indication that the church consisted of an educated class, predominantly Gentile in character (1:8–15).

3. *When was it written?* Paul speaks of his own missionary career. He indicates that he feels he has completed his work between Palestine and Rome and that he now desires to take his message to Spain. He wants to visit the Roman church and secure their support for his further endeavors. Before he comes, however, he must return to Jerusalem to deliver the collections he has gathered. This would place the time of writing at the end of Paul's third missionary journey and before his arrest in Jerusalem, late in 55 or early in 56 C.E.

4. *Why was it written?* Some have speculated that Paul had been accused throughout his ministry of preaching an incomplete Gospel because he did not require converts to adopt the practices of Judaism. Preparing to visit a church closely associated with Peter, one that had been formed among Roman Jews who would have been sympathetic to the Judaizers' views, Paul felt the need to explain himself fully to a community whose support he desired. Using the skills of his rabbinic training, he systematically built his case to show its reasonableness. He prepared a full statement of his understanding of the meaning of the Christ event in history, hoping to quiet his critics. The impact, of course, was much more far reaching, for the letter of introduction became the classical statement on the subject for much of subsequent Christian history.

5. *In light of the above, what was Paul's message?* It is obvious that the answer is not a simple one. The clue is found early, however, as the theme of all that is to follow is stated:

> For I am not ashamed of the Good News: it is the power of God saving all who have faith— Jews first, but Greeks as well—since it is what reveals the justice of God to us: it shows how faith leads to faith, or as scripture says: "The upright man finds life through faith." (1:16–17).

The remainder is a systematic development of that theme, showing how Paul understands the course of **salvation history** to flow through human events.

It will be helpful to remember the presuppositions of the Judeo-Christian tradition.

Paul remains firmly entrenched in that view of history, which understands God as involved in the history of the creatures he has made. With that in mind, let us examine Paul's case:

a. *The Human Situation is one of alienation: Sin (1:18–3:20).* The opening section deals with the problem of sin. Two things should be noted. The first is the universal nature of the problem. If Yahweh is Lord of all, then all humanity, being sinners, are alienated from him. The Jews have the Law as their measure, but those without the Law are not without a measure. The creator is revealed in his creation, a revelation not always recognized or honored by humankind. There is strong ground for natural theology in this section.

Second, Paul is not hostile to Judaism as such. The Jews are alienated by their measure, as are the Gentiles by theirs. All are judged by what they know, and all are found wanting. Sin is sin, and all are sinners, Jew and Gentile alike. Relying on his Jewish heritage, Paul quotes extensively from the psalms to make that point.

b. *God has provided a means of reconciliation: Faith (3:21–4:25).* God has revealed his will, and he has provided the means of overcoming the alienation created by the violation of that will. The means is faith in what God has done: that is, providing the adequate sacrifice (his son) to eradicate the consequences of human sin. One must not forget the sacrificial system of the Judaism of which Paul was a part. The purpose of sacrifice was to atone or make amends for the violation of Yahweh's will as revealed in his law. The ritual of sacrifice included the understanding of what constituted an appropriate sacrifice, as well as the need for true repentance for one to be returned to right standing. The concept includes the ideas that God is just and that justice must be satisfied. Paul says that God has himself provided the means of that satisfaction by the gift of his son. Faith becomes the complete surrender of one's life to that new reality, an act that God counts as actual righteousness. One stands righteous before God by accepting the gift that God has provided. Paul uses the example of Abraham, as he had in Galatians, quoting Genesis 15:6: "Abraham put his faith in God, and his faith was considered as justifying him."

c. *The results of faith are salvation (5:1–8:39).* Saved from God's anger, one can look forward to future glory in a personal state of reconciliation. Rehearsing the concept of salvation history indigenous to Judaism, the idea that sin entered the world through Adam, Paul adds the chapter introduced by Christianity: the idea that in Jesus' sacrificial death comes the possibility of overcoming one's former inheritance. Sin is more universal than merely violation of the Law; sin includes all. Freed of the domination of sin by the gift of Christ's sacrifice, one is released from the slavery of that sin to the freedom of righteousness.

Now free to serve "in the new spiritual way," one is led to examine the Law. The Law defines sin; it is not the cause of sin. While the Law is good, it does not rule life. Sin has become the dominant force in life, and sin causes sins. The spirit of Christ, however, freed humans from the domination of sin, to live lives dominated instead by that spirit. Christ rules where sin once ruled. All this is a gift freely provided by God himself.

d. *But what about the Jew? (9:1–11:36).* Paul's concern is now directed toward another portion of salvation history, the choosing of the Jews as God's elect. "Has God changed the rules?" Paul asks. His answer is complex and needs to be examined carefully. Paul casts his argument in the fashion of a rabbi expounding the Law, and his answers are not to be discerned until the end of the presentation.

Paul offers a series of possible answers. Perhaps, for example, it is not the physical descendants of Abraham who are the chosen. You can list the other possibilities for yourself. Each argument is built on the scriptural heritage of Judaism, and each makes its own case. Also note the conclusion, in which Paul says that the rejection of the Christian vision by those who have chosen to remain Jews and God's response to that rejection remain a mystery. Having noted that God still loves the Jews, that they remain his chosen, Paul concludes by quoting Isaiah (40:13):

Who could ever know the mind of the Lord? Who could ever be his counselor? Who could ever give him anything or lend him anything?

Certainly one could not argue from this that Paul felt that the Jews were lost from God's plan of salvation. But neither is it clear what Paul believed to be the climax of salvation history for those who remained Jews.

e. *So, how shall we live? Ethics (12:1–15:13).* Lest any reader conclude that Paul has dismissed the ethical dimension of life by contending that one is justified by grace through faith, he makes quite clear that such is not the case. Ethics, guided by the rule of love, remains of paramount importance.

A number of scholars have questioned whether Chapters 15 and 16 properly belong to Romans. Some ancient texts do not harmonize in these two chapters, although the problems with Chapter 15 are not as severe as those of 16. Certainly 15:1–6 seems to complete the thought begun in Chapter 14, but it is difficult to detect other problems in Chapter 15 without textual comparisons. Chapter 16 does raise questions even for the casual reader, particularly knowing that Paul had never been to Rome. It is difficult to connect Phoebe to Rome unless we assume that she was dispatched to deliver the letter, and others named are more easily associated with the church at **Ephesus.** While nothing included creates major problems, it is likely that Chapter 16 did not belong to the original letter.

FIVE OTHER LETTERS OF PAUL

Most scholars agree that 1 Thessalonians, **Philemon,** and Philippians belong to the genuine works of Paul. There is less agreement in regard to 2 Thessalonians and Colossians. This does not mean that they are not as important as the others. Each of Paul's works provides a piece of the mosaic that gives us a complete picture of the man and his message.

1 Thessalonians

◆ **READ** *The First Letter of Paul to the Church in Thessalonika*

Some have questioned the authenticity of 1 Thessalonians because of its failure to use the Hebrew Bible, a document Paul quotes often elsewhere, and the absence of a discussion of justification by grace through faith, a repeated theme in many of Paul's other works. This letter has always been in the list of Paul's collection, however. The problems can be resolved by noting that Paul wrote the church to address a specific problem and limited his remarks to that problem. As in his other letters, he wrote for very practical reasons, which dictated the content in each case. The letter itself provides most of the necessary clues.

Writing to a church he had founded and among whose members he had lived, Paul indicated concern for the continued well-being of the Thessalonians in the face of persecution. Unable to revisit the church, he had sent Timothy in his place. The report of that visit brought Paul great joy at the steadfast faith of the community. It also brought a question from the community regarding the fate of those who died before the return of Jesus, an event Paul and his followers seemed to expect in the very near future. Paul attempts to explain to the community that those who had died would be at no disadvantage, that they would share equally in the event with those who remained alive. He seems to quote from Jesus' own teaching on the subject (4:13–18). Giving encouragement for those remaining to get on with life, he reminds them that no one can know the time of the end. He counsels them to be patient with those who have taken to despair or idleness in their misunderstanding of the implications of the teaching about the return, urging them to maintain the spirit of love and support that has characterized the community. This letter contains the basis of the theology of the "Rapture," important to some segments of the modern Protestant movement (3:20–21).

2 Thessalonians

◆ **READ** *The Second Letter of Paul to the Church in Thessalonika*

Criteria for Evaluating Claims to Authorship. No great harm can come from considering 2 Thessalonians with Paul's genuine works. In fact, if the rule of thumb is to reject tradition only when the evidence becomes very powerful, one would have to say that the arguments for and against Paul's authorship of 2 Thessalonians seem to balance out. If the evidence against authorship is not overwhelming it is perhaps better to rely upon the traditional assumptions about the epistle and leave it with Paul's genuine letters. Those who excluded it from that category, however, cite the following among their reasons:

1. The amazing similarity of the two Thessalonian letters, making the second appear to be almost a paraphrase of the first.

2. The seeming discrepancy between the eschatology of the first letter (5:1–11) and the second (2:1–12).

Those who affirm Paul as the author suggest in response:

1. That the second letter was trying to clarify the first, thus accounting for the similarity.

2. That rather than contradicting the first letter, 2 Thessalonians complements its teaching. The emphasis changes, but the point of view does not.

Both 1 and 2 Thessalonians have as a major purpose the clarification of Paul's teaching on the last days, particularly the problems involved with the delay of **parousia**. Whether the second letter was written by Paul or by a later author in his name, the point of view remains constant. The first letter includes several matters; the second directs itself more exclusively to one point.

Content. The letter deals with the last days. Reviewing what the Thessalonians had been taught in the first letter, the author attempts to clarify what has been understood as Paul's view—or what has been passed on in the name of Paul—but is now rejected as his teaching. In the process he hopes both to encourage those who have become despondent and to correct those who have become idle while anticipating a quick end to history. Finally, he encourages patience as people grope with the problems.

Philippians

◆ **READ**   *The Letter of Paul to the Church in Philippi*

The church at Philippi, founded by Paul, may well have consisted totally of Gentile Christians. Written at about the same period as the Corinthian letters, Philippians seems to be two separate letters, now combined: The second letter is 1:1–3:1, the first is 3:2–4:23. Verse 3:2 provides the clue that Paul wrote on more than one occasion. Reading the book as two letters helps to distinguish between purpose and message.

Letter One (3:2–4:23). Paul deals mainly with the problem of the Judaizers, those he refers to as the "cutters" (3:2). Perfection, he says, comes through faith, not the Law. The letter directs itself, as well, to some local church problems, particularly disputes among some members. Here Paul seems to have been released from prison.

Letter Two (1:1–3:1). The second letter seems to have been written from prison, to thank the church for a gift Paul had received from them through Epaphroditus. With the gift, Paul had also received news from the church. Judaizers had come and, although they had met with little success, Paul felt the need to reiterate the Gospel he had planted. Verses 6–11 of Chapter 2 seem to quote a familiar early Christian hymn, leading some to speculate that Paul composed such hymns for use in the churches he founded and guided. He was having to send Epaphroditus home, and the letter seems also designed to make that return more comfortable.

Philemon

◆ **READ**   *The Letter from Paul to Philemon*

This personal letter, written from one individual to another, is somewhat set apart from Paul's other letters. The contents provide our best clue to its purpose. It is an appeal to Philemon, who was either the owner of the slave **Onesimus** or the pastor of the church in Colossae (the point is not entirely clear), on the occasion of Onesimus' return to Colossae. The details of the affair are found in the short letter, as well as Paul's advice in the matter.

Colossians

◆ **READ** *The Letter of Paul to the Church in Colossae*

Those who hold Colossians to be one of Paul's genuine works often regard it as a postscript to the return of Onesimus. Although many argue that in language and style it is very different from Paul's other works, thereby bringing into question its authenticity, it is quoted in Ephesians more often than any of Paul's other letters. Since the author of Ephesians, who is believed to be responsible for the original collection of Paul's letters, considered Colossians to be the work of Paul, its many citations in Ephesians are strong testimony to how it was viewed in the first century. That argument alone is enough to overcome the objections of those who would assign it to another author.

The Colossian church was the place to which Onesimus returned. This letter would be an appropriate follow-up to the action Paul took in sending the slave back to his master. In the letter Paul reminds the church of the message he has proclaimed among them, while warning them against false teachers. After discussing the problem of heresy, the points of which are clear in Paul's refutation, he outlines proper ethical behavior among Christians, including the relationship of slave and slave holder—presumably because of the Onesimus affair. Written while Paul was imprisoned, the letter to the Colossians well could be the last we have from his pen. It is especially helpful in achieving a sense of the presence and nature of early Christian heresy.

PAUL'S CONTRIBUTION

Although Paul did not create Christianity, he gave expression to it in its first generation of existence. He was also one of those most responsible for its spread beyond Judaism. His mode of operation was much like that of the rabbis of his day, and he was strongly influenced by the Jewish tradition that had formed him. Since his interpretation of the Christ event in history was to become a standard by which Christianity would continue to understand itself, his significance in shaping the expression of Christianity for future generations cannot be overstated.

However, Christianity was founded by those who preceded Paul in the faith. Its founding was based on the belief that Jesus was the Messiah and was supported by the common experience of the resurrection among the earliest disciples. Belief in the resurrection was the one thing all Christians had in common. From the resurrection they looked back on the life of the man they believed to have overcome death and found further clues to his messiahship. More and more early believers sought to keep alive the "Jesus of history" as the "Christ of faith" took control of their lives. Paul used stories about him, as well as memories of his teaching, but not as fully as some might have hoped. With the death of the eyewitnesses, the followers of Jesus felt the necessity of keeping his memory alive and free from distortion. That literary process is what we next examine as we turn to the Gospels, stories about the historic Jesus that include the meaning for humankind of the Jesus of faith.

STUDY QUESTIONS

1. How does a knowledge of Paul's Jewish background help one understand his presentation of Christianity?

2. Discuss the importance of Paul to the spread of early Christianity beyond the borders of Palestine.

3. Explain how and why Paul's letters are important to our understanding of early Christianity.

4. Discuss the basis of the tension that existed between Paul and some Palestinian Jewish Christians in regard to his views on what specifically was required of one who became a Christian.

5. Explain Paul's letter to the Galatians, using the time it was written, the audience to whom it was addressed, and the purpose of the letter as the basis of your response.

6. Explain what Paul means when he speaks of justification through faith.

7. What is the basis for the theory that 1 and 2 Corinthians are really a larger body of Paul's letters?

8. Why is Paul's letter to the Romans considered his most important work? Include in your discussion clues from the letter itself.

9. Explain Paul's advice to the Corinthians on marriage in the context of the times.

10. Based upon what Paul wrote in Romans 9–11, how would you characterize his attitude toward the Jewish faith he abandoned?

SUGGESTED READINGS

Achtemeier, Paul J. *Romans* (John Knox Press, Atlanta, 1985).

Barclay, William. *The Mind of St. Paul* (Harper & Row, New York, 1958).

Barrett, C. K. *Freedom and Obligation: A Study of the Epistle to the Galatians* (Westminster Press, Philadelphia, 1985).

Beare, F. W. "Romans, Letter to the," *The Interpreter's Dictionary of the Bible*, Vol. 4 (Abingdon Press, Nashville, 1962).

———. *St. Paul and His Letters* (Abingdon Press, Nashville, 1962).

———. "Thessalonians, First Letter to the," *The Interpreter's Dictionary of the Bible*, Vol. 4 (Abingdon Press, Nashville, 1962).

Bornkamm, G. *Paul* (Hodder and Stoughton, London, 1971).

Coggan, Donald. *Paul: Portrait of a Revolutionary* (Crossroad, New York, 1985).

Duncan, G. S. "Philippians, Letter to the," *The Interpreter's Dictionary of the Bible*, Vol. 3 (Abingdon Press, Nashville, 1962).

Gilmour, S. M. "Corinthians, First Letter to the," *The Interpreter's Dictionary of the Bible*, Vol. 1 (Abingdon Press, Nashville, 1962).

———. "Corinthians, Second Letter to the," *The Interpreter's Dictionary of the Bible*, Vol. 1 (Abingdon Press, Nashville, 1962).

Goodspeed, Edgar J. *Paul* (Winston, New York, 1947).

Johnston, G. "Colossians, Letter to the," *The Interpreter's Dictionary of the Bible,* Vol. 1 (Abingdon Press, Nashville, 1962).

Knox, J. "Galations, Letter to the," *The Interpreter's Dictionary of the Bible,* Vol. 2 (Abingdon Press, Nashville, 1962).

Lyman, M. E. "Philemon, Letter to," *The Interpreter's Dictionary of the Bible,* Vol. 3 (Abingdon Press, Nashville, 1962).

Malherbe, Abraham J. *Paul and the Thessalonians: The Philosophic Tradition of Pastoral Care* (Fortress Press, 1987).

Morrow, Stanley B. *Paul: His Letters and Theology: An Introduction to Paul's Epistles* (Paulist Press, New York, 1986).

Purdy, A. C. "Paul, the Apostle," *The Interpreter's Dictionary of the Bible,* Vol. 3 (Abingdon Press, Nashville, 1962).

Talbert, Charles H. *Reading Corinthians: A Literary and Theological Commentary on I and II Corinthians* (Crossroad, New York, 1987).

NINE

THE SYNOPTIC GOSPELS: STORIES ABOUT JESUS

THE GOSPELS DEFINED

This chapter deals with three of the four evangelical accounts of the life and teachings of Jesus. The gospels are the sole literary form found only in Christianity and, as such, deserve special attention. Although they are certainly influenced by their historic predecessors in the Hebrew Bible, especially the historic books, they are without formal literary precedent as far as is known.

Mark, Matthew, and Luke have come to be called the synoptic Gospels. Synoptic means "to view together" and, because these works are so similar, they can be viewed together. The Gospel of John, on the other hand, has little literary similarity to the first three and will be considered separately.

The form of the gospel was invented by the author of the Gospel of Mark and imitated by those who produced the later gospels. This rather ordinary man, who does not appear to have been formally educated and shows little acquaintance with the forms of the higher literature of his day, simply set out to record the story of Jesus as it was known by contemporaries. Using Mark's story and following his style, the authors of Matthew and Luke did the same a bit later. Though the author of John tended to present his story in more dramatic form, he was influenced by those who had already completed their works.

What method of writing did the author of Mark use? He blended event with meaning, relating stories about Jesus to the meanings of the stories. Convinced that Jesus was indeed the long-expected Messiah, he wrote the Gospel to convince others of the significance of the events that had led to that conviction.

The Gospels are not simple histories of the life of Jesus. They reflect the faith of a community as they try to bolster that faith and gain converts. Taking the view of history as the arena in which God makes himself known, they are in some respects like the so-called historic books of the Old Testament. They use history to speak of things beyond history, to address its meaning. History again becomes the vehicle to speak further of God, using as the symbol and instrument of revelation the

Jesus of history/Christ of faith. Just as 1 and 2 Chronicles highlight the life of David to speak about Yahweh's intentions, the Evangelists use Jesus to speak about God's continuing revelation of himself.

This does not mean that the history itself has no meaning, or that it is not history. To the writers of the Gospels it is in the concrete events of history that God operates, and in that sense they do not differ from their predecessors. Yet history had already become more than events, people, or places. It had taken on the significance that is provided by the "eyes of faith." History told through the "eyes of faith" has intention, the intention of producing faith. If one could understand the true meaning of the events, these authors believed, those who were exposed to the story would believe as well.

For example, the individual Gospel writers obviously cared more about the meaning of an event than about when that particular event might have occurred. You will find numerous examples where setting, time, or participants change as an event is reported. Note the different settings for Jesus' response about which are the most important of the Laws (Mark 12: 28–31, Matt. 22:34–40, Luke 10:25–28). In Luke the Parable of the Good Samaritan is added to the end of the encounter. Jesus' teaching about the Law was what was important to the writers, not the setting in which it occurred or the particular person to whom it was addressed.

THE OCCASION FOR THE GOSPELS

Jesus of Nazareth lived in the first century of the common era. Shortly after his execution by the Romans, a group of Jews, most of whom had been associated with him in his lifetime, came to believe that he was the promised Messiah. That belief was based chiefly on the conviction that Jesus had risen from the dead. The first generation of this group of believers was also convinced that Jesus would return soon to usher in the kingdom of God. This idea is reflected throughout much of the New Testament, from the letters of Paul to the book of Revelation.

As far as is known, there was no formal writing about the life of Jesus in the first generation of Christianity. There were probably some oral and written traditions about Jesus, more likely related to his teachings than to his life. We can also assume that fairly well-developed accounts of his passion and resurrection existed in oral tradition. As the first (eyewitness) generation of Christians began to die, and since Jesus had not returned as expected, the need to keep the remembrance of him and what was believed about him became more important. These realities created the occasion for writing the first Gospel, Mark, and played a role in the composition of the other three, as well. The church had already begun the process of remembering both the person and the meaning his presence represented in history. The stories would vary, both because of the audiences to which they were addressed and because of the primary purpose for which each was written. They still had much in common, fueled by a common faith.

Ancient tradition tells us that the Gospel of Mark was written by a companion or secretary of Peter, on the occasion of Peter's death, to preserve what Peter had taught about Jesus. Though another tradition places Matthew as the first written gospel, there is good reason to believe that Mark's recording of Peter's teachings was indeed the beginning of the gospel tradition.

The similarity of the accounts of Mark, Matthew, and Luke is striking. In places they parallel one another word for word; at other places there are only subtle differences in the telling. Matthew and Luke have more material than does Mark, and together they include almost everything Mark reports (though not always at the same place in the narrative). Matthew and Luke have material in common that is not found in Mark, and each of these two has material found only in its own account.

THE INTERRELATIONSHIP OF THE GOSPELS

The question of the literary relationship of the synoptic Gospels is one that has raised questions among students of the New Testament over the centuries. Pious students of the Bible have generally assumed that the scriptures were inspired, that God was the ultimate author, even if the words were transcribed by human hands. However, in the past centuries, as humanity became intrigued with the history of things, it has tried to develop means to get to that history. Out of this attempt came the development of the critical tools of scholarship. It was not long before religious scholars began to use such tools in the study of their own traditions. Among these tools were literary and historic criticism, which were especially helpful in finding answers to such questions as who wrote a work, to whom was certain material addressed, or when or why was a particular work produced. Though the conclusions drawn from such endeavors must be classified as intelligent speculation, rather than fact, they have led to new ways of viewing the traditions of which we are all inheritors. They have also led some to question the validity of some traditions that have generally informed our ideas about the gifts from the ancient past, the beliefs we have always held about them.

The Critical Problem

Much of what has been believed about the Bible was derived from the ancient tradition that affirmed Moses as the author of the Pentateuch and held that no book included in the Hebrew Bible was written after the time of Ezra and Nehemiah. It represents what was believed about the books of the Bible as they became the scripture of the Judeo-Christian tradition. This tradition was generally accepted until the period of modern scholarship, which began to question some of its long-held assumptions. Even then, the purpose of raising critical questions about the Bible or the tradition surrounding it was not to discredit the Bible. Rather, scholars hoped that through the use of scholarly tools they might understand the scriptures better. That hope continues to be the major motivating factor for those primarily involved in such scholarship.

None of us can read intelligently without bringing our own critical faculties to bear on the material at hand. Sometimes this exercise is quite conscious, as when we are studying a poem for an English assignment, and at other times it is less conscious. Just as we always measure our understanding with that of others, so we measure our critical conclusions with those who have explored the same territory. We do not say "No!" to the past without good reason. The rule of thumb should be basically to trust what tradition asserts of the past until it is no longer reasonable to do so. Of course it sometimes may be wise to question tradition, but not simply because it arose out of another generation. If the bias of a particular tradition's creators can be determined, then it may seem as if they might have shaped tradition to support that bias. However, the fact that they reported what they did might make it more reliable, especially if it would have been better for them if other circumstances had prevailed rather than those they reported. In the case of the Gospels of Mark and Luke, tradition assigns the authorships to persons who were not eyewitnesses to the life of Jesus or to events they report. Although the founders of those traditions report that Mark was secretary to Peter and his companion, and that Luke was an associate of many who were eyewitnesses, they do not attempt to pretend that the authors of those Gospels were indeed present at the events they report. That in itself makes the claims of those who passed on the traditions about the authorships of those Gospels more trustworthy to some, for clearly the early Christian community preferred to rely on the accounts of eyewitnesses. "Why would they attribute the authorship of a Gospel to a noneyewitness when it would be better to believe that it was written by a firsthand observer?" they would reason.

There is a certain amount of arrogance in the modern world that tends to reject the past simply because it is the past. It assumes that we have better tools and are more objective than earlier generations. We have already used these tools with some caution in exploring various aspects of the Bible, and now you can apply your own critical tools to make conclusions as we share alternative views. There is seldom a single final conclusion on which everyone agrees, and you deserve to know what informs those who draw different conclusions from the same information.

Earlier we noted that tradition assigned the Gospel of Matthew the place of the first of the written gospels. Later came the assertion that Mark was written first, with Matthew and Luke coming later. What is correct? Most now agree that Mark was written first and that the authors of both Matthew and Luke used Mark when composing their own works. To understand the basis of this more recent assumption, you must know something of the work of the German New Testament scholar B. H. Streeter, first published in English in 1930.

Streeter's Hypothesis

Dr. Streeter formulated **Streeter's hypothesis** as he attempted to solve what he called the **synoptic problem.** Tradition had affirmed Matthew as the first Gospel. The closest tradition surrounding Mark was simply silent on the matter, while another, less reliable source, referred to Mark as an abridgment of Matthew.

However, when Streeter applied some of the tools of literary criticism to the synoptic Gospels, he made some rather remarkable observations that led to his hypothesis.

Streeter set the gospels side by side, as is done in a **gospel parallel.** Some of the more important findings that emerged from this comparison were as follows:

1. That almost all (all but three paragraphs) of Mark is included in either Matthew or Luke (Mark 3:26–29, 8:22–26, 9:49–50).

2. That material common to both Matthew and Luke is not found in Mark.

3. That Matthew and Luke have material exclusive to themselves, not found in Mark or John.

4. That when there is chronological order to the synoptic Gospels, Mark seems to provide that order.

5. That when the Gospels of Matthew and Luke disagree (as to time, place, how much was said, etc.), Mark provides the place of agreement. Mark provides the agreement and Matthew and Luke never agree together against Mark.

6. That the literary similarities do not extend to John.*

From this and other evidence, Streeter decided that Mark was written first and that the authors of both Matthew and Luke used Mark as a major source when they composed their works. He suggested that Matthew and Luke had another common source, probably a writ-

---

*To make your own visual observations see Burton H. Throckmorton, Jr., Ed., *Gospel Parallels, A Synopsis of the First Three Gospels,* 2nd ed. (New York: Thomas Nelson and Sons, 1957). You can quickly observe where the Gospels do parallel, where each has its own unique material, what is added or changed by the various authors when they use material common to all three, and so on.

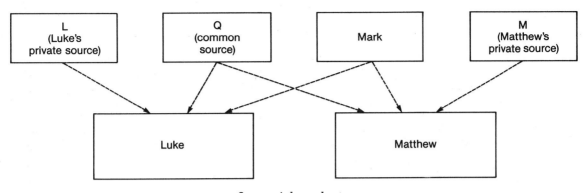

Streeter's hypothesis.

ten source consisting mainly of the sayings of Jesus, a source he designated as "Q" (*quelle* is German for source). Finally, he concluded that Matthew and Luke each had a private source, available only to him individually, which was reflected in the material found exclusively in the respective works. Thus, Streeter illustrated the literary relationship of the synoptic Gospels schematically as shown in the figure above. Streeter proposed a proto-Luke, an earlier edition of the third Gospel; the theory does not enjoy universal acceptance, however, nor is it necessary to this discussion.

Streeter's hypothesis convinced most scholars that Mark was the first gospel and, in turn, raised other questions about traditional assumptions. Why, for example, would a disciple (Matthew) depend so heavily on the work of Mark, who was not an eyewitness, in composing his own work? (As we see later, modern scholarship finesses this objection by contending that the disciple Matthew did not directly write the Gospel that bears his name.)

Although there have been numerous attempts to refute or replace Streeter's hypothesis, it has stood well the test of time. The original propositions continue to offer the best explanation of what many conclude to be the literary relationship among the three synoptic Gospels.

New Testament scholars, however, have not stopped at the observations of Streeter. They seek answers to the questions we tackled in our analysis of the letters of Paul. The attempt to arrive at such answers would not detract from the works, they believe, but would provide a means of better understanding their original message. An example of this type of scholarship led Perrin to suggest that the Gospel of Matthew was originally addressed to the Pharisaic community at **Jamnia** late in the first century. He suggests that Matthew was engaging in dialogue to try to convince those Pharisees that Jesus was the true Messiah, very much in the tradition of true Judaism and not without regard for the Law, of which the Pharisees remained the guardian.* As can be seen, such an explanation does not have to distort history but can clarify Matthew's expanded resurrection account, which made possible the refutation of the charge that Jesus' body might have been stolen from the grave (see Matt. 27:62–66), as well as his strong emphasis on Jesus' ethical teachings reported in the Sermon on the Mount.

---

*Norman Perrin, *The New Testament: An Introduction* (New York: Harcourt Brace Jovanovich, 1974), pp. 170–171.

This review of the synoptic Gospels relies on the observations of many scholars. You are not, however, incapable of making independent observations, always incorporating a test of the reasonableness of any assumption. The process is not new, for it has been in existence almost as long as the books themselves have been used as scripture. In the final sense, the concept of "tradition" (what has been believed about these works) is simply the reporting of the answers those of earlier ages have provided. New conclusions are measured against traditional assumptions. One rejects the idea that Matthew was the first Gospel, for example, or that Moses was the sole author of the Pentateuch, only if the evidence to the contrary is overwhelming, making it less than reasonable to accept the traditional assumption. The ultimate judgment belongs to the individual who has considered the alternatives.

You are now asked to read all of the Gospel of Mark and portions of Matthew and Luke. Try, as best you can, to dismiss from your mind any prior familiarity with these works. That familiarity lends itself to a blending of the accounts and tends to blur the distinctive features of each. While it is true that Christian theology is based on all its scripture, many important observations need to be made about that theology by approaching the individual works separately. By observing how Matthew and Luke used Mark, and noting how they use their common material or the material unique to them, you will be able to understand each one more fully.

MARK

The Origins of Mark

According to tradition, when the apostle Peter died, his companion Mark undertook to record Peter's recollections so that they would not be lost. The very fact that this work is not attributed to an eyewitness, but to someone who recorded the older man's memory, tends to support tradition. That same tradition tells us that Mark did not write an orderly account, yet both Matthew and Luke seem to rely on its order in the composition of their works. It is possible that the originator of the tradition was familiar with all the Gospels (or at least the synoptics), and noting that they did not always follow the same order, simply assumed that Mark, a noneyewitness, was less reliable at such points than the authors he believed to be eyewitnesses. We can only know what was believed and taught about these works early in the second century when the tradition was formed.

If Mark was indeed the first Gospel, as most now believe, and if it does report the reminiscences of Peter, as tradition asserts, it is most interesting to observe both what it does and does not include. The shortest of all the stories about Jesus, it begins with the baptism of Jesus by John the Baptist and the start of the public ministry of Jesus. It does not include an account of Jesus' birth, or any events of his life before he reached full adulthood. The first half of this short account reports the ministry of Jesus, the last half, his journey to Jerusalem and the fateful last days in that city. Finally, if Mark indeed ends at 16:8 as most scholars now believe, it includes no account of any of the postresurrection appearances of Jesus that are reported by the other Evangelists. Brief to the point of frustration for those who want more detail about the life of him they believe to be God's instrument of human salvation, Mark well could represent the most vivid picture available to us of what earliest Christianity remembered and taught about Jesus as Messiah. That, in itself, makes the book of enormous value. It will also aid in understanding how that teaching was expanded as new narratives were subsequently produced.

Let us, for the present, concentrate on the

Gospel of Mark, appropriating its story as it is. An outline of its contents is a useful beginning:

I. Introduction (1:1–8)
II. Baptism and Temptation (1:9–13)
III. Ministry in Galilee (1:14–7:23)
IV. Journey to Jerusalem (7:24–10:52)
V. Events in Jerusalem (11:1–13:37)
VI. Passion Story (14:1–16:8)*

One would do well to concentrate on what this story about Jesus reveals. Read it as if it were the only information you have on the life of Jesus. That approach will help you focus on the elements that the author believes to be crucial in the understanding of Jesus as Messiah. Go through the story step by step and list what Mark tells. At the end you will have the picture this Evangelist intended to paint. Only after you have done that will you want to read this text further and share what others believe they have observed in the story.

Principal Features of Mark's Gospel

✦ **READ** *The Gospel According to Saint Mark*

1. The author makes quite clear in verse 1 whom he believes Jesus to be, "Jesus Christ, the son of God." As one reads the remainder of the story the identity of Jesus as Messiah, either in self-proclamation, or in the recognition of others, is not so clear. That contrast is an important clue to understanding where the author of Mark bases his faith in Jesus as Messiah.

2. The revelation to Jesus about his role, at the time of his baptism, was a private event: *"he* saw the heavens torn apart . . ." (1:

10–11, italics supplied). This is consistent with Mark's representation of Jesus as downplaying any public outcry as to his messiahship.

3. Jesus' ministry is defined as proclaiming the kingdom of God. "The time has come," he said, "and the kingdom of God is close at hand. Repent, and believe the Good News" (1:15). Jesus did not preach about himself, but about the coming of the kingdom. That is what he called people to believe. This, too, remains consistent throughout.

4. Those who first experienced Jesus' ministry viewed it as something new and possessed with authority (1:27).

5. Jesus never explicitly claimed to be the Messiah and forbade others to make such claims for him (e.g., 1:25, 1:34).

6. Jesus is portrayed as a preacher, who was also a healer of extraordinary power (e.g., 1:38, 1:40–43).

7. Much of Jesus' ministry was among the outcasts of society. Such associations put him into conflict with the religious establishment (2:15–17).

8. Jesus' ministry did not follow the patterns of Jewish orthodoxy, another point that created conflict with the established religion (e.g., 2:18–22, 23–28, 3:1–6).

9. Jesus' ministry was misunderstood by his own family, who thought he was out of his mind (3:20–21).

10. The misunderstanding of Jesus penetrated even his teaching, a concept that continues throughout the story (4:10–12).

11. Jesus used the parable as a method of teaching (4:33–34).

12. The miracles that Jesus performed did not lead all those who witnessed them to an immediate understanding of his messianic role (4:41).

---

*Many scholars believe that verses 9–20 of Chapter 16 constitute a later addition to the Gospel. The ancient manuscripts considered to be the most reliable end the story at 16:8.

13. Jesus emphasized the importance of faith to those who would profit from his ministry (5:21–34).

14. In preaching of the kingdom, Jesus called those who would be its inheritors to repent (1:15, 6:7–13).

15. Even those closest to Jesus failed to grasp the significance of his life or ministry as they were experiencing it (6:45–52).

16. Jesus' teaching on the Law went beyond the accepted standards of the day, again causing conflict with Palestinian Judaism (7:1–13).

17. The nearer Jesus moved toward his fate, the more open he became about his role (8:27–38).

18. Jesus did not seem to claim equality with God, even if he had a sense of his Messianic role (10:17–22).

19. The **passion story** accounts for a full third of Mark's Gospel.

20. There was a strong apocalyptic dimension to Jesus' teaching about the kingdom of God, an event he seemed to expect in the near future (9:1, 13:1–37).

21. Jesus is portrayed as interpreting the meaning of his own death (14:22–25).

22. Jesus was accused of blasphemy by the Sanhedrin because he claimed to be the Messiah (14:53–65).

23. The story in Mark ends with the finding of the empty tomb, not with resurrection appearances (see earlier note on this).

The Gospel of Mark is not a neutral document, but one hoping to convey faith from one who already possessed such faith. Putting the foregoing observations together can help one reach some understanding of what the author was attempting to accomplish as he retold the story of the "Jesus of history," who had already for him become the "Christ of faith."

Our Résumé of Mark

From the beginning the author has told us what the story is about: "The beginning of the Good News about Jesus Christ, the Son of God" (1:1). Having made that assertion, he tells about John the Baptist. Jesus appears, is baptized, deals with temptation, and begins his ministry. The nature of Jesus' ministry is revealed immediately. "After John had been arrested, Jesus went into Galilee. There he proclaimed the Good News from God. 'The time has come,' he said, 'and the kingdom of God is close at hand. Repent, and believe the Good News'" (1:14–15). Here Jesus did not call for belief in himself, but for belief in the Gospel he preached.

The brief account has several types of material. Much of the teaching (parables, etc.) is done in the context of Jesus' conflict with established Judaism. Most of the healings and exorcisms provide occasions for a fleeting recognition of Jesus as Messiah, though early in the story those who seem best able to recognize Jesus in that role are the demons. The miracle stories tell us what Jesus did, yet they did not provoke recognition in their original audience of Jesus as Messiah. By the middle of Chapter 8 the author has Jesus on the road to Jerusalem, to face his final days. Chapters 14–16 recount those days in Jerusalem, the betrayal, arrest, trial, and crucifixion, concluding with the story of the empty tomb.

A Special Theme. One is struck by a recurring theme in Mark. Although we are told who Jesus is in the very first verse, we are also told that most who encountered him during his ministry did not immediately recognize him as Messiah, and the few who did were counseled to be silent. This theme has been titled the **"messianic secret"** by many biblical scholars.

Some suggest that there is a question in Mark as to Jesus' own messianic consciousness. The point is interesting, but less clear than the much more distinguishable secret

The Sea of Galilee, site of much of Jesus' early ministry.

motif, and many disregard it altogether, citing the voice from heaven reported early in Mark. The messianic secret is expressed throughout the Gospel, some examples being:

1. Jesus warns demons to tell no one (1:25–26).

2. His own family doesn't understand (3:20–21).

3. He counsels Peter to silence (8:27–30).

4. He admonishes silence after the **transfiguration** (9:2–9).

5. After a series of miracles, climaxed when Jesus walks on water, there is still no recognition (6:45–52).

Mark painted a picture of a Jesus who did all sorts of marvelous things and yet was not recognized as Messiah. On top of that, this portrait makes it quite clear that Jesus made no public claims of being the Messiah. He preached not of himself, but the Gospel of God. He did not call persons to believe in him, but in that Good News.

The Demand for Faith. It is fair to say that if Christianity had only the Gospel of Mark to guide its understanding, its theology might be quite different. What would it be? It would be a theology based on an empty tomb, a theology with a strong demand for faith. Its creeds would not include:

1. A **trinity**

2. A **virgin birth**

3. Strong messianic claims by a historic Jesus

4. Strong reliance on miracles as proof of messiahship

The theology of Mark is based on a simple gospel of faith—a faith that had served the life of those who first told it. It proclaims that Jesus can be understood as Messiah only by the faith called for by an empty tomb. If proofs had not been effective in Jesus' lifetime, how would they convince others? Jesus' own people, the Jews, had him crucified. His disciples often did not understand him. The final proof was the empty tomb, and acceptance of that proof required an act of faith. (We continue to assert that the Gospel of Mark truly ends at 16:8, as most scholars believe.)

Obviously any segment of Christianity that existed when Mark was written would have known the traditions that included accounts of postresurrection appearances of Jesus. Mark simply chose not to use them. Why? The entire Gospel provides the clue. In Jesus' own life miracles, exorcisms, healings, or teachings did not convince the world that he was the Messiah. For Mark the resurrection provided the prism through which all else could be understood, but even that event demands faith. No number of stories about appearances of the risen Jesus would convince anyone if walking on water had not.

The simple story that Mark tells of Jesus, whom he believes to be the Messiah, the son of God, testifies to all the essential elements: Jesus' messiahship is proclaimed in all he did and said, and finally and fully in his resurrection. As clear as that might seem to some, its reality for Mark does not come in external proofs, but in the act of simple faith. He knows that without faith, there is no conviction, so he concludes history with an empty tomb, a demand for faith.

MATTHEW

◆ **READ** *Chapters 1–2, 5–7, and 28 of the Gospel According to Saint Matthew*

The sections of Matthew you have been asked to read are for the most part portions of material exclusive to that author. The exception is the portions of the Sermon on the Mount found in the other synoptic Gospels. You are not discouraged from reading the entire Gospel; indeed, you should do that soon, if not now. As you move from an introduction to a more serious and complete study of the Bible, many more elements available in such a story will become obvious. This beginning should help you recognize some of the elements you will want to pursue later. Singled out for your attention now are portions of Matthew that point to its particular theme or message. First, however, you should know some of the tradition that surrounds what was perhaps the favorite gospel (in terms of use) of the early church.

The Origins of Matthew

As reported earlier, tradition had assumed Matthew was the first written Gospel and Mark an abridgment of it. This is not a very satisfactory explanation for Mark, and you might rightly ask why Mark excluded such important elements as the birth stories, the Sermon on the Mount, or the postresurrection appearances. A more logical explanation is that Matthew is an expanded account, whose author included matters of importance known to all the early followers of Jesus but simply not reported by Mark.

That same tradition assigned the authorship to the disciple Matthew, thus making it the work of an eyewitness. Most modern scholars assume instead that the author was an unknown first-century Christian who had or used the name Matthew. They assume that either he was himself named Matthew, or he was associated with the community over which the disciple Matthew had presided. If the latter were true, then the work could indeed be in the tradition of Matthew even if that disciple were not the author. These scholars reject the disciple as author based on the strong use of sources by the author, especially the heavy dependence on Mark, a noneyewitness. The most that can be said is that the gospel was associated very early with the disciple Matthew, and there must have been some reason for this connection. If he was not its author, there is good reason still to believe the message it contains is not unrelated to his influence. Although no one can identify the author with certainty, one can assume the work stands in the tradition of Matthew.

The work itself offers clues to its origins. The Gospel of Mark is obviously one source of Matthew. Two other major sources are easily identified, those designated "Q" and "**M**" by Streeter. "Q," which consists mainly of sayings of Jesus, well could have been in written form in very early Christian history, or it could have been part of a strong oral tradition. The fact of its existence is clear, though its form is still debated. The "M" material, which is exclusive to this Gospel, might or might not have existed in another form before Matthew was written. Either it is the literary product of the author or it existed separately, and the author used it as he did Mark and "Q." If it had a separate existence, it would not be unreasonable to assume a development out of the tradition surrounding the ministry of the disciple Matthew and reflective of his theology, just as Mark is said to reflect Peter's presentation. That would make Matthew in the tradition of Matthew, perhaps more representative of the intent of the original designation of the Gospels by name than indicative of actual authorship.

All such speculation about biblical authorship is hampered by our lack of information of the life and fate of individuals after the period of Jesus' ministry. It is not totally clear how many disciples there were, who they were, or what became of them. Interest in such matters arose fairly late in Christianity, and tradition is neither clear nor always consistent. The New Testament is not particularly helpful, for it focuses on Jesus and the movement that grew as a result of him. What information it does provide is selective and intends something other than reporting the fates of the disciples.

Most scholars now suggest that Matthew was written between 80 and 90. This assumption is based on the idea that it used the Gospel of Mark and, therefore, must have been written after that material had begun to be circulated among the broader Christian community. The same scholars are in less agreement, however, over why it was written.

Why did gospels continue to be produced after Mark? Either they were independently produced without knowledge of the existence of the others or there were other reasons. If Streeter is correct in his assertion of a literary interdependence of at least three of these works, there must have been reasons beyond the simple recording for posterity of the events surrounding the life of Jesus. Because we have no other means to make such a determination, we must look to the Gospels themselves for clues. These can be found by analyzing the content each author chose to include, or exclude, as well as the way he used the material. Careful observation reveals many things about each of the books, while circumstances to which they were addressed add a further dimension to our understanding.

Audience and Purpose

To whom was Matthew addressed? You should attempt to answer that question as you read. Was the audience Jewish or Gentile, or a combination of both? What kind of assumption does the author make? What kinds of questions does he address? What bias is he trying to overcome? You should be sensitive to the many clues in the text. To what audience would this presentation make the most sense, be the most convincing? The answers to such questions have been important in the way Matthew has been understood over the years.

For one who relies on tradition to learn the answers to these questions, the Gospel of Matthew provides a good example of how tradition is not always helpful. Tradition asserts of Matthew, for example:

1. That it was the original gospel, Mark being an abridgment

2. That it was written originally in Hebrew or Aramaic

3. That it was written in Jerusalem

4. That its author was the disciple Matthew

Most scholars now believe:

1. That Mark was the original gospel, and Matthew used it as a source

2. That Matthew was written in Greek, though the author may have used Hebrew or Aramaic sources

3. That it was more likely written in Syrian Antioch, or somewhere beyond the borders of Palestine

4. That its author is unknown, though he could have been influenced by the tradition of the disciple Matthew

These later assumptions come from a critical analysis of the tradition and the work itself. If they are correct, they might well bring a different understanding of the purpose and meaning of Matthew's contents. Let us, for example, look at Norman Perrin's contention that Matthew was originally directed to the Pharisaic community at Jamnia after the fall of Jerusalem, to demonstrate that Jesus stood very much in the Jewish messianic tradition. Such an understanding would explain many of Matthew's additions as well as its particular point of view. It would, for instance:

1. Explain the addition of Matthew's first two chapters in which:

   a. Jesus' lineage is traced back through David to Abraham, the father of Judaism.

   b. The virgin birth is claimed, supported by scripture from Isaiah.

   c. The story of the wise men is told, enriched by a quotation from Micah.

   d. The flight into Egypt is reported, incorporating a quotation from Hosea.

   e. The story of the killing of male children is added, supplemented with a quotation from Jeremiah.

   f. The location of Jesus in Nazareth is reported, with an affirmation that this is in keeping with the tradition of the prophets.

2. Explain the observation of many scholars that Matthew seems to present Jesus as a new Moses:

   a. By the story of the slaying of the firstborn

   b. By relating Jesus to Egypt

   c. By the Sermon on the Mount

   d. By having Jesus reinterpret the Law

3. Explain Matthew's way of using the Hebrew Bible, especially his oft-repeated formula, "to fulfill."

4. Explain Matthew's expanded resurrection account, especially the addition of witnesses beyond the Jewish community.

5. Explain the fivefold division of Matthew (sections II–VI in the Jerusalem Bible), paralleling the five books of the Law.

It is evident that a student's approach to and understanding of any work are influenced by the assumptions made about the audience and purpose of that work. The books of the Bible are no different in that respect from any literature, and the assumptions become crucial. A continued study of the Bible will involve dealing with such questions and the ways different investigators have come to answer them.

Our Résumé of Matthew

Two features of Matthew's account are particularly striking. The first is the many references to the Hebrew scriptures used to show Jesus as fulfilling Jewish messianic expectation. Many believe also that the very construction of the Gospel is a conscious parallel of the fivefold division similar to the Pentateuch. Jesus, presented as a new Moses, delivers the Law from the mountain, as it was intended to be understood. Second, there is strong emphasis on Jesus' continuity with the Jewish tradition of which he was a part. Called by some both the most pro-Jewish and anti-Jewish of the Evangelists, Matthew is perhaps best understood as an attempt to convince an audience sympathetic to Judaism that the teachings of Jesus represented Judaism as God had intended it.

If Matthew was written as late as most now suggest, 80 or later, it came after Paul's strong influence on the Christian church had become widespread. Paul's emphasis on the concept of "justification by grace through faith" could well have seemed to some to be a rejection of the tradition of the Law. The Jesus of Matthew would certainly do much to correct any such impression. The remarkable chapters we now call the Sermon on the Mount, Chapters 5 through 7, are particularly clear on this point. Jesus becomes the master Law giver, taking it beyond the literal, in an approach that could almost be called Pharisaical. The author of Matthew has obviously grouped many of the ethical teachings of Jesus in this section, as he often grouped materials to make a point, breaking the order of Mark to do so.

The Sermon on the Mount sets the theme for the rest of the work. Beginning with the **Beatitudes** (5:3–12), the role of the Law is consistently highlighted. Jesus begins the sermon by identifying attributes that are pleasing to God, implying that God will reward those with whom he is pleased.

The first "M" material found in the sermon is enlightening, for it defines Jesus' relationship with or attitude toward the Law:

"Do not imagine that I have come to abolish the Law or the Prophets. I have come not to abolish but to complete them. I tell you solemnly, till heaven and earth disappear, not one dot, not one little stroke, shall disappear from the Law until its purpose is achieved. Therefore, the man who infringes even one of the least of these commandments and teaches others to do the same will be considered the least in the kingdom of heaven; but the man who keeps them and teaches them will be considered great in the kingdom of heaven." (5:17–19)

Immediately follows a series of sayings peculiar to Matthew which all begin, "You have learned how it was said" (referring to a particular Mosaic law). Laws about killing, adultery, and swearing are mentioned. Jesus does not suggest that these laws no longer apply. Rather, he apparently extends the Law beyond the act proscribed to address the very motivations in human relationships.

After dealing with that segment of the Law, and apparently giving affirmation to it, the other "M" material in the sermon addresses such issues as to how one practices piety; the manner of alms giving; when, where, and why one prays; and fasting. Taken in sum, this material creates a picture of Jesus acting very much like a Pharisee in addressing the Law from the point of view of its spirit rather than in its literal sense.

The picture of Jesus as a new Moses begins to emerge. It is brought into sharper focus in the remainder of Matthew's Gospel. Particularly striking is the series of "kingdom" parables found beginning in Chapter 13. They remind us repeatedly that the kingdom is related to what one does. Note the parable found only in Matthew, near the end of this section:

"And so the kingdom of heaven may be compared to a king who decided to settle his accounts with his servants. When the reckoning began, they brought him a man who owed ten thousand talents; but he had no means of paying, so his master gave orders that he should be sold, together with his wife and children and all his possessions, to meet the debt. At this, the servant threw himself down at his master's feet. 'Give me time,' he said, 'and I will pay the whole sum.' And the servant's

Church of Loaves and Fishes located above the Sea of Galilee on the
site believed to be the place Jesus fed the five thousand.

master felt so sorry for him that he let him go
and canceled the debt. Now as this servant
went out, he happened to meet a fellow servant who owed him one hundred denarii; and
he seized him by the throat and began to
throttle him. 'Pay what you owe me,' he said.
His fellow servant fell at his feet and im-
plored him, saying, 'Give me time and I will
pay you.' But the other would not agree; on
the contrary, he had him thrown into prison
till he should pay his debt. His fellow servants were deeply distressed when they saw
what had happened, and they went to their
master and reported the whole affair to him.
Then the master sent for him. 'You wicked
servant,' he said. 'I canceled all that debt of
yours when you appealed to me. Were you not
bound, then, to have pity on your fellow servant just as I had pity on you?' And in his
anger the master handed him over to the tor-
turers till he should pay all his debt. And that

is how my heavenly father will deal with you
unless you each forgive your brother from
your heart." (18:23–35)

There is a strong internal consistency to the
message of Jesus found in his ethical teachings
of the Sermon on the Mount and in his teaching about the kingdom of heaven. In both cases,
there is a matter of judgment involved. Some
even speak of his ethical teachings as a "kingdom ethic," affirming that the ethic proposed
has a direct relationship to the kingdom. That
is, the kind of behavior that qualifies as pleasing
to God renders one eligible for his kingdom.

If Jesus is pictured as a "new Moses," the
"new" must be emphasized. It is precisely the
different view of the role and function of Law
that Matthew seems to be emphasizing, imply-

ing that the Law of Moses had been misapplied and therefore failed to function as it was intended. The Law in Judaism expresses the bounds of the covenant relationship with God. Jesus seems to suggest throughout Matthew that the Law has become a standard by which Jews measure themselves, not that which indicates how they are measured by God. The Law, Jesus suggests in the Sermon on the Mount, is not a set of rules, but a way of life that guides attitudes as well as actions. People must not only refrain from committing adultery, they must avoid doing what adultery represents, treating others as objects to be used to satisfy their needs. Looking at someone with lust relates to how one regards others; it is an attitude that is reprehensible, just as an improper action. Jesus, in Matthew, delivers the Law in relation to its intention, not its letter alone.

This major point is illustrated throughout the ethical teachings, as well as in the kingdom parable above. How does that parable end? "And that is how my heavenly father will deal with you unless you each forgive your brother from your heart" (18:35). Matthew consistently pictures Jesus as Law giver, showing how the Law was intended to function in Judaism, not how the Gospel seems to infer it had come to function. Even in Matthew's final scene, reported only in this Gospel, the picture remains consistent. After the resurrection Jesus meets his disciples on the mountain (another glance at the parallel with Moses) and gives his great commission:

> "All authority in heaven and on earth has been given me. Go, therefore, make disciples of all the nations; baptize them in the name of the Father and of the Son and of the Holy Spirit, and *teach them to observe all the commands I gave you.* And know that I am with you always; yes, to the end of time." (28:18–20; emphasis supplied)

From the beginning to the end the Jesus portrayed in Matthew says that the Law remains important. It is not a dead letter, simple rules to be followed, but a law that leads individuals to live in ways that are pleasing to God, who will share his kingdom with the righteous. It is not a religion hostile to Judaism, but one consistent with the most important characteristics of that religion.

Certainly this is but a portion of the richness of this small volume. These few sections can only begin to introduce you to Matthew's Gospel, which you will want to pursue in greater depth.

LUKE

Unique Features of the Third Gospel

✦ **READ** *Chapters 1–2, 9:51–18:14, and 24 of the Gospel According to Saint Luke*

As with Matthew, the sections of Luke you have been asked to read are material for the most part exclusive to that Gospel. You will also want to read the entire work soon if you do not take time to do so now. Some important information about Luke will help you as you seek to understand it in its own context:

1. The New Testament books of Luke and Acts are believed to have been written as a single book. Division probably took place in the second century when the New Testament began to be canonized.

2. Tradition assigns the authorship of these works to Luke the physician who, like Mark, has never been regarded as an eyewitness to the life of Jesus, a point made in the works themselves.

3. The books are addressed to **Theophilus.** This common Greek name means literally "beloved of God." Some suggest an intention to address the total Christian community, but most scholars feel that the term "your excellency" (1:4) identifies Theophilus as a person in a position of authority in the Roman Empire.

4. The gospel is believed to have been written between 80 and 95. Many date it in the time of Domitian. (More later on this.)

5. Luke's story in the opening chapters is entirely different from Matthew's.

6. After the introduction the author generally follows the order of Mark until **Luke's "special section"** (9:51–18:14), in which is found a large portion of "L" material.

7. The work returns to the order of Mark until near the end, when the author provides more of his own information.

8. Miracles play an especially significant role in Luke, in sharp contrast to Mark, and provide a means of identifying Jesus as Messiah.

9. There is a strong emphasis on eyewitnesses in Luke, as well as the creditability of such witnesses.

10. The Jews are perhaps cast in their most villainous role in Luke.

11. Luke puts strong emphasis on Jesus' innocence of any crime, a theme continued in regard to the early Christians in Acts.

12. The original work (Luke-Acts) seems to divide history into three eras: the era of the Law and the Prophets, ending with John the Baptist; the era of Jesus, which ends with his ascension; the era of the Church, which will continue until his return.

13. Though the author of Luke makes use of the Old Testament, his use differs slightly from that of the author of Matthew.

14. The very existence of Acts further distinguishes Luke from the other synoptic Gospels.

Clearly all these points are important and have implications for one's understanding of this work. The reader will want to explore these areas in more depth after finishing an introductory study of the Bible, but knowledge of their existence can help now in placing this work in the context in which it was written and can lead to a clearer initial understanding.

Implications of the Unique Features

Let us explore some of the implications of the elements distinguishing Luke from Mark and Matthew by a review of the points enumerated above.

1. Assuming that the author did not end his story at the point of the other synoptic Gospels, he must have had a reason for continuing. The combined work (Luke-Acts) has been called by some the first Christian **apology,** suggesting that its purpose was to defend or explain Christianity as Judaism properly understood, true Judaism as it ought to be practiced. This is witnessed to not only by the life of Jesus and the miracles he was able to perform, but by the continued manifestation of the spirit of God in the life of the church. What Jesus had done, the church continued to do.

2. The honor accorded this work, never claimed to be an eyewitness account, attests to the importance and value Luke held in early Christianity. Indeed, the author reports in his opening (1:1–4) that he relies on outside sources, a comment important to understanding the work itself. Though Luke has come to be associated with the church at Jerusalem (and thus with Peter, James, et al.), as well as with Paul, the Evangelist himself makes no issue of this.

3. The identification of Theophilus is crucial in how one comes to understand the work. If we assume that Theophilus was a Roman official who had some control over the fate of the

Christians, it is easy to establish a context for Luke-Acts. His being a Roman authority would also explain the particularly harsh attitude expressed toward the Jews, the villains of the piece who do not deserve the favor of the Romans.

4. The time of the writing is as important as the recipients. If Luke-Acts was written at the time of Domitian's persecutions of Christians many pieces fall into place. Judaism was an "official religion" of the Roman Empire and, as such, exempt from the emperor worship demanded by Domitian. As far as we know, actual "emperor worship" was not unlike a modern loyalty oath. However, like their predecessors, the Romans had learned the importance to the Jews of the worship of one God and did not force them to violate their consciences in this matter. When Christians were viewed merely as a Jewish sect, they enjoyed the exemption of the Jews. As they achieved a separate identity, however, they could no longer claim a Jewish privilege. They either would have to be given their own status or, as Luke seems to argue, be regarded by the Romans as the true Jews.

5. Luke's opening chapters differ from Matthew's because his purpose is different. Matthew carries his genealogy back to Abraham, Luke (in Chapter 4) to Adam. The citing of Adam as the father of all humanity would explain why Christianity now includes so many Gentiles (maybe a majority by the time of Luke), and would argue implicitly that a true Jew is one who does God's will, not simply someone born into the family. The point is made strongly later in Luke's "special section," perhaps best illustrated by the parable of the Good Samaritan. Many of the incidents Luke reports are of highly creditable people within the established Jewish community witnessing to Jesus as Messiah. God Himself,

through the angels, also reveals just who Jesus is.

6. The "L" material in Luke's so-called special section is composed mainly of parables not found elsewhere in the New Testament. It opens with a story of Jesus' rejection by a Samaritan village because they recognize him as a true Jew. Following are mainly "kingdom" parables that seem to identify those who please God and thus inherit his kingdom. The most powerful are the parables of the Good Samaritan (10:29–37), the prodigal son (15:11–32), and the Pharisee and the publican (18:9–14). Taken in sum they seem to argue that those who claim God's blessing do not always receive it, but those who follow God's intention do, thus being real Jews.

7. Each time Luke strays from the order of Mark, most often by adding to that story, he does so with purpose. Even a casual reader can surmise that part of his purpose is to champion the integrity of the religion that Jesus taught over and against that represented by the Jews of Palestine.

8. Jesus' miracles in Mark did not immediately convince anyone that Jesus was Messiah. An act of faith was required. In Luke the miracles not only bring recognition of Jesus' messiahship but are one cause for his widespread following among the Jews, a sign that he was special.

9. Eyewitness reports are important in Luke. The credibility of the witnesses is well established, as are the events they witness and report. Note the stories of **Simeon** (2:25–35) and **Anna** (2:36–38) as early examples.

10. If Christianity makes the claim as the true Judaism that should enjoy the status of an "official religion," obviously Judaism must be seen as having abandoned its intended role. Luke-Acts seems constantly to make such a case. A poignant illustration is found in Chapter 12 (1–12), although examples abound throughout.

11. Neither Jesus nor any of his followers is ever found guilty of any crime by the Roman courts, according to Luke-Acts. The Jews are the accusers and, finally, the judge and the jury. Although Pilate, the governor of Judaea, finds no criminality in Jesus, this Roman official gives in to the demands of the Jews and orders **Barabbas** released and Jesus crucified. Afterward, the Roman centurion at the cross is quoted as saying, "This was a great and good man" (23:47). The same theme is continued in regard to the early church leaders in Acts. The Christians are innocent of any crime other than offending established Judaism by proclaiming Jesus as the promised Messiah.

12. The division of history into eras places Christianity in the ongoing scheme of God's intentions. Jesus is portrayed as beginning a new chapter in a continuing history, not displacing Judaism but moving it beyond the confines of the past as God again enters history and reveals himself. The Church (in Acts) becomes the final expression of that continuing revelation, witnessed to by the demonstration of the presence of God's spirit in its midst.

13. The author of Matthew cites the Old Testament to show how Jesus fulfilled Jewish messianic expectation. Luke's uses the Old Testament differently, often placing the quotations in the mouths of the characters who, by their use, connect past and present. In both cases the intention is to identify Jesus as the Jewish Messiah. Luke simply let his witnesses perform the task.

14. The presence of Acts as a part of the original account testifies strongly to the intentions of the author. While Matthew seems to try to convince Jews that Jesus is the Messiah and a proper extension of Judaism, Luke seems to attempt to convince those outside Judaism. Just as God had manifested himself in Jesus, a point testified to by those within Judaism, he continued in that manifestation in the life and ministry of the ongoing church. What Jesus began was continued by those who followed him in the church. God's presence was demonstrated in such ways as the spirit at **Pentecost** (Acts 2:1–36), the miraculous releases from prison (e.g., 5:17–21), and the ability to perform miracles like those of Jesus (e.g., 9:32–42). Paul, once the chief antagonist of Christianity within Judaism, had become its chief missionary spokesman after a dramatic conversion experience. The respected Rabbi Gamaliel counsels that if the new Christian movement is not of God, it will die of its own accord. Luke seems to have a broader audience in mind as he has Gamaliel saying of Christianity, "but if it does in fact come from God you will not only be unable to destroy [Peter and the other apostles], but you might find yourselves fighting against God" (Acts 5:39).

Our Résumé of Luke

Taken as a whole, Luke-Acts portrays Christianity as the Judaism God intended it to be. Regardless of whether this work was written as an apology for the church, it served needs far beyond that function from its very early existence. Regardless of whether it helped to convince the Romans that Christianity ought to be given the status of an "official religion" (apparently such status was not granted until the fourth century), it reminded the Christian community of its heritage and the continuing evidence of God's presence among them, for encouragement in times of persecution.

Viewing history as ongoing, Luke-Acts assumes that God has always been present in its midst. In each stage of history God has revealed himself, first in the Law and prophets, most perfectly in Jesus, and finally by the presence of his eternal spirit manifest in the life of his followers. Jesus is the link between the past and the future, for it is in his life and teaching that all is to be understood.

The author states clearly that he is relying on tradition to make his case. The picture that he paints affirms that Christianity is not a new movement begun in the first century, but is rather the long-established heritage of Judaism as God himself intended it.

Luke's story begins with the account of the birth of John the Baptist, adding details not available elsewhere and bearing striking similarity to the story of the beginnings of Judaism with the birth of Isaac to Abraham and Sarah. Tying the birth stories of John and Jesus together as a continuing drama defines more fully each character and his role in God's plan. The integrity of the stories is affirmed by a hoard of unimpeachable witnesses. One almost gets a sense of reading a well-prepared legal brief in which all the facts are established in anticipation of challenge. Using the story that has been reported already by Mark, this author makes important additions to the briefer account, an account that might not serve his purpose. To achieve his purpose, the author of Luke-Acts must make use of all materials available to him.

Having supplied detail not before published of events surrounding the circumstances of Jesus' birth and an event of childhood, the author takes up the story as told by Mark. He uses the order and detail of Mark more faithfully than does the author of Matthew, and both his deletions and additions form an important clue to what he is proclaiming. Most significant, perhaps, of the additions are those found in Luke's "special section" (9:51–18:14):

9:51–56	The inhospitality of the Samaritan village.
9:59–60	"Let the dead bury the dead."
10:17–20	The return of the seventy-two.
10:29–37	The Good Samaritan.
10:38–42	Mary and Martha.
11:5–8	The friend at midnight.
11:27–28	The blessedness of Jesus' mother.
12:13–21	The rich fool.
12:47–48	The servant's wages.
13:1–9	Repentance or destruction.
13:10–17	The healing of the woman with a spirit of infirmity.
13:31–33	The departure from Galilee.
14:1–6	The healing of a man with dropsy.
14:7–14	Teaching on humility.
15:11–32	The prodigal son.
16:1–8	The unjust steward.
16:14–15	The hypocrisy of the Pharisees.
16:19–31	The rich man and **Lazarus.**
17:7–10	The servant's wages.
17:11–19	The healing of the ten lepers.
17:20–21	On the kingdom of God.
18:1–8	The unjust judge.
18:9–14	The Pharisee and the publican.

Much of this added material is obviously parabolic, teaching who it is that pleases God and who, thus, will enjoy the fruits of his kingdom. In addition, it is in this section that Jesus sets his face toward Jerusalem, his journey becoming the occasion for a large body of teaching. As with Mark, the narration of these last days dominates the story in terms of length and importance, for it is in those days that the role and mission of Jesus are most fully interpreted. What is true of Mark can also be said of Luke; each is a passion story with a long introduction.

It is not without significance that Luke

begins his "special section" with the story of Jesus' rejection by the Samaritan villagers. Note the reason: Jesus was on a pilgrimage to Jerusalem, thus a part of the Orthodox Jewish community. The enmity of the outcasts of Judaism, the Samaritans, is testimony once again that Jesus was regarded as a part of ongoing Judaism.

Three of the most remembered parables of Jesus throughout Christian history are found only in this section of Luke: the parables of the good Samaritan, the prodigal son, and the Pharisee and the publican. Though they have internal consistency with the other material found in this section, one has to wonder about the source of these powerful stories and why, if they were known by the other Evangelists, they were not included in the other synoptic accounts. Whatever their source, their purpose remains the same, to make clear Jesus' teaching about who was pleasing to God. As for the parable of the Good Samaritan, the beginning of the story is found in both Mark and Matthew. Jesus is asked by a lawyer (a Pharisee in Matthew; a scribe in Mark) what he must do to inherit eternal life. The response is that he must love God and his neighbor. But the story continues in Luke when the lawyer, seeking to justify himself, asks the question, "Who is my neighbor?" Jesus responds with the parable, and afterward he asks who proved to be the neighbor in the story. The lawyer answers, "The one who took pity on [the unfortunate traveler]" to which Jesus responds, "Go, and do the same yourself."

What if the question were changed to "Who was the best Jew?" Would that alter the point of the story? Would the best Jew be the priest or the Levite who had the outward symbols or the one who did what was pleasing to God? Could not the same point be made for the other two parables as well? Elsewhere in Luke's account (11:37–44) Jesus is criticized by the Pharisees for not washing before a meal, and he responds by chiding the Pharisees for their neglect of "justice and the love of God." Criticized for healing a man with dropsy on the sabbath, he again questions the accusers' true compassion (14:1–6). Again and again the case made in Luke is that the religion practiced and taught by Jesus is both more pleasing to God and consistent with his intentions than the loveless application of which he accuses the Pharisees. Like Matthew, Luke makes his case for Christianity as Judaism as God intended, but Luke is speaking to an open-minded Gentile audience. Surely, he seems to argue, any reasonable person can determine the merits of the case.

You have been asked to read the closing portions of Luke, incorporating material found exclusively in his work. Christianity has always based its belief in Jesus as Messiah on faith in his resurrection from the dead. Look at Luke's additions to the accounts you have already read. He establishes a strong link with ongoing Jewish messianic expectation:

> Then he said to them, "You foolish men! So slow to believe the full message of the prophets! Was it not ordained that the Christ should suffer and so enter into his glory?" Then starting with Moses and going through all the prophets, he explained to them the passages throughout the scriptures that were about himself. (24:25–27)

Jesus' postresurrection appearances are also affirmed by a veritable cloud of witnesses, not just the disciples. The resurrection, like everything that affirms Jesus as Messiah, is a totally public event.

Luke, of course, does not end his story here. In Acts he amplifies his report of the ascension, then continues with the story of the church. As Jews bore witness to Judaism, so the church continues to bear witness to the present and the future. God remains his own best witness by the observable presence of his spirit in the life and work of the church.

Thus, we have the picture. In the Gospel of Luke, Jesus is the Messiah, fulfilling the old and giving direction to the new. We have the testimony of countless witnesses not only of his words, but of his deeds. That testimony remains visible by the active presence of the spirit manifest in the life of the church. Luke would argue, "How could anyone dispute such overwhelming evidence? Christianity is Judaism properly expressed. If any have deserted their heritage, it is the Jews." For Luke the image of Jesus is that of a bridge linking the past and future through himself.

THE GOSPEL WITHIN THE GOSPELS

Now that you have read the individual Gospels with an effort toward determining the particular purpose and message of each, you need to become aware of another dimension of the study of the Gospels. Christianity is not based on any individual Gospel, but rather on the combined picture drawn by the four Gospel accounts of the life of Jesus in the New Testament. While each Gospel has its own emphasis, and while some Christians tend to be partial to one specific Gospel, the proclamation that is the central message of Christianity—that Jesus is the Christ—is drawn from all four Gospels. Because that is so, and because every Gospel is somewhat different (as you have already observed in studying the three synoptics and as you will see again when studying the Gospel of John), throughout history there has been a continuing debate among some Christians as to how the Jesus of the Gospels is to be understood, or what belief in him as the Christ requires of the believer. While this text is not designed to deal with all of these issues, it does not seem appropriate to leave our study of the synoptic Gospels without making you aware of some of the questions or issues that arise out of such a study.

The first question one encounters when wrestling with the presentation of Jesus in the Gospel accounts is whether he was a self-proclaimed messiah. If one had only the Gospel of Mark as a source, the answer, as you have seen, would more than likely be "No." The answer becomes more difficult with the presentation of Jesus in Matthew and Luke, and by the time you read the Gospel of John at the end of this study you will discover that the issue becomes only more confusing. Are the accounts contradictory? Some argue they are. Some argue that in Mark we have more of an account of what Jesus taught about himself, in John more of an account of what the church taught about him. Obviously it is not that simple. In the presentation of Jesus in Mark, Jesus had a sense of messianic awareness, even if he did not proclaim himself messiah throughout his public ministry. His message, that of preparing people for the coming of the kingdom of God, conveyed a sense of preparing for the messianic age in first-century Palestine and at least in that way affirms a messianic dimension to his ministry.

Questions like this one are endless, but some of the more common ones that you will want to explore as you continue your own studies will include:

1. What do the Gospels ask a person to do in response to their proclamations (i.e., What do the Gospels assert one has to do to become a Christian?)? What do they ask readers to believe about Jesus or do in response to that belief? Is there a single answer, or should one seek clues in all four Gospel accounts?

2. As portrayed in the various Gospels, what did Jesus teach about himself? Did he claim equality with God, did he suggest that he was a God? What did Jesus ask people to do in response to his message or to their understanding of who he was or what he was about? How is this question different from the one above?

3. What did Jesus teach about the Law? Are the demands made of human behavior in the Sermon on the Mount meant to be a new Christian ethic, a set of rules one is to follow as a Christian, or an ethic that can be followed only after the kingdom of God has been established upon the earth? Is the Sermon on the Mount reflective of Jesus' ethical teachings as a whole, or is it a construction by the author of Matthew to convince Jews that Jesus took the Law seriously? What do the individual Gospels and the Gospels as a whole suggest about this subject?

4. Did Jesus have a growing sense of messianic awareness during his days of active ministry (as might be implied in the Gospel of Mark), or was there a strong sense of messianic awareness throughout his ministry, as implied in the Gospel of Luke? How was he understood by the audiences to which he addressed himself during the period of his ministry? Did they think of him as a messiah then or later? How does one resolve what seem to be contradictory portrayals of the Jesus of history found in the various Gospel accounts?

5. What do the Gospels imply Jesus taught about the kingdom of God? Was it something that was to come in or near his own lifetime, in the far distant future, or was it an *experience* more than an event, an experience available to every individual in his or her own lifetime? Does this teaching differ among the Gospels or is it consistent in all of them?

As in other areas, you can make your own list from your own observations. The questions above are but samples of the kind of issues that arise as one encounters the various Gospel accounts of Jesus as the Christ.

Some view the raising of these issues as improper: The Gospels are not contradictory, they assert—they are complementary. The reason these issues seem like problems to some,

they contend, is because those persons do not understand that each Gospel simply provides another dimension to the life of Jesus as the Christ of faith. To call them problems is really a reflection of the lack of religious insight on the part of those who would raise the question.

Whatever your perspective, divisions within Christianity are often most easily explained by the fact that not everyone comes to the same understanding of the material studied; an entire body of literature has been produced concerning the portrayal of Jesus in the individual Gospels. Not all religious communities that use the Bible as scripture understand it in the same way. The gospel understood and proclaimed out of the Gospels does indeed vary within various segments of the Christian community.

ACTS

✦ **READ**   *Chapters 1–12 of the Acts of the Apostles*

Before we move on we need to look briefly at the second part of Luke's Gospel, the Acts of the Apostles. If Acts was written, as most now believe, as a whole with the Gospel, it simply extends the story of Jesus to the study of the first generation of the church.

Organization

The first part of Acts (Chs. 1–12) reports on the birth and growth of the church in Palestine. The second part (Chs. 13–28) deals with the missionary activities of Paul, far beyond Palestine.

Acts is not simple history, although in broad strokes it probably provides a fairly helpful overview of how Christianity formed itself, the problems it encountered, and how it spread throughout the Roman world. It should be read, however, in the same way you read the Gospels. Its purpose is not simply to report history, but to proclaim the faith that Christianity is indeed Judaism as Yahweh intended it. Its stories, rooted in history, proclaim that the presence of God in the midst of his church is visible in that history, both in the acts of its adherents and in the survival and prospering of the movement that proclaims Jesus as Messiah.

The stories include:

1. The story of the ascension (1:1–11)

2. The birth of Christianity, including the occasion of Pentecost (1:12–3:26)

3. The struggle with the Jews as the Christian sect grew (4:1–5:42)

4. The early missions (6:1–8:40)

5. The conversion of Saul (9:1–30)

6. Other events in Palestine (9:30–12:25)

7. The ministry of Paul (13:1–28:31)

As many have observed, the work might better be titled "Some of Acts of Some of the Apostles." It is selective, for history is obviously not its main purpose. It is more accurate to call it a continuing apology for early Christianity as true Judaism, beginning with the story of Jesus and continuing through the first generation of the church founded on the belief that Jesus was the true Messiah.

Acts as a History of the Early Church

Most scholars do not rely on Acts as their only source of information about the first generation of Christianity. This book does not tell us the fate of most of the apostles, nor does it tell us how Paul died, although the author must have known, since he compiled his record after the death of most of the first generation of Christians and because he was Paul's friend. The account of the **Council of Jerusalem** (Acts 15) does not totally harmonize with Paul's reporting of the same event in Galatians, and some have raised other questions about the historic reliability of Luke's second volume.

It must be remembered that Luke does not claim to be an eyewitness to all he writes about (Luke 1:1–2), and only in the "we" sections of Acts (Acts 16:11 ff) is there any indication that the author was present at the events reported. Not writing for history, Luke still uses the arena of history to set his story. In that sense, he does take history seriously, and we can safely assume that he gives a general, though incomplete, picture of how Christianity began and grew in the time from Jesus' death until early in the seventh decade of the common era.

That history can be outlined as follows:

I. Jesus Ascends to Heaven (Acts 1:6–11).

II. Church Founded at Jerusalem (1:12–4:37).
   A. The replacement of Judas (1:15–26).
   B. The Spirit of Pentecost (2:1–36).
   C. The first converts (2:37–47).
   D. Evidence of the Spirit in the church (3:1–5:42).

III. The Early Church (6:1–12:25)
   A. Diaspora Jews included in Christianity (6:1–7:60).
   B. Missions outside Jerusalem (8:4–8:40).
      1. Samaritans included (8:4–8).
      2. Diaspora Jews included (8:26–40).
   C. Conversion of Saul (9:1–30).
   D. Peter's vision: Gentiles included (10:1–48).
   E. The church at Antioch (11:19–30).
   F. Peter's arrest and deliverance (12:1–35).

IV. Paul and His Missionary Activity (13:1–28:31).
   A. First missionary journey (13:1–14:28).
   B. The Jerusalem Council (15:1–35).
   C. Second missionary journey (15:36–18:17).
   D. Third missionary journey (18:18–20:38).

E. Journey to Jerusalem, arrest, and trial (21:1–26:32).

F. Journey to Rome (27:1–28:31).

This outline shows that Christianity began as a sect within Judaism. Its first converts were fellow Jews from Jerusalem, followed by Diaspora Jews who returned to Jerusalem to live. Moving outside Jerusalem, it next spread to the despised Samaritans, the Diaspora Jews from beyond the borders of Palestine, and finally non-Jews (Gentiles). The church at Antioch seemed to be the first to include a significant number of Gentiles and, for that reason, it was there that the name "Christian" began to be applied to the group. The name identified persons who were no longer simply a Jewish sect, among whom were some unacceptable to traditional Judaism.

The missionary activities of Paul beyond Palestine began in the midst of the Diaspora Jewish community. It spread from there to the "God fearers" and, only later, to other Gentiles. By the end of Paul's missionary career Christianity had spread from Palestine all the way to the capital of the Roman Empire. It had achieved an identity of its own and was well on its way to becoming an important religious force in the Western world. What is clear in Acts, as it was in Luke, is that the author believes that those Jews who accepted Jesus as the Christ were those most pleasing to God. He also asserts that Christians were those whom God had blessed in their endeavors, interceding time and again in history to deliver them from unjust punishment. The visible presence of God's spirit is but another manifestation that God affirms this new community that affirms Jesus as Messiah.

Though written for other purposes, Acts has provided us with a helpful view of how this initial thrust occurred, showing that expansion was both a blessing and a curse. No longer able to appeal to a common religious heritage among its adherents, the remainder of Christian history faced the problems brought by the inclusion of such a divergent community. The next works we examine help illustrate the problems and responses to those problems provided by the expanded environment in which Christianity was to exist.

STUDY QUESTIONS

1. What is a Gospel?

2. Describe the "synoptic problem" and indicate how its solution is helpful in our study of the synoptic Gospels.

3. How would you explain the "messianic secret" as a major theme in the Gospel of Mark?

4. Explain the idea that Mark is a passion story with a long introduction.

5. Discuss why it is suggested that the theme of the Gospel of Mark might be "a demand for faith."

6. Explain the basis upon which some suggest that the original Mark ended at 16:8.

7. Discuss Matthew in light of the suggestion that the original audience of this Gospel was the Pharisaic community at Jamnia.

8. How would you describe Jesus' attitude toward the Law as portrayed in Matthew?

9. Discuss the Sermon on the Mount as a key to the understanding of Matthew's Gospel.

10. Identify the major portions of Matthew that are unique to that Gospel and indicate what in that material might be helpful in one's understanding of its purpose or message.

11. What is meant when one speaks of the Gospel of Luke as the first Christian apology?

12. Discuss the significance of the fact that in Luke no one associated with early Christianity is ever portrayed as being found guilty of any crime, despite such accusations by the Jews.

13. What is important about the "special section" of Luke to our understanding of the purpose and message of that Gospel?

14. What insights are provided to the purpose and message of Luke in the materials found only in his volume?

15. Why is it significant that Luke and Acts were probably once a single book?

16. Discuss Acts as a history of the first generation of Christianity.

SUGGESTED READINGS

Beach, Curtis. *The Gospel of Mark* (Harper & Row, New York, 1959).

Best, Ernest. *Mark: The Gospel as Story* (T and T Clark, Edinburgh, 1983).

Bornkamm, G., G. Barth, and H. J. Held. *Tradition and Interpretation in Matthew* (Westminster Press, Philadelphia, 1963).

Bultmann, R. *History of the Synoptic Tradition* (Harper & Row, New York, 1968).

Cadbury, J. H. "Acts of the Apostles," *The Interpreter's Dictionary of the Bible*, Vol. 1 (Abingdon Press, Nashville, 1962).

Conzelmann, H. *The Theology of St. Luke* (Faber and Faber, London, 1960).

Cranfield, C. E. B. "Mark, Gospel of," *The Interpreter's Dictionary of the Bible*, Vol. 3 (Abingdon Press, Nashville, 1962).

Davies, W. D. *The Sermon on the Mount* (Cambridge, New York, 1966).

Grant, F. C. "Matthew, Gospel of," *The Interpreter's Dictionary of the Bible*, Vol. 3 (Abingdon Press, Nashville, 1962).

Kingsbury, Jack Dean. *Matthew as Story* (Fortress Press, Philadelphia, 1986).

Orchard, Bernard, and Harold Riley. *The Order of the Synoptics. Why Three Synoptic Gospels?* (Mercer University Press, Macon, 1987).

Rowlingson, D. T. "Synoptic Problem," *The Interpreter's Dictionary of the Bible*, Vol. 4 (Abingdon Press, Nashville, 1962).

Streeter, B. H. *The Four Gospels: A Study of Origins* (Macmillan, New York, 1930).

Swanson, Reuben J. *The Horizontal Line Synopsis of the Gospels* (Western North Carolina Press, Dillsboro, 1975).

Taylor, V. "Luke, Gospel of," *The Interpreter's Dictionary of the Bible,* Vol. 3 (Abingdon Press, Nashville, 1962).

Throckmorton, B. H. *Gospel Parallels* (Thomas Nelson, Camden, N.J., 1952).

Tiede, David L. *Luke: Augsburg Commentary on the New Testament* (Augsburg Press, Philadelphia, 1988).

Tyson, Joseph B., Ed. *Luke-Acts and the Jewish People* (Augsburg Press, Philadelphia, 1988).

TEN

OTHER LETTERS AND A SERMON

THE NATURE OF THE MATERIAL

Scholars have much less certainty about the authorship of the books studied in this chapter, the date they were written, or the audience to which they were addressed than they have about the earlier works we have examined. Questions have surrounded these works since their first consideration for inclusion in the New Testament; thus those who raise doubts about, for example, their authorship are not to be regarded as irreverent upstarts who do not take the Bible seriously. Each of these works had some problem in being accepted into a permanent place in Christian scripture. However, these books are not less valuable than the remaining books of the New Testament, for once they became secure within the canon they shared equal authority with their companions.

It is important to remember that all the works now part of the Bible carry the authority of scripture for those who *accept* the Bible as their scriptures. Those who established the canon used criteria they believed to be met by all the works they included. They had resolved for themselves any lingering questions about the authenticity of the works; they had come to accept their claims of authorship. The inclu-

sion of the books we study accurately reflects what was believed about them in the fourth century of the common era. Even if a work was not written by the author it claims, it is no less valuable to our understanding of early Christianity, nor contrary to its tradition. If those who decided on the authenticity of an individual work had found it not in the spirit of the ongoing tradition they were dedicated to uphold, they simply would not have included it, a practice well established by the works known to have been excluded. The presence of any book says it was considered to be consistent with and reflective of the continuing tradition contained in the scripture as a whole and what that scripture represented. Thus, the authors we refer to as anonymous did not write with the intention of deceiving anyone; to write in the name of Paul, or Peter, or another apostle was instead an effort to protect and pass on the tradition that rested on these early leaders. Such authors, if they were other than those the works claim, sought to speak in the name and spirit of those who had been present at the forming of the tradition.

The works discussed in this chapter are all identified as letters or epistles, and all but one (Hebrews) make internal claim to authorship.

Probably, however, Hebrews should not be considered a letter, for it is more like a sermon or religious tract. The letters we discuss under the classification of the **catholic Epistles** differ from the letters of Paul in that they are not addressed to specific audiences. They were obviously written for widespread circulation among the Christian community, a point not without importance in the assumptions made by modern scholarship about them.

The letters that identify their author as Paul but were not included in our earlier discussion, of course, are generally assumed to have been written by others. The dating of all these works, which is a matter of broad speculation, is discussed only in connection with particular works for which the issue is important.

The works are divided into three categories: the **Paulinists,** the catholic Epistles, and a sermon or tract (Hebrews). This division is somewhat artificial, but it is a convenient way to consider the material. Paulinist material makes an internal claim to Paul's authorship, but there is enough contrary evidence that seems to outweigh the claim. These letters probably were written in the name of Paul after his death, in the spirit of that portion of the tradition over which his strong influence continued. The catholic Epistles are addressed to a universal (catholic) audience. This grouping does not imply that the works have much else in common unless further commonality is specifically identified. Hebrews, the sermon or tract, is dealt with separately simply because it is significantly different in literary form.

THE PAULINISTS

The works that make an internal claim to have been written by Paul but are now believed by many not to be the product of that apostle are as follows:

Ephesians

1 and 2 Timothy

Titus

Their authorship has been questioned on the basis of observations made from critical examination of style, language, theology, and the historic circumstances the letters address. In the case of the **pastoral Epistles** (1 and 2 Timothy, Titus), early skepticism surrounding the source of these letters has also been an important consideration in the denial by some that they are genuine works of Paul.

As indicated earlier, scholars need to be conservative in their rejection of tradition. When we rely on what tradition has to say about a certain work, we must be ready to ask about the reliability of that tradition. And you have already learned that all tradition is not equally strong. Therefore it is appropriate to ask where a tradition originated, who formed it, and on what information it was based. Did the originators report their own information or pass along what they had received? How reliable are their sources? Did the tradition originate near the time of the event reported, or later? Obviously the answers to such questions will be important tools in one's testing of the reliability of tradition. Obviously, too, critical judgments about the answers are necessary before a conclusion can be drawn.

How reliable is a given work in telling us about itself? If a work claims to be written by Paul, do we have the right to reject its own testimony? The answer is the same as our response to the question about the reliability of tradition. Namely, we accept the claim of a work until it is no longer reasonable to do so. As with tradition, a single item that would call an assertion into question usually is not enough to lead to rejection. Only an accumulation of points that question the assertion and cannot be set aside in a reasonable manner will induce most scholars to consider rejection of what a tradition, or a work itself, asserts.

Criteria for Evaluating Claims to Authorship

The kinds of critical questions applied to these works have led many (not all) serious scholars to reject both established tradition and the internal claims of the works in regard to the authorship of Paul. Despite some disagreement on specific points, the major reasons can be summarized as follows.

Language. Many scholars conclude that the vocabulary of the so-called Paulinist works is not that of Paul. Comparing the letters that all accept as those of Paul, they point out significant numbers of words in the questioned works that do not appear in the others. Since each letter has its own purpose and audience, and since the subjects vary with such changes in circumstance, the expanded vocabulary is not in itself sufficient to cause us to dismiss the authorship of Paul. The number of new words, however, is a critical factor, and Ephesians introduces more than ninety.

In addition to the words selected, their usage is significant. For example, we can compare Paul's use of the word "faith" in Romans or Galatians and then observe how it is specifically defined in Hebrews (another work later attributed by some to Paul). "Would the same author use this word both ways?" is the question the scholar is bound to ask. You should take advantage of such scholarly observations and then make personal critical judgments.

Style. What is the author's literary style? Does he write in short, concise sentences in one letter and use long, complex sentences in another? Style is hard to determine when reading works in translation, but it is not impossible to evaluate. Style alone has never been a deciding factor in rejecting any work as Paul's, but it has

been added to the accumulated evidence that has led to rejection of long-held assumptions about some of them. The best example is found in Ephesians, where long involved sentence structure is unlike that of the other works accepted as belonging to Paul.

Historical Circumstances. Does the work fit into the known or assumed circumstances of the times of the purported author? Is it reasonable to assume that the reflected history of these works is in keeping with our best knowledge of the time and circumstances of Paul? This, of course, is not an easy question. History of first-century Christianity is elusive at best, and some assumptions about that history held until just a few decades ago have been seriously challenged. In addition, much of what we assume about that history is derived from the New Testament itself and includes the assumptions about when a particular work was produced and by whom. What was the fate of Paul? Was he released from house arrest in Rome (as perhaps implied at the end of Acts), and did he do further missionary work in Spain, only to return to Rome to be arrested again and finally martyred? The truth of the matter is that the answers to these questions are not firmly known; yet the way they are answered often strongly informs a reader's final conclusions about particular works.

Theology. Is the particular work consistent with what is known of the theology of an individual? Would Paul, for example, speak of the "holy apostles," or give them a place of special honor, as is done in Ephesians? Would he speak of the apostles as founders of the church?

Evaluating the Evaluations

The foregoing suggestions indicate the kinds of questions that have been asked. As can be imagined, serious and competent scholars do not agree on the answers, nor do similar answers always produce the same conclusions. Some, for example, acknowledge a difference in language and style but assert that it does not weigh conclusively against Paul's authorship. Different conclusions can be drawn from the same evidence, resulting in assertions and counterassertions, conclusions and counter-conclusions. Both are included in our discussion so that you can make independent judgment in regard to specific works.

EPHESIANS

Criteria for Evaluating Claims to Authorship

◆ **READ** *The Letter of Paul to the Church at Ephesus*

Ephesians is a letter that makes internal claim to have been written by Paul (1:1) and yet is considered by many scholars to be the work of another person. Those who argue against Paul's authorship include the following among those points that lead to their conclusions:

1. Ephesians contains more than ninety new words not found in the earlier epistles considered genuinely the work of Paul.

2. The style is not typical of Paul. This work contains long, involved sentences, unlike the more concise style in Paul's other letters.

3. It depends heavily on Colossians.

4. Its theology is not Pauline. The high honor given to the "holy apostles" does not reflect Paul's prevailing attitude implied elsewhere.

5. The author seems more like his non-Jewish audience (2:1–6) than the Paul with strong Jewish roots of the other materials.

Those who defend Paul's authorship counter:

1. Paul's use of secretaries, as on other occasions, is not indicated here. The difference in language in this work can be attributed to his penning the letter in his own hand.

2. Unlike Paul's other works, Ephesians seems more like a sermon than a letter. After a brief salutation, Paul addresses a community to whom he cannot preach in person but with whom his relationship is well established. That would account for the difference in style.

3. Romans and Galatians display the same kind of similarity. Colossians and Ephesians could have been written close together in time.

4. Paul had a high regard for tradition and constantly used it in the works considered genuine. Surely he had high regard for those who were original bearers of that tradition, the apostles.

5. Verses 1–6 of Chapter 2 do not necessarily suggest that the author is not Jewish. Paul could be simply identifying himself with humanity in general.

These arguments, and others involved in this debate, must be considered fully before reaching a decision about Paul's authorship. Even those who suggest that Paul is not the author, however, concede that the work reflects the spirit of Paul. Many accept the idea that it was originally prepared by the person who collected Paul's correspondence, as a cover letter to introduce the readers of the Epistles to the mind and spirit of Paul. Although Paul's theological statement represented by his letter to the Romans would itself provide a good introduction, the countersuggestion above has enjoyed nearly equal acceptance. The works included in the so-called Paulinist letters probably would not have been accepted into the canon if they had been perceived as violating the spirit of Paul. The early church fathers found nothing in the discrepancies we have described to warrant the exclusion from the canon of these works.

Content

The theme of Ephesians is unity. Some might say it is Christian unity, but perhaps it is best expressed as an assertion that the Christ event is the unifying religious force in human history. In the Christ event God has acted decisively to make salvation available to all the world, making Christianity all-inclusive (circumcised and uncircumcised, Jew and pagan). Unity is found in Christ. The theme is set in the introductory hymn (1:3–14). It is developed throughout the remainder of the chapters and perhaps most fully expressed in 4:1–6. All else is understood in relation to this concept of unity. This is no less true of the later ethical chapters. In sum, it is in the Christ event that God's purposes have been finally fulfilled, and its consequences are available to all regardless of original station in life. It is in the fulfillment offered in the Christian life that humankind can enjoy existence as it was intended, filled with harmony with others as well as with the God who offers it.

If Paul is not the author of Ephesians, still the work is in no way contrary to his teachings in his other epistles. While it does not focus on the concept of justification by grace through faith, neither does it belittle it. Rather it speaks of what the Christ event has done in making all equal before God. The Christ event is God's expression of his love for humankind, and the appropriate response is to accept that love and live a life worthy of that love. No one is more special than anyone else; all deserve the treatment that love issues forth. We should treat one another as God has treated us. Finally, we should recognize that we have been renewed, given new life, by the expression of God's love toward us, and our everyday life should express that. Our identity comes in being children of God; it is what binds all humans together, and our behavior should reflect that reality as an act of gratitude and witness.

You may want to review the outline of Romans; although it may seem much different, you may be surprised at the remarkable harmony reflected in those two works. If both are reflective of Paul's overall theology, as most suggest, they serve that role well. One might well be the summary of Paul himself, the other the summary of one who would honor Paul by circulating his work and introducing his thoughts in this letter.

1 AND 2 TIMOTHY, TITUS: THE PASTORAL EPISTLES

◆ **READ** *The Letters from Paul to Timothy and Titus*

The pastoral Epistles have a history of their own. They were not included in the list of Paul's letters assembled by the heretic **Marcion** when he made what some consider the first attempt to canonize the New Testament in the middle of the second century. Some early Christians accused Marcion of excluding these letters for his own devious reasons. An equally plausible explanation is that these letters were not known to him, because they were not in Paul's collected letters available to him. Although Bishop Irenaeus did list them in his list of works attributed to Paul later in the same century and indicated that they were being circulated among some Christians and were accepted as being written by Paul, they did not appear in all such lists during the next century. They seemed to have a literary history of their own, a history separate from the other works of Paul. They either appeared together in such lists, or they were excluded together, suggesting to some that they were being circulated apart from Paul's other collected works before they joined that larger collection in some quarters. Some question as to whether they should be attributed to Paul remained, even among those who had the letters available to them and listed them with Paul's other works. One has only to review that history to realize that these three epistles enjoyed less acceptance as genuine works of Paul than any of the other works attributed to him or circulated in his name. Their presence or absence in canonical lists over the first centuries, as well as the early debate that surrounded them, has always made their inclusion among Paul's collected works a debatable issue.

The term "pastoral Epistles" reflects a presumed preoccupation with church order. Careful reading, however, makes clear that such order is not the main subject matter. The main issue is orthodoxy, and the works refute contemporary heresies, not fully described, whose elements can be detected in the refutations.

Criteria for Evaluating Claims to Authorship

Those who reject Paul's authorship do so for several reasons, some of which are included below:

1. The Paul reflected in the pastoral Epistles is quite different from the man observed in what are considered to be Paul's genuine letters. The author of the pastoral Epistles seems to view religion as acceptance of a body of authoritative teaching, accompanied by a morality based on such acceptance. The genuine Paul, they assert, viewed religion more in terms of experience that later encouraged one to make individual moral judgments.

2. The pastoral Epistles lack a strong eschatological dimension.

3. The language of these epistles is more akin to second-century Christianity than it is to Paul's other works.

4. The descriptions of the church in the pastoral Epistles imply a much more highly developed institution than existed in the time of Paul.

5. The strong presence of heresy reflects a period of history beyond the time of Paul, probably as late as the second century.

6. The activities of Paul reflected in these epistles seem to be out of sequence with those in the accepted letters and in Acts. They also suggest a second imprisonment of Paul in Rome, an allegation not verifiable by history.

Those who do accept Paul's authorship would respond:

1. The theology of the pastoral Epistles is reflective of Paul. If the purpose is to refute heresy, it would be natural to emphasize right belief. Ethical exhortation is typical of Paul, and the exhortations included here are in the spirit of the purpose of the works, not contradictory to what he had always done.

2. Paul seemed to have concluded that Jesus would not return as soon as he had once expected, perhaps not in Paul's own lifetime. Since this change in attitude is reflected in what are considered Paul's genuine works, the absence of the expectation of Christ's early return here is not uncharacteristic.

3. Paul dictated most of his letters to secretaries, yet the personal letter to Philemon, which is accepted as genuine, gives no evidence of having been dictated. The language of the pastoral Epistles could be accounted for in that sense, for there is no indication that these personal letters were dictated.

4. We do not know with certainty the extent of the church's institutional development in Paul's time. The description in Acts, especially the church in Jerusalem at the time of the ordination of Stephen (Acts 6), might be taken to reflect rather mature organization very early in church history.

5. As with church structure, the presence and extent of heresy in early Christianity are diffi-

cult to date. There were obvious tensions in Paul's own time in regard to right belief. Who is to say that full-fledged heresies were not present during the apostle's ministry? Some would argue that Paul would consider the Judaizers heretics and would attack them as false teachers.

6. There are no discrepancies that cannot be resolved. Some tradition does indeed include missionary activity after Paul's first imprisonment in Rome, though it is a weak tradition and might have arisen out of an early attempt to authenticate the pastoral Epistles. There is no direct information to absolutely affirm such activity.

As can be seen, convincing arguments can be made on both sides, and you should investigate them all before drawing conclusions. Nothing in the pastoral Epistles themselves strongly violates the spirit of Paul as we know him. The works seem, however, to be more in the spirit of Paul than the product of his life. They contain nothing that contradicts what we know of Paul, but many elements suggest a period of Christianity more fully developed than the fledgling church of Paul's time. Paul probably would not have found it necessary to be so formal in instructing trusted coworkers who were absent only for a time. It is more likely that the letters were intended for a wider audience, a church that would profit from the influence of Paul in matters of great importance.

Content

A survey of the contents discloses a unity of material, which has led some to suggest that the division into separate letters is a literary device, that as a whole they can be considered a single encyclical address. Because they now exist as three, however, we may review them in their present state.

1 Timothy has a number of references to false teachers (heresies). First mentioned in 1:3–7, the subject is reintroduced in 4:1–16, 6:3–10, and finally 6:20–21. Church order and religious behavior are best understood in relation to the overriding concern for orthodoxy. Read the work in its entirety to discover its overall point of view. There is a strong regard for established tradition, which the author seems to be teaching rather than defending.

2 Timothy is also preoccupied with false teaching. Again expressing a strong regard for established tradition, 2 Timothy (3:14–17) highlights the appeal to scriptural authority reflecting what many believe to be the way the Hebrew Bible was regarded and used in the new Christian community. (Those verses have become proof texts for some modern Christians who argue the infallibility of all scripture.) As in 1 Timothy, the heresies are described as they are being refuted. The refutation again appeals to what has been established, a plea for orthodoxy.

Titus, like its companions, is concerned about false teachers. The elder is specifically defined as one who "can be counted on for both expounding the sound doctrine and refuting those who argue against it" (1:9). The moral instruction found in the remaining portions seeks to make clear the behavior expected of a true believer.

Two final observations are appropriate. First, these letters seem to have been produced during a period when Christians were being persecuted. The suggestion to pray for rulers (1 Tim. 2:1–2) and the reminder to be obedient to officials (Titus 3:1) indicate to some scholars that the letters are post-Pauline because such advice would have been timely in and after the reign of Domitian. The second has to do with instructions regarding women. 1 Timothy 2:9–15, for instance, has been used to help keep women in their place for centuries. However, these injunctions simply reflect the social attitudes of the times; they do not represent anything other than the advice of the author (2:1), never purporting to be a command from the Almighty. While the author does not view women as men's equals, neither does his attitude seem to coincide with that of Paul, who recruited some women to be leaders of local churches. The presence of these verses is another convincing argument to some that Paul is not the author.

THE CATHOLIC EPISTLES

James

1 and 2 Peter

Jude

The Nature of the Material

The term "catholic Epistles" refers to the idea that these epistles are addressed to a general audience, for circulation among a group of churches. Perhaps the most prominent common feature of these works is their collective struggle to be included in the New Testament canon. They were not totally accepted as scripture until well after the beginning of the fourth century, partly because of the controversy surrounding their origins, the tradition about them being less strong than with other New Testament works.

New Testament scholars believe that all these works were produced very late in the New Testament period, although there is no consensus on either date or authorship. Obviously 2 Peter was written after Paul's letters were in circulation and were finding acceptance as scripture (2 Pet. 3:15–16). That circumstance, however, would place 2 Peter beyond the lifetime of its purported author. But despite the controversy surrounding the catholic Epistles, these works are a valued part of the New Testament. Their inclusion in the canon gives them the status and authority of scripture, though they have not always enjoyed the same popularity as less controversial works among all Christians. Martin Luther, for instance, called the Book of James an "epistle of straw" and suggested that it probably should not be in the New Testament.

JAMES

✦ **READ** *Chapters 1–3 of the Letter of James*

The epistle of James was originally attributed to James, the brother of Jesus, a leader of the early church in Jerusalem. Most scholars now argue that we cannot be certain of its authorship. The work does, however, reflect the spirit of James as he is portrayed in Acts. That James seems to have been closely associated with the "circumcision party," a group in early Christianity that advocated that to be a Christian one must first become a Jew, be circumcised, and continue to be bound by the Law in at least such things as diet and Temple worship.

History

James did not receive mention in New Testament canonical lists until the third century, when **Origen** included his letter, though indicating some question about its authorship. Its place was not secure until the late fourth century, but even that did not prevent Luther's attack in the sixteenth century. The question of authorship has always been the central problem. The letter achieved general acceptance only when there was wide agreement that the James identified as author was the James who was the brother of Jesus.

The certain identity of James remains a difficult problem. A number of Jameses appear in the New Testament, and little is known of any of them. Probably best known are the two identified as disciples (James, son of Zebedee, and James, son of Alphaeus) and James, the brother of Jesus. James, the brother of Jesus, the person to whom this epistle is attributed, is mentioned in the Gospels, and some things are told about him in Acts. Although there is no indication that James was a follower of Jesus during the Galilean ministry, it is known that he achieved a position of leadership in the Jerusalem church. There is no direct report about his fate, but according to a strong tradition, he was martyred by the Jews in Jerusalem in the seventh decade of the common era. Roman Catholics, who hold the concept of the perpetual virginity of Mary, do not regard James of Jerusalem as the full brother of Jesus; yet attempts to identify him as a cousin or stepbrother of Jesus are not consistent with the way he is mentioned in the New Testament or with subsequent tradition.

Although James is associated with the branch of early Christianity that stressed its emergence out of Judaism, it is unfair to portray him as rigid, for he is credited in Acts 15 with reaching a compromise with Paul on what would be required of Gentile converts to Christianity. Nevertheless, it is fair to say that James worked best among Palestinian Jews and was most comfortable with the expression of Christianity practiced by that segment of the growing religious community.

The letter itself received no recorded attention until it was identified in a list of Origen's early in the third century. Its place in Christian scripture remained in dispute for almost two centuries. Although public discussion of this work always centered on the issue of authorship, the contents of the epistle were also a matter of concern.

Content

Martin Luther, among others, has described James as an argument against Paul's doctrine of justification by grace through faith. Those who hold such a view understand the letter as an argument for a return to a more Jewish kind of Christianity, in which the Law still held a place of central importance. Because the author of the letter obviously had Paul's teachings in mind (cf. James 2:14–26 with Romans 4:1–25), they conclude he is attempting to rebut Paul's doctrine. However, the letter itself suggests other ways to understand it.

The theme of the epistle is the "righteous of God," perhaps better stated as the kind of righteousness of which God approves and will therefore reward. The writer makes very clear that such righteousness comes from doing, not merely believing. The idea that faith without works is "dead" (see 2:17) can be taken to be the key to the epistle. Although some argue that in making this point the author supports the notion of righteousness through works refuted by Paul, it can just as well be argued that he is attempting to remove some distortions of Paul's teaching that had appeared. Some early Christians may have taken Paul's words so literally that the church fathers felt the need for clarification. The author was likely a member of a group that regarded James as its spiritual leader and wrote in his name to emphasize the importance of total commitment to one's new life in Christ, a commitment finally and most completely expressed in one's daily life. Paul, however, argued no less, as indicated by the amount of space he devoted to the ethical sections of his letters.

Thus, rather than viewing the epistle of James as a refutation of Paul, we can view it as an affirmation of Paul. Both Paul and the author of James have as the standard of Christian ethics the "law of love," and both argue that faith justifies. James seems to correct a view of faith as being simple right belief, arguing that true faith can be measured only in the fruits it produces in life. He attacks the lack of expression of love in concrete reality, as well as the expression of relationships honoring some persons over others. The virtues of true righteousness are best expressed in the life of faith in which the law of love prevails.

James provides an excellent example of how equally sincere persons can differ greatly in interpretation.

1 PETER

History

◆ **READ** *The First Letter of Peter*

Unlike its companion 2 Peter, 1 Peter has a history of wide acceptance since its first appearance on canonical lists. It was long attributed to the apostle Peter, although it did not appear on all the lists until late in the canonical period. On the basis of its contents and the circumstances it addresses, however, most scholars now believe it was produced late in the New Testament period by an unknown author.

The epistle identifies its author as Peter, apostle of Jesus Christ. Its audience well could have been facing persecution as a direct result of the Christian faith (2:13–17; 3:13–17; 4:12–19), as occurred during and after the reign of Domitian. Whenever it was written, the expectation of the parousia remains (4:7–11), evidence to many that Christians hoped for the imminent return of Jesus well into the second century.

A popular theory among twentieth-century New Testament scholars is that 1 Peter was originally a baptismal sermon, preached on the initiation of Gentile converts into the Christian community. Certainly no harm is done to the essential message if the letter is read with that view in mind. The writer himself states his purpose: "I write these few words to you . . . to encourage you never to let go this true grace of God to which I bear witness" (5:12). A baptism would be an appropriate occasion for such encouragement.

Content

This book is a tight blending of theology and the ethics that flow out of it. Founded on the proclamation of Jesus as Lord, attested to by his resurrection from the dead, it not only teaches important beliefs, it also gives instruction about how the life of faith is to be lived in a hostile world. Proper behavior, including serving as a witness to those outside the faith, can produce its own fruits. (It can also reduce the hostility of the civil authority, perhaps lessening persecution.) The ethics are not unlike those suggested by James, and like those seem to be rooted in the "law of love." An especially interesting point is that this small work contains a unique revelation. It is here that the doctrine of Christ's descent into hell is found (3:18–19, 4:6), the reference that in the spirit he went to preach to the spirits in prison.

2 PETER

History

◆ **READ** *The Second Letter of Peter*

2 Peter had a more difficult journey toward inclusion in the New Testament canon. Mentioned in the discussion of Origen, at the beginning of the third century, it was acknowledged even then as the subject of dispute. It was not included in many subsequent lists, and apparently did not enjoy widespread circulation or honor until near the time of its inclusion in the New Testament canon in the fourth century. Its history is the most difficult to establish of all the New Testament works. In addition, its heavy reliance on the epistle of Jude raises more questions than it answers. Addressing a community struggling with the problems caused by the continued delay of the parousia, the author quite clearly intends his audience to believe that the words are those of the apostle Peter. Yet those who regard style

and language find that this work fails all tests for being the work of the same author as 1 Peter. Most modern scholars believe it to be a product of the mid-second century, when much of the rest of the New Testament was already in use as scripture by Christians.

The arguments that surround 2 Peter are many, and most agree that it deserves the skepticism with which it is surrounded. It may not have been written by Peter, but a study of its contents will show that it is very much in the tradition of that apostle. Indeed, it has possessed the authority of scripture since its official inclusion in the canon.

Content

An outline might prove helpful for our discussion:

  I. Greeting (1:1–2)

 II. The Promises and Demands of God (1:3–11)

III. The Long-Established Witness (1:12–21)
   A. The apostles (12–18)
   B. The Old Testament (19–21)

IV. The Fate of Those Who Would Lead Others Astray (2:1–22)

 V. The Answer to the Doubters (Apocalypse) (3:1–13)

VI. The Conclusion (3:14–18)

In the greeting the author identifies himself as Simon Peter, the apostle. Since no specific audience is addressed, a general audience is implied. Immediately that audience is reminded of what God has done and what they must do in response, the very doing an assurance that they will not fall away. The validity of the testimony is found in the witness of the apostles, as well as that of established scripture. Note the attitude about scripture as inspired. Those who argue from the point of view of the total inspiration of scripture often use verses 20 and 21 of Chapter 1 as a proof text.

A condemnation of false teachers comes next. Those who lead others astray will surely face the judgment of God. Immediately follows the real purpose of the letter. Chapter 3 deals with the problems caused by the delay of the parousia and reminds the people of what they were taught in the past, relying on the tradition of the prophets and, later, of the apostles, who received their instruction directly from Jesus.

In the conclusion the author reminds the audience of relevant parts of Paul's letters but warns that these difficult passages are subject to distortion. These verses may be an allusion to some of the heresies of **gnosticism** of the second century.

The letter has a single purpose: to deal with the problem of the delayed parousia. Its purpose is served by establishing the authority of tradition in this matter, while condemning those who would distort that tradition. Not only is apostolic authority important, but so is the proper understanding of authoritative teaching. What better way to understand than in the name and spirit of one of the church's most prominent leaders? While it cannot be said that Peter is the author of this work, nothing in it violates the spirit of Peter or what we know of the tradition he helped form.

JUDE

History

◆ **READ** *The Letter of Jude*

Most studies deal with the epistle of **Jude** before 2 Peter because many believe that Jude is a source used by the author of 2 Peter. Like 2 Peter, Jude was not universally accepted in the early church, and the relation of the two epistles has not been fully established. If Jude was used by 2 Peter, that use would affirm its strong standing early among some Christians.

Who is Jude? He identifies himself in 1:1 as "servant of Jesus Christ and brother of James." His work is included in the New Testament because those who determined the content of that canon believed that it was written by Jude, another brother of Jesus. The author does not claim to be an apostle, for when he refers to the apostles he does not include himself. If he were indeed a brother of Jesus, it would be strange for him not to claim this identity in his opening. He does say that he is a Christian, a brother of a James who was probably known and honored by the original recipients of the letter. The letter, like the others in this group, does not designate an audience, although there is some indication that it had a particular segment of the community in mind.

Content

The letter is an attack on a form of heresy to which its recipients are being exposed. The nature of the heresy is not totally clear, but it appears to relate to the scandalous behavior of certain libertines. The letter recalls the tradition of which the recipients are a part, warns them of the pollution, and condemns the polluters. It uses the Book of Enoch for one of its quotations (1:14–16), indicating that that pseudepigraphical work (see Postlude) was still being used like scripture by some. Warning that the heretical behavior being attacked was a sign of the time of judgment drawing near, it counsels Christians not to abandon their faith in the face of temptation.

A SERMON: HEBREWS

The Nature of the Material

Though the Jerusalem Bible identifies Hebrews as "a letter addressed to a Jewish-Christian community," it is hardly a letter. It is much more like a sermon or a theological tract. Ascribed by tradition to Paul, it makes no claim to authorship within its own pages. Addressed to an audience steeped in the Jewish tradition, it establishes Jesus as the true successor to that tradition, not merely an extension of it. Hebrews is unlike the letters attributed to Paul in style, form, or **Christology,** leading most to designate the work as anonymous. Like the catholic Epistles, it was not universally known or used in Christianity until near the time of its inclusion in the canon (based on the belief that it was authored by Paul).

Many argue that Hebrews was not addressed to a Jewish audience, suggesting that its theology is much more akin to the Gentile Christianity of the postapostolic age. The majority, however, point out its extensive use of the Hebrew Bible, as well as its very theme, which would be of little interest to those who were not close to the roots of Judaism.

Hebrews is a highly theological work. Some scholars contend that the author ranks with the authors of John and Paul as one of the most original theologians in the New Testament. That, alone, makes it a volume deserving more than passing attention.

Content

✦ **READ** *The Letter to the Hebrews*

The work outlines itself in a fairly simple manner:

I. Jesus as Superior to All Predecessors (1:1–4:13)

II. Jesus as True High Priest (4:14–6:20)

III. The Sacrifice of Jesus (7:1–10:18)

IV. A Call for Continuance in Faith (10:19–12:29)

V. Final Exhortations and Salutation (13:1–25)

What makes Hebrews so much like a sermon is its theological affirmation followed by an appeal to moral response. This approach is consistent throughout, making the whole appear as a single exhortation, which it probably was. The question "So what?" is answered immediately in every instance. Scholars who conclude that the appropriate audience for such a sermon was a community faced with the perils of persecution view the book as a call for faithfulness, with the promise of rewards. They therefore classify it as apocalyptic literature. There is much in Hebrews to support that interpretation, and regardless of its original intention, it serves that purpose well.

The work begins by affirming the greatness of Jesus over all God's former revelations. Jesus is depicted as superior to the angels, as the only one who can bring redemption. Next he is proved to be the superior high priest, and it is established that he is a part of the superior priesthood of **Melchizedek,** greater than the later Levitical priesthood.

The order of Melchizedek becomes the occasion to show how the sacrifice of Jesus becomes superior to and supersedes the old sacrificial system of the established Levitical priesthood of Judaism. Christ is the mediator, as well, of a "better" covenant, founded on "better" premises. Using the imagery of the new covenant theology of Jeremiah (31:31–34), the author shows the superiority of that covenant and the rewards it offers.

The next portion includes a call for perseverance and seems a logical conclusion to all that has preceded. Included in this section is a definition of faith (Chapter 11) that seems to many to be much more Jewish than Pauline, faith here being a kind of steadfastness in the face of travail, or steadfast obedience.

The admonitions to continue in steadfast love and obedience are followed by final greetings. It is in the last lines that a hint of this work's relationship to Paul is revealed. Some even suggest that the whole of Chapter 12 is an addition, though there is no wide acceptance of that speculation.

In this chapter we have reviewed a wide variety of material essentially unrelated except for a common faith. We first looked at the works purportedly written by Paul, although many question whether they are actually his works. Next we reviewed the catholic Epistles, which share in common only that they are addressed to general audiences, and therefore are best understood in their individual contexts. Last we examined a unique form of literature called a letter but which is more likely a sermon from early Christian history whose authorship remains a mystery.

We are now left with five New Testament works that will conclude our study. What they have in common is the person to whom they have been attributed, the apostle John. As you will discover in the next chapter, even that has been subject to question.

STUDY QUESTIONS

1. Identify the epistles designated as Paulinists and discuss the major reasons that some would exclude the group as a whole for consideration as genuine letters of Paul.

2. What are the catholic Epistles and why have they been so designated?

3. Discuss what it is that makes the epistle to Hebrews unique, including in that discussion the content of the epistle.

4. What are the pastoral Epistles, how are they related to one another, and what makes them controversial?

5. Indicate the problems associated with the epistle of James as you discuss the origin and content of the letter.

6. What seems to be the relationship of 2 Peter and Jude, and how are those two works best understood?

7. Discuss the content of Ephesians and why some suggest it was written as a cover letter to Paul's collected works as they were being circulated among the broader Christian community.

8. Using the pastoral Epistles as your source, describe as much as possible the contents of the heresies that are addressed by the author of those epistles.

9. Explain why some might consider the epistle of James an effort to correct Paul's teaching about justification by grace through faith, or at least an effort to correct how that teaching might have been understood by some early Christians.

SUGGESTED READINGS

Barnett, A. E. "James, Letter of," *The Interpreter's Dictionary of the Bible*, Vol. 2 (Abingdon Press, Nashville, 1962).

Becker, J. C. "Jude, Letter of," *The Interpreter's Dictionary of the Bible*, Vol. 1 (Abingdon Press, Nashville, 1962).

————. "Pastoral Letters, the," *The Interpreter's Dictionary of the Bible*, Vol. 3 (Abingdon Press, Nashville, 1962).

————. "Peter, Second Letter of," *The Interpreter's Dictionary of the Bible*, Vol. 3 (Abingdon Press, Nashville, 1962).

————. *The Church Faces the World* (Westminster Press, Philadelphia, 1960).

Bruce, F. F. *The Epistle to the Hebrews* (Eerdmans, Grand Rapids, Mich., 1964).

Collins, Raymond F. *Letters That Paul Did Not Write: The Epistle to the Hebrews and the Pauline Pseudepigrapha* (Glazier, Wilmington, 1988).

Dibelius, M. *The Pastoral Epistles* (Fortress, Philadelphia, 1972).

Dinkler, E. "Hebrews, Letter to the," *The Interpreter's Dictionary of the Bible*, Vol. 2 (Abingdon Press, Nashville, 1962).

Goodspeed, E. J. *The Meaning of Ephesians* (University of Chicago Press, Chicago, 1933).

Johnston, G. "Ephesians, Letter to the," *The Interpreter's Dictionary of the Bible*, Vol. 2 (Abingdon Press, Nashville, 1962).

Kelly, J. N. D. *A Commentary of the Epistles of Peter and Jude* (Harper & Row, New York, 1969).

Laws, S. *The Epistle of James* (Harper & Row, New York, 1981).

Van Unnik, W. C. "Peter, First Letter of," *The Interpreter's Dictionary of the Bible*, Vol. 3 (Abingdon Press, Nashville, 1962).

ELEVEN

IN THE NAME OF JOHN

Five books in the New Testament have been in some way related to the apostle John. Revelation identifies its author as "John," the fourth Gospel is attributed to the apostle John, and there are three letters attributed to John by title. The association of these five books with one man, John, is based on the traditions that have followed them since they were first known and used in the very early Christian community.

Elements in some of the works themselves suggest common origins. Moreover, tradition has attributed them to John the apostle, and this view is shared by many modern biblical scholars. Yet even if the books were not produced by the same author, they still seem to have some common roots. It is useful to examine these common elements before looking at the individual documents.

COMMON ELEMENTS

Those who accept all these works, or perhaps only the Gospel and the letters, as being the work of the apostle John cite the following points:

1. Similarity in style in the Gospel and the letters

2. Similarity in doctrine in the Gospel and the letters

3. Internal claims of authorship in the works

4. Consistency with the history as it is known at the time of John

There is less agreement in regard to the place Revelation holds within this group, and indeed the arguments that disassociate it from the others are much more widely accepted (see below).

Even the casual reader can note the differences from the other works in the New Testament of the Gospel and 1 John. It is in those differences that some believe they find internal consistency, leading them to accept the idea of common origins. Many who are not willing to accept common authorship, however, concede the place of these works in the tradition of John the Apostle.

TRADITIONS ABOUT JOHN

It is important to review what tradition tells us of John, for his life beyond the time of Jesus is crucial in determining whether he could have

183

written the works attributed to him. We know of John, of course, first through the Gospel accounts. He is mentioned as well in Acts and in Paul's letter to the Galatians. Although he is identified with his brother James as one of the "**sons of thunder,**" the Gospel of John portrays him in a somewhat softer light. In Acts and Galatians he has significant leadership responsibilities in the early church at Jerusalem. The New Testament does not reveal John's fate, although Acts reports the martyrdom of his brother James (12:2). According to tradition, John moved to Ephesus, was banished for a period to the island of **Patmos,** and returned to live out his days in Ephesus, where he composed the works attributed to him. It is thought that John died at an old age of natural causes.

The reliability of this chronology, however, falls into some question, for some of it apparently stemmed from attempts to reconcile tradition with the works attributed to John himself. His presence in Ephesus and his long life present a less serious problem than does his time on Patmos. Some have suggested that the tradition about Patmos is based completely on the belief that John the Apostle was the author of Revelation and that part of the tradition comes from the book of Revelation itself. Many regard the entire tradition as fairly reliable by whatever standards we have available to test such reliability. Certainly if the information is accurate, it makes more plausible the claims that he is somehow connected to some or all of the works attributed to him.

THE GOSPEL OF JOHN

Problems Supplied by the Gospel

♦ **READ** *The Gospel According to Saint John*

The problems surrounding the Gospel of John since its known presence in the Christian community in the early second century have never concerned its origins. The tradition of John's authorship has been secure from a very early period in the Gospel's history. The problems have always centered on its content—the differences it presents with the synoptic Gospels, as well as its theological point of view. One has only to read its first chapters to note that it is indeed very different from its New Testament companions.

Some of those differences are worth considering at the beginning of our discussion:

1. The Gospel opens with a prologue that is a theological affirmation linking Jesus with the logos, seemingly as God himself. Jesus as the "**word**" became fully human in his earthly life. Strongly incorporated in the affirmation of who Jesus was/is is the clear distinction between Jesus and John the Baptist, the latter only a "witness" to the former, as the Baptist himself testifies.

2. It lacks the virgin birth stories of Matthew and Luke, though it has always been believed to have been the last of the written Gospels.

3. There is no report of the baptism of Jesus by John the Baptist. Rather the Evangelist uses the encounter described in Chapter 1 (19–34) to affirm Jesus as the one for whom John has been preparing the way.

4. It omits the story of the temptation.

5. The order of events and the length of Jesus' ministry differ from that of the synoptics.

6. The miracles, beginning with the opening of Jesus' ministry at the wedding at Cana, are identified as **signs** that testify to his identity as Messiah.

7. Jesus is portrayed as visiting Jerusalem throughout his ministry, in contrast to his one visit at the climax of his ministry reported in the synoptic accounts.

8. Jesus is portrayed as teaching by the use of long discourses, not primarily through parables as indicated elsewhere.

9. Jesus is much more the self-proclaimed Messiah in John than in Mark, Matthew, and Luke.

10. John contains a large amount of material not found in the synoptic Gospels.

11. The literary style differs greatly from that of the other Gospels.

12. Jesus' own country is Judaea in John, not Galilee, as in the other accounts.

13. The cleansing of the Temple occurs at the beginning of Jesus' ministry in John.

14. John does not include the story of the transfiguration.

Modern scholarship is not the first to note or deal with these and other differences. Clement of Alexandria, early in the third century, spoke of John as the "**spiritual Gospel,**" suggesting that John knew that the outward facts had been presented in the earlier Gospel accounts and that he had written this work at the urging of his own disciples and the spirit of God. This hypothesis helped explain for Clement and the early church some of the troublesome differences. The fourth Gospel was obviously composed for a different purpose and did not repeat much of what had already been reported. The author of John himself supports this explanation: "These are recorded so that you might believe that Jesus is the Christ, the son of God, and that believing this you may have life through his name" (20:31). The earlier Gospels had similar goals, but in John there is a more self-conscious effort to achieve that purpose, perhaps for a different audience.

The primary audience of the Gospel was quite surely Gentile, people who had had some association with the Hellenistic religions of the day. Perhaps the Gospel was originally addressed to Gnostic heretics in early Christianity, for the author employs some Gnostic features, particularly the use of contrasts of light and darkness, good and evil. It should not be surprising that these elements troubled some second-century Christians, who feared that their presence in the canon might encourage rather than refute some forms of gnosticism. These qualities even led some to resist the inclusion of John in their tradition of scripture. The very presence of these elements, however, made the Gospel an ideal tool for presenting Christianity to a non-Jewish world, thus accounting for its early and continued popularity within the broader Christian community.

Gnosticism itself is an elusive subject for New Testament scholars. Because gnosticism was deemed a heresy by early Christianity, much of the work that was produced by Gnostic philosophers was destroyed by the Church. Much of what is currently known about the Gnostics is based on the writings of the early church fathers who spoke of the heresies as they were refuting them. Nevertheless, some general information about the world view represented within the Gnostic community is important for an understanding of the works associated with John.

"Gnostic" is rooted in the Greek word *gnosis,* which means knowledge. One of the elements most Gnostic groups had in common was an apparent claim that their particular knowledge or understanding of the Christ event in history was essential for salvation. It seems that this knowledge itself held the key to salvation. In that sense, it was not unlike the mystery religions of the Greco-Roman world contemporary to early Christianity. One cannot help but be struck by the similarity of the approach to the life of Jesus and Christian theology expressed in the literature written in the name of John to this phase of gnosticism, and one could conclude that in this respect the material is gnosticlike. It would certainly be appropriate to address an audience that held Gnostic views.

If superior or saving knowledge was the only common element among Gnostics, they might never have been branded heretics. After all, there is much emphasis throughout Christianity on the elements of right belief. The second common element embedded in various Gnostic expressions is, therefore, much more important to our understanding of the heresy of which Gnostics were accused. That element was the denial of Jesus as a human. Influenced by Greek philosophy, particularly the thought of Plato, they asserted that if Jesus were truly human he would have been polluted by the imperfections of the material world and could not have been perfect. Thus, they asserted, he only appeared to be human, while remaining divine.

Note the **logos theology** found in the literature of John, in which there is a strong emphasis on the humanity of Jesus, while his divine nature is also confirmed. Some have described this theology as paradoxical, appearing to contradict itself while, in fact, not being contradictory. It becomes difficult to think of Jesus as a human (becoming flesh), and at the same time as the preexistent Christ (Jesus as the Word): How can one be fully human and yet divine? The question provides a basis for different ways of understanding Jesus and of making religious proclamations about him; indeed, the understanding of the Gospel is a point of continued debate among Christians. This again demonstrates why it is important to deal with biblical literature within the historical context that produced it.

Many New Testament scholars assert that this Johannine literature was addressed to an audience that was influenced by gnosticism and that the author(s) of these biblical works used Gnostic categories to dispute the contentions of the heresy. There was not, of course, a single Gnostic heresy. There were as many heresies as there were Gnostic leaders. Some scholars have suggested that there were probably more than a hundred Gnostic groups in the early centuries of Christianity. These groups viewed the world as evil, only the transcendent as perfect. Highly dualistic in their world views, they surfaced wherever Christianity had penetrated the Greco-Roman world.

It is now assumed that the Gospel of John was written in the last decade of the first century of the common era, its original audience being the Christian church at Ephesus. A palm-sized fragment of the Gospel found in Egypt that has been dated in the early second century seems to affirm such a dating. That is, the Gospel must have been known and broadly circulated by the date established for the fragment. Gnosticlike in some respects, it also became Christianity's best refutation of gnosticism. One can imagine its important role in an area where those heresies seemed to thrive.

Answers to the Problems

Let us return to the elements of John that have been identified as different from the earlier Gospel traditions and make some further observations:

1. The prologue, designated by some as the "Hymn to the Word," is indeed unique to this Gospel. This author, however, is not doing anything different from the author of the Gospel of Mark, who opens his work with the words, "The beginning of the Good News about Jesus Christ, the Son of God." In both instances the author is making quite clear who he believes Jesus to be. The logos theology of John's introduction remains consistent throughout the remainder of his Gospel and is affirmed often from the mouth of Jesus himself. Jesus, in his human form, became the agent through whom God could be fully revealed. One with God, the agent of God's creation in his preexistence, in fully human form he becomes the agent of God's disclosure of himself to the human community. Though that revelation was not accepted by all, those who did/would accept it found in it the "power to become children of God" (1:12), as well as the "grace and truth" (1:17) of God.

2. For Matthew and Luke the virgin birth is an affirmation of Jesus' messiahship, a fulfillment of Old Testament prophecy. John identifies Jesus as Messiah through his power to perform miracles, through his resurrection, and through his own testimony about himself. He does not deny the virgin birth; in fact, there seems to be a shadow allusion to it in 1:13. He simply does not emphasize it.

3. There is an obvious attempt in this Gospel to distinguish between Jesus and John the Baptist. Some have seen this emphasis as evidence that the Evangelist was refuting the claims of a sect that honored the Baptist as Messiah. Another explanation would be that Jesus, the preexistent one, who had now taken on human form, was not in need of the baptism John offered. This "chosen one of God" (1:34) who was not baptized by John serves as an argument as well for the claim that Jesus was superior to John.

4. The absence of the temptation story, found in all three synoptic Gospels, has puzzled many. The explanations of those who have tried to show that the author of John knew and used Matthew, Mark, and/or Luke have not been wholly satisfactory. Although there is some evidence that John shares the tradition used by the authors of the other Gospels, there is no agreement as to the extent of John's sources, nor is it clear how he used those sources. If the authorship can be related to the apostle John at a time near the end of a long ministry, even if the final author was someone else, John was probably both a carrier and one of the creators of any early Christian tradition. Having the task of making into Christians a predominantly Hellenistic population, such a person would draw from that tradition elements he considered important to the task, but not necessarily everything available. Thus he omitted the temptation story for reasons that are not clear to the modern reader.

5. The question of order penetrates the study of all the Gospels: They use history, but they are not bound by it in an absolute sense. Matthew and Luke stray from the order of Mark to accomplish their respective theological purposes. The problem is complicated in John by this Evangelist's extension of the time of Jesus' ministry. John reports three years as opposed to Mark's one. Both problems can be partially resolved by recognizing that John seems to include portions of Jesus' ministry that overlap that of John the Baptist (see 3:22–36), whereas the synoptic Gospels begin this portion of their stories after the arrest of John. But even that explanation is not wholly satisfactory. The early church begged the question by concluding that this "spiritual" Gospel ought not to be considered as "historic" as the others. Thus we can say with certainty only that all the Gospels are primarily declarations of faith, not essentially history books. They use history, and history can be found within them, but history is not their first purpose. John, the least "historical" Gospel, serves as an excellent example of the problem of using the Bible as history in the literal sense of that term.

6. John builds his story around seven signs, which he says were given by Jesus to show his messiahship. The first six signs performed by Jesus were:

a. Changing water into wine (2:1–11)

b. Saving the son of a royal official (4:46–54)

c. Curing a man at the pool of Bethzatha (5:1–9)

d. Feeding five thousand with five loaves and two fishes (6:1–15)

e. Healing a man blind from birth (9:1–12)

f. Raising Lazarus from the dead (11:1–44)

The signs produced faith for believers, but were rejected by those who refused to believe. They were intended to reveal Jesus as Messiah, a point emphasized in the text itself (see

2:11–12). The testimony of resurrection itself, the seventh and perfect sign, becomes the ultimate witness to Jesus as Messiah for the author of this Gospel.

7. The order of events and the length of Jesus' ministry differ from their presentation in the synoptic Gospels. One cannot easily rectify these discrepancies. To argue that Jesus may have begun a ministry before his association with John the Baptist, that the messianic dimension of that ministry was assumed or declared at his encounter with John, or that the other earlier explanations suffice, does not do justice to the problem. It is obvious that the authors of Matthew and Luke had some regard for history as reflected in their respect for Mark's order. There has to be another explanation to John's "history," and, whatever it is, it will very likely be found in John's theological considerations.

8. The answers to the questions already posed might help us understand the form of Jesus' teaching as presented in John as well. Most serious scholars believe that Jesus' primary mode of teaching was by the use of the parable. Why is that not reflected in John? Perhaps it is, but not directly. No one would argue that Paul did not have access to the teachings of Jesus, though he does not quote them directly, as in the synoptic Gospels. Paul's emphasis, in common with all the New Testament authors, is on the meaning of the Christ event in history. He proclaims that event in his own way and has not been accused of distorting its meaning. If indeed the author of John was one of the original disciples, or even if he only stood within the tradition of that disciple, what we might have is the reflective understanding of what the "Jesus of history" meant as the "Christ of faith" and how that message could be most clearly communicated to its intended audience. John's Gospel certainly has accomplished such a purpose for the ongoing Christian community without doing damage to the other traditions that have accompanied it throughout history.

9. There is not as much conflict in how Jesus represented himself to the world as might first appear. John makes explicit what the others have implied in regard to Jesus' messianic claims.

10. The question about John's sources cannot be answered adequately. There is no agreement among scholars about whether he used the synoptic materials or drew from the same sources the authors used. It is unlikely that any of the Evangelists included all the material available to them. If a writer was an eyewitness (as early tradition asserts about Matthew), was somehow related to the tradition of an eyewitness (as was believed about Mark), or simply had available all the existing Gospels and current tradition about Jesus (as was assumed about Luke), it is not unreasonable to assume that the author of John could produce such a work without exhausting the earlier accounts.

11. The style is individual, indicative perhaps both of author and audience. The author's style has some commonality with **Philo of Alexandria,** the first-century Jewish philosopher, or the authors of the Dead Sea scrolls. It is certainly appropriate for an audience primarily a part of the Hellenistic world, or perhaps a part of an early Gnostic community.

12. There are no adequate answers to the question of why the author of John locates Jesus in Judaea, beyond those already suggested for similar questions.

13. The same response holds with respect to the time of the Temple cleansing. The inclusion of the story by John at all is testimony of a tradition about that event held in common with the synoptic Gospels.

14. The absence of the story of the transfiguration is puzzling, especially because the disciple John is said to have been present at that event in the synoptic accounts. Perhaps the author of John felt that the story would be less impressive to Gentiles than to Jews—but no one can accuse John of abandoning the Jewish heritage of Jesus at other places. There seems no satisfactory explanation. The absence simply has to be reported.

Content

The Gospel of John can be divided into five sections:

I. The Prologue (1:1–51)

II. The Signs (2:1–12:50)

III. The Prelude to the Passion (13:1–17:26)

IV. The Passion (18:1–20:31)

V. The Epilogue (21:1–25)

The Prologue (1:1–51). As can be detected by the presentation in the Jerusalem Bible, verses 1–18 seem to be an ancient hymn, probably composed by the Evangelist. The hymn identifies Jesus as the "word," makes the initial identification of John the Baptist, and describes the latter's role. Verses 19–34 continue the distinction between John the Baptist and Jesus. The remaining verses, 35–51, include further testimony about Jesus as Messiah from the mouth of the Baptist and name the disciples. (Note the difference in the twelve here: John gives Nathanael in place of the Bartholomew, found in the other Gospels.)

The Signs (2:1–12:50). The signs give internal continuity to Section II. While some detect a sense of chronology here, chronology does not seem to be the dominant element. Rather, it appears that John selects a series of incidents in the ministry of Jesus, with order at most a peripheral concern. Beginning with the changing of the water into wine (first sign) and mov-

ing to the raising of Lazarus (sixth sign), each occasion affirms Jesus as Messiah. Interspersed is testimony from Jesus and from those around him of his messiahship and its meaning. Jesus is the vehicle through whom God is best known, the most complete and final revelation. Jesus makes that claim for himself, and it is affirmed by John the Baptist. Found throughout are dialogues between Jesus and others in which his messianic claim and mission are identified, often followed by a monologue by Jesus for the purpose of clarification. The signs themselves become occasions at times for Jesus to make clear the meaning of his messianic role.

The view of Jesus as the preexistent Christ, now in human form, the vehicle for revealing God to the world, remains consistent with the concept developed in the prologue to the Gospel. What has been said about Jesus and what he now says about himself is affirmed more fully by the wonder-working powers he is able to display.

The Prelude to the Passion (13:1–17:26). In much of Section III Jesus instructs his disciples about the future, his coming passion and its meaning, and the proper response to achieve the benefits of his presence among them. There is a strong demand for faith and obedience. This section is a teaching section, in which Jesus teaches about the meaning of his life as Messiah.

Appropriately, the section concludes with the long "**priestly prayer**" (17:1–26), in which Jesus interprets again his life, anticipates the future church, and defines that church as the vehicle for God to continually be made known, as well as the locus of God's salvation. It is perhaps our clearest clue to the theological viewpoint of the author.

The Passion (18:1–20:31) As elsewhere in the Gospels, the details of John's version of the passion do not totally coincide with the earlier accounts. However, all four Evangelists differ in presenting this material, each adding to a common tradition in significant ways. You will note both similarities and differences. John, for example, reports more postresurrection appearances, accounts not found elsewhere. The closing verses of Chapter 20, where the author reveals why this Gospel was produced, seem to be the conclusion of the testimony.

It is clear that the author of John wanted to attest to a physical resurrection, although at the same time the exact nature of the risen Christ remains unclear. Thomas is convinced by touching the wounds, a physical act; yet Jesus twice appears to the disciples in a room described as closed, a more spiritual manifestation. What is consistent is the humanity of Jesus, even in his resurrected form. The remainder of John's view on the nature of the resurrected Christ is a matter of continuing speculation.

The Epilogue (21:1–25). Many view the final chapter as a later addition, since the preceding verses (20:30–31) give the impression of a conclusion. If Chapter 21 is an addition, it was probably inserted before the Gospel was in general circulation, perhaps by the same author, for all copies of the Gospel available to us out of the past contain twenty-one chapters. It has been suggested that this addition was an afterthought, or arose out of a need to affirm within the church the authority of Peter as a leader of the church. It has been further suggested that the author identifies himself in this section as an eyewitness to substantiate the authority of all that he has reported. Chapter 21 is similar in style and in language to the preceding chapters. One will note how much the details of this Gospel involve Jesus' last journey to Jerusalem, his trial, crucifixion, and resurrection. The strong emphasis on this part of the life of Jesus is consistent with the other Gospel accounts and shows again how central

belief in the resurrection was to early Christianity's claim to Jesus as messiah.

Authorship

Who did write this Gospel? Probably it was someone of Jewish background, addressing a Gentile audience. This work has always been associated with the apostle John, and it claims to be the work of an eyewitness in Chapter 21. Tradition places its composition in Ephesus and says that John lived there after retiring from his active ministry. If one can accept even portions of the tradition about this Gospel and its author, it is not difficult to imagine it to be the work of a disciple in the role of missionary whose goal was to win outsiders to his faith. And indeed, tradition has always asserted it to be the work of John the apostle, composed at the end of a long and fruitful ministry among Gentiles.

If it is true, as some have suggested, that the author of John was fully aware of the accounts of the other Evangelists and that in telling his story he used those Gospels to clarify their spiritual meaning to his Hellenistic audience, it is also true that he did not harm those stories in the retelling. John makes the same affirmation as the other Evangelists, though in a very different form. It certainly does not damage the tradition that surrounds it to view this Gospel as the effort of one who has taken the message of the Christian faith beyond the community in which it was originally proclaimed to convince others of its validity, while being careful to preserve its ultimate meaning.

THE LETTERS OF JOHN

✦ **READ** *The Three Letters of John*

Three letters in the New Testament are attributed to John. None of the three directly identifies its author, although the second and third letters say they are from "the Elder," identified by later tradition as John. Most agree that all three have enough in common in style, vocabulary, and subject matter to have come from the same person. Unquestionably the author was an influential leader in the churches to which these works were addressed, and there are no overwhelming reasons to dissociate them from the apostle to which tradition attributes them. There is harmony with the logos theology expressed in the Gospel of John and the first letter. Even if that letter was not written by the same author, it is clearly compatible with that Gospel. Surely all emerged out of the same community, if not from the same pen, and that would in itself explain their close association over the years. They are indeed in the tradition of John.

The casual reader may have some difficulty in identifying the elements that have convinced most scholars that the Gospel and the letters, particularly the last two, have so much in common. Let us look at the letters, both to understand their purpose and to see what establishes their commonality.

1 John

1 John has been described as a Christian manifesto. It lacks the salutation and the conclusion of a letter, standing more like a sermon or theological tract than an epistle. Its purpose is obviously to teach sound doctrine, while at the same time correcting what many now view as a heresy. The author was certainly more intent on passing on orthodoxy than on attacking heretics, however, and was probably convinced that the former would overcome the latter.

The outline provided in the Jerusalem Bible is as good as any for examining the work itself. It begins with the logos theology found in John's Gospel, an introduction one might title a "Hymn to Christ." The next three sections constitute the three main points of the sermon:

I. Walk in the Light (1:5–2:29)

II. Live as Children of God (3:1–4:6)

III. Love and Faith (4:7–5:12)

Section I begins with what some believe to be a claim of an eyewitness (1:5). Its main point is that those who claim to live in the light must reflect that light in their lives. They must break with sin, keep the commandments, detach themselves from worldly distraction, and renounce false teachers. In the final point we have a clue to the nature of the heresy that is being denied (2:22 ff), apparently some form of early gnosticism that denied the true humanity of Jesus.

Section II reiterates Section I. Again the hearer is called to break with sin, keep the commandments, and guard against heretics.

The appropriation of right belief becomes manifest in human behavior, for people are to love one another. Proper belief leads to love, for God is love. This is the application of belief found in Section III.

Note the tension expressed in all three sections. The struggle between good and evil, light and darkness, is similar to that found in the Gospel of John. As in the Gospel, response in faithful acceptance of Jesus as Messiah will eventuate in God's blessing, namely eternal life, the very hope that has motivated the composition of this work.

The concluding verses (5:13–21) reaffirm what has already been said; they are a declaration of sound doctrine and a warning to those who would abandon it.

2 John

This next short work is much more like a letter than 1 John. The author identifies himself as the "Elder" and the recipient as the "Lady, the chosen one," suggesting to some a particular (unidentified) church.

The letter seems to attack a heresy that is bringing chaos within the church. It counsels remembering the law of love and rejection of heresy. The heresy is a form of gnosticism, "refusing to admit that Jesus Christ has come in the flesh" (1:7). As in the first letter the heretics are identified with the Antichrist, a term peculiar to the works associated with John.

3 John

In this personal letter the author again calls himself the Elder; the recipient is his friend Gaius. The occasion is an internal church problem that centers on the question of authority. The letter makes the lines of authority clear and supports the ministry of someone called **Demetrius** against the slanders of a certain **Diotrephes.**

Some have suggested that 2 and 3 John are individual letters that accompanied 1 John when it was originally circulated. The sermon or tract may have been circulated among the churches of Asia Minor with the intention of establishing an orthodoxy, accompanied by separate letters sent to deal with pressing problems in individual communities as well. 2 John addresses a local heresy, whereas the subject of 3 John is a problem among the local leadership. The author, who hoped to visit the churches soon, intended the letters as a preliminary approach to difficulties that he would deal with in a more direct and personal way. The letters lend themselves well to such a view.

One could question why 2 and 3 John are even included in the Bible. There are certainly no new and profound religious insights in either. There is hardly anything religious about 3 John at all. Perhaps the best explanation is that the three letters circulated together at the beginning of their history. Perhaps they were being delivered at the time the apostle John passed away. All were saved in honor of John, believed (or known) to be their author. It never

occurred to anyone to distinguish between the three, and all three continued to be shared among the Christian community because they were believed to reflect the work of that apostle. Thus they remained to be included in the first Christian canon.

REVELATION

✦ **READ** *The Book of Revelation*

Some might say that we have saved the best for last. Others would prefer to ignore altogether the presence of the Book of Revelation, which has been surrounded by controversy since its inclusion in the canon of the early Christian church. It can hardly be ignored, however, despite its controversial nature, for it is a significant part of the study of Christian scripture.

Questions Surrounding Revelation

Although this study of Revelation includes it with the works of John, and the work identifies itself as having been written by someone named John, its author probably was not the apostle John. Revelation varies significantly in style and thought from the other works associated with the name of John. The author states that the revelation he is reporting occurred when he was on the island of Patmos, which tradition associates with the apostle. As reported earlier, that association is tenuous at the least, perhaps developed with the belief of those forming the tradition that Revelation was the work of the apostle. The author does not seem to claim to be an apostle, nor does there seem to be any internal evidence that he was an eyewitness to the life and ministry of Jesus. He does say that he was a Christian preacher (1:9), bound to the Christian community by a common loyalty to Jesus.

The book could well have been written in the same period as the other works attributed

The Valley of Armageddon as viewed
from the site of Ahab's palace at Megiddo.

to John (i.e., in the last decade of the first century of the common era), though some propose that it should be dated in the time of Nero (i.e., before 70 C.E.). There is no question that it was written to a church facing persecution, more likely the widespread persecution of the late first century than the limited persecution experienced under Nero.

The book is the only complete apocalyptic work in the New Testament, though the apocalyptic view is certainly found elsewhere in the Christian portion of the Bible. Chapter 13 of Mark is a good example of such an expression. More like the Hebrew Bible Daniel than any other biblical work, Revelation applies symbols to past, present, and future history. Convinced that the signs point to nearness of the end of time, the author reports the vision he says that he received to prepare the faithful for that end.

The apocalyptic view had been a part of the Judeo-Christian heritage at least since the time of the composition of the Book of Daniel. Du-

alistic, at least to some degree, it holds a rather pessimistic view of the course of human history. Embedded in it is a belief that history as we know it will end, an event brought about by God himself, and only then will God's will prevail. At the end God will reign, evil will be destroyed, and the righteous will prevail. There is good evidence that John the Baptist, Jesus, and Paul, as well as most of early Christianity, incorporated the apocalyptic view of history into their theology. Jesus' strong emphasis on the kingdom of God is but one expression of that. The general expectation of the early return of Jesus among primitive Christianity is another. In that sense, the Book of Revelation can be viewed as very much in keeping with the thought of first-century Christianity, and acceptance of a date either slightly earlier or later for its writing would not offer serious historical problems. Although never the dominant theological force in either Judaism or Christianity, so-called apocalyptic sects have been present in most generations of their respective histories. Some scholars have called earliest Christianity an apocalyptic sect within Judaism, a description that has some merit.

Christian apocalyptic thought certainly cannot be dissociated from its Jewish roots, its strong reliance on the Book of Daniel being quite easy to demonstrate. Some Christians used Daniel to prove that Jesus was/is the Messiah, while they viewed Revelation as a clue to the time of his expected return, a time when they believed God would establish his final reign on earth.

Interpreting Apocalyptic Literature

People have come to interpret apocalyptic literature in many ways. Some look to it for clues to end times. Others regard it as so symbolic as to be beyond comprehension. Those who believe it contains clues to future history do not always agree on the meaning of its symbols. In almost every generation there have been some in the Judeo-Christian tradition who have believed that their moment was the one symbolized in the apocalyptic pages of scripture, that their days were, indeed, the last days. Christianity in particular has had a succession of apocalyptic sects, often led by those who claimed to be able to interpret the symbolic language. A flourishing of apocalyptic sects in the past century or so has resulted in the forming of permanent church groups such as the Seventh Day Adventists, Jehovah's Witnesses, and the Church of Jesus Christ of Latter Day Saints (the Mormons). Dominant in all has been a particular understanding or interpretation of the apocalyptic portions of the Hebrew and New Testament.

Traditionally the Christian community has interpreted apocalyptic literature in general and Revelation in particular in four major ways.

1. A view that Revelation must be understood in the context of its own time and the events

symbolized in its pages as having already taken place.

2. A view that only a portion of the revelations have occurred and that the work offers clues to the remaining portion of human history.

3. A view that the book is best understood spiritually, and no attempt should be made to interpret it in the context of history.

4. A view that the book is prophetic and its prophecies are yet to be completely fulfilled.

Perhaps the most helpful way to understand Revelation is to place it into the context of its own time, as we have attempted to do with all the other books of the Bible, examining what we know about it as well as what it tells us about itself.

History of the Work

The Book of Revelation was known and circulated in Christianity at least by the mid-second century. From its inclusion in early canonical lists it was generally assumed to have been written by John the apostle. Those who rejected apostolic authorship did so more because of contents than for other reasons. Popular among the montanists, second-century heretics who claimed direct oracular revelations from God for their teaching on ascetic prophecy, asceticism, and eschatology, the book was rejected by some as being part of what they considered heretical teaching. Its inclusion in the canon affirms that the church itself did not brand its contents heretical, although its encouragement of a spirit of **millennialism** in the early church fostered the spirit of controversy that seems always to have surrounded it. As in the case of the Gospel of John, Revelation's place in scripture was questioned more because of how it was understood and used by some than because of what it actually contained. Indeed, interpretation remains the issue that makes Revelation perhaps the most controversial book of the Bible.

As is the case with other books that did not enjoy early unanimous acceptance and yet are now a part of the tradition of scripture, its merits outweighed other concerns and it assumed its place. Those merits, of course, are found in the book itself and deserve consideration in the proper context.

Time, Place, Audience, and Circumstances

Revelation was written in the first century. It addresses itself to the "seven churches" located in Asia Minor, and its author tells us he received the vision he reports while on Patmos. The book contains visions of the last days, a time when the forces of good and evil have their last horrible encounter, with good triumphing, evil being punished, and the kingdom of heaven finally established permanently on the earth. In the struggle the faithful are tested, and those who abandon their faith will have eternal punishment. Such a message is especially important for people who are suffering persecution because of their faith, as occurred during the reign of Domitian at the end of the first century.

As far as we know, Christians did not encounter widespread persecution until that late period. While there was some very early persecution of the Christians by the Jews in Palestine, with the intention of wiping out a dangerous heresy within Judaism, it does not seem to have gone beyond Palestine, or even to have been very systematic or of long duration within those borders. The persecution of Christians by Nero seems to have been a short-lived episode centered in and around Rome and not affecting Christians elsewhere. It was not until the time of Domitian that Christians suffered broad-based official persecution simply because they were Christians, as discussed in Chapters 7 and 9. It is believed that the Book of Revelation addressed the Christian community in such stressful times.

Judaism had experienced a similar situation little more than two centuries before. The Temple was desecrated, and Jews were asked to renounce their faith. Some resisted, and the resulting Maccabean War had won them their freedom. Judaism's most famous apocalyptic work, the Book of Daniel, is believed to have been written in the midst of those events. The author of Daniel had rehearsed the history of Judaism, using symbols to portray the past and present, and had concluded that the times were indeed the prelude of the messianic age. He urged faithfulness, promising reward to those who would stand fast and punishment to those who forsook Yahweh.

The Book of Revelation continued the apocalyptic theme it had inherited. It dealt with past, present, and future history. Convinced that Yahweh was the "Lord of history," and as such controlled the destiny of the world, it spoke out of that faith to those whose faith could bring them death. Like the author of Daniel, the author of Revelation believed his days included signs of the end. "Happy the man who reads this prophecy, and happy those who listen to him, if they treasure all that it says, because the Time is close" (1:3). In the worst of times, a word of comfort and encouragement is pronounced.

A View of Interpretation

Those who take the foregoing view of Revelation will seek to find in the history of the first century clues to many of the symbols contained in the book. It has been suggested that apocalyptic writers deliberately veiled their message in symbols so that those outside the faith, who would not understand the symbols, would not know that their days were numbered. The faithful would understand and would be encouraged by the message of hope, the message that they would prevail.

The Book of Revelation survived in the

early Christian community because those who had it as their possession found it meaningful. The same was true of subsequent generations. The message of Revelation is quite simple: Remain faithful and God will reward you; abandon your faith and God will abandon you to the forces of evil, with all the consequences such rejection entails. No matter how the symbols are interpreted, the message remains essentially the same. It is a message of the trustworthiness of God as the continuing "Lord of history."

There does not have to be agreement about all the symbolism in the book for readers to agree that in the view of this author the beginning of the end has arrived. Evil has prevailed too long; the innocent have suffered too much. God is ready to reassert himself, to take complete and final control. For those who survive, by the grace of God, there is a future in which things will be as God always intended, a new Jerusalem, a new heaven, a new earth. Loyalty will be rewarded in a life of abundance and peace. Those who abandon God will bear the consequences of exclusion from the fruits of God's victorious triumph. The choice made has eternal implications: Not only those living in the day of victory will be rewarded, but all who have maintained the faith. Unfaithfulness will have its consequences on the day of judgment as well, consequences that cannot be avoided by an early death (20:1–21:8).

Such a message would certainly have had an impact on people facing death for their beliefs. It also is a message that has a timeless quality, for every generation must face its own test of faith. It is also a message very consistent with the faith expressed from the beginning of our study, one that would be affirmed by the prophets, by Jesus, and by his apostles. It contains all the elements of the theology articulated by Moses and all who followed him. It is a fitting ending to the articulation of that theology expressed throughout the scripture of the Judeo-Christian tradition.

Regardless of whether Revelation holds the secret of the time and place that history as we know it will end, it holds the view that how one lives matters greatly. That alone makes it of value for those who use it as an authority for their lives. Its vision may have been intended primarily to support Christians facing death for their first-century faith, but it has served a much broader purpose for continuing Christianity. A book of comfort and devotion, it has called people to faithfulness over the years, while assuring them of the faithfulness of the God it proclaims. Read with that in mind, Revelation is less frightening and more comforting. Even more, it is more consistent with all that has preceded it and remains in harmony with the spirit of the scriptural tradition of which it is a part.

Such a view makes Revelation less than some would have it be and more than it is claimed to be by those who would dismiss its importance. Much more, it makes this work comprehensible to every generation

Before we end our study of the Bible, you will want to know how this body of literature reached us from the ancient past. It is also important to know how it achieved its status as scripture. The history of those events is the subject of the Postlude of our study.

STUDY QUESTIONS

1. Who is the John to whom the works of the New Testament are attributed, and what is known about him as a historic figure?

2. Discuss the common elements found in the literature written in the name of John and either defend or refute the idea of studying this collection of literature together.

3. Identify the elements of the Gospel of John that separate it from the synoptic Gospels.

4. Define the term *gnosticism* and discuss how a general understanding of the subject might help one understand the works associated with John.

5. How does the author of the Gospel of John relate the use of miracles (signs and wonders) to the ministry of Jesus and his basic identity as messiah?

6. Explain Chapter 21 of John as a later addition to the Gospel, indicating what in that chapter and in the earlier material leads some to suggest such an idea.

7. How would you describe the contents and relationship of 1 John with the Gospel of John?

8. Discuss the Book of Revelation as the most complete apocalyptic work in the New Testament.

9. How does a sense of late first-century Christian history affect how one might understand the Book of Revelation?

10. Discuss the overall message of the Book of Revelation using the work itself to justify your response.

SUGGESTED READINGS

Bowman, J. W. "Revelation, Book of," *The Interpreter's Dictionary of the Bible*, Vol. 4 (Abingdon Press, Nashville, 1962).

Bultmann, R. *The Gospel of John: A Commentary* (Westminster Press, Philadelphia, 1971).

————. *The Johannine Epistles* (Fortress, 1973).

Caird, G. B. *A Commentary on the Revelation of St. John The Divine* (Harper & Row, New York, 1966).

————."John, Letters of," *The Interpreter's Dictionary of the Bible*, Vol. 2 (Abingdon Press, Nashville, 1962).

Collins, Adela Yarbro. *Crisis and Catharsis: The Power of Apocalypse* (Westminster Press, Philadelphia, 1984).

Filson, F. V. "John, The Apostle," *The Interpreter's Dictionary of the Bible*, Vol. 2 (Abingdon Press, Nashville, 1962).

Fiorenza, Elisabeth Schussler. *The Book of Revelation: Justice and Judgment* (Fortress Press, Philadelphia, 1985).

Kysor, Robert. *John: Augsburg Commentary on the New Testament* (Augsburg Press, Minneapolis, 1986).

Layton, Bentley. *The Gnostic Scriptures: A New Translation with Annotation and Introductions* (Doubleday, Garden City, N.Y., 1987).

Sanders, J. N. "John, Gospel of," *The Interpreter's Dictionary of the Bible,* Vol. 2 (Abingdon Press, Nashville, 1962).

Smith, D. Moody. *John,* 2nd ed. (Fortress Press, Philadelphia, 1986).

POSTLUDE

We have examined the Bible from beginning to end, from Adam to Armageddon. That examination has suggested how the literature was produced and how it reached its final form. It has not included a full discussion of how each work achieved the status of scripture for the Judeo-Christian tradition, nor has it recited the history of the transmission of the Bible from ancient to modern times. Neither has it recognized the books produced by both the Jewish and the Christian communities that had some status as scripture for at least portions of those communities until the limits of their respective canons were officially established. Those subjects are appropriate for the conclusion of our study.

THE FORMING OF THE JEWISH AND CHRISTIAN CANONS

Judaism began using at least portions of the Hebrew Bible as scripture as early as the period of the Babylonian exile (587 B.C.E.). However, the final canon of the Hebrew Bible was not officially established until the Council of Jamnia in 90 C.E. Christianity shared the Hebrew Bible with Judaism and began at the same time to produce its own scripture. It seems that the letters of Paul were being used like scripture by some Christians by the end of the first century, the Gospels and remaining works achieving that status somewhat later.

Defining the Canon

"Canon" comes from the Greek word *kanon*, which is similar to *kanna*, meaning reed. The reed was used as a measuring device in the Greco-Roman world and the word "canon" is associated with measure. The canon of the Bible consists of the works that have been measured by the respective religious communities and been found to meet the criteria by which they were evaluated. The occasion and purpose of the setting of the limits of the canon, as well as the standards of measurement by which those books now in the canon were established, are important.

Historical Background

The Jewish Canon. If Judaism used some of the Hebrew Bible like scripture from the time of the Babylonian exile, it is also true that all the current Hebrew Bible enjoyed semiofficial scriptural status long before the Council of Jamnia. As a matter of fact, Judaism had an even broader scriptural tradition than the works now included in the Jewish canon.

We do not know precisely how this scriptural tradition was established, but we can make some fairly intelligent assumptions. The process began, of course, as the literature was formed. It would not be surprising to discover that the literature revealing the Covenant and the Law carried the authority of scripture very early in the national history of Judaism, beginning at least with the discovery of the scroll of the Law in the Temple in 621 B.C.E. From the time of the Babylonian exile the religious tradition of Judaism seemed more to be refined than to be shaped. Even the postexilic prophets relied on their predecessors in the tradition as they spoke to new times. As far as we can tell, the prophetic role was all but abandoned after the time of Ezra and Nehemiah, with Judaism depending on the word of Yahweh revealed in the so-called prophetic period to understand the past, interpret the present, and guide the future. The publishing of the Septuagint, the Greek translation of the Hebrew scriptures, gives us our best clue to the literature regarded as having the authority of scripture at that time. Some of the books included in that tradition of scripture did not become a part of the final Jewish canon, as will be shown, and some works that were being used with the authority of scripture were not in the Septuagint.

The Christian Canon. Christianity began with an established scripture, the Hebrew Bible. The religious literature of the first years of Christianity was not produced to replace that scripture. Rather, it was for the purpose of teaching and guiding the early Christian community as it awaited the soon-expected return of Jesus. As Christianity spread into the Gentile world, that literature had to be used to correct false teachings, to give guidance to the new communities, and to provide a sense of order. Paul's circulated letters were playing such a role at least by the early second century, but they did not then enjoy the status of scripture.

A heretic, the Gnostic Marcion, can really be credited with moving New Testament literature to the status of scripture. Marcion supported his mid-second century heresy by publishing what we might call the first New Testament. He included in that collection many of the letters of Paul and a blending of

the Gospels. Though he and his heresy were rejected by the church, it became clear that many Christians were relying on the literature of early Christianity as having the authority of scripture. At that point the church fathers began to publish lists of literature, commenting on the reliability of the various works. Those lists became the foundation for the official New Testament canon established and accepted by Christianity in the last years of the fourth century. As was the case with the Hebrew Bible, not all works that had been used as scripture by all portions of the Christian community were included in the final canon.

We are dependent on the writings of the church fathers to put together the history of how the Christian canon was shaped. Many provide us with lists of the books accepted by all, those in dispute, and those that were simply rejected. The third and fourth centuries saw those lists achieve a consensus, and at the end of the fourth century that consensus was affirmed: by the Council of Hippo in 393 and by the Council of Carthage in 397. The New Testament now stood with the Hebrew Bible as the official scripture of Christianity.

THE STANDARDS OF CANONICITY

How, one might ask, did the councils determine what ought or ought not be included? The obvious answer is that they relied on what time and tradition had already done; they used what had been in use. Yet the criteria for the choices were more complicated. Neither Judaism nor Christianity included all the works that were being used like scripture in their own traditions.

The Council of Jamnia

The limits of the Jewish canon were established by a council of Pharisaic Jews meeting at Jamnia in 90 C.E., when Judaism was facing an-

The Wailing Wall, foundation wall of the Temple Mount in Jerusalem where modern Jews offer prayers of thanksgiving for their return to their Holy Land.

other crisis in its long history of crises. The events of history had dashed their hopes and crushed their spirit. Jerusalem and the Temple had been destroyed by the Romans in 70 C.E. as a result of continued Jewish resistance to the Roman occupation of their land, and Jews were barred from even the ruins of the Holy City. Except for the Pharisees, the major sects of Judaism described in Chapter 7 seem to have disappeared, and a heretical sect was claiming to be Judaism properly understood, proclaiming that the Messiah had come and was soon to return, and using the scriptures of Judaism to support its assertions.

The Council of Jamnia was not convened for the sole sake of placing limits on the Jewish canon. That was only one of its results. It really was dealing with the problems facing Judaism and attempting to give direction to its

future. It was an effort to understand and control how Judaism would survive as a religion. It also was an assertion of what would serve as authority for Jews in matters of religion, setting buffers to protect them from both friends and enemies. In that sense, it was to define Judaism from that time forth.

The canon established at Jamnia excluded a number of works that until that time had carried the authority of scripture for at least some Jews. You know already that some of the works found in the Septuagint are not now in the Jewish canon. Excluded as well were other works that had enjoyed for a short moment in Jewish history the status of scripture for some, works we classify now as the Pseudepigrapha (see below).

The Pharisees wanted to establish criteria by which to measure what works ought to be included in their scriptures. The works accepted were believed to meet criteria such as the following at the time the decisions were made:

1. The idea that the period of prophetic inspiration ended at the time of Ezra and Nehemiah

2. The restriction that nothing known to have been originally composed in a language other than Hebrew would be included

As you can recall, the period of Ezra and Nehemiah preceded the period of Hellenization. Hellenization, with its philosophy of blending the best from every culture, could have had a subtle influence on Judaism, distorting it from the faith Yahweh had intended. It would be best, obviously, to avoid that possibility by closing the window of scriptural authority before the opportunity for distortion had arisen. Judaism was already a religion of the book; it was simply a matter of deciding when the last chapter of the book had been written. The same reasoning applied to the criterion that the original language of composition must have been Hebrew. Greek had become the language of the Mideast after Hellenization, and obviously any work composed in Greek must have been written after the period of prophetic inspiration.

The Councils of Hippo and Carthage

Christianity, like Judaism, was using its scripture as scripture long before the limits of its canon were officially decided. Again, the decision makers were largely confirming what tradition had already established. The Council of Hippo and the Council of Carthage affirmed what was already set by usage, and with their decisions excluded the possibility of including other Christian works still known within the Church. Their criteria, which had been established by predecessors who had been devising

canonical lists for the past two centuries, included the following:

1. The work must be by an eyewitness or one closely associated to an eyewitness to life and teachings of Jesus.

2. The work must not dispute what had become established as orthodox teaching.

Orthodoxy has of course been established by the writings themselves. However, other writings did exist, and had seen some use as scripture within the Christian community, which supported ideas that had been branded as heresy and were now officially excluded from further consideration. Some, but not all, of these works compose the **New Testament Apocrypha.**

In setting the limits of the scripture produced by the Christian community, the church fathers also indicated the limits of its Old Testament. It had used throughout its history the Septuagint version of the Hebrew Bible and as a result included in its Old Testament those works included in that version at these councils. It was only at the time of the Protestant Reformation that some Christians began to relegate the works of the Jewish Apocrypha to nonscriptural status, accepting as their Old Testament the works identified by the Jews as scripture.

PSEUDEPIGRAPHA AND NEW TESTAMENT APOCRYPHA

Pseudepigrapha

Some books used like scripture by a portion of Judaism for at least a period of history are not now a part of either the Jewish or the Christian Bible. These works are classified as the Pseudepigrapha. Most of these works were composed between 200 B.C.E. and 200 C.E. Many have been attributed to such famous characters as Adam, Enoch, and Moses, and the name

"Pseudepigrapha" indicates the current belief that often these works were written under fictitious names. Having origins in both Palestinian and Diaspora Judaism, the only true commonality shared by the Pseudepigrapha is failure to achieve canonical status.

Included in the pseudepigraphal works produced in Palestine are:

Testament of the Twelve Prophets

Psalms of Solomon

Lives of the Prophets

Jubilees

Testament of Job

Enoch

Martyrdom of Isaiah

Paralipomena of Jeremiah

Life of Adam and Eve

Assumption of Moses

Apocalypse of Baruch

Included in the works of Diaspora Judaism are:

Aristeas

Sibylline Oracles

3 and 4 Maccabees

Slavonic Book of Enoch

Greek Apocalypse of Baruch

New Testament Apocrypha

Of the numerous works produced during the early centuries of Christianity, some carried the authority of scripture for some segment of Christianity but never achieved broad acceptance or became a part of the general scriptural heritage. More numerous than the similar works produced in the Jewish community, these works varied in type from gospel, to letter, to apocalypse. Those that are known to us we designate as the New Testament Apocrypha.

Many of these works were never held in high regard by most of the Christian community. They were recognized as inauthentic by the generation in which they were produced. Works such as these generally tried to fill in the details of the life of Jesus, the so-called silent years, to add to or change belief, or to report new visions. Other works were held in high regard and used by the Christian community, but never were regarded as having the authority of scripture because it was always known that their authors were not eyewitnesses. Another group served to authenticate the ideas of a particular heresy and were rejected by ongoing Christianity, along with the related heresy.

We know of some nineteen Gospels, twenty-four Acts, seven Epistles, six Apocalypses, ten Gnostic writings, and five other works circulated among some segments of Christianity in its first centuries.

THE TRANSMISSION OF THE BIBLE THROUGH THE CENTURIES

The final piece of the puzzle contains the information about how the Bible reached us from the ancient past. You already know how it was preserved and passed on in ancient Judaism and some of how that process was duplicated in Christianity. How did the process continue beyond the biblical period?

The most obvious answer is that the Bible was preserved and passed on by the religious communities that cherished it as scripture. At the same time it was translated from one language to another to make it accessible to whatever community regarded it as sacred. Diaspora Jews translated the Hebrew Bible into Greek; Roman Christians translated the Greek New Testament into Latin. Generation after generation passed on those scriptures by piously copying the manuscripts for others.

One could well imagine that in translating and copying the original manuscripts distortions might have occurred. Yet modern scholars have discovered that the copies are remarkably free from error or change, probably because they were regarded as sacred, not to be tampered with by the copyists.

Judaism and Christianity remained the guardians of their respective scriptures. Translations into the common tongue of a particular people did not take place until near the sixteenth century, and then only among Protestants. It was when such translation began to take place that renewed attention was paid to the ancient biblical manuscripts and the reliability of such materials. These endeavors eventually led to other areas of modern biblical scholarship and criticism, as described earlier.

When the Bible began to be translated into modern languages, some manuscripts commonly available were all the aid the translators had, perhaps along with the Latin Vulgate and the Hebrew Bible. Subsequent translators worked from the same sources, plus the original translations themselves. Only in the past hundred years have new translations depended heavily on the most ancient manuscripts. The judgment of the meaning of obscure Hebrew or Greek phrases depends, as it has always, on the best judgment of the particular translator(s).

Translations themselves have usually involved the joint efforts of a number of scholars who have decided the best way to reexpress a particular thought written in one language in another language. Though it is not impossible for a single person to translate the Bible, the most highly regarded translations have been those of a group of translators, often both Jews and Christians, an effort reflected in the translation of the Jerusalem Bible for example. Not only is accuracy a prime criterion, but an effort to keep the sense of beauty and power of the original language has been a prime objective.

You now have a basic understanding of the process of transmission of the Bible; however, serious students of the Bible will want to pursue this subject further.

CONCLUSION

You now know something of what the Bible is, what it contains, and how it got to us. You also should have a deeper understanding of Judaism and Christianity, the communities that produced and passed the Bible on to us. The information prepares you to begin any serious study of the Bible and should not be regarded as an end in itself. You know now what questions to ask and where to begin to find the answers. It is my hope that this book will launch you toward asking those questions and finding those answers.

STUDY QUESTIONS

1. Explain how the Bible in its individual parts functioned in the religious communities it served before it achieved the final status as the scripture of those communities.

2. Describe the steps that led to the canonization of the Hebrew Bible.

3. Explain the idea that Christianity began its history with a scripture common to Judaism. Why did it take a while for Christianity to develop its own literary tradition?

4. Define the terms *Pseudepigrapha* and *New Testament Apocrypha* and explain why these works did not achieve final scriptural status for the communities they served.

5. Explain what it was about the books in the Bible that made them so important to the communities they served that they achieved the status of scripture for those communities.

6. Discuss the possible problems created in Bible translations, as opposed to the problems arising from preserving the Bible in the original languages in which it was written. Why is it important to understand these issues?

7. What is meant by the suggestion that the Bible is the final *product* of the Jewish and Christian communities that produced them rather than the *foundation* upon which those communities are based, particularly in regard to one's understanding of the process of canonization?

8. Identify the most important question that remains unanswered for you as you conclude this introductory study of the Bible.

SUGGESTED READINGS

Barclay, William. *Introducing the Bible* (Abingdon Press, Nashville, 1979).

Beare, F. W. "Canon of the NT," *The Interpreter's Dictionary of the Bible,* Vol. 1 (Abingdon Press, Nashville, 1962).

Enslin, M. S. "Apocrypha, NT," *The Interpreter's Dictionary of the Bible,* Vol. 1 (Abingdon Press, Nashville, 1962).

Fritsch, C. T. "Pseudepigrapha," *The Interpreter's Dictionary of the Bible,* Vol. 3 (Abingdon Press, Nashville, 1962).

McDonald, Lee Martin. *The Formation of the Christian Canon* (Abingdon Press, Nashville, 1988).

Pfeiffer, R. H. "Canon of the OT," *The Interpreter's Dictionary of the Bible,* Vol. 1 (Abingdon Press, Nashville, 1962).

GLOSSARY

Aaron Brother of Moses, first high priest of Israel. Served as spokesman for Moses.

Abednego Name given by the Babylonians to Azariah, one of the companions of Daniel, cast into fiery furnace (see Dan. 3:12–30).

Abijah The Hebrew Bible mentions several persons by this name: the younger son of Samuel (1 Sam. 8:1–9); the son of Becher, a Benjaminite (1 Chron. 7:8); the head of the eighth division of the Aaronic priesthood (1 Chron. 24:10); the king of Judah who succeeded Rehoboam (2 Chron. 13).

Abimelech There are two characters in Hebrew Bible with this name: a king of Gerar identified in the Abraham story (Gen. 20–21, 26), and the son of Gideon who had an abortive kingship over a portion of Israel during the time of the Judges (Judges 9).

Abraham The first Jew, the one from whose seed Jews identify themselves (Gen. 12:1–3). Genesis describes Abraham as the foundation for God's chosen people, himself chosen by Yahweh.

Absalom The third son of David (2 Sam. 3:3) whose tensions with his father led to open warfare with his father, resulting in David's temporary flight from Jerusalem. David prevailed, Absalom was killed, leading to David's memorable lament (2 Sam. 19:1).

absolute law One of two kinds of Law found in the ethical demands of Hebrew Bible (cf. Conditional Law). The unqualified command "Thou shalt not kill" is an example. This is the most common type of Law for Judaism.

Additions to Esther The portions of the Book of Esther not found in the most reliable Hebrew manuscripts but given in the Septuagint version of the Hebrew Bible.

Adonijah The fourth son of David, and the king's legitimate heir. Adonijah's aspirations to the throne set him into conflict with Solomon's supporters, and led to the consecration of Solomon as king before David had died (1 Kings 1:5–53).

Ahaz King of Judah (2 Kings 16:1) during period of Assyrian domination. He was king of Judah when Israel fell to Assyria, and it was to him that Isaiah addressed his famous Immanuel prophecy (Isa. 6–13).

Ahijah The most prominent person of this name in the Hebrew Bible is the prophet from Shiloh, who played a part in the division of Israel and Judah when he supported Jeroboam in his opposition to Rehoboam (1 Kings 11:26–40).

Ai A Canaanite city whose major claim to fame was as the site of the defeat of the Israelites soon after the Battle of Jericho (Josh. 7–8).

Alexander the Great Alexander III of Macedon, a heroic king who established the Greek Empire and instituted Hellenization, a cultural phenomenon that had profound impact on later history. Born in 356 B.C.E., Alexander died at the age of thirty-three, having changed in his short span the language and culture of much of the world.

Alexandrian Jews The Diaspora Jewish community located in Alexandria, the capital city of Egypt during the Hellenistic and Roman periods.

Amorites A group that occupied a portion of Canaan at the time it was invaded by the Hebrews; they remained traditional enemies of the Jews.

Amos A seventh-century prophet of Israel.

Anna The woman identified as the wife of Tobit in the Apocrypha. In the New Testament she is the Jewish prophetess who affirms the infant Jesus as the Messiah (Luke 2 : 36–38).

Antiochus IV King of the Seleucid dynasty of Syria, 175–164 B.C.E. Antiochus claimed to be Zeus reincarnate, and his policy of heavy-handed Hellenization led to the persecution of Palestinian Jews and caused the Maccabean revolt.

apocalypse A religious writing about the coming of the end of time. The books of Daniel and Revelation are the most complete examples of such literature in the Bible.

apocalyptic age The "age to come," when history will end as we know it and the kingdom of God will be established.

apocalypticism Form of dualistic religious thought found in late Judaism and throughout Christianity, seemingly rooted in Persian Zoroastrianism. It views history as involved in a cosmic struggle between good and evil. Satan leads the forces of evil, God the forces of good. It anticipates a final cosmic conflict in which good prevails over evil and the kingdom of God is established.

apocalyptic literature Writings about the coming of the end of time; they are dualistic in

nature, highly symbolic, and affirm the eventual triumph of good over evil.

Apocrypha That portion of Jewish scripture found in the Septuagint but not included in the Jewish canon adopted at Jamnia in 90 C.E. Its works were used by the early Christian community as scripture, but have not generally carried the status of scripture among most Protestants.

apocryphal works Besides the Hebrew Apocrypha, a number of literary works produced in the early Christian community were used like scripture at least by some until the New Testament was canonized. Excluded from that canon, these works are little known today.

Apollos An early Christian minister associated with the church at Corinth, founded by Paul (1 Cor. 1 : 12).

apology/apologia A writing in defense of the Christian faith, usually presenting a detailed historical explanation to defend what might otherwise be misunderstood.

apostle One who was directly commissioned or called by Jesus to carry on his ministry. All the Gospels and Acts mention the "twelve"; Luke (Chap. 10) cites the appointment of an additional seventy-two, and Paul claimed such status (Gal. 1 : 1) based on his religious experience on the road to Damascus (Acts 9 : 1–30).

Ark of Covenant A major religious symbol in Jewish history. Originally constructed by Moses, it housed the "two stones" on which were the Ten Commandments. It was believed to represent the invisible presence of Yahweh among his people and remained a major cultic symbol for Israel until its mysterious disappearance from historic reference during the monarchical era, perhaps as late as the period of Jeremiah.

Artaxerxes Persian king who commissioned Nehemiah to return as governor of Jerusalem.

Artaxerxes I (465–425 B.C.E.) was the son of Xerxes. Artaxerxes II (404–359 B.C.E.) was the son of Darius II of Persia. It is not clear which Artaxerxes the story of Nehemiah refers to.

Assyrians The predecessor to Babylon, a civilization that achieved the status of a major power in the Mideast during the separate monarchies of Israel and Judah. Assyria defeated Israel in 721 B.C.E. and subdued but did not destroy Judah at the end of the eighth century B.C.E. Both Assyria and Babylon occupied the territory that lies within the borders of modern Iraq.

Athaliah Daughter of Ahab and Jezebel, she became Queen of Judah for six years (2 Kings 11), breaking the line of David for that period. She ascended the throne on the occasion of the death of her son King Ahaziah, and remained until overthrown by supporters of Joash, who was of the line of David.

Baal Name of the god(s) of Canaan. Generally associated with fertility cults, the word can be translated simply as deity. An accompanying name generally specified a local or national deity.

Babylonia The successor to the Assyrian Empire, which occupied the same territory but had Babylon as its capital and reached the height of its power under Nebuchadnezzar. Babylonia defeated Judah, destroying Jerusalem and the Temple in 587 B.C.E. and taking the Israelite leaders into exile.

Babylonian exile Period during which the citizens of Judah were exiled in Babylon after their defeat by Nebuchadnezzar, usually dated 587–539 B.C.E.

Balaam A Moabite seer or prophet who was called to curse Israel as it was about to invade Canaan (Num. 22:5 ff). Instead, he was used by Yahweh to bless Israel.

Barabbas The criminal who was released by Roman authorities to placate the Jews after Jesus' trial (Matt. 27:15–26; Mark 15:6–15; Luke 23:13–19; John 18:39–40).

Baruch Probably the secretary to the prophet Jeremiah (Jer. 36:4 ff), his name is also associated with pseudepigraphical works of Baruch and the Apocalypse of Baruch.

Bathsheba A wife of David (2 Kings 11:1 ff); mother of Solomon. David arranged her first husband's death so he could marry her.

B.C.E. Before the common era. The common era is that period of history shared by Judaism and Christianity, and B.C.E. indicates the years before the birth of Jesus as determined by the Julian calendar, which divided history at the year then believed to have been the year of Jesus' birth.

Beatitudes A literary form that begins with word "blessed" and continues to praise individual piety as pleasing to God and worthy of reward. Beatitudes are found in both the Hebrew Bible and the New Testament.

Bel and the Dragon One of the Hebrew Bible's apocryphal works; included in the Book of Daniel in the Septuagint but not found in many Protestant Bibles.

Benjaminites Members of the tribe of Benjamin. The story of their exclusion from the other tribes of Israel is recalled in Judges (19:1 ff). The Benjaminites later joined the tribe of Judah to form the nation of Judah.

Bethlehem A town in Judah; the home of David and the birthplace of Jesus.

Bible The collection of writings of the Judeo-Christian tradition that carry the authority of scripture for those traditions.

Bildad One of the three friends of Job (8:1).

Boaz The husband of Ruth and the great-grandfather of David (Ruth 4:18–22).

Book of the Acts of Solomon A source used

by the Deuteronomic historian that is identified in 1 Kings.

Books of the Annals of the Kings of Israel One of the sources believed to have been used by the Deuteronomic historian. Mentioned in 1 and 2 Kings, it evidently was the official court history of Israel.

Book of the Annals of the Kings of Judah One of the sources believed to have been used by the Deuteronomic historian. Mentioned in 1 and 2 Kings, it evidently was the official court history of Judah.

Book of Wisdom One of the books of the Apocrypha.

Canaan The land occupied by the Canaanites, lying between the Jordan River and the Mediterranean Sea, which was invaded by the tribes of Israel and became the land of Israel.

canon The list of the books accepted as scripture by a religious body.

catholic Epistles The letters in the New Testament that are addressed to a general audience: James, 1 and 2 Peter, and Jude. Some also include 1, 2, and 3 John in this category.

C.E. "Common era." The years of the Judeo-Christian tradition.

Chloe A close associate of Paul from the church he founded in Corinth; she seems to have had leadership responsibilities among the Corinthians (1 Cor. 1:11).

Christ event Term used to describe Christianity's understanding of the meaning of all the events surrounding the life, death, and resurrection of Jesus.

Christ of faith Term used to describe how Jesus is understood or interpreted by New Testament authors as they report his life.

Christianity The religion that emerged from Judaism in the first century based on the belief that Jesus was/is the Messiah long expected by the Jews.

Christology Term used to describe how Jesus is interpreted as the Christ (Jewish Messiah).

Chronicler The name given to the author/editor of 1 and 2 Chronicles, Ezra, and Nehemiah.

Cilicia The name used during the period of emerging Christianity to designate a large geographical district located in the southeastern coastal section of Asia Minor.

conditional law Law that is based on the circumstances named; it takes the form: If you do so and so, then you must . . . This type of Law is found in the Hebrew Bible, though not as prominently as absolute law.

convocation at Shechem The occasion on which Joshua led the tribes of Israel in a covenant renewal ceremony (Josh. 23–24).

Corinth The chief city located on the Isthmus of Corinth, capital of the Roman province of Achaia, and site of one of the churches founded by Paul.

Council of Jamnia The group of Pharasaic Jews who met in Jamnia in 90 C.E. and determined the limits of the Jewish canon.

Council of Jerusalem A meeting between Paul and the other leaders of the Christian church at which were decided the requirements of Gentile converts to Christianity (Acts 15:1–29; Gal. 2:1–10).

court prophets Representatives of the official religion(s) of a land, these prophets acted as religious advisers to the king. They were common throughout the Near East during the Hebrew Bible period. Nathan was the court prophet to David.

covenant A binding promise or oath that sets conditions for a continuing relationship. The covenant most well known in the Bible (Exod.

19:3–8) describes Israel's covenant relationship with Yahweh.

cultic life The way in which a religion carries out its beliefs in the arena of worship; the ritual of a religion.

cultic prophets Members of a professional group of prophets who were responsible for the teaching and preservation of the religious tradition, supplementing the liturgical responsibilities of the priesthood.

Cyrus of Persia The leader of the Persian Empire who defeated the Babylonians and allowed the Jews to return to their homeland.

Damascus The Palestinian town associated with the conversion of Paul (Acts 9:1–30).

Daniel The subject of the Book of Daniel, a Jew who purportedly served as a wise man/counselor in the court of Nebuchadnezzar and gained fame by his loyalty to his religion in the face of persecution.

Danites One of the twelve tribes of Israel, not well regarded by the Deuteronomic historian. Samson was a Danite.

Darius King of Persia (522–486 B.C.E.) who allowed the reconstruction of the Temple in Jerusalem, as described in the Book of Ezra.

David The second king of Israel. Yahweh promised through the prophet Nathan that David's royal line would endure. The line of David became closely associated with Jewish/Christian messianism.

Deborah One of the twelve Judges of Israel during the period of the tribal confederation.

Demetrius A Christian leader who receives the affirmation of John the Elder in 3 John.

Deuteronomic history (historian) The term applied to the material found in the Hebrew Bible in the Books of Joshua through 2 Kings (except for Ruth). The term "Deuteronomic historian" identifies the author/editor of that material.

Diaspora Jews The Jews who did not return to Palestine after the Babylonian exile but remained faithful Jews.

Diotrephes A Christian of ill repute who was associated with the community to which 3 John was addressed.

disciples Followers of Jesus including, but not limited to, the twelve apostles.

Domitian Roman emperor (81–96 C.E.) under whom first widespread persecution of Christians took place.

Eastern Church The portion of Catholicism that separated from Rome in 1054. The denominations resulting from that separation are usually referred to as the Eastern Orthodox tradition.

Ecclesiastes One of the books of the Hebrew Bible that is part of the wisdom literature of Judaism. It is nontraditional in its approach to classical Hebrew wisdom.

Ecclesiasticus One of the books of the Apocrypha.

ecstatic prophets In a form of prophecy alluded to in the Hebrew Bible (1 Sam. 10:9–12), the prophet seemed to be seized by the spirit of Yahweh, thrown into a spirit of ecstasy out of which he prophesized.

Edomites Residents of Edom, a territory located between the Dead Sea and the Gulf of Aqabah. The Edomites were constant enemies of the tribes of Israel.

Eli The priest/leader of Israel in the last days of the tribal confederacy. Eli raised his successor, Samuel.

Elihu The fourth person in the Book of Job who tries to convince Job that since he was suffering, he must have sinned (Job 32:2 ff).

Elijah Ninth-century Hebrew prophet active in the kingdom of Israel. Particularly remembered for his encounters with Ahab, Jezebel, and the Baal prophets, Elijah later was viewed in the Judeo-Christian tradition as the herald of the Messiah.

Eliphaz Another of the three friends who argue with Job about whether Job is indeed righteous (Job 2:11).

Elisha The successor to the prophet Elijah; his influence helped establish the Jehu dynasty in Israel.

Ephesus An ancient city located on the Aegean coast near what is now Izmir; site of one of the churches founded by Paul.

Ephraim One of the sons of Joseph and a **half-tribe** of Israel. In later Hebrew Bible literary tradition it becomes synonymous with Israel.

epistle A formal letter, one of the literary forms found in the New Testament.

eschatology Term used to describe the Bible doctrines about the end of time.

Esdras, 1, 2 Books included in the Apocrypha.

Essenes A Jewish sect in existence during the life of Jesus. It is believed that they wrote and preserved the Dead Sea Scrolls. Some have suggested that John may have been associated with Essenes before he began his ministry of baptism.

Esther Jewish heroine of the exile whose story is recorded in the Book of Esther.

evangelists The writers of the four Gospels, Matthew, Mark, Luke, and John.

exegesis The explanation of a portion of scripture based on critical exposition.

exilic The term used to describe events that took place in the history of Judaism during the period of the Jews' exile in Babylon (587–539 B.C.E.).

Exodus The second book of the Bible. The totality of all the events surrounding the Hebrew escape from Egyptian enslavement.

experienced history Describing history in light of one's personal perception of its meaning.

"eyes of faith" Term describing a way of understanding history based on the presuppositions provided by one's religious viewpoint.

Ezekiel A prophet of Israel in the sixth century B.C.E.

Ezra The priestly leader of Israel who, with Nehemiah, helped establish the religious understanding of Judaism after the exile.

faith Belief in something beyond the self. Trust or belief in the assertions or the revelations of a given religion.

"Fall" Word used to describe the descent of humanity into the state of sin or alienation from Yahweh. The event is described in Genesis 3.

form criticism A critical method that is applied to material in an effort to recapture it in as close to its original form as possible.

Galatia Both a region in a province of the Roman Empire located in central Asia Minor, and an area of activity by Paul on his first missionary journey.

general Epistle A letter or epistle that is addressed to a general rather than a specific audience; also known as catholic Epistle.

Gentiles People who are not Jews; term first applied to those outside the Jewish faith before the birth of Christ.

Gideon Highly popular Judge of the era of the tribal confederacy whose exploits led the people of Israel to try to make him their king (Jud. 6:1 ff).

gnosticism Term used to describe a number

of religious philosophies that existed within and outside the Judeo-Christian tradition in the years during which Christianity emerged from Judaism. The word *gnosis* (knowledge) characterized a common belief that one is saved by correct (and often secret) knowledge. Most systems were dualistic, distinguishing between the world (evil) and the spirit (good).

"God fearers" People who associated with and followed many of the practices and religious beliefs of the Diaspora Jewish community without actually becoming converts to that community.

Gomer Wife of Hosea; a temple prostitute of the Baal religion before she became his bride.

gospel parallel A book that sets the synoptic Gospels side by side to facilitate a comparison of their order, content, similarities, and differences.

Gospel Literally, "good news." A literary form exclusive to the New Testament in which events in the life of Jesus are reported to affirm the belief in his messiahship. The first four books of the New Testament are the Gospels of Matthew, Mark, Luke, and John.

Greco-Roman world The sociopolitical matrix of early Christianity. Controlled politically by the Roman Empire, its common language was Greek and it inherited the products of the years of Hellenization.

Habbakuk Prophet of Judah in the sixth century B.C.E. who proclaimed the importance of individual righteousness and the promise of individual judgment by Yahweh. It was he who first spoke of justification by faith.

Haggai A postexilic prophet, he encouraged the rebuilding of the Temple at Jerusalem after the Jews had returned from their Babylonian exile.

half-tribe A term that refers to that portion of the tribe of Manasseh that chose to remain east of the Jordan after Israel occupied Canaan. The other half of the tribe settled in central Canaan.

Haman The dreaded enemy of the Jews who attempted to have them exterminated during the reign of Ahasuerus of Persia. The story is reported in Esther.

Hasidim/ic Strict observers of the Jewish law who formed the major resistance to the Hellenistic policies of Antiochus IV; they were the forerunners of the Pharisees.

Hasmonaean dynasty The Jewish kings who ruled Palestine from 142 to 63 B.C.E. The dynasty began at the end of the Maccabean wars.

Hebrew Interchangeable with Israelite; a name the Israelites applied to themselves, also used by others to identify them in the Hebrew Bible period. It is the name of the ancestor of Eber and may derive from that. More likely it is derived from *habiru*, the word that refers to a class of mideastern inhabitants neither slave nor free, who were often landless and nomadic.

Hebrew Bible That portion of the Bible produced within the Jewish community before the common era and used as scripture by the entire Judeo-Christian community.

Hellenization The spreading of the Greek culture across the lands conquered by Alexander the Great. The "civilizing" of that world continued into the Christian era, characterized by the use of Greek as the common language and honoring the Greek view of life.

heresy Wrong belief. Heresy is determined by those who have the responsibility for maintaining a tradition and protecting it from distortion.

hermeneutics The final step in the use of critical tools when the meaning of a text is interpreted.

Hezekiah The king of Judah (715–689 B.C.E.) honored as the pious ruler who saw Judah and Jerusalem through the siege by the Assyrians (701 B.C.E.).

historical criticism The attempt to place material in the context in which it was produced, to better understand its original message.

Holy Spirit The third person of the Trinity in Christian theology, it refers to the spirit of God as it dwells in Jesus and, later, in members of the Christian community.

Hosea The prophet who used his marriage to Gomer as illustrative of Yahweh's relationship with Israel.

House of Jehu One of the two major dynasties during the period of monarchy in Israel. It began with Jehu in 842 B.C.E. and continued until the death of Jeroboam II in 746 B.C.E.

House of Omri The first major dynasty in the history of Israel's monarchy. It began with Omri in 876 B.C.E. and ended with the revolt of Jehu in 842 B.C.E.

Huldah A seventh-century prophetess who was consulted by Josiah regarding the authenticity of the scroll found in the Temple in 721 B.C.E. (2 Kings 22:14).

Isaac The second patriarch; the son of Abraham and Sarah, the father of Jacob and Esau.

Isaiah Eighth-century prophet of Judah who introduced the messianic dimension into prophetic theology.

II Isaiah Isaiah 40–55, believed by many to be the work of a fifth-century prophet carrying on the tradition of Isaiah.

III Isaiah Isaiah 56–66, believed by some to be the work of a postexilic prophet.

"Isaiah School of Theology" A term used to describe the continuing influence of the prophet Isaiah beyond his own time, particularly as reflected in Isaiah 40–66.

Ishmaelites The descendants of Ishmael, son of Abraham and his concubine Hagar. They lived in Canaan at the time it was invaded by Joshua and became enemies of the Hebrews.

Israel The name given to Jacob after his encounter with the supernatural, and used to designate the twelve tribes of Israel as descendants of the sons of Jacob (Gen. 32:22 ff). Also, the name given to the land of Canaan by the Hebrews after their conquest. The northern portion of that land after the division of the monarchies at the end of the reign of Solomon.

Jacob Son of Isaac, twin to Esau; he was renamed "Israel" and his twelve sons became the twelve tribes of Israel. It was through Jacob the seed of Abraham was passed.

James Identified in the Gospels as a brother of Jesus and in Acts as one of the leaders of the early Christian church in Jerusalem. He seems to have been sympathetic to the Judaizers. There are two other Jameses of importance in the New Testament: One James was the son of Zebedee and the brother of John, a disciple of Jesus. The other James is identified as the son of Alphaeus and was one of the original twelve disciples.

Jamnia Site (near present-day Tel-Aviv) of the conference of Pharasaic rabbis who set the limits of the Jewish canon in 90 C.E.

Jehoiachin One of the last kings of Judah; exiled to Babylon by Nebuchadnezzar in 597 B.C.E.

Jehoiakim King of Judah (609–598 B.C.E.); martyred either by the Babylonians or their sympathizers. His original name was Eliakim but was changed to Jehoiakim by Pharaoh Neco.

Jeremiah The prophet active in the sixth and fifth centuries, best remembered for his theology of a "new covenant written on the heart."

Jericho According to the story in Joshua (6: 1–27), the scene of Israel's first major victory in their invasion of Canaan.

Jeroboam I The first king of Israel after the division of Israel and Judah (922 B.C.E.). Jeroboam II was the last ruler of the House of Jehu.

Jerusalem The city that served as the capital of Judah and the site of the Temple; the Holy City of the Judeo-Christian tradition.

Jesse The father of King David.

Jesus The personal name of the man Christians believe to be the Messiah, the "Christ."

Jesus of history The portion of the life of Jesus reported in the New Testament, which scholars believe helps in drawing the picture of the historical figure Jesus.

Jew An inheritor of the Jewish religious tradition, which was preserved and passed on by the surviving nation Judah and its descendants.

Jezreel Name of the first son of Hosea (Hosea 1:4), reflecting Yahweh's displeasure of the slaughter of Jews at Jezreel by Jehu.

Job The pious Edomite about whom the Book of Job is written.

Joel The late Hebrew Bible prophet who is credited as author of the Book of Joel.

John The "disciple whom Jesus loved." He and his brother James, son of Zebedee (the "sons of thunder") were among the original twelve apostles. Tradition asserts he is the author of the Gospel of John and 1, 2, and 3 John, as well as the Book of Revelation.

John the Baptist Identified in the New Testament as the contemporary herald of Jesus' messianic ministry. He came from a priestly background but functioned more in the role of prophet. According to the synoptic Gospels, Jesus began his public ministry after being baptized by John.

Jonah Purportedly a Jewish missionary to Nineveh, Jonah is the subject of the Hebrew Bible book that bears his name.

Joseph Husband of Mary and father of Jesus. Also, in the Hebrew Bible, the favorite son of Jacob; he was sold into slavery by his brothers and became a prominent aide to an Egyptian Pharaoh. He was later reconciled with his family and it was through him that his family settled in Egypt.

Joshua The successor to Moses, who led Israel's invasion of Canaan.

Josiah The boy king of Judah who came to power after the period of Assyrian domination. It was during his reign that Judah experienced great religious reform, culminating in a cleansing of the Temple in 621 B.C.E.

Judah The smaller of the two nations of Jews after the division of Israel in 922 B.C.E. Its capital was Jerusalem and the Temple was the center of its worship life.

Judaism The name of the religion of the Jews. It reflects the survival of religion, as later shaped in the nation of Judah.

Judaizers Members of the early Christian community who believed and taught that one had to become a Jew to be a Christian. They are referred to as the "Circumcision Party," for they wanted to require circumcision of Gentile converts to Christianity.

Jude Identified in the Gospels as a brother of Jesus; according to tradition, author of the New Testament work of that name.

Judeo-Christian Term applied to those things Judaism and Christianity hold in common.

Judges Military leaders during period of tribal confederacy; they functioned much like American Indian war chiefs, having no hereditary claim to their leadership role.

Judith The book of the Apocrypha that celebrates the feats of the Jewish heroine whose exploits it reports.

"kingdom ethic" The idea that the ethics of Christianity have a direct relationship to the coming of the kingdom of God, either by helping one achieve the kingdom, or as the ethic that will be practiced in that kingdom.

kingdom of God The acknowledgment of God as sovereign king of the world. It is particularly prominent in apocalyptic thought, which anticipates the time when the kingdom will be realized on earth.

"L" The designation of the material that is found only in the Gospel of Luke as discussed in Streeter's hypothesis.

Law The totality of the rules and regulations in the Pentateuch, which Jews understand as setting the bounds of their covenant relationship with Yahweh; sometimes used to refer to the first section of Jewish scripture: Genesis, Exodus, Leviticus, Numbers, and Deuteronomy.

Lazarus The friend whom Jesus is reported to have raised from the dead (John 11:1 ff). Another Lazarus was a beggar, a subject of a parable found in Luke (16:19–31).

legends Stories that come to us from the past, generally regarded as being rooted in history even if not historically verifiable.

Levites Members of the tribe of Levi, they carried the responsibilities of the priesthood in Hebrew culture.

literary criticism The means by which a text is examined to determine its original form or source.

literary tradition The literature of culture that has been written down, preserved, and passed on (cf. *oral tradition*).

liturgy The established or guiding form prescribed for a service of worship.

logos theology Refers to the concept found in writings of John in which Jesus is identified directly with the "Word" or "Logos" (John 1:1 ff).

Luke According to tradition, the author of the Gospel of Luke and the Acts of the Apostles. An early convert, he was associated with most of the major leaders of the first generation of Christianity.

Luke's "special section" The material found in Luke 9:51–18:14, so called because much of it is found only in this Gospel.

"M" Material found only in the Gospel of Matthew, designated to distinguish it from other common materials shared by the synoptic Gospels in Streeter's hypothesis.

Maccabean revolt The guerrilla war waged by the Jews against the oppressive policies of Antiochus IV. Victory came in 165 B.C.E., and Palestine was freed from outside control for the last time in ancient history.

1, 2 Maccabees Two books of the Apocrypha that share views of the events surrounding the Maccabean revolt.

3, 4 Maccabees Two books of the Pseudepigrapha whose origins and purposes are less clear than those of 1 and 2 Maccabees.

Malachi Name given to the last book in the Hebrew Bible, the work of a late (fifth-century) prophet.

Manasseh King of Judah during a period of Assyrian domination (687–642 B.C.E.); the history of his rule reflects the reality that Judah was a vassal of Assyria.

manna The honeylike substance supplied by Yahweh to the Hebrews to provide nourishment during their journey through the wilderness (see, e.g., Exod. 16:31–35).

Marcion A second-century Christian heretic who is credited with producing the first canonical list for the New Testament. It was in opposition to Marcion that more orthodox Christians began to produce their own canons of the New Testament.

Mark The person tradition affirms as the author of the Gospel of Mark. A noneyewitness to the life of Jesus, but an early convert to Christianity, companion to Paul and finally secretary to Peter, from whose reminiscences the Gospel was purportedly written.

Matthew One of the original twelve apostles, whom tradition credits with the authorship of the first Gospel.

Melchizedek A Canaanite king/priest mentioned in Genesis (14:18–20) whose priestly heritage the author of the New Testament Book of Hebrews asserts is superior to that of the Levites and with which he associates the priesthood of Jesus.

Meshach Name given by the Babylonians to Mishael, one of the companions of Daniel who survived the ordeal of the fiery furnace (Dan. 3:12–30).

Messiah The one expected at the end of time, the "annointed one" who will help usher in the kingdom of God.

"messianic secret" The concept implied in the Gospel of Mark that Jesus did not publicly claim to be Messiah and asked others to make no such proclamation for him.

Messianism The theology that surrounds the concept of messianic expectation in the Judeo-Christian tradition.

Micah Late eighth-century prophet of Judah, a contemporary of Isaiah.

Midian; Midianites Descendants of Abraham through his third wife Keturah. Jethro, father-in-law of Moses, was a Midianite.

millennialism The views surrounding the meaning of Revelation 20:4–6 when Christ is to establish a thousand-year reign following his victorious return to earth.

Miriam Sister of Moses and Aaron; credited as author of Song of Victory (Exod. 15:20–21) after the Israelite victory at the Red (Reed) Sea.

Mishnah A collection of Jewish oral law gath-ered between the first century B.C.E. and the third century C.E., it formed the basis of the later Gemara, the second portion of the Talmud.

Moabites Traditional enemies of the Israelites who occupied the land east of the Dead Sea and south of the Jordan River.

monarchy The period when Israel and Judah enjoyed national independence and each was ruled by a king.

monotheism The belief in a single God.

moral law Law that governs the moral behavior of individuals or groups.

Mordecai The cousin of Esther who, in the book of that name, worked with Esther to keep Haman from obliterating the Jews in the Persian Empire.

Moses The leader of the Jews out of Egyptian exile, through whom Israel received the Law and the Covenant.

myth A story whose major intention is to explain the meaning of life in relation to its understanding of that which is the ultimate cause. The story may or may not be rooted in history.

Nahum A Hebrew prophet of the preexilic period.

Naomi Israelite mother-in-law of Ruth, whose religion Ruth adopts as her own.

Nathan The court prophet of Israel at the time of David.

national religion A religion identified with a particular people located in a particular place or nation. Nationhood and the religion are generally interconnected.

Nazareth The Palestinian town in the territory of Galilee where Jesus grew up.

Nebuchadnezzar King of Babylon who defeated Judah in 587 B.C.E. and sent most of Judah into exile.

Nehemiah Governor of Jerusalem in the mid-fifth century B.C.E. who was responsible for rebuilding the wall around the city and, with Ezra, helped to reestablish and define surviving Judaism.

Nero Roman emperor (54–68 C.E.) who was responsible for the period of persecution of Christians traditionally assumed to have resulted in the martyrdom of Peter and Paul.

New Testament The scriptures of Christianity used exclusively by the Christian denominations.

New Testament Apocrypha Those literary works produced by the early Christian community and used by some segment of that community as scripture for a period of time. They were not included in the official canon of the New Testament as determined by the Councils of Hippo and Carthage.

Nineveh Capital of Assyria, whose destruction in 612 B.C.E. signaled the collapse of the Assyrian Empire. The city to which Jonah was sent (Jon. 1).

nomadic Wandering; a description of people who do not possess land of their own.

nontraditional wisdom Literature whose contents seem to question the assumptions of traditional Hebrew wisdom.

Obadiah One of the minor prophets whose writings were probably produced in the fifth century B.C.E.

Obed Son of Ruth and Boaz; father of Jesse; grandfather of King David.

"official religion" Term used to describe a religion allowed by the Roman Empire to function without government interference.

Old Testament The Christian term for the Hebrew Bible (see *Hebrew Bible*).

Onesimus The slave for whom Paul interceded in the epistle to Philemon.

oracles The speaking of what is understood to be a divine revelation.

oral tradition The traditions of a culture or religion that are passed on by word of mouth from generation to generation (cf. *literary tradition*).

Origen A prominent Alexandrian Christian of the third century who was a scholar and leader of the catechetical school in Alexandria.

Orpah The Moabite daughter-in-law of Naomi who decided to remain in her own country when her sister-in-law Ruth returned to Israel with Naomi.

orthodoxy Right belief, as defined by the accepted officials of a religious tradition.

Palestine The name by which Israel was known to outsiders before and after the period of the monarchy.

Palestinian Judaism The Judaism practiced among the Jews who returned to the Holy Land after the Babylonian exile.

parables A form of speech similar to an allegory; a brief narrative told to make the point of an object lesson.

parousia The event of the coming of the end of time.

passion story The telling of the events surrounding the trial and crucifixion of Jesus.

Passover A major festival of Judaism, celebrating the deliverance of the Jews from Egyptian bondage.

pastoral Epistles The name sometimes applied to 1 and 2 Timothy and Titus by those who understand their common overriding interest to be church order.

Patmos An island in the Icarian Sea, identified by the author of Revelation as his location when he received the visions reported.

Patriarchs Those forefathers of the nation of Israel: Abraham, Isaac, and Jacob.

Paul (Saul) The Jewish convert to Christianity credited with spreading Christianity among the Gentiles during the first generation of Christianity. He is also credited with authorship of a significant number of New Testament books.

Pauline Christianity The name applied to the type of Christianity that attributes much of its thought to the interpretation of the works of Paul as they define the meaning of the Christ event in history.

Paulinists The name applied to the unknown authors whose works in the New Testament attribute themselves to Paul, although most modern scholars seriously doubt that they were written by Paul.

Pentecost A Jewish festival celebrated the seventh week after Passover to commemorate the gathering of the grain harvest. In Christianity it is the seventh Sunday after Easter and celebrates the bestowal of the Holy Spirit on the church at Jerusalem (Acts 2).

Pentateuch The first five books of the Hebrew Bible, sometimes called the five books of Moses.

Pharisees The most popular sect in Palestinian Judaism at the beginning of the Christian era, it survived the destruction of Jerusalem and the Temple in 70 C.E. and helped give shape to modern Judaism.

Philemon The churchman to whom Paul addressed his epistle interceding for the slave Onesimus.

Philistines Known as the "sea people," their origins are unknown. They occupied the coastal section of Canaan at the time of its invasion by Israel and remained enemies of Israel for many years.

Philo of Alexandria Influential Alexandrian Jewish philosopher who was a contemporary of Jesus. Philo's works show the influence of Hellenization on Diaspora Judaism.

popular prophets The name applied to the prophets in the Hebrew Bible who reportedly said what the people wanted to hear rather than pronouncing the authentic judgment of Yahweh.

postexilic The period of Jewish history that follows the return of some Jews to their Holy Land after the Babylonian exile until the beginning of the Christian era (539–6 B.C.E.).

Prayer of Manasseh A short apocryphal work consisting of fifteen verses purporting to be the prayer of the repentant King Manasseh.

preexilic The period of Jewish history that precedes the exile of the Jews in Babylon (before 587 B.C.E.). It generally is used in relationship to the period of the written prophets, so its beginning can be assumed to be about 750 B.C.E.

priesthood The religious officials of Israel, members of the tribe of Levi, whose responsibility it was to carry out the cultic activities of the Temple, mediating between Yahweh and the people of the Covenant.

"priestly prayer" The prayer of Jesus reported in John (17:1–26) in which Jesus defines his own role as mediator.

promised land The land of Israel for the Jews, so called because of the promise of the land made by Yahweh to Abraham. It was formerly known as Canaan.

prophet One who speaks for Yahweh, always with a sense of call and directly in relationship to God's will for his people.

Prophets The classification given by Judaism to the second section of Jewish scripture: The former Prophets include Joshua, Judges, Samuel, and Kings; the latter Prophets include Isaiah, Jeremiah, Ezekiel, Hosea, Joel, Amos, Obadiah, Jonah, Micah, Nahum, Habakkuk, Zephaniah, Haggai, Zechariah, and Malachi.

"Prophetic School of Theology" Term used to

describe the ongoing prophetic tradition of Israel and Judah, implying that that tradition was formal and continuing.

Protestant Bible Any translation of the Bible that follows the practice of the Protestant tradition of either placing the Hebrew Bible apocryphal works between the Hebrew Bible and the New Testament or removing them from the Bible altogether.

Proverbs Sayings that give expression to cherished facts or values of society, used to teach the facts or values to new generations.

psalms Hebrew poetic liturgy used in the context of worship to give expression to the continuing relationship between Yahweh and his people.

Ptolemy Philopator One of the last of the Ptolemaic kings (221–203 B.C.E.), he was denied entry to the Jerusalem Temple by the Jews. As a result, he later persecuted Jews.

Purim A popular Jewish festival celebrating the survival of Judaism during the Persian period, as recounted in the Book of Esther.

"Q" The designation B. H. Streeter applied to the materials that are common to the Gospels of Matthew and Luke, but not found in Mark. Most of this material consists of "sayings" of Jesus.

redaction criticism The critical effort to separate in a literary work the sources used by the author/editor and the material he actually wrote.

Rehoboam Son of Solomon who succeeded his father to the throne and under whom Israel and Judah were divided into two separate nations. Rehoboam ruled Judah.

religious law Law that has to do with how one's religion is to be expressed in the activities of life.

remnant theology That portion of the theology of the literary prophets of Israel and Judah that proclaims that Yahweh will preserve and allow to prosper a remnant of his chosen people who have lived within the bounds of the convenant relationship and have kept the Law.

"revealed" Term used to describe a religion whose affirmations are believed to come through direct revelation from the deity rather than through reason or other means.

revelation The means by which God through his own initiative makes himself known.

ritual law Laws that have to do primarily with the form worship is to take.

Ruth The Moabite daughter-in-law of Naomi who became an Israelite, married Boaz, and was the great-grandmother of King David.

Sadducees One of the major sects in Judaism at the beginning of the Christian era. Its members were the conservative aristocracy of Palestinian Judaism whose principal interest was in the worship activities of the Temple.

salvation history Term used to describe the Judeo-Christian view of history that God's continuing relationship with humankind has as its object the reconciliation of salvation of creatures with or by the creator.

Samaritans Those residents of the area of Palestine called Samaria after the fall of Israel in 721 B.C.E. who thought of themselves as Jews but were not considered Jews by other Palestinian Jews because of their unorthodox religious practices and their questionable family heritages.

Samson The mythiclike Judge who singlehandedly destroyed the Philistines after he had become their captive (Judg. 14–17).

Samuel Described as prophet, priest, judge, and almost king, successor to Eli in the last days of the tribal confederacy, who anointed Saul and then David as the first kings of Israel.

Sanhedrin The court in Jerusalem that governed Jewish religious life during the late Hebrew Bible period until the fall of Jerusalem in 70 C.E. It had seventy-one members, the majority of whom were Sadducees; its presiding officer was usually the high priest.

Saul Hebrew Bible: the first king of Israel; New Testament: the name of Paul before his conversion to Christianity.

scribes Teachers of the Law in postexilic Judaism, they probably also kept the Jewish scriptures alive by making copies, which were passed on to future generations.

scripture The sacred literature of a religion, which is considered authoritative in matters of faith and practice.

Septuagint The name applied to the oldest Greek translation of the Hebrew Bible, so named because of the seventy witnesses to Moses' receiving the Law.

Sermon on the Mount The material found in Chapters 5–7 of Matthew, consisting of a sermon on religious ethics that Jesus preached from a mountain.

servant passages The writings of II Isaiah in which the messianic figure is cast in the role of a servant (42:1–4; 49:1–6; 50:4–11; 52:13–53:12).

Shadrach Name given by the Babylonians to Hananiah, one of the companions of Daniel who experienced the ordeal of the fiery furnace (Dan. 3:12–30).

Shechem Site (near present-day Nablus) of the tribal convocation described in Joshua 24.

Sheshbazzar Descendant of David who led the Jews out of Babylonian exile under the Edict of Cyrus of Persia.

signs Term applied to the extraordinary feats Jesus is reported to have performed in the Gospel of John, which served as testimony to his role as Messiah.

Simeon The devout Jew described in Luke (2:25–35) who was a witness to the infant Jesus as the promised Messiah.

Solomon Son of David, third king of Israel, remembered for his great wisdom.

Song of Azariah in the Furnace A book of the Hebrew Bible Apocrypha describing the religious devotion of those who survived the ordeal of the fiery furnace described in Daniel (3:12–30).

Song of Songs Also known as Song of Solomon; a collection of wedding poetry out of ancient Israel.

Song of the Three Young Men Another apocryphal addition to the Book of Daniel.

"sons of thunder" Name applied to the two disciple brothers, James and John.

"spiritual Gospel" The name applied to the Gospel of John by some early Christians in an effort to explain why it differed from the synoptic Gospels.

St. Jerome Fourth-century Christian scholar whose voluminous works provide a great deal of information about the early history of Christianity.

Streeter's hypothesis The attempt of B. H. Streeter to explain the literary relationship between the Gospels of Mark, Matthew, and Luke.

Susanna An apocryphal addition to the Book of Daniel.

synagogue A place of public worship for Jews away from the Temple. A creation of the Babylonian exile, this institution made possible the continued practice of Judaism.

syncretism The fusion of the ideas or practices of a variety of religions.

synoptic Gospels The Gospels of Mark, Matthew, and Luke; the term acknowledges the striking similarities among those three accounts of the life of Jesus.

synoptic problem The difficulty of determining the literary relationship among the synoptic Gospels.

Tarsus The birthplace of Paul: a city on the southeast coast of Cilicia in Asia Minor.

Temple The center of the worship life of Israel, it was located in Jerusalem and was the only place at which sacrifices could be offered. First built in the tenth century B.C.E., it was finally destroyed in the first century of the common era.

Ten Commandments The ten laws given to Moses (Exod. 20:1–17); known as the Decalogue.

testament Usually synonymous with "will," this term could have been used in Greek as another name for covenant. The latter usage is implied in the designations Old Testament and New Testament.

textual criticism The study of a writing to discover as nearly as possible the original form in which it was first produced.

Theophilus The person to whom Luke-Acts is addressed, most likely an official of the Roman Empire who might or might not have been a Christian.

Timothy One of Paul's chief and most trusted aides on his missionary journeys.

Titus A companion and co-worker of Paul.

Tobias The son of Tobit and a chief character in the apocryphal Book of Tobit.

Tobit A devout Jew of the Diaspora whose story is recounted in the Book of Tobit.

Torah Sometimes used to refer to the books of the Pentateuch; also used as a reference for all of the scripture of Judaism: the Hebrew Bible.

tradition The memory of the past, preserved, either orally or in literary form, and passed on because it is regarded as having value for succeeding generations.

tradition of the prophets The commemorative materials, both oral and written, which kept the memory of the prophets of Israel alive and preserved their point of view for future generations.

traditional wisdom The point of view reflected in much of the wisdom literature of the Hebrew Bible; in its prophetic view of history the rewarding of good and the punishment of evil are assumed.

transfiguration An event described in the synoptic Gospels (Matt. 17:1–9; Mark 9:2–10; Luke 9:28–36): On his last journey to Jerusalem, Jesus was glorified by God in the presence of Moses and Elijah.

tribal Describing a society structured in small groups, often the immediate or extended family, whose commitment to the community is essential to its existence.

tribe of Judah The tribe of which David was a part, one of the twelve tribes of Israel and the chief tribe involved in establishing the nation of Judah.

tribes of Israel The descendants of the twelve sons of Jacob and the people who became the nation of Israel.

trinity Term representing the Christian idea that God is manifest both in unity and in diversity: One God coexists as Father, Son, and Holy Spirit.

"true" prophets The prophets who in the judgment of Judaism spoke in behalf of Yahweh, not for themselves.

universalism An expression of religion that is not limited by the boundaries of nation, race, or sexual preference that often separate people and ideas.

virgin birth The assertion found in the Gospels of Matthew and Luke that Jesus was conceived by the spirit of God, not in the natural biological way.

Vulgate The Latin translation of the Bible done by St. Jerome at the end of the fourth and the beginning of the fifth century C.E. It was made the official version of the Bible for Roman Catholics at the Council of Trent in the sixteenth century.

"We" section of Acts That portion of the Book of Acts beginning in Chapter 16 where the narrative turns to the first person, indicating that the author was present at the events he was reporting.

wisdom The means by which one can know the way of the gods or God.

wisdom tradition The preservation of the collected wisdom of the culture of Israel in both oral and literary form.

"word" In the Hebrew Bible, the means by which Yahweh makes his will known in the Law and the prophets; in the New Testament the Gospel of John expands the term to include Jesus as such a manifestation.

world religion A religion that is not bound by national or ethnic considerations but which can be expressed by people regardless of circumstance or location.

Writings The classification given by Judaism to the third section of Jewish scripture: Psalms, Proverbs, Job, Song of Songs, Ruth, Lamentations, Ecclesiastes, Esther, Daniel, Ezra, Nehemiah, and 1 and 2 Chronicles.

Xerxes A Persian king (486–465 B.C.E.), son of Darius I.

Yahweh The name of God revealed to Moses on the occasion of the encounter of the burning bush (Exod. 3:13–15).

Zealots A sect that arose in postexilic Judaism most noted for radical attitudes toward political domination by nonPalestinians and their activist approach to the goal of ending the political domination of the Romans.

Zechariah Name that appears frequently in the Hebrew Bible identifying, for example, one of the postexilic prophets.

Zedekiah The prophet who promised Ahab victory over the Syrians (1 Kings 22:1–28); also, king of Israel after Jehoiachin (2 Kings 17 ff). He was blinded by the Babylonians and taken into exile at the time of the fall of Jerusalem.

Zephaniah A late preexilic prophet.

Zerubbabel One of the two leaders of the early postexilic period who can be identified with the line of David.

Zophar One of the three friends of Job (11:1).

INDEX

Aaron, 27, 29, 90, 91
Abdon, 35
Abednego, 91, 109
Abijah, 83
Abimelech, 35, 39
Abraham, 14, 16, 19, 23–24, 26, 137
Absalom, 41
Absolute law, 28
Acts of the Apostles, 120, 125, 126, 127, 157–158, 159, 160, 161, 164–166
Adam, 21, 159
Adonijah, 43
Ahaz, 63
Ahijah, 45
Ai, 35, 38
Alexander the Great, 16, 107, 113, 115
Alexandrian Jews, 110
Amos, 25, 55, 56, 58, 59–60
Anderson, Bernhard W., 26
Anna, 159
Antichrist, 192
Antiochus IV, 100, 101
Apocalypse, 12
Apocalyptic age, 121–122
Apocalyptic literature, 12, 193–194, 195
Apocalyptic world view, 100, 101–102, 112
Apocrypha, 3, 12, 103, 106–110
  New Testament, 203
Apostles, 118
Ark of Covenant, 29
Artaxerxes, 110
Assyrian
  domination of Israel, 10, 15, 16, 43, 47, 50, 58, 63
  domination of Judah, 48, 50, 64
Athaliah, 48, 83
Azariah, Song of, 109

Baal, 46
Babylon, 2, 15, 66, 67
  creation story of, 20, 21

domination of Judah, 16, 43, 49, 63–64, 75
  Persian defeat of, 76, 77, 80
Babylonian exile, 5, 8, 10, 11, 12, 13, 59, 67, 68, 73–76, 83, 101, 109
Balaam, 29
Barabbas, 160
Bar-Kochba, Simon, 114
Baruch, 65, 109
Bathsheba, 41, 42, 58, 83
B.C.E. (before the common era), 3
Beatitudes, 155
Bel and the Dragon, 109
Benjaminites, 39
Bethlehem, 119
Bible. See also Hebrew Bible; New Testament; Septuagint; names of specific books
  approaches to, 1–2
  historical development of, 9–11
  as history, 2, 3–4, 8
  lands and peoples of, 14–19
  meaning of, 6–7
  order of, 4–5, 12–14
  origin of, 7–8
  preservation and transmission of, 203–204
  as religious document, 1, 2, 7
  scholarly study of, 8–9, 145
  as scripture, 2–3, 7, 10, 11–12
  translations of, 5, 106, 107, 204
Biblos, 6
Bildad, 96
Boaz, 98
Book of the Acts of Solomon, 2
Book of the Annals of the Kings of Israel, 2, 45, 49
Book of the Annals of the Kings of Judah, 2, 45, 49
Book of Wisdom, 108
Burning bush, 27

Canaan, 14, 16, 24, 29. See also Israel; Palestine
  invasion of, 16, 37–38
  name of, 14, 116

Canon
  Christian, 200, 202
  defined, 199
  Jewish, 6, 10, 12, 199–200
Carius, 82
Catholic Epistles, 170, 176–180
  James, 176–178
  Jude, 179–180
  Peter, 178–179
C.E. (common era), 3–4
Chaldeans, 14
Chloe, 132, 134
Christ-event, 121, 124, 173
Christ of faith, 120, 124
Christianity, 1, 2, 3, 5, 6. See also Jesus; New Testament
  apocalyptic view in, 193–194
  apology, 158
  birth of, 117–122
  interpretation of Hebrew Bible, 11, 12
  Judaism as root of, 1, 3, 12, 16, 117, 118
  Judaism as Yahweh intended, 155, 158, 159, 160, 162, 163, 165
  Pauline, 118, 125
  persecution of, 175, 178, 193, 195
  spread of, 120–121, 166
Christology, 180
Chronicles, 2, 41, 83–85
Circumcision
  Christianity and, 127, 128–129, 131
  covenant of, 24, 27
Clement of Alexandria, 185
Colossians, 140
Conditional law, 28
Convocation at Shechem, 38
Corinth, 132
Corinthians, 129, 131–135
Council of Carthage, 200, 202
Council of Hippo, 200, 202
Council of Jamnia, 6, 10, 106, 114, 199, 200–201
Council of Jerusalem, 106, 165

Council of Trent, 107
Covenant, 6, 7, 10
    with Israel, 19, 26, 28–29, 30, 33,
        55–56, 61, 65
    and Law, 19, 25, 26, 28–29, 30,
        53, 57, 91–92
Creation story, 20, 21, 30
Crucifixion, 160
Cultic life, 50
Cultic prophets, 58
Cyrus of Persia, 62, 76–77, 80, 81,
    83

Damascus, 126
Daniel, 64, 69, 90, 91, 100–102,
    193, 195
    additions to, 109
Danites, 39
David, 26, 37, 40–41, 42, 48, 49,
    57, 58, 83, 85, 88, 98
Dead Sea Scrolls, 113
Deborah, 35, 38, 39
Demetrius, 192
Deuteronomic history, 37, 41, 45,
    49–51, 53, 56, 57, 58, 74, 100
Deuteronomy, Book of, 11, 29
Diaspora Jews, 107, 108, 110, 113,
    203
Diaspora Judaism, 12, 75, 80–81,
    120, 129, 166, 203
Diotrephes, 192
Disciples, 125, 153
Dome of the Rock, 16
Domitian, 122, 159, 175, 178, 195

Eastern Church, 106
Ecclesiastes, 93–95
Ecclesiasticus, 106, 108
Ecstatic prophets, 57
Edomites, 67, 76
Egypt, 14, 15, 24, 27–28, 32, 49,
    110
Ehud, 35
Eli, 39, 40
Elihu, 96, 97
Elijah, 45, 57, 58, 69, 79
Eliphaz, 96
Elisha, 45, 57, 58
Elohim, 11. See also God
Elon, 35
Ephesians, 140, 171, 172–173
Ephraim, tribe of, 39
Epistles, 12. See also Catholic Epis-
    tles; John, letters of; Paul,
    letters of; Paulinists
Eschatology, 100
Esdras, 6, 106, 109–110
Essenes, 113

Esther, 99–100
    additions to, 108
Evangelists, 124
Eve, 21
Exegis, 9
Exodus, 9, 19, 25–28, 29, 30,
    31–33
Experienced history, 26
Eyes of faith, 32
Ezekiel, 56, 66–67, 74, 75–76, 78,
    102
Ezra, 40, 72, 74, 75, 76, 81–83, 84,
    85, 97, 109, 113, 202

Faith, 2, 7
    Christ of, 119, 120, 124, 150,
        151–152
    eyes of, 32–33
    Mark on, 151–152
    Paul on, 66, 136–137, 177
Fall, The, 21
Flood story, 20, 21, 22
Form criticism, 9

Galatia, 130
Galatians, 126, 129, 130–131
Gamaliel, 126, 160
Genesis, 2, 4–5, 9, 14, 19–33, 56
Gentiles, 118, 120, 121, 166, 185, 190
Gideon, 35, 39
Gilgamesh, 14, 16
Gnosticism, 179, 185–186
God
    Kingdom of, 118, 164
    names for, 8, 11, 27
    of New Testament, 89, 136–137,
        160, 162, 173, 196
    scripture as word of, 2, 7
God fearers, 117, 121, 166
Gomer, 60
Good Samaritan, 159, 162
Gospel parallel, 146
Gospels, 12, 118, 119, 124. See also
    Acts of the Apostles
    defined, 143–144
    interrelationship of, 145–148
    of John, 119, 143, 163
    of Luke, 8, 119, 143, 144, 145,
        146–147, 157–163
    of Mark, 8, 119, 143, 144, 145,
        146, 147, 148–152, 163, 193
    of Matthew, 8, 119, 128, 143,
        144–145, 146–147,
        152–157, 163
    occasion for, 144–145
    spiritual, 185
    Streeter's hypothesis, 146–147, 153
    synoptic, 124, 143–166

Graf-Wellhausen hypothesis, 11
Greco-Roman world, 121, 185
Greeks, 15, 112, 115–116. See also
    Hellenization
Gregory XIII, Pope, 4

Habbakuk, 55, 56, 66
Haggai, 56, 68, 82
Haman, 99
Hammurabi's Law, 16
Hasidim, 113
Hasmonaean dynasty, 108, 113
Hebrew Bible, 3, 5, 6, 10, 11. See
    also Bible; names of specific
    books
    Apocrypha, 106, 107
    canon of, 199–202
    Christian interpretation of, 11,
        12
    historical development of, 9–10
    of late period, 87–103
    literary criticism of, 8
    order of, 12, 13
    as "scripture," 12
Hebrews, 170, 171, 180–181. See
    also Canaan; Israel; Palestine
    conquest of Canaan, 37–38
    in Egypt, 27–28
    in Sinai, 28–29
    Sumerian origins of, 14
Hellenization, 10, 107, 113, 202
Heresy, 120, 121, 175, 179, 180,
    185–186, 192
Hermeneutics, 9
Hezekiah, 48, 63, 77
Historical criticism, 9
Holofernes, 107, 108
Holy Land, 75
Hosea, 55, 56, 58, 60–61
Huldah, 48, 55
Hyksos, 14

Ibzan, 35
Immanuel, 63
Immanuel prophecy, 63
Isaac, 23, 24, 26
Isaiah, 48, 50, 55, 56, 57, 61–64, 78
Isaiah II, 56, 61, 63, 68, 76–79, 80,
    120
Isaiah III, 61, 69
Isaiah School of Theology, 62
Iscariot, Judas, 114–115
Ishbaal, 41
Israel. See also Canaan; Judah; Pal-
    estine; Prophets
    Assyrian domination of, 10, 15,
        16, 43, 47, 50, 63
    under David, 40–41, 42

division of, 10, 16, 43, 46
Egyptian domination of, 14, 15
era of Judges, 38–39
geography of, 16–17
as Holy Land, 14, 16
internal/external strife in,
    45–47, 50
under Jerusalem, 45
Kings of, 44, 45, 49
Persian domination of, 16, 76–78
postexile, 75
religious tradition of, 7–8, 10,
    49–50, 55
return from Babylon, 74, 76, 78,
    80, 81–82, 113
role of prophets in, 45, 53–54, 58
under Samuel, 39–40
under Saul, 40
under Solomon, 42–43
tribes of, 16
wisdom tradition in, 90–92
Israelites. *See* Hebrews

Jacob, 23, 24, 26
Jair, 35
James, 176–178
James (brother of Jesus), 126, 176,
    177, 180
Jamnia, 146, 154
    Council of, 6, 10, 106, 114, 199,
    200–201
Jehoahaz II, 49
Jehoiachin, 49
Jehoiakim (Eliakim), 49
Jehoshaphat, 83
Jehu, 45–46, 60
Jehu dynasty, 44
Jephthah, 35
Jeremiah, 55, 56, 57, 64–65, 67, 72,
    102, 103, 109
Jericho, 38
Jeroboam, 43, 45, 83
Jeroboam II, 97
Jerusalem, 83. *See also* Temple
    fall of, 103, 109
    as Holy City, 16
    Paul in, 126, 136
    restitution of walls, 82
    return to, 10, 68, 74
    siege of, 63
Jerusalem Bible, 5, 12, 13, 35, 36n,
    99, 100, 106, 180, 191
Jeshua, son of Sirach, 108
Jesse, 40, 98
Jesus, 6
    birth of, 4, 26–27, 186–187
    Christ of faith, 119, 120, 124,
    151–152

crucifixion, 160
disciples of, 125, 153
    and eyewitness tradition,
    121–122, 125, 144, 145, 146,
    159, 190, 202
    of history, 112, 119–120, 140,
    144
humanity of, 186
and Judaism, 154–155, 159–160,
    162
and Law, 21, 127, 128, 155,
    156–157, 164
as Messiah, 10, 11, 62, 63, 78,
    117, 118, 120, 121, 124, 140,
    149, 150–151, 152, 160, 162,
    164, 187–188, 189
    self-proclaimed, 163
miracles of, 149, 150, 151, 159,
    160
parables, 119, 120, 155–156, 159,
    162, 188
passion, 189–190
resurrection of, 135, 140, 144,
    151–152, 157, 162, 188, 190
Sermon on the Mount, 128–129,
    147, 152, 155, 156, 157
as the "word," 184, 186
Jethro, 28
Jews, converts to Christianity, 118,
    120–121, 166. *See also*
    Judaism
Jezreel, 60
Job, 25, 95–97
Joel, 56, 68–69, 82
John
    Gospel of, 119, 143, 163,
    184–190
    letters of, 190–192
    traditions about, 183–184
John the Baptist, 26, 113, 119, 150,
    161, 184, 187, 188, 189, 193
Jonah, 69, 97–98
Joseph, 24–25, 90, 91
Josephus, 110
Joshua, 8, 14, 16, 35, 37–38,
    49–50, 57
Josiah, 48, 50
Josiah, King, 10, 11
Judah, 14
    Assyrian domination of, 48, 50,
    64
    Babylonian domination of, 16,
    43, 49, 63–64
    under David, 41, 48
    division from Israel, 10, 16, 43,
    46
    geography of, 16–17
    Kings of, 44, 45, 48–49, 50, 83

prophetic school in, 50, 58, 61
religious tradition of, 10, 49, 50,
    55
Judaism, 1, 2, 3, 6. *See also* Hebrew
    Bible; Israel; Palestine
    Alexandrian, 110
    in apocalyptic world view, 100,
    101–102, 112
    and Babylonian exile, 5, 8, 10, 11,
    12, 13, 59, 67, 68, 73–76, 83,
    101
    in covenant relationship, 19, 26,
    28–29, 30, 33, 55–56, 61, 65
    definition of, 75, 82–83, 84–85,
    97, 98, 99
    Diaspora, 12, 75, 80–81, 107,
    108, 110, 113, 120, 129, 166,
    203
    diversity within, 116–117
    Jesus and, 154–155, 159–160,
    162
    messianism in, 62, 63, 68,
    78–79, 112, 116
    monotheism of, 78–80
    as natural religion, 5, 67, 73
    Palestinian, 113–117, 122, 127,
    129, 159, 160, 203
    postexile, 112–116
    prophetic theology in, 54, 55–57
    Pseudepigrapha, 202–203
    purity of, 84
    as root of Christianity, 1, 3, 12,
    16, 117, 118
    and salvation history, 137
    sects, 113–115, 201
    separateness of, 84, 85
    survival of, 72–73, 75, 100
    within Roman Empire, 113, 114,
    115, 122, 159
    as world religion, 5, 65, 66, 68,
    69–70, 73n, 75, 113
Judaizers, 127, 139
Jude, 179–180
Judeo-Christian tradition, 1, 2, 4, 6,
    8, 12, 16, 22–23, 62, 66, 88, 89,
    90, 92, 100, 102, 110, 119, 194,
    196
Judges, 35–36, 37, 38–39, 49–50,
    54, 57, 98
Judith, 106, 107–108

Kingdom ethic, 155–156, 159
Kingdom of God, 118, 164
Kings, 2, 5, 8, 36, 42, 43, 45, 47, 49,
    53, 54, 56, 57, 65, 84, 90

Laban, 24
Lamentations, 65, 102–103

Law, 7, 13
    absolute, 28
    conditional, 28
    Covenant and, 19, 25, 26, 28–29,
        30, 53, 57, 91–92
    of Hammurabi, 16
    Jesus and, 21
    moral, 28
    Paul and, 127–129, 131
    religious, 28
    ritual, 28
Law, Book of, 48, 50, 55, 200
Legends, 12
Letters. See Catholic Epistles;
    John, letters of; Paul, letters of;
    Paulinists
Levites, 8, 45, 83
Literary criticism, 8–9
Literary tradition, 4, 7, 8, 9, 10
    prophetic, 55, 56, 59–69
Liturgy, 12, 88–89
Logos theology, 186, 191
Luke, 127
Luke, Gospel of, 8, 119, 143, 144,
    145, 146–147, 157–163. See
    also Acts of the Apostles
Luther, Martin, 107, 110, 176, 177

Maccabean Revolt, 100, 101, 108,
    195
Maccabees, 107, 108, 110
Malachi, 56, 69, 82
Manasseh, 5, 48, 50, 55, 64, 84
    prayer of, 106–107, 110
Manna, 28, 32
Marcion, 173, 200
Mark, Gospel of, 8, 119, 143, 144,
    145, 146, 147, 148–152, 163,
    193
Matthew, Gospel of, 8, 119, 128,
    143, 144–145, 146–147,
    152–157, 163
Melchizedek, 181
Meshach, 91, 109
Mesopotamia, 14
Messiah
    Jesus as, 10, 11, 62, 63, 78, 117,
        118, 120, 121, 124, 140, 149,
        150–151, 152, 160, 162, 164,
        187–188, 189
    self-proclaimed, 163
Messianic secret, 150–151
Messianism, 62, 63, 68, 78–79,
    112, 116
Micah, 56, 64
Midian, 27
Millennialism, 194
Miriam, 28

Mishnah, 114
Moabite, 98
Monarchy, 7, 9. See also Kings
Monotheism, 78–80, 121
Moral law, 28
Mordecai, 99, 108
Mosaic law, 28–29, 59
Mosaic tradition, 53, 54, 55, 56, 57,
    59, 69, 73
Moses, 5, 6, 7, 14, 19, 20, 25–33
    authorship of Pentateuch, 30
    prophetic role of, 53–54, 55, 57
    story of, 26–30
    view of Yahweh, 79
    as wise man, 90, 91
Myths, 12

Nahum, 56, 65–66
Naomi, 98
Nathan, 41, 42, 55, 57
Nazareth, 119
Nebuchadnezzar, 49, 90, 91, 101, 107
Nehemiah, 40, 72, 75, 81–83, 84,
    85, 97, 109, 113, 202
Nero, 122, 193
New Testament, 3, 6, 7, 20,
    117–118, 203. See also Bible;
    names of specific books
    canon of, 200, 202
    God of, 89
    historical development of,
        10–11, 87
    order of, 12, 13, 124–125
    as "scripture," 12, 118
Nineveh, 107
    fall of, 66
Nomadic culture, 7
Numbers, 29

Obadiah, 56, 67–68
Obed, 84, 98
Official religion, 122, 159
Old Testament. See Hebrew Bible
Omri dynasty, 44, 45, 60
Onesimus, 139, 140
Oracles, 63
Oral tradition, 4, 7, 8, 9, 10
Origen, 176, 178
Orpah, 98
Orthodoxy, concept of, 45, 48
Othniel, 35

Palestine, 14, 16. See also Canaan;
    Israel; Judah
    early church in, 165–166
    name of, 115–116
    in Roman Empire, 113, 114, 115,
        122, 159, 160, 201

Palestinian Judaism, 113–117, 122,
    127, 129, 159, 160, 203
Passion, 189–190
Passover, 28, 48, 84, 107
Pastoral epistles, 170, 173–176
Patmos, 184, 192
Patriarchs, 9, 23–25
Paul, 10, 11, 14, 165, 188, 193, 200
    authorship of Paulinist works,
        170, 171, 172, 173, 174–175,
        176
    conversion of, 126, 160
    on faith, 66, 136–137, 177
    influence on Christianity, 121,
        125, 140
    and Law, 127–129, 131
    letters of, 5, 118, 121, 125,
        129–140
        Colossians, 140
        Corinthians, 129, 131–135
        Galatians, 126, 129–130,
            135–138
        Philemon, 139
        Philippians, 139
        Romans, 127, 129–130,
            135–138
        Thessalonians, 138–139
    missionary journeys of, 121, 127,
        128, 135–136, 166
Pauline Christianity, 118, 125
Paulinists, 170–176
    Ephesians, 171, 172–173
    pastoral Epistles, 170, 173–176
Pentateuch, 7, 8, 9, 11, 13, 19, 20,
    25–33, 56
Pentecost, 160
Perrin, Norman, 2, 147, 154
Persia, 15, 16, 100, 113
    defeat of Babylon, 76
    Esther in, 99–100
    religious toleration under, 76–77
Peter, 127, 144, 145, 148, 178–179,
    190
Pharaoh, 27–28, 90, 91
Pharaoh Neco, 49
Pharisees, 21, 108, 114, 116, 120,
    146, 154, 162, 201–202
Philemon, 139
Philippians, 139
Philistines, 16, 40
Philo of Alexandria, 188
Pilate, 160
Plagues, 28, 32, 68
Priesthood, 10, 39–40, 74, 83, 181
"Priestly prayer," 189
Promised Land, 29
Prophetic theology, 54, 55–57,
    69–70

Prophets, 97. *See also* specific
    names
    contribution of, 69–70, 72
    court, 58
    cultic, 58
    defined, 53–54
    early, 57–58
    ecstatic, 57
    exile, 59, 75–83
    literary, 55, 56, 59–69
    political role, 45, 48, 53, 54
    popular vs. true, 65
    postexile, 59
    preexile, 59
    sanctuary in Judah, 50, 58
    tradition of, 53, 54–57, 69–70, 74
    true, 10, 65, 69
Prophets court, 41
Proverbs, 92–93
Psalms, 12, 88–90
Pseudepigrapha, 202–203
Ptolemy Philopator, 110
Purim, 99, 108

Qoheleth, 93
Qumran, 114

Rachel, 26
Redaction criticism, 9
Rehoboam, 43
Religious law, 28
Remnant theology, 55
Resurrection, 135, 140, 144,
    151–152, 157, 162, 188, 190
Revealed religion, 2
Revelation, 118, 184, 192–196
Righteous One, 113
Ritual law, 28
Romans, 15, 16, 127, 129–130,
    135–138
Rome
    Jews under, 113, 114, 115, 122,
        159
    persecution of Christians, 122,
        159, 160, 175, 178, 193, 195
    religions of, 121, 185
Ruth, 75, 85, 88, 98

Sadducees, 108, 113–114, 116
Saint Jerome, 107
Salvation history, 136, 137
Samaritans, 47, 82, 117, 118, 166
Samson, 39
Samuel, 26, 36, 38, 39–40, 41, 53,
    54, 57

Sanhedrin, 114
Sarah, 26
Satan
    apocalyptic view of, 100, 101
    and Job, 95–96
Saul, 16, 37, 40, 41, 54, 57
Scribes, 118
Scripture, 1, 2–3, 5, 6, 10, 11–12.
    See also Bible; Hebrew Bible;
    New Testament
Sects, 113–115, 201
Septuagint, 6, 12, 106, 107, 112,
    113, 200, 201
Sermon on the Mount, 128–129,
    147, 152, 155, 156, 157
Servant passages, in Isaiah, 78–79
Shadrach, 91, 109
Shamgar, 35
Shechem, convocation at, 38
Sheshbazzar, 81
Simeon, 159
Sin, 22
    Paul on, 136, 137
    seven sins, 93
Solomon, 16, 42–43, 49, 83, 90,
    102, 108
Song of Azariah, 109
Song of Miriam, 28, 30
Song of Songs, 102
Song of the Three Young Men, 109
"Sons of Thunder," 184
Streeter's hypothesis, 146–147, 153
Suffering, human, 95
Sumerians, 14
Susanna, 109
Synagogue, 10, 74
Syncretism, 107
Synoptic Gospels, 124, 143–166
Synoptic problem, 146

Talmud, 114
Temple, 11, 43, 45, 83
    cleansing of, 48, 50
    cultic prophets in, 58
    destruction of, 74, 201
    Dome of the Rock, 16
    liturgy in, 88, 90, 102
    rebuilding of, 81–82
    scroll found in, 48, 50, 55, 200
    second, 88, 102
Ten Commandments, 28
Testament, 6. *See also* Hebrew
    Bible; New Testament
Textual criticism, 9

Theophilus, 157–159
Thessalonians, 138–139
Timothy, 132, 138, 173–176
Titus, 127, 173–176
Tobias, 107
Tobit, 106, 107
Tola, 35
Torah, 19
Tower of Babel, 22
Traditions, 7–8, 10, 21
Tribal setting, 8
Tribes of Israel, 16

Ur, 14

Vulgate, 107

Wisdom
    defined, 90
    in Israel, 90–92
    literature of, 92–97
    nontraditional, 93–97
    traditional view of, 91–93
Wisdom, Book of, 108
Wisdom tradition, 90–92
"Word, " Jesus as, 184, 186
Writings, 12, 13

Xerxes, 82, 99

Yahweh, 7, 8, 9, 10, 11, 16, 37, 38,
    39, 40, 41, 43, 48, 97, 98
    in apocalyptic world view, 100,
        101, 102
    in burning bush, 27
    Covenant with Israel, 19, 26,
        28–29, 30, 33, 55–56, 61, 65
    God of history, 30, 32, 37, 50, 69
    images of, 45
    and monotheism, 78–80
    in prophetic theology, 53, 55, 57,
        59, 60, 62, 64, 66, 67, 68–69,
        73, 75, 76, 78
    in Psalms, 89, 90
    and wisdom tradition, 91, 93, 94,
        95–96, 97

Zadok, 113
Zealots, 114–115
Zechariah, 56, 68, 83
Zedekiah, 49
Zephaniah, 56, 64
Zerubbabel, 68, 110
Zophar, 96